GASTROPOLIS

Arts and Traditions of the Table: Perspectives on Culinary History
ALBERT SONNENFELD, SERIES EDITOR

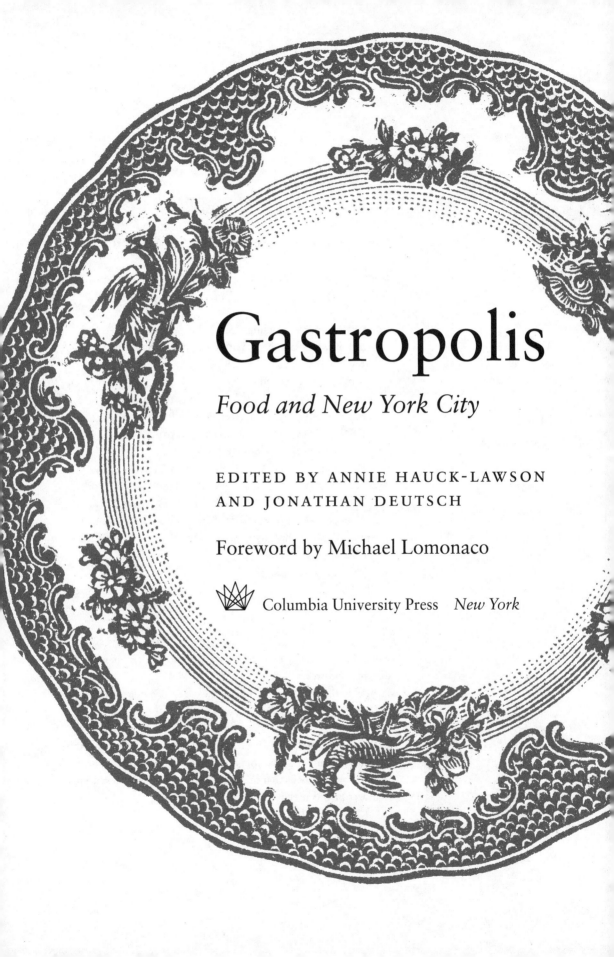

Gastropolis

Food and New York City

EDITED BY ANNIE HAUCK-LAWSON
AND JONATHAN DEUTSCH

Foreword by Michael Lomonaco

Columbia University Press   *New York*

Columbia University Press
Publishers Since 1893
New York Chichester, West Sussex

Library of Congress Cataloging-in-Publication Data
Gastropolis : food and New York City / edited by Annie Hauck-
    Lawson and Jonathan Deutsch.
        p. cm. — (Arts and traditions of the table: perspectives on
    culinary history)
    Includes bibliographical references and index.
    ISBN 978-0-231-13653-2 (cloth : alk. paper)
    ISBN 978-0-231-51006-6 (e-book)
    1. Food habits—New York (State)—New York—History.
    2. Food in popular culture—New York (State)—New York.
    3. Food—Social aspects—New York (State)—New York.
    4. Cookery—New York (State)—New York. I. Hauck-Lawson,
    Annie. II. Deutsch, Jonathan, 1977–   III. Title. IV. Series.
      GT2853.U5G37 2008
      394.1'209747—dc22
                                                    2008023536

♾

With gratitude to my dear family and friends: my "pit crew."
You nourish my food voice. You rock! (AH-L)

To my family. (JD)

CONTENTS

FOREWORD

EACH SEPTEMBER, when I was growing up in Brooklyn, we put up tomatoes that my father had grown in our backyard. Putting them up meant filling sterile glass jars with this valuable crop of home-grown Romas, which served to tide us over through the winter so that the Sunday "gravy" (Brooklyn Italian American for a particular pasta sauce, only we didn't call it pasta, but *maccheroni*) would have the rich taste of the sun, unlike the flaccid tomatoes that came packed in cans.

We had two peach trees in the same, small yard. Their fruit was best enjoyed after being bathed in red wine or put up in their own jars with some sugar, later to enjoy as a midwinter treat when nary a stone fruit was in sight, long before globalization brought us long-distance, gas-treated fruits from thousands of miles away. There was nothing as sweet and delicious as those peaches. Except, of course, the ripe, black figs from the two ample fig trees or the raspberries and blackberries from the bushes that grew beside the rear fence, just next to our neighbor's berry bushes, whose fruit she turned into Austrian compotes, like those her mother had made before they fled the combat of World War II. She also taught my mother, a Sicilian mama to the core, how to make dill pickles as only she, a Jewish mother, could do.

Green beans, tomatoes, basil, parsley, cucumbers, eggplants, and sweet bell peppers filled our yard every summer, all grown from seeds that had germinated in our cellar in the waning days of winter before the warm days of spring arrived. Those seedlings lived not far from homemade sausages made in late fall that were curing into dry *salumi*, hanging very near barrels of homemade wine, made from California grapes shipped to New York each autumn for Italian immigrant winemakers like my grandfather Salvatore.

My childhood sounds as though pulled from an ancient history book, not lived in Brooklyn in the late 1950s and early 1960s. My mother, Mary, was born to Sicilian immigrant parents on the Lower East Side and spoke the Sicilian dialect until she was five, when she learned English. My father, Frank, immigrated to the United States, leaving Sicily behind at the age of fifteen. We were urban-agrarian before it was part of the green movement. My mother cooked every day, using many ingredients from our backyard in season and from our cold-cellar stores of home-cured and preserved foods. Of course, the chickens, rabbits, and even Thanksgiving turkey were all free range from the live-poultry market, "harvested" to order. Meat from the butcher shop was cut from the sides of midwestern beef hung to dry; sausages were made from pork that likely came from heritage breeds before they were in vogue; fresh Jersey eggs were candled right in front of us; and espresso was brewed from beans from the coffee roaster whose only business was roasting coffee daily.

In *Gastropolis: Food and New York City*, Annie Hauck-Lawson and Jonathan Deutsch lead me to realize that I was not alone in this unique way of seeing and eating and that these experiences define me through my food voice, which has been unstoppable. It took shape during my childhood in my Brooklyn neighborhood, where the fusion of great Jewish delicatessens and dairy stores, next to the Italian *salumeria* and *latticini*, down the block from the Mittel-European sweet shop that made ice cream and the market that sold fish brought fresh from the dock, and on whose side streets plied 1940s-era trucks from which was sold produce grown in the Hudson Valley conspired to make food the central focus of my life.

Today, whether in my home kitchen or in my restaurant, my cooking is rooted in a Brooklyn-New York–laced story that draws on the diversity I have been exposed to, having eaten my way through this city, my hometown, transforming me as curing and aging do *salumi*; great ingredients, all ground and mixed together, with time and patience, yield something different and entirely original. And so in my own food voice, with my New York–cured taste, I feel as though I have become a part of the city and, with luck, contribute to and mentor the formation of someone else's food voice.

Taking my food voice to the streets, as a chef and restaurateur, came later in life. While I didn't know that was where I was headed, I wasn't surprised when I arrived. In my late twenties, tiring of life as a struggling actor, I found my true voice in cooking, by way of Brooklyn, earning my degree in hospitality at the New York City College of Technology in the 1980s. Since boyhood, I have sought out the New York food experience, traveling the boroughs in search of a perfect, usually ethnic meal. As the city's world population has grown, so have my tastes for the authentic from around the globe. I have long believed that New Yorkers can taste their way through most of the cuisines of the world without leaving the five boroughs. This global connection has influenced the food I cook at home as well as in the restaurant. I credit the food of New York for having informed and helped me find my own personal voice, the food voice that I rely on each day for my livelihood. And I know that I am not alone in this experience; I know many chefs who seek out ethnic-food markets to find the authentic ingredients they need to create their own style of cooking. New York is like an incubator for great cooking, recognized around the world for being a center of innovation—with great chefs, ethnic markets, and farmers' markets—and a catalyst for creativity. You can find your true food voice in New York; you just need a guidebook like *Gastropolis*.

MICHAEL LOMONACO
EXECUTIVE CHEF/PARTNER
PORTER HOUSE NEW YORK

PREFACE

THE IMAGE, identity, history, and soul of many American cities can be captured in the foods that have come to define their unique culinary landscapes. It is almost impossible to envision these cities without the sights, smells, sounds, textures, and tastes of the edible environment overtaking the individual: the charred-molasses barbecue of Kansas City, the heft of a golden Chicago pizza, the feel and peel of a spicy New Orleans crawfish boil. Perhaps nowhere else in the United States is this more the case than in New York. The social, political, and cultural climate of the city is inextricably linked to the foods that have immigrated here from around the world, along with the people who brought them, to start a new life in this most diverse city. From the iconic bagel, pizza, cheesecake, and knish, and from low-keyed, beloved neighborhood eateries or world-renowned restaurants and gourmet destinations that draw millions to the city annually, the flavor of New York City is in its food.

Whether you find yourself extracting the last slurp from the paper cup at the Lemon Ice King in Corona, eating fiery Jamaican jerk chicken fresh off the oil-drum grills at Badoo's in Flatbush, or enjoying a cool ocean breeze with a Nathan's hot dog in hand on the Coney Island boardwalk, New York City allows the edible sensibility of traveling the world, tasting re-created homeland flavors of any of more than 200 countries, prepared by speakers of more than 140 languages. Far from offering inspired reflections of authentic cuisine alone, this diversity hosts combinations and flavors that work in New York: Cuban-Chinese, Russian banquet hall with sushi bar, halal Afghani and kosher Afghani. These foods respond to the unparalleled resources and resourcefulness of New York and New Yorkers.

From the first Native Americans in the region to the present, New Yorkers have formed relationships with food that have helped shape the identity of their great city.

A "food voice," what people eat or avoid, often can say as much about them as their own words can.[1] From rural to suburban to urban New York, food has been a ready medium for expressing identity through food voices in a mutual relationship between food resources and the preparers' skills.

The need for food is not only the primary biological drive of humans, but also a central and potent channel of communication carrying intentions, meanings, and larger forces that influence the way we eat. Culture, religion, psychology, nutrition, agriculture, economics, marketing, history, and politics converge at the table to tune our food voices and shape how we eat. Decisions about food procurement, preparation, and service are often negotiated in ways that address gender, class, labor, and cultural identities.

The diversity and complexity of our relationships with food are felt saliently in New York City, which at one time had a geographic landscape rich in food sources. People, influenced largely by their skills and tastes in bringing together food cultures from around the world, have long interacted with the city's land and maritime resources to make the flavors of New York unique. Through food-centered activities—growing, procuring, cooking, celebrating, sharing, and dining—this city of more than 8 million, encompassing more than three hundred square miles and boasting a population that represents nearly every culture in the world, has individual and collective food voices competing to be heard. Often a cacophony, at times in harmony, New York City's food voices tell the story of immigration, amalgamation, and assimilation with their concomitant interplays between tradition and change, individual and society, and identity and community. Food and eating serve both as a process by which these changes occur and as one entrée to understanding the people of New York and their worlds.

This collection of essays presents a variety of thought on the ways in which New Yorkers experience food and asks: What are the food voices of New Yorkers saying? From the pre-European Lenapes clamming on what is now Staten Island, to hedonists eating sashimi off a latex-covered woman in the contemporary avant-garde Manhattan food scene, food experiences in New York City are colorful, rich, and, in Claude Lévi-Strauss's words, "good to think."[2]

Theoretical Orientation: The Food Voice

The concept of the food voice means that what people choose to procure, prepare, and eat—and what they do not eat—can reveal much about their identity and culture. Often, the food voice expresses what the spoken voice struggles to articulate. In other instances, the food voice itself can tell a story about its speaker's experiences.[3]

Scholars have been listening, directly or indirectly, to food voices tell stories of migration, assimilation, and resistance; changes over time; and personal and group identity. In short, human experiences can be conveyed through what foods are eaten, avoided, and no longer or more often eaten and, of course, through what is produced and prepared and how it is produced and prepared. Perhaps most obviously, food choices—what a person or group decides to produce, prepare, and consume—can represent a conscious affirmation and expression of a personal identity,[4] a group identity,[5] an ethnic identity,[6] or a national identity.[7] Beyond who we are, our food voices are often politicized in the form of food protests, philosophies of eating, and socially conscious food choices to express how we feel and what we want.[8] The food voice can work in tandem with the spoken and written voice in order to enact a holistic representation of identity, politics, and human experience.[9]

Remaining Questions

When we proposed writing this book and after later critiques by others, some questions continually resurfaced: What's so special about New York? Couldn't you write this book about another place? About London, Washington, D.C., or Beijing? What about Ames, Iowa? The answer, of course, is a resounding yes. Food voices heard through stories, histories, tensions, cooks, and eaters are everywhere, and they can and should be captured everywhere.

But at the same time, there *is* something special about New York. It has been a key point of entry, both past and present, to millions of new Americans. It is home to many of the world's elite and many more of the world's poor. It possesses an iconic status in film, music, literature—and the food world.

So while New York's food stories may not be unique, they are vital. In a collection as wide-ranging as this one, a number of themes emerge that transcend the limitations of time, inner or outer borough, or ethnic enclave: land and water use, immigration and identity, and what New York food is where it will go from here.

What This Book Is Not

Writing about the foodways of New York can be a lifelong project. In a city with more than 8 million people, each with his or her food styles and stories, the food scene is bound to be diverse, dynamic, stratified, and confusing. What we and our contributors in this book try to provide are tastes of these styles and stories or, stated in a more New York way, noshes.

This book is not a guidebook, although it may make you want to visit many of the places described in it. This book is not a cookbook, although it may inspire you to prepare new dishes. This book is not a textbook, although scholars and students should find it useful.

This book is not representative. We hope to show a broad image of the city and explore all five boroughs. We do not focus solely on "ethnic" food, nor do we restrict ourselves to the city's famous restaurant culture. Rather, this book tells stories of hunger and plenty, of indigenous people and recent immigrants, of cooking for a family and cooking for a world, of New Yorkers hailing from both six continents and New

xvi   York itself. So even though it may not be possible to provide a representative portrait of the foodways of New York City, we have offered, we hope, a compelling one.

ANNIE HAUCK-LAWSON

JONATHAN DEUTSCH

NOTES

1. Annie Hauck-Lawson, "Foodways of Three Polish American Families in New York" (Ph.D diss., New York University, 1991).

2. Claude Lévi-Strauss, *Totemism* (Boston: Beacon Press, 1963).

3. Annie Hauck-Lawson, "When Food Is the Voice: A Case Study of a Polish-American Woman," *Journal for the Study of Food and Society* 2 (1998): 21–28; Annie Hauck-Lawson, ed., *Food, Culture and Society: An International Journal of Multidisciplinary Research* [Special Issue: Food Voice] 1, no. 1 (2004).

4. Meredith E. Abarca, *Voices in the Kitchen: Views of Food and the World from Working-Class Mexican and Mexican American Women* (College Station: Texas A&M University Press, 2006); Thomas A. Adler, "Making Pancakes on Sunday: The Male Cook in Family Tradition," in *Foodways and Eating Habits: Directions for Research*, ed. Michael Owen Jones (Los Angeles: California Folklore Society, 1983), 45–54; Arlene Voski Avakian, ed., *Through the Kitchen Window: Women Writers Explore the Intimate Meanings of Food and Cooking* (Boston: Beacon Press, 1997); Carole M. Counihan, "What Does It Mean to Be Fat, Thin, and Female in the United States?" in *Food and Gender: Identity and Power*, ed. Carole M. Counihan and Steven L. Kaplan (Amsterdam: Harwood, 1998), 76–92.

5. Jonathan Deutsch, "'Eat Me Up': Spoken Voice and Food Voice in an Urban Firehouse," *Food, Culture and Society: An International Journal of Multidisciplinary Research* 1 (2004): 27–36; C. Paige Gutierrez, "Cajuns and Crawfish," in *The Taste of American Place*, ed. Barbara G. Shortridge and James R. Shortridge (Lanham, Md.: Rowman & Littlefield, 1998), 139–44; José E. Limon, "Carne, Carnales, and the Carnivalesque," in *Dancing with the Devil: Society and Cultural Poetics in Mexican-American South Texas* (Madison: University of Wisconsin Press, 1998), 123–40.

6. Benay Blend, "'I Am an Act of Kneading': Food and the Making of Chicana Identity," in *Cooking Lessons: The Politics of Gender and Food*, ed. Sherrie A. Innes (Lanham, Md.: Rowman & Littlefield, 2001), 41–61; Donna R. Gabaccia, *We Are What We Eat: Ethnic Food and the Making of Americans* (Cambridge, Mass.: Harvard University Press, 1998); R. Ray, "Meals, Migration, and Modernity: Food and Performance of Bengali-American Ethnicity" (Ph.D. diss., State University of New York at Binghamton, 2001).

7. Amy Bentley, *Eating for Victory: Food Rationing and the Politics of Domesticity* (Urbana: University of Illinois Press, 1998); Jeffrey M. Pilcher, *Que Vivan los Tamales! Food and the Making of Mexican Identity* (Albuquerque: University of New Mexico Press, 1998); Yael Raviv, "National Identity on a Plate," *Palestine–Israel Journal of Economics, Politics and Culture* 8–9 (2002): 164–72.

8. Carol J. Adams, *The Sexual Politics of Meat: A Feminist-Vegetarian Critical Theory* (New York: Continuum, 1990); Warren J. Belasco, *Appetite for Change: How the Counterculture Took on the Food Industry* (Ithaca, N.Y.: Cornell University Press, 1993); Jane Dusselier,

"Does Food Make Place? Food Protests in Japanese American Concentration Camps," *Food and Foodways* 10 (2002): 137–65.

9. Louise DeSalvo, *Crazy in the Kitchen: Food, Feuds and Forgiveness in an Italian American Family* (New York: Bloomsbury USA, 2004); Cara De Silva, ed., *In Memory's Kitchen: A Legacy from the Women of Terezin* (New York: Jason Aronson, 1996); Hasia R. Diner, *Hungering for America: Italian, Irish and Jewish Foodways in the Age of Migration* (Cambridge, Mass.: Harvard University Press, 2002).

ACKNOWLEDGMENTS

OUR GOAL as coeditors of this collection was not to represent *the* food voices of New York, a daunting task, but to offer readers thoughtful and interdisciplinary perspectives on some of New Yorkers' relationships with and activities regarding food, past and present, that have served to make food in New York a rich and important part of its character.

The strength of this book is in its contributors. Working on food and culture in New York City is a dream. The passion, the expertise, the talent, and the depth of roster are a Luger burger or *café con leche* away. All the authors of this book contributed many hours and a great deal of thoughtfulness to realize this project, and they have done so graciously and with humor, which was important to us as first-time editors! We are delighted to be able to share the private pleasures we have had in working with these words. This is their book: Babette Audant, Jennifer Berg, Mitchell Davis, JC Dwyer, Mark Federman, Jessica Harris, Annie Lanzillotto, Martin Manalansan, Anne Mendelson, Damian Mosley, Fabio Parasecoli, Ramona Lee Pérez, Janet Poppendieck, Nan Rothschild, Joy Santlofer, Harley Spiller, and Suzanne Wasserman. What a talented collection of wisdom about food in New York City! Two of our contributors deserve special mention: in addition to writing pieces for the book, Cara De Silva and Andy Smith supported us from the start.

We also would like to thank Warren Belasco and Fred Kaufman for their valuable comments, as well as the anonymous reviewers of the proposal and manuscript, whose comments further shaped this book. We have special appreciation for Juree Sondker, our editor at Columbia University Press, who planted the seeds for this project and encouraged its growth to fruition.

xx   Our colleagues in our respective departments of the City University of New York, Health and Nutrition Sciences at Brooklyn College (Annie), and Tourism and Hospitality at Kingsborough Community College (Jon), along with our chairs over the course of this project, Drs. Leslie Jacobson and Janet Grommet at Brooklyn and Drs. Stuart Schulman and Richard Graziano at Kingsborough, provided valuable space and support to allow this book to happen.

Finally, of course, thanks to our families: starting right at home, Danny (who thought up the title *Gastropolis*—awesome, Lawson), Alana, and Phillip (Annie); Molly, Emma, and Alice (Jon), who even as we write this are understanding and patient with this project and the time and attention it demands.

GASTROPOLIS

Fusion City

From Mt. Olympus Bagels to
Puerto Rican Lasagna and Beyond

CARA DE SILVA

TO OUTSIDERS, the problem seemed frivolous. The solution even more so. But to a New Yorker, both concern and response were entirely appropriate. The crisis in the food tent at the Smithsonian Folklife Festival during New York on the Mall—the sudden lack of New York water for authentic New York bagel and pickle making—was clearly a state of affairs requiring emergency measures.

To ensure his supply, Steve Ross of Coney Island Bialy & Bagels had sent thirty-six gallons of hometown water to Washington. But when Herman Vargas of Russ & Daughters, Manhattan's more-than-ninety-year-old appetizing store, borrowed some for its Lower East Side brine, Ross began to run out. Enter the New York City Department of Environmental Protection, which, on hearing of the problem, airlifted containers of Big Apple water to the capital. "Ridiculous," I heard one person say. But we New Yorkers understood. Even if we did it with a smile.

Few of us may know why Acqua Naturale New York, our tap water, is so good, so critical to the taste of foods produced here, but we are aware that it is a composition of elements that come together naturally and create something unique, not unlike ourselves, the inhabitants of what is arguably the world's greatest city. In a way, that water, brought here from all over the state as we are brought here from the earth's four corners, symbolizes New York itself.

So when I "listen" to what in this book has been called the "food voice"—a term coined by Annie Hauck-Lawson to refer to each individual's food-and-drink patterns—the rush of water is part of what I hear. But I also hear in it the collective food voice of the city, formed by a chorus more than 8 million strong. Listen hard and you will hear it, too, the whole greater than the sum of its magnificent parts, yawping, as

Walt Whitman would say, but also melodious, exhilarating, seductive, irresistible, vigorous, compelling. And endlessly mutable.

In approach, and in the multiform style and content of its chapters, *Gastropolis: Food and New York City* reflects the diversity of the city it depicts. Turn its pages and you move across time and history, from the city's pre-beginnings to today; turn them again and you are introduced to facets of its food life through archaeology, sociology, food studies, anthropology, and personal narrative.

The book explores "The Orient Express," a subway line. An archaeological dig. Russ & Daughters. The history of pushcarts. Restaurant dining and identity. Heritage Tourism in Harlem. A sensory approach to a street. The city's avant-garde food scene. The dilemma of hunger. The Lenape Indians. The venerable Port Arthur Restaurant. A collection of ten thousand Chinese take-out menus. New York iconic foods ("When I was a young man, no bigger than this, / a chocolate egg cream was not to be missed," sings Lou Reed in tribute to one of them). And, in addition, offers memoirs of growing up African American, Polish American, and Italian American in the city's boroughs.

This is a study of our town's inflections. Its gastronomic utterances. Of why it sounds (and tastes) the way it does. And these accounts work both to introduce those elements and to conserve them. No easy task. Listen to Walt Whitman on the subject. "A New York journal a few days ago," he wrote in *Preserving Tradition,* an essay for the *Brooklyn Eagle,* "made the remark in the course of one of its articles that the whole spirit of a floating and changing population like ours is antagonistic to the recording and preserving of what traditions we have of the American past. This is probably too true."[1] Neither Whitman nor the other journalist is likely to have been referring to foodways, but they easily could have been. And what was true for America was even more the case for New York.

As a writer with a deep interest in food and its meanings and history, and also as a native New Yorker, passionate about my city from its most grimy to its most tony bits, this way of looking at NYC (a logo recognized the world over) is special to me. For a dozen years, when the food, foodways, and food people of the city were my full-time beat for one of its newspapers, I would tramp the streets in disbelief that someone was paying me to do this privileged work. And when I would take a friend or colleague from elsewhere to one of our ethnic neighborhoods, I would wait expectantly for the yelp of wonder that always followed our emergence from the subway: "Cara, I feel like I took a plane to get here!" And then I would beam with native pride. I still do.

As a consequence of that joyful period (as well as exploring I have done since), when I picture my hometown, I see what everyone else sees, of course, but I also see a city map whose signposts are *thalis* (metal trays holding small bowls of Indian fare), grills, steamers, woks, pots, cleavers, *tagines,* samovars, markets, and restaurants, all of which delineate its beguiling highways and byways.

My mental slide show includes Mt. Olympus Bagels, my favorite New York food sign. When I see it, I picture Zeus and Hera on their thrones, glasses of nectar in hand, having Sunday breakfast on the mountaintop along with the whole family. Perhaps to them, as to us, it is a bagel and a schmear that is the real ambrosia. (A related sign, in the window of a Greenwich Village bagel shop, also has a place in my gallery. Meant to make passersby think the store's version of this Jewish, and now American, specialty is the best, it lyrically enthuses, "Our bagels are baked at dawn in an Italian bakery.")

Other pictures flash through my mind. There is the Burmese temple atop the bean sprout factory in Brooklyn, where the abbot's birthday is being celebrated with offerings of Coke and American birthday cake. Gypsies eating pastrami sandwiches at Juniors in Brooklyn. *Laamb* (Senagalese wrestling) in Central Park as propitiatory milk is spilled over the combatants. Ganesha, the Elephant God, at the Hindu temple in Flushing with a tasty *laddoo* in his hand. A Brooklyn factory at night, rain pounding on the corrugated-metal roof, and its rudimentary tortilla-making rig at rest for a moment. Boxes being carried off airplanes by couriers bringing immigrants lonely for the taste of home, dishes prepared by their mothers and wives. The city's ball fields where, whether the game is soccer or baseball, some of its best ethnic food is to be had. And the fancifully nicknamed "Spaghetti Park," even today a bastion of Italian American life in increasingly Hispanic Corona Heights.

Change carousels and up comes the image of an SRO (single-room occupancy) immigrant hotel where a friend and I are sitting on a bed to eat delicious, but illegally prepared, African food. The *casitas,* or clubhouses, in East Harlem, the Lower East Side, and the South Bronx where club members cook whole roast pig. Crusty *banh mi.* (Think Vietnamese heroes. Grinders. Subs.) Spicy red bean soup eaten to the sound of domino tiles being slapped against tables in a West Indian restaurant. A menu offering Thai Chicken, Jewish Style. Latina women on street corners with homemade tamales or arepas or empanadas being sold from pots in their shopping carts. And Shanghai soup dumplings in which the soup is in the dumpling and not the other way around.

New York foods. And New York food voices. It would take a book the size of all the borough telephone directories put together to list every one. Each an expression of culture. Each loaded with meaning. Each completely distinctive. Each an element of New Yorkerness, representing the sui generis amalgam of people who call the city home.

If America was never quite "the melting pot" that Israel Zangwill dubbed it in his 1908 play of that name, still the phrase came to express a political and social ideal, if not an absolute reality. And because our immigrant heritage was, as it still is, a huge element of our identity, for many years the melting pot was an important part of the construct, a piece of how we, as Americans and as New Yorkers, thought of ourselves. But though we have been together in the crucible for centuries, and have mingled and combined, in fact, we have never quite melted.

In his 1938 book, *Around the World in New York,* Konrad Bercovici wrote:

New York! A fold that has multiplied one hundred and twenty times the original size in a hundred years. A fold that has increased itself not from within, of its own kind, but from without, from people of all nations, coming from all directions. . . . Crowding one another, and fusing against their wills slowly with one another, without ever becoming a compact whole.[2]

Not a perfect description, certainly not always against their wills, but, in many ways, on the mark.

And it is that kind of commingling, one in which merging does not rule out the retaining of distinctions and the building of new ones, that began to fascinate me as I wandered the streets of my hometown, "Fusion City," a place seasoned with a singular spice blend of *ras el hanout* and hot dogs, asphalt, spirit, skyscrapers, traffic, and grit.

That fascination has never stopped. How could it? Exploring a neighborhood, learning to understand it, watching its foodways change shape and mingle under the press of urban forces is still a special pleasure for me.

Pervasive though it is in New York, I never set out to make fusion a focus. Initially, it was more a matter of accretion of information, acquired not by intent, but by circumstance and observation. Work, and then curiosity and delight, took me to locations where I saw it constantly, and the process, whether natural or manipulated, gradually became a regular subject of thought.

Ultimately, however, I realized that the ethnic beat I walked for my newspaper was not my introduction to fusion, and that I had first encountered it, as most New Yorkers do, in streets both elegant and mean, where it was, and is, simply a given. However, the real beginnings came even earlier, in my own immigrant family, when my artsy Polish Jewish mother, transported to New York, served maple syrup to accompany her blintzes and her matzo brei.

What she was doing, combining the New World and the Old, was not unusual, and on these shores must certainly have begun in New Amsterdam when the already diverse population—it is said that more than seventeen languages were spoken in a settlement of only a thousand people—needed substitutions for what couldn't be easily had, or, as was often the case early on, simply needed food.

And certainly there came a day when some Dutch goodwoman, wanting a change, threw some local berries into her *olykoeks,* the progenitors of our doughnuts, as Andrew F. Smith points out here. There were also Native American corn and cornmeal to explore. And if a bottle of Japanese soy sauce was common on the tables of the rich in Amsterdam, as early as the seventeenth century, used to add saltiness and more flavor to soups and meat dishes, might it not ultimately have come here, as well?

The English arrived. The Jews. The Africans. Germans. Irish. Italians. West Indians and East Indians. Russians. Poles. Chinese. Latinos. Southeast Asians. The Spanish. And still more. And with each arrival, then as now, the pattern was repeated, and the city further fortified by the power of diversity.

Fusion in New York has been in full swing for centuries. With every war, with every change in the immigration laws, with every revolution, with every flight to freedom and away from hunger, and with every search for a better life, the city's foodscape has shifted.

Over the years, as a result of increased understanding of the processes at work here in Fusion City, my own interpretation of the term "fusion" has broadened substantially, growth that really began with Mt. Olympus Bagels. The sign made me aware that where food is concerned, fusion goes far beyond the usual, and far too limited, definition. "A style of cooking that combines ingredients and techniques from very different cultures or countries," says the *American Heritage Dictionary,* most inadequately.

For me, the name, cleverly suggesting bagels of mythic quality to the population at large, while marking them for local Greeks as in some way the food of home, quintessentializes certain aspects of urban fusion—the movement of foods from one ethnic group to another. The way food is used as an identity marker. Or as a form of ethnic signaling. The effects of commerce. Of mingling. And those, of course, are only the beginnings. Come with me now and see.

An immigrant travels with luggage of several kinds. There are suitcases packed with practical goods and memorabilia (for example, a handwritten cookbook, a *lefse* rolling pin, or a gefilte fish pot, such as those in the museum on Ellis Island), and there is the baggage carried only in the mind, which contains flavors, aromas, and images from the kitchens of homeland and family.

Of the 12 million people who came to Ellis Island between 1892 and 1954 (the vast majority by 1924, when the National Origins Act reduced the flow), forming the most momentous migration in history, one-third stayed in New York, adding to the already pulsating mix.

If at first they attempted to cling to foods they knew, or that resembled those they knew, and offered comfort through their familiarity, they were, ultimately, forced toward change by circumstance; by contact with other ethnic groups even within their own tight enclaves (at that time, the Lower East Side was one of the most crowded places on earth); by the urging of misguided social workers; and by the power of enculturation.

That process had been under way even before they began their lives here. Creolization, whether created by epochal forces such as mass migration, or by a single immigrant leaving home, begins at the airport or pier, when a sense of "us" and "them" is first established. On arrival, language, clothes, mores, manners, traditions, ways of thinking, consumption patterns, always at risk, are at once clung to, and slowly, and to varying degrees, altered, the process helped along not only by societal pressures, but also by the natural inclinations of immigrants themselves, impelled to move on out, to taste the new, and to be, and act, a little bit American.

Inevitably, food culture is part of that negotiation. The accommodation starts when immigrants, especially the first to arrive, must use the ingredients available in the new country to make the dishes of the old. In that sense, ethnic foods are often, and inescapably, fusion foods. (The irony is that, at first bite, we tend to regard anything ethnic as traditional. Indeed, we use the term "ethnic" as a measure of cultural authenticity. Yet in some sense, the word implies dilution. Or at the very least, difference.) Of course, the larger the group grows, the more likely that the real thing can be found here, but that is still not always the case. Sometimes fusion is simply the result of making do, a matter of substitutions made for economy or simplicity.

And so it happened that years ago, while dining on *fejoaida* in a Brazilian eatery in Manhattan, I noticed something oddly out of place among the flavors. Because it was easier to get at the time, the chef was substituting pastrami for the *carne seca* with which the dish is traditionally made. Writing a column about Eritreans in one of the city's Eritrean-owned restaurants (most often simply identified as Ethiopian),

I wondered of what the *injera* (fermented tablecloth bread that is one of the staples of that cuisine) had been made. I knew the traditional grain, teff, a relative of millet, was not yet easily available here. The waitress responded to my question with a smile, "Why Auntie Jemima, of course." Then the market for teff grew, and today "Aunt Jemima *injera*" is most often replaced with the more authentic variety, just as the *fejoaida* is most often made with *carne seca*. Yet even now, sometimes Aunt Jemima or pastrami is made to do.

The new New Yorkers have, in general, been part of the huge influx of peoples from Asia, the Caribbean, Latin America, and eastern Europe that began after a change in immigration law ended the quota system in 1965 and that was fed, too, by the fall of the Soviet Union and the breakup of Yugoslavia. Today, these immigrants, in company with those who came before them, have been creating an even more varied society, one so heterogeneous that even we, whose roots from the beginning were set down in immense diversity, and who live in its midst, are unlikely ever to have experienced anything like it before.

If the notion of the melting pot was contested by some almost from its inception, it has never been more in question than now. These days, metaphors are more likely to invoke a mosaic or a salad or a stew, in which each component remains separate, distinct, while at the same time becoming part of a whole. They reflect the idea of pluralism, of a multiethnic society, in which the heritage of each immigrant group is to be maintained, with little pressure to shed it in order to become A New Yorker, and no need to cohere except in ways that are much more minimal than in the past. Today, the fact that you are an immigrant may actually be the thing that most makes you feel you are an American and deeply a part of New York.

Boris Fishman, a Russian émigré, put it tellingly in the *New York Times:*

Modern America is kind to ethnicity. A hundred years ago, when the country was less certain of itself, the greenhorns who sailed from Eastern Europe for the tenements of the Lower East Side were expected to assimilate and lose themselves to America's cultural largess. Today, immigration has so thoroughly redefined the American narrative that I feel American precisely because I am an immigrant. New York has subsumed ethnicity so thoroughly that I feel more American than a Russian plowing through a plate of blintzes at the Russian Vodka Room.[3]

But blintzes and other good things to eat remain part of the story. While reinventing New York (and again confirming its centuries-long role as a destination for people around the world), the new immigrants are also reinventing New York food—as did their Irish, Jewish, and Italian ancestors a century ago. By adding their dishes to the city's already heavily laden table, they are creating a feast even more various than any that has preceded. And we New Yorkers, like little birds with beaks open, are ready to savor every aspect of it.

Its initial force, of course, is still in immigrant communities where, if we could peep into home kitchens, we might find not only the traditional foods we would expect, but jerk pork tossed with spaghetti, French fries flecked with *za'atar,* or Puerto

Rican lasagna heavy with cilantro and green chiles (lasagna is a tabula rasa for many ethnic groups).

Perhaps the process begins in the schoolyard when Pedro tries what Ahmed is eating and goes home and demands it from his mom. Or arises out of practicality when both parents are working and there is a product on the market that resembles the original, even if it is American made (and originally from somewhere else entirely). Thus mozzarella often stands in for any white cheese. And pita is often substituted for any flatbread, or, as in a case that Annie Hauck-Lawson learned about from a student, refrigerator biscuit dough stands in for that in Chinese steamed buns.

The compounding can result, too, from immigrant creativity and the lure of new ingredients. When a Ukrainian-born woman learned I was doing a story about her East Village neighborhood, she approached me in the street to offer her recipe for the best-ever pierogi. Reaching for my notebook, I began to write, sure this would be the version I would run home to make. Temptee Whipped Cream Cheese was the first ingredient. Velveeta was the last.

It happens when ethnic neighborhoods are contiguous and their borders are like the borders of foreign countries, with all that lies on the other side. It happens, as with earlier generations, out of yearning to be American and like everyone else. (The Pakistani-style Thanksgiving turkey I once saw for sale in Manhattan's Little India was a wonderful example of the ethnicized version of the holiday, as defined by immigrants for whom it is the turkey that is iconic, the thing that makes the meal American, but who think nothing of surrounding it with Chinese fried rice, curried vegetables, *foo foo,* or *kapusta.*)

And it can also come about while rehearsing to be American. At a Taiwanese banquet, roast beef was served alongside traditional fare, so diners could practice for their new lives in Flushing, Queens.

The adoption of foreign techniques is another form of fusion—say, the use of stir-frying to cook non-Chinese dishes—or the use of new cooking implements—for example, the wok. Or see Anne Mendelson on the Lenapes' adaptation of iron kettles after the arrival of the fur traders, providing the Indians for the first time with a long-lived cooking utensil.

Fusion can even be a matter of proportion. The combining and changing increase when ingredients that were an extravagance back home become more available or affordable. Meat, perhaps eaten once a week or a month, or used largely for flavor in the countries of many who passed through Ellis Island, fell into this category when, here, it became the central ingredient of the meal, and a powerful symbol of pride and plenty.

And, of course, substitutions may be made for religious reasons. A kosher restaurant in New York that once served Jewish deli on one side of the center aisle, and Chinese food (a Jewish favorite) on the other, also made its sweet-and-sour pork with pastrami. Muslim diners sometimes frequent halal Chinese restaurants run by non-Muslim Chinese. And the late-night halal cart at Fifty-third Street and Sixth Avenue, which began business many years ago to feed Muslim cab drivers, has won itself a fan base of non-Muslim eaters described by the owner as largely American or Spanish.

And sometimes it is simply a matter of who is doing the cooking. Many immigrants—people who were engineers, accountants, or teachers in their own country—open simple restaurants here because they cannot get a job or cannot speak English. And quality or authenticity or respect for tradition are not always the first priorities—especially when a vitiated version of the original can be a selling point. After I had written a story about Vietnamese restaurants in Manhattan's Chinatown, one owner confided in me with delight that he had finally found the right way to serve his customers *nuoc mam,* the fermented fish sauce that characterizes Vietnamese cuisine. "Now," he said contentedly, "we dilute it with flat 7-Up."

Inevitably, fusion occurs when the variety of foodstuffs available grows larger with each new influx from around the globe and changes the already complex foodscapes of the city, as it always has. And those foodstuffs often have complex histories of their own. Of course, the swap meet didn't begin here. Many of the foods that have added to the amazing ferment in the city's kitchens arrived in New York already fused.

After all, cuisines have been converging and forming unions since day broke on the world's first civilizations, and new combinations have been created with every war, at every colonial outpost, and with every movement across borders, whether by force or in search of a better life. In the city's Peruvian restaurants you will find *tallarín verde* (*tallarín* from the Italian *tagliarini*), served tossed in a pesto-type sauce made with spinach. In those of the Trinidadians, you see curry powder, and dishes such as roti that show the Indian influence on the island's foods. In another restaurant, say Jamaican-Chinese, it is the use of ginger and stir-frying that mark the effect of the island's Chinese population. An Ethiopian or Eritrean restaurant in New York will sometimes have spaghetti on the menu, a throwback to the time when Italy was the colonial power there.

Combine Spanish, Chinese, Indian, Japanese, and American influences with a basically Malay cuisine, and you are eating in Filipino Jackson Heights or along First Avenue and Fourteenth Street in Manhattan. *Nonya* cooking, the food of the Straits Chinese, is a nineteenth-century Singaporean product of marriages between Chinese men and Malaysian women who blended their husbands' native fare with Malaysian and Indonesian techniques and flavors. In the "purely" Malaysian eateries of New York, it is the mélange of Malay, Chinese, and Indian cooking that offers historical insight.

Whether created through empire and expansion or indentured labor (brought to work railroads or sugar plantations) or by miscellaneous other causes, such fusions defined the cooking of the immigrants from these countries long before they arrived on American shores. Yet odds are, something new was added here.

During the heyday of Ellis Island, if one immigrant carried her recipe for rugelach in her head and heart and the muscle memory of making it in her hands, others brought, to name just a very few, pizza, pasta, pita bread, and bagels, all of which were adopted and adapted. And still today, one of the primary ways that the fare of hyphenated Americans—whether New York's Mexican-Americans, Italian-Americans, Russian-Americans, or even Americans who have lost the hyphen—develops and spreads is simply through exposure.

Moreover, fusion results whether foreigners come to our tables—or we come to theirs. It happens when people travel for business or pleasure or even military purposes, enjoy the local food, and come back wanting to have it at home. And once adopted and adapted, whether under these or other circumstances, it draws the rest of us as well. During the 1939 World's Fair, which had a pronounced effect on the city's food culture, foreign cuisines were offered for nationalist and political reasons, as well as commercial ones. Thus New Yorkers who had never been abroad could taste dishes from afar and learn to crave them. "If you care for variety, there are approximately twenty restaurants in the Foreign Government area, where France, Italy, Norway, Sweden, Poland, the Soviet Union, and even the Dutch East Indies among others, will offer their favorite delicacies," said the *Official Guidebook*.[4]

Of course, it was not only the place in which fusion most obviously makes itself manifest—that is, the home kitchen, whether that of new immigrants or native-born New Yorkers—that I kept turning over in my mind in the course of this years-long adventure.

I thought about many other manifestations of it, one of which was pizza and the pizzeria—yes, the pizzeria. If creations such as smoked salmon pizza with mascarpone served at high-end restaurants are one kind of pizza fusion, there is also another, more basic. Pizzerias have been ethnicizing their product and fusing ingredients and styles for years. If New York pizza is pizza by the slice, it is frequently also pizza made ethnic. The pie's eternal popularity and the fact that the pizzeria business has relatively low startup costs has long made it attractive to immigrants. After Gennaro Lombardi opened the first New York pizzeria in 1905, pizzerias became a foothold occupation not only for Italians, but for Greeks (prominent here in the restaurant business) and Arabs (and even South Americans and, occasionally, Chinese or Indians). They still are. And their pizzerias do not make only Italian American pizza. Often, and increasingly it seems, in keeping with the growth of our interest in the food experience writ large, they make it their own.

In the pizzerias of New York, I have had Greek pizza with feta; Israeli pizza topped with falafel; double-crusted Indian vegetarian pizza; pizza topped with *pebril*, a Chilean sauce; Argentinian pizza topped with *faina*, a chickpea flour pancake with Italian origins (a combination eaten here, but created there because of Argentina's large Italian population). And the city has long had a "pitzeria" owned by an Iraqi, in which the toppings come on pita bread.

Often, though, the ethnic statement appears not only in the form of toppings, but also in the form of small bites from home. The Salvadoran owner may also sell *pupusas*; the Chilean owner, empanadas; the Yemenite owner, *malawach*.

And I also saw that fusion is not only about immigrants. Learning about one another's cuisines, even among those who are native born, can produce related effects. Sometime ago, waiting for a friend at the bottom of that great stage, the staircase of the Metropolitan Museum, I heard a man approach a woman with a flirtatious line that was certainly original, if not unique. "I wonder," he asked, "if I could I persuade you to cook for me?" "What would you like?" she replied, happy to join in the game. A list of his favorites followed—pork chops and gravy, grits, sweet potato pie—but although she was nodding, he suddenly stopped to reconsider. Then, surveying her face, he continued, a big smile on his own: "Actually, I think it would be better if you made me chicken soup, gefilte fish, and some rugelach. After that, I will teach you how to make the rest." Gasping with pleasure at this New York exchange, they slapped their thighs, spun around, and laughed out loud until they cried. And to me those two New Yorkers, shouting with delight on upper Fifth Avenue, and connecting through the cuisines into which they were born, is also fusion, and yet another aspect of the city's multilayered, multifaceted, multiflavored food voice.

Through writing about fusion and lecturing about it, I came to realize that, too, in the past several decades something had been added to the city's usual gastronomic free for all. In both concept and reality, the fusion process was taking place faster and at many more levels, and to a greater degree than ever before, happening not only naturally, through immigration and through exposure to one another's cuisines, as it always has, but also through contrivance, the result of our enthusiasm for it, chef creativity, globalization. And, in particular, commercial forces.

Fusion was a gastronomic idea whose time had come, we all latched onto it, and the melding became dazzlingly visible, affecting local delis to supermarkets, luncheonettes to fine-dining restaurants, big food companies and small, and how and what we ate (and eat), from the lowliest table to the finest.

Of course, when a particular cuisine or culture is in vogue, and much imitated by others, dishes are reformulated to suit perceptions of the marketplace. The desire to be modish, on the part of both restaurateur and diner, is a great determinant. And so it was here.

As any New Yorker knows, the panino (or as we call Italian grilled sandwiches here, a panini [the plural erroneously used as a singular]) has taken the city. A few months ago, lunching in the Meatpacking District, one of Manhattan's "hot" areas, I saw a Cuban panini featured on the menu. Composed of regular ham, cheese, and tomato, it was neither a Cuban sandwich nor an Italian one, and to top it all off, literally, it was also served with salsa, adding a south-of-the-border note. A sign in a restaurant window in Midtown offered a Reuben panini—corned beef, sauerkraut, Swiss cheese, and Russian dressing, a classic New York sandwich (whether by adoption or through invention) made to sound more trendy by serving it in the style of the moment. My favorite? The greengrocer on my corner, among whose offerings is an "Italian" panino made with *bulgogi,* a style of grilled beef often referred to as the national dish of Korea.

At the fine-dining level today, chefs romance the city's increasingly bold palates with fusion dishes born both out of brilliance and out of folly—for example, a dish of eggplant topped with soy sauce, mozzarella, and kiwi at a restaurant best left unidentified. (Although more freewheeling and also more globalized now, chef mix and match is not entirely a new phenomenon. Seventy years ago, Le Perroquet, a French restaurant in Manhattan, was offering diners "Steak Vermont," a dish of beef topped with cheese. Not, however, American Cheddar, as one might expect in a dish so named, but rather French Roquefort.) In skillful hands, however, fusion cuisine can at once seduce, entertain, and startle. Consider the parsnip tart with quinoa, hazelnuts, and bok choy at WD-50; the luscious foie gras ravioli served with a green cabbage marmalade at Le Cirque; or the dish of Vietnamese "minestrone" with charred pineapple and cilantro found at Spice Market.

In restaurants and on menus, fusion also happens linguistically and notionally with the loosening and deterioration of meaning in food terms and the incorporation of culinary catchphrases to mean other things. At Spice Market, "minestrone" had at least been placed in quotation marks, suggesting that it wasn't exactly authentic. But other chefs are less careful. For example, anything raw and thinly sliced, even vegetables, is likely to be called a "carpaccio"; anything layered, a "napoleon"; or any legume puree, "hummus." And recently, I heard a woman order a caffe latte "with almost no milk, please." A heavily milky coffee drink whose very name in Italian means "coffee with milk" was being requested without milk. And even more amazing, the barrista knew exactly what she meant.

However, it may be the bill of fare at an Italian restaurant in Rockefeller Center that trumps them all. The lounge menu features something called "Italian sushi," defined, rather startlingly, as sushi-inspired tapas. In just those few words, there are two terminological extensions, or dilutions, of meaning, sushi and tapas, and the mixing of three cultures: Italian, Spanish, and Japanese. Moreover, when you scan the list of offerings, you see that two of the four "sushi-inspired tapas" are meat—prosciutto and *bresaola*—and one is very un-Italian smoked salmon, Italianized by the addition of buffalo mozzarella.

The culinary combining appears unstoppable. From the Spanish rice knishes I saw long ago at Mrs. Stahl's Knishes in Brighton Beach to the Polish empanada (kielbasa and sauerkraut–filled) I saw a few weeks' ago in Hells Kitchen. From the "We serve grits" notice at a Korean luncheonette, to Irish breakfast served in an Indian-owned diner, to pretzel croissants, cappucino in Chinatown, and a BLT burrito, food here, as always, continues to reflect the gastronomic pandemonium that is New York. The city that never sleeps is, in addition, the city that always eats. And its restlessness and energy keep its foods and foodways constantly coalescing, but always in motion.

Yet this current infusion of fusions, this diffusion of fusions, this effusion of fusions, and this confusion of fusions are as much a matter of fission, a blowing apart, as they are of a bringing together. And soon enough, they, too, will change. Just stay tuned to the city—murmuring and roaring and, of course, chowing down—and it will tell you, between bites, just what is coming next.

NOTES

1. Walt Whitman, "Preserving Tradition," in *Walt Whitman's New York, from Manhattan to Montauk,* ed. Henry M. Christman (New York: New Amsterdam Books, 1989), 3.

2. Konrad Bercovici, *Around the World in New York* (New York: Appleton-Century, 1938), 3–4.

3. Boris Fishman, "Where Is Home, If the Place You Come From No Longer Exists?" *New York Times*, November 21, 2004.

4. *Official Guidebook of the New York World's Fair, 1939* (New York: Exposition Publications, 1939).

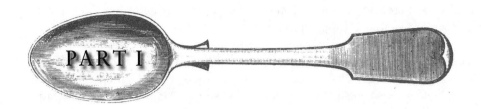

Places

"PLACES," PART I of this book, situates New York City in time and place. We invite readers to imagine the city's food life before asphalt paved the region. Imagine five hundred years ago, people indigenous to Brooklyn summering along the shorelines now known as Brighton, Gerritsen, and Manhattan beaches plus Coney Island, gathering and preserving clams and oysters. Imagine early European settlers living in downtown Manhattan, buying their meat, dairy, and vegetables from farmlands that today comprise the five boroughs. What evidence of our predecessors' eating—bones, pots, china, shells—remains under the city streets, and what stories do they tell?

In her Sophie Coe Prize–winning essay "The Lenapes: In Search of Pre-European Foodways in the Greater New York Region," Anne Mendelson opens this section with a natural history of the region and a description of native foodways. She meticulously follows the development of the region's water, animal, and land resources and focuses on the Lenape people's engagement with these resources for food. Her chapter will help readers understand the formation of New York City's geography and the Lenape people's foodways.

Mendelson's chapter ends with the virtual extinction of the Lenape people, driven to demise by trade, disease, and colonization, although the region's abundance of food remained. In "The Food and Drink of New York from 1624 to 1898," Andrew F. Smith continues the history with the story of the early European settlement in the region, focusing on foodways and food trade, through the city's consolidation in 1898.

Next, Nan A. Rothschild presents an archaeological study of the food history of urbanizing New York—that is, what the many new New Yorkers or, more accurately, New Amsterdammers, ate—in "Digging for Food in Early New York City."

From several sites around the city, Rothschild pieces together a foodways picture shaped by such factors as supply, race, and class.

Each of this book's parts includes a food voice narrative of personal perspectives on food and the city. Part I concludes with Annie Hauck-Lawson's "My Little Town: A Brooklyn Girl's Food Voice," the story of her "food-centric" family in Brooklyn and her lifelong engagement with the local food supply. Hauck-Lawson's narrative begins with her childhood memories of her family's growing and gathering food and continues with her encouragement of her students and her own children to be an active part of the city's agriculture, fishing, and gathering.

The Lenapes

In Search of Pre-European Foodways in the Greater New York Region

ANNE MENDELSON

HOW FAR can we ever reconstruct the food of peoples who have been obliterated? More precisely, preliterate peoples who have been obliterated as societies, along with the physical environment that virtually defined their civilization, including their foodways? Where do we look for evidence in such cases, and how trustworthy is it?

One such group was the Lenape Indians, whom some would call "Munsees" or "Lenni Lenapes." From perhaps 900 or 1000 to the early seventeenth century, the Lenapes, who formed subgroups within the larger Algonquian linguistic group, lived in a swath of the Northeast between eastern Pennsylvania and the western ends of Long Island and Connecticut. Their richest territories lay on and around the Lower Hudson River between about present-day Albany and the river mouth. Lenapes occupied what is now Greater New York when the Dutch arrived to found New Netherland colony in 1624.

Much is either known or discoverable about their food, but much is not. The four major sources of evidence are

- The natural history of the region[1]
- Lower Hudson Valley archaeological remains from the last pre-European era, the so-called Late Woodland period (about 1000 to 1600)[2]
- Early firsthand, if gap-ridden, European colonists' accounts of the Lower Hudson Valley peoples[3]
- Documented foodways of the Lenapes' close or less close neighbors, other northeastern peoples who either received fuller early descriptions or even now preserve much of their culture, including the practice of traditional crafts[4]

Our only abundant and consistently reliable evidence comes from the first of these. Despite some limited uses, the rest present serious interpretive puzzles. The evidence from natural history, however, tells us in great detail what the first peoples of the Greater New York region had to eat and why it was there in the first place. It also helps us evaluate more problematic kinds of evidence and grasp in what ways the Lenapes' food supply resembled neighboring peoples' or was unique.

The foundations of this region's pre-European food resources were laid when the Wisconsin ice sheet, the last of four tremendous glaciations that covered much of North America starting around 3 million B.C.E., stopped advancing southward and began withdrawing toward the North Pole, perhaps sometime between 15,000 and 12,000 B.C.E. Its southern terminus lay directly atop parts of modern New York City. Even Manhattan parks still have glacial mementos like great scarred gashes rasped across rocky surfaces, or the odd boulder bulldozed from Quebec to an alien background. On a broader scale, we can still glimpse the outlines of terminal moraines. These long ridges of rocky rubble carried southward and dumped along the leading edge of the ice now stretch from eastern Long Island into Queens, Brooklyn, and Staten Island and westward through and beyond New Jersey.

Over a six- or seven-thousand-year period, the aftermath of the ice sheet's retreat left the Greater New York region—later the main Lenape territory—with the most stupendously plentiful, diverse, and annually sustained food supply of any area on the East Coast. This blessing arose from two sources: the land-based and water-based environments. The first broadly resembled other northeastern regions. The second was unique.

The Land and Its Resources

On terra firma, postglacial events in the Hudson Valley followed a general pattern found from the Atlantic coast into the Midwest. Several thousand years passed before the slowly departing ice sheet ceased to depress North American temperatures. Gradually the climate warmed enough to support subarctic tundra vegetation—sedges, mosses, and lichens—that was followed in centuries or millennia by various small flowering plants. Later the first large evergreens invaded the landscape, chiefly spruce, hemlock, and several kinds of pine. Finally came the great northeastern climax hardwood forests, which stretched for hundreds of miles from the coast inland and were dominated by chestnut, hickory, and oak trees that commonly reached heights of eighty to one hundred feet.

When temperatures had rebounded to something like present levels, the Greater New York region, directly astride the southernmost edge of the ice, was left with a climate partly overlapping that of New England to the north and the Chesapeake–Tidewater region to the south but less seasonally extreme than either. Plants earlier restricted to opposite sides of the glaciated–nonglaciated divide now could cross the former boundary of the ice's advance. The Lower Hudson Valley ended up with a rich mixture of species found everywhere east of the Mississippi, southern species uncommon in colder areas, and northern species uncommon in warmer areas.

From the time the great hardwood forests appeared, perhaps by 5000 or 4000 B.C.E., they formed not one uniform environment but a patchwork of environments resulting from natural events like wildfires, windstorms, and droughts. The fall of even one tree could affect other plants' chances of colonizing some spot. When thousands of trees at once were destroyed by, say, a lightning strike and fire, many acres of ground might be laid bare, opening the way for grasses and other ground plants that thrived in direct sunlight while allowing still others to establish themselves on edge zones between forest and clearing.

Over a century or so, any piece of open ground would be invaded by different annual and, later, perennial flowering plants, then successively by other kinds of growth, including briar canes, shrubs and bushes, junipers, larger evergreens, and, finally, hardwood trees. In the pre-European Northeast, the "forest primeval" really consisted of incalculably varied large or small tracts at particular stages of succession. Their different kinds of growth attracted different kinds of creatures, from insects to large herbivores; these in turn attracted other members of the food chain.

This pattern obtained in the whole of eastern North America from southern Canada almost to the Gulf Coast, and more particularly in the Northeast from Quebec west to the Great Lakes and south to the Carolinas. With local variations like the particularly diverse biological endowment of the Lower Hudson Valley, all the pre-European Indians of the Northeast drew for food on many of the same animal and plant species.

Their knowledge of what lived alongside them directly mirrored an existence somewhere between settled and roving—which brings us to one of the aforementioned interpretive difficulties. Undoubtedly some of the northeastern peoples were more sedentary or more mobile than others; that issue directly impinges on the question of when agriculture reached different areas. Archaeological evidence unfortunately tells us less about food than about some other aspects of Late Woodland culture. The main problem is that most plant remains—unless hard-shelled or partly carbonized by charring—quickly decay in the climate of the Northeast. Bones are more durable and hence more abundant at excavation sites that seem to represent either settlements or encampments. This makes it difficult to reconstruct the relative importance of plant and animal foods in people's diets, or to surmise how far the members of any community ranged in search of either. Current scholarship suggests that the New York–area Lenapes remained a particularly mobile group down to the arrival of the Dutch.[5]

Early colonists' reports, which fill in the archaeological gaps to some extent, indicate that most northeastern peoples, including the Lenapes, lived in bands of anywhere from a few dozen to a few hundred members, each moving about a range or territory of a few dozen square miles that was mentally mapped out to include many different kinds of terrain. At some seasons of the year, the whole band resided in something recognizable to Europeans as a "village"; at others, everybody or some task force would move to various locations convenient to wild plant or animal resources. They intimately knew everything that grew, walked, crept, or flew throughout every square yard of their beat.

The animals that the northeastern Indian peoples used for food were pretty much anything that breathed and moved.[6] Certainly creatures the size of deer would have been intrinsically more attractive targets than field mice. But we have no evidence of any special taboos against particular animals or birds. All the creatures in question were wild except for dogs, whose place in the diet is little understood. People ate them on special occasions like the feast featuring "a fat dog" prepared in Henry Hudson's honor in 1609 somewhere around today's town of Hudson in Columbia County, but it is not clear whether dog was everyday fare.[7]

Among the wild creatures, the American white-tailed deer would have stood at the top of any pre-European food hierarchy. Part of the reason was the skill and stamina required for the chase, which was the province of men. Like other game animals, deer were most often hunted at the onset of winter when they were fattest. No part of the animal went unused, from horns and hooves to guts and teeth. The sinews furnished bowstrings; the bones, the makings of many implements including kitchen tools like spoons.

The only other large game animal of comparable importance was the American black bear. What the native peoples—and some later Americans into the early twentieth century—especially admired about it was the richness imparted by a heavy layer of fat, much like the richness of pork before agribusiness helpfully bred the fat (and flavor) out of it.

The northeastern Indians' love of fat struck even the Dutch and the English, neither of whom carried any brief for lean diets. By far the best source was bear, but some smaller creatures were also valued for their fat, including raccoon, lynx, and particularly beaver. It was an honor for a guest to be served beaver; it was a royal honor to be offered the tail, which had a particularly succulent consistency and would be considered a rare delicacy by American frontiersmen at least through the nineteenth century.

The New York region also supported an extraordinary range of birds. All—from small shore birds and songbirds to diving birds, raptors, and gulls—were regularly or sometimes taken for food, as were their eggs in the spring nesting season. Huge flights of migratory waterfowl—wood ducks, mallards, redheads, canvasbacks, mergansers, widgeons, Canada geese, snow geese, and whistling swans, among others—came through the Lower Hudson Valley area during spring and fall. Adriaen Van der Donck, the eponymous Jonckheer (squire) of Yonkers, wrote in the 1650s that in spring, swans crowded the edges of local waterways in such multitudes as to look like white drapery.[8]

The bird of birds was the wild turkey, found from Central America to Canada. From early European descriptions, the birds were larger than most modern farm-raised turkeys as well as wilier and more resourceful. They could fly only a few hundred feet at a time, but they were very long-legged and ran like the wind. Contrary to common assumption, they seem to have been not stringy and tough but richly fatty; the males developed a particularly heavy layer of fat over the breast in late fall, the main turkey-hunting season.[9]

As everywhere in the Northeast, the plants used for food included most things that weren't actively poisonous or horribly unpalatable—and many that were, since people were skilled at processing unpromising materials to remove toxins or bitter alkaloids. The Indians also knew how to encourage the growth of different plants by simple but effective methods of environmental management that also affected animal habitats in the great ecological patchwork of the forest. The management technique most noted by Europeans was setting controlled fires in hardwood ranges during fall and spring. This not only cleared the understory of brush to make tracking game easier but created fertile conditions for some small food plants. Burning could also help maintain areas of open ground where useful plants like wild strawberries flourished or preserve edge zones—a magnet for grapevines—between forest and other growth. People also understood the usefulness of simply turning over a bit of ground with a hoe made by fastening a clamshell to a stick; annual plants that seeded themselves on the spot could be encouraged to come up yearly, in a practice foreshadowing more systematized forms of agriculture and domestication.[10]

All tending and gathering of plants was done by women, as were some other kinds of harvesting, like collecting shellfish. In general, men seem to have been responsible for what had to be actively pursued; women, for whatever stood still to be gathered. Their knowledge of plants reflected the mobile or partly mobile way of life that took virtually every member of any band from end to end of the group's recognized range in the course of the year. An informal taxonomy of the major food-plant types in the New York region would run thus:

• *Annual plants bearing small, hard seeds with fairly good amounts of protein, some fat, and some starch*. These probably were the most concentrated sources of vegetable protein in very early times. They included a kind of goosefoot (member of the *Chenopodium* genus) thought to have been similar to the Mexican *huauzontle* but gathered at a maturer stage; one or two members of the *Amaranth* genus; and "little barley," a cousin of European barley.

• *Annuals with tender young leaves and shoots that were boiled and eaten as we treat spinach or asparagus*. For most of these, the only gathering season was spring; later they were either too woody or too toxic. Amaranth and goosefoot could be gathered at this stage, though it meant forgoing the more valuable seeds of the mature plant. People also collected young pokeweed, milkweed, or cattail shoots; marsh marigold; wood sorrel; and various ferns at fiddlehead stage.

• *Starchy roots and rhizomes (some of which also had edible shoots)*. People ate the roots of Solomon's seal, jack-in-the-pulpit, a plant called "wild ginger" (no relation to real ginger), and the American groundnut (unconnected with peanuts, which are called "groundnuts" in some countries). Many aquatic roots were harvested, including cattail roots (which had a mucilaginous substance useful for thickening and binding mixtures), the plant called "arrowhead," sweet flag, and several kinds of pond lilies. The only native root vegetable later used in American cookery was the Jerusalem artichoke, perhaps because it required less processing before cooking than some of the others.

• *Fruits and berries from trees, vines, and shrubs*. These had enormous importance for all the Indian peoples, for several reasons. First, they were among the few foods that anyone could pick and eat without the laborious processing that most other plant foods required. They were also the best local sources of vitamin C. Among the best fruits of the Northeast were splendid white and purple grapes; cranberries, blueberries, and huckleberries; and several members of the *Rubus* genus (raspberries and blackberries). Where fire had cleared the ground there were enormous fields of strawberries, which were described by Europeans as ambrosially delicious, and apparently were bigger than today's wild strawberries. People also ate native gooseberries and currants, beach plums, bitter but edible kinds of cherries, and several reputedly quite good relatives of the European hawthorn.

• *Tree nuts.* Because the dominant hardwood trees of the Lower Hudson Valley were chestnut, hickory, and several species of oak, huge crops of nuts rained down on the earth every fall. The now decimated native chestnuts (by report, richer and sweeter than European chestnuts) were an important starchy vegetable used as we might use potatoes or beans. Acorns were treated in somewhat the same way. Some were quite bitter and took a lot of processing to be palatable, but those from the white oak and chestnut oak were mild-flavored and rich in oil. There were several kinds of hickories—in this region, principally shagbark and shellbark—as well as black walnuts, butternuts, beechnuts, and American hazelnuts.

All the plants mentioned were native wild species, though several benefited from management techniques that at some point might have approached cultivation. Like the other Indians of pre-European North America, the Lenapes had three others—maize, beans, and squash—that were neither native nor wild. But discussing their place in Lenape foodways means raising murky questions about the relative importance of mobile and sedentary ways among the different peoples of the Northeast. Sedentism is, by definition, a requirement for growing domesticated plants, but we do not know how attracted the Lower Hudson Valley predecessors were to the idea.

Contrary to popular wisdom, tending domesticated species is not such an unqualified improvement over exploiting wild ones as to make any society in its right mind stop foraging and start farming overnight. The process usually takes centuries or millennia, during which any individual people maintains its own equilibrium between the two according to local circumstances.[11] There is much evidence that peoples living near the coast generally reached a different balance from counterparts farther inland. But in Lenape territory, some inlanders had at least partial access to coastal benefits. It does not make sense to discuss the role of maize, beans, and squash in their lives without first understanding an entirely different source of food that could have fed everyone in the region of Greater New York the year round.

The Waters and the Question of Agriculture

The Wisconsin ice sheet's land-based effects in the vicinity of Greater New York were tame compared with what it did to the local waters in both its bulldozing advance and its slowly melting withdrawal. Where the rock-studded underside of the ice rasped over the ground, it scoured out innumerable kettle-hole depressions, the site of the area's many later ponds and swamps. As the glacier retreated, enough meltwater poured from it to bring the Atlantic coastline more than a hundred miles westward and to create innumerable tidal pools and backwaters that formed their own little ecological niches. Huge meltwater lakes submerged hundreds of square miles of ground before vanishing or subsiding into wetlands like Hackensack Meadows, formerly one of the great shellfish-spawning grounds of the Northeast.

The most dramatic of all the glacial resculptings was performed on an ancient river gorge. The weight of the ice (a thousand to several thousand feet thick) moving over the existing gorge like some monstrous reaming tool gouged it out into a great valley that would become a fjord—that is, a drowned river valley running inland from the sea—after the glacier's retreat let the ocean tides wash 160 miles inland, past the nearest stretch of the Appalachian Mountain system around West Point, New York. This fjord, better known as the Hudson River, is unique on the East Coast. Carrying the tides as far north as the natural barrier of Cohoes Falls at Troy, where the Mohawk River empties into it, the Hudson forms the longest and best link between the Atlantic and the trans-Appalachian interior anywhere on the East Coast. Long before European sailing ships appeared on the scene, its tides helped cement the separate bands of Lenape relatives living anywhere between Lower New York Bay and the vicinity of modern Albany.[12]

The Hudson was probably the greatest single factor in giving the Lenapes—even some of the inlanders—a food supply surpassing that of any other northeastern people. Other water habitats played their part. Freshwater lakes and streams provided brook trout, catfish, crayfish, and much more. The far richer coastal waters yielded—among many other kinds—blackfish, sea bass, weakfish, sheepshead, several herring relatives, mackerel, Spanish mackerel, summer flounder, winter flounder, monkfish, a few shrimp species, oysters, scallops, mussels, lobsters, hard-shell and soft-shell clams, razor clams, whelks, and blue crabs. But over and beyond all these, the Hudson was the reason for tremendous seasonal migrations of anadromous fish—those that live in saltwater but must spawn in fresh or brackish water. The most important were shad, striped bass, and sturgeon, the object of annual Lenape journeys to known fishing grounds along the river.[13]

Of course, the same species appeared in other rivers and played a major role in other groups' foodways. In spring, peoples everywhere decamped en masse to all rivers that offered good spawning conditions. What was unique was the sheer size and complexity of the Hudson. No other river was host to such massive numbers of fish at a time or abutted so varied an assortment of additional water habitats; in no other river did shifting gradations of salinity suitable for different species unfold over such distances. (The water is usually salt or brackish up to about eighty miles from the Lower Bay.) If any complement to the Hudson's resources were needed, it was filled by the annual migration of salmon into Long Island Sound and the Connecticut River, the southernmost East Coast salmon-spawning river.

The complex of water-based resources including the two rivers, the coast, and all the other local aquatic environments furnished not only the richest supply of animal protein in eastern North America but the one best spread out over the year. People did dry much of the spring fish catch to put by. But virtually the year round, they also had a fresh supply of creatures like winter flounder, mussels, oysters, and clams. Other coastal peoples enjoyed some of the same advantages, but to a much lesser extent, while the peoples who dwelt inland far from the Lower Hudson depended more heavily on the seasonally limited supply of game animals.

How does the Lower Hudson Valley's good fortune bear on the question of agriculture? The answer is that hunter-gatherers—as the Lenapes surely were throughout most of their existence—are unlikely to switch to sedentary farming unless they see it as a hedge against seasonal want. Otherwise, they are much better off as is, because farming—especially grain farming—places great demands on a society.[14]

In the Northeast, groups at inland locations like the Susquehanna Valley are thought to have begun growing domesticated crops well before 1000. Early evidence in coastal areas seems to date from some four centuries later.[15] This is why we cannot assume that the Lenapes ate like their sedentary and agriculture-minded counterparts elsewhere, much less like Native American peoples who survive today on terms far removed from hunter-gatherer economies.

Three plants—corn, beans, and squash—were the basis of pre-European agriculture throughout North America. (A less important plant, the sunflower, is of unclear status in this region.) These resources did not simply arrive one day on everybody's doorstep. They are natives of the Mexican tropics, from which people carried them every mile of the way to southern Ontario—they could not have survived on their own in the wild—over a period of many centuries. People did not adopt them everywhere with uniform speed. Those who first did so apparently were inlanders whose meat supply fluctuated seasonally in the absence of livestock animals. Coast dwellers not only had virtually year-round access to fish but, as the archaeologist Lynn Ceci pointed out thirty years ago, tended to live on soils less hospitable to farming than those of the interior.[16]

Even inland, the switch to agriculture cannot have been simple. Squash and beans were fairly easy plants to grow and use. Not so the most important member of the trio: maize, or corn. The kind in question was not sweet corn but an offshoot of an exceptionally hard, dense strain called "Northern Flint," which was seldom eaten fresh, since it was more valuable (and flavorful) in dried and ground form. No cultivated grain requires more work than flint corn—not only painstaking care at every stage from planting to harvesting, but also complex processing afterward (drying, shelling, treatment with alkali, dehulling, redrying, pounding, sifting) to convert it into something nonperishable and suitable for cooking.

The Equilibrium Disturbed

Even if all the northeastern peoples eventually would have gone over to agriculture, they were not left to do so on their own. At around 1500, their situation began to be changed by a phenomenon often called "contact," or "Contact" with a capital "C": the quiet infiltration of European barterers into Indian territorial ranges in the coastal Northeast and eventually the interior. Maintaining prudent silence about their doings to their own governments or potential competitors, adventurers from France, England, and elsewhere started buying furs on an ever-increasing scale in exchange for trade stuffs like woven cloth, glass beads, iron kettles, and steel knives. Because of these surreptitious dealings, European artifacts were already widespread in the Northeast by the time more official visitors—for instance, Hudson in 1609—began showing up. Hunter-gatherer societies close to the coast were the first to develop an appetite for such goods, but the search for pelts rapidly expanded inland. Within a generation or two, the entire northeastern population of fur-bearing animals began to shrink.[17]

Such early exchanges of furs for "trifles" (as the voyagers called their trade goods) were so unequal as to be no exchange at all. Only one side—the Europeans—possessed an endless supply of manufactures irresistibly desirable to the other. The Indians had no product of their own civilization that the foreign fortune-hunters prized as eagerly as the natives prized cloth and kettles. For such wares, they were willing to divert immense time and effort from their earlier hunter-gatherer economies to the commercial-scale pursuit of beaver, foxes, and the rest, incidentally decimating the supply deeper inland and having to work harder to bring in smaller catches. This vicious cycle, carried on with wampum as transregional and transnational currency, probably hastened the transition from foraging to farming in some regions with good soils while giving coastal peoples an incentive to rely for more of their food on trade with agricultural societies inland.[18]

It should now be clear why the natural history of the Lower Hudson Valley furnishes solider insights into pre-European foodways than other avenues of investigation—the meager and often ambiguous archaeological record, the example of other northeastern peoples with no Hudson River, or what the Dutch colonists saw the locals cooking and eating in communities already ravaged by Old World diseases. Nonetheless, we can piece together some important fragments of the culinary or gastronomic picture from these sources. One significant aid to reconstruction is the fact that all the peoples of the Northeast shared not only elements of a common larder but similar technological means, resulting in much the same arsenal of cooking equipment and techniques.[19]

How Did They Cook?

The Indians of the Northeast at the point of Contact were what archaeologists call "Neolithic" or "Late Stone Age" peoples; that is, they possessed advanced stone tool–making skills and some knowledge of agriculture grafted onto a hunter-gatherer way of life. Except for stones and clay, their material culture was almost wholly derived from the native wild plants and animals of the forests. As the first Europeans to wander into the region found, they had no metalworking technology—and thus no cooking methods involving pots able to conduct heat or withstand temperatures above the boiling point of water. One culinary consequence is obvious: until fur traders brought iron kettles, no native people could fry or sauté anything in fat, or even brown food in a pan before stewing it.

With certain exceptions, the materials they possessed for making cooking pots and other implements were short-lived: woven bark strips, woven reeds or plant fibers, skin pouches, or clay. Even this last was not particularly durable, for it could not be fired at anything above the temperature of a wood fire and tended to crack with repeated use. The only really long-lasting vessels were tubs made of hollowed-out log sections, which people used for cooking by putting in the ingredients and water, then adding smallish stones previously heated in the fire; as they cooled, more would be added.[20] Not surprisingly, the Lenapes and other northeastern peoples depended heavily on porridges, stews, soups, and dishes uniting elements of all these.

Other Native American cooking methods usually involved dry rather than moist heat and employed materials derived from what was at hand in people's everyday surroundings. People did stone-baking or -grilling by heating a rock enough to sear anything that came in contact with it. This was a fine way of cooking small or flat fish, not-too-thick slabs of meat, or flat cakes of meal.

For direct fire-roasting or -grilling, a method more suitable for large thick fish or large pieces of meat, people put the food on wooden spits to hold over the flames or on simple frameworks of peeled twigs or branches to prop up next to the fire. Doing this slowly over a partly damped fire, preferably of green wood, which gave off a lot of smoke, resulted in a kind of roasting/smoking that, along with sun-drying, was one of the few pre-European preservation methods.

Another means of roasting or baking well suited to small thin pieces of food was in the live embers of a fire, a method used with corn to make a highly portable but sustainable and, by Dutch report, delicious trail ration. If the food—say, a small fish or cake of meal—was put in *tout nu,* it cooked by dry heat alone. If it was wrapped *tamal*-style in leaves or husks, enough moisture would be trapped inside to create a little steaming action. People may well also have practiced clay-baking, a method (independently invented in many parts of the world) in which they completely sealed something like a whole fish or bird in a jacket of wet clay and put the entire thing in the fire, where the food steamed inside the coating. Eventually, they retrieved it from the embers and cracked off the baked clay, to which any unwanted scales or feathers would cling.

The only other moist-heat method was a kind of pit-cooking akin to a modern clambake, most likely reserved for large occasions. The cook or cooks dug a hole in the ground and lined it with stones, on which they built a fire. When the layer of stones was red hot, they arranged the food on top, covered up the pit, and let the contents cook in the live steam for many hours. Probably this would have been the best way of cooking very large pieces of meat other than spit-roasting, and the best way of cooking a medley of different ingredients other than pot-boiling.

Before cooks could apply any of these cooking methods, most foods required an enormous amount of processing—skinning or scraping; repeated boiling or steeping to leach out poisons or bitter juices; pounding or grinding to soften tough fibers, separate kernels from hulls and husks, or break down anything obstinately hard. The tools for these tasks were everyday objects subjected to very simple modifications.

Clamshells made excellent scoops and spoons and also could be chipped or ground to produce a fine edge for cutting or a rough edge for scraping. A skilled woman could skin and cut up any meat animal from a deer to a rabbit with a clamshell "knife." The most important grinding tools were rocks and wooden mortars. To convert a rock into a grinder, a person selected a large, flat one that could be hollowed out (using a smaller stone) into a shallow concavity. Plain water might leach out harsh flavors from some foods; repeated treatment with hot water would mellow others. For the stubbornest cases, people used lye, the all-purpose household chemical of many preindustrial households; lye was made by dissolving plant ashes in water, and its exact composition varied with the nature of the plant.

The stuff of other implements was always at hand. Most could be easily made, discarded, and replaced: trimmed sticks to stir the pot or fashion into spits and grilling racks, empty turtle shells or dried gourds to use as bowls, good-sized bones and horns to carve into spoons or paddles, small sharp bones for use as pins or needles. Such tools were not meant to last forever, something that people didn't expect even of a house. Clearly, lack of durability is not terribly disadvantageous for most of the basic *batterie de cuisine* in a hunter-gatherer society. But the native peoples quickly began to find it so as the pressures of Contact, with the appearance of new devices like iron pots, started propelling them toward a more sedentary existence.

But What Did It *Taste* Like?

None of this information tells us the one thing that most people would like to know about any unfamiliar cuisine: the way that flavors and textures register on the palate. Potential clues are very few; most Europeans who described the Indians of New Netherland alluded too briefly to the food or cooking to give us much to chew on.

One anonymous Dutch fur trader who ventured into Mohawk–Seneca country in December 1634 and January 1635 noted down much of what he ate. Some of the details may also be applicable to Lenape food, though the inland-dwelling Iroquois Confederacy peoples undoubtedly depended more on settled agriculture and stored food than did the Lenapes of the Lower Hudson Valley. Allowing both for the Dutch habit of attaching convenient Dutch names to New World items (the narrator's "salmon" may or may not be that fish) and for the twentieth-century English translators' clumsy vagueness in rendering food-related terms, this account still conveys much that we would not know otherwise.

A brief glossary gives the "Maqua" (Mohawk) words for foods including bread, beans, maize, fish, salmon, meat, flour, "The bacon," "The fat," "The grease," and "The bone." The bacon in question was made (without salt) of smoked dried bear meat, and the nameless traveler ate it several times in a six-week journey. At one point, he and his companions helped themselves to some fleeing Indians' "bread"— probably some kind of cornmeal ash cake—"baked with beans." Later they saw "Sinneken" (Seneca) women trying to sell dried and very bad-smelling fresh salmon. (If it really was salmon, it must have come from coastal Connecticut.) They paid wampum for "a very fat" turkey that a local chief then cooked for them, "and the grease he mixed with our beans and maize." On another occasion, "we were invited to buy bear meat"—the Mohawks fattened bears in cages—"and we also got half a bushel of beans and a quantity of dried strawberries, and we bought some bread [cornbread], that we wanted to take on our march. Some of the loaves were baked with nuts and cherries and dry blueberries and the grains of the sunflower." A couple of weeks later, "I bought four dried salmon and two pieces of bear bacon that was about nine inches thick; and we saw thicker, even. They gave us beans cooked with bear bacon to eat to-day, and further nothing particular happened." Near the western end of the Mohawk Valley, friendly villagers offered him white hare cooked with walnuts and—a rare treat for Europeans in those parts—"a piece of wheaten bread" brought by an Indian recently arrived from Fort Orange (Albany).[21]

Adriaen Van der Donck, in *The Representation of New Netherland* (1650) and *A Description of the New Netherlands* (1655), tried to construct more connected portrayals of the natives' food. Our single best source of information is his account in the second work, though Jeremiah Johnson's 1833 translation shows little command of English kitchen terminology. We can't assume that Van der Donck himself would have noticed the same things as an eagle-eyed home cook, but plainly he had taken intelligent notice of his neighbors' ways:

> Their common food is meat, and fish of every kind, according to the seasons, and the advantages of the places where they reside. They have no pride, or particular methods in preparing their food. Their fish or meat they usually boil in water, without salt, or smout [rendered fat], and nothing more than the articles yield. They know of no stewing, fricasseeing, baking, frying, or the like methods of cooking, and seldom do they warm up or boil any food, unless it be small pieces of meat or fish, when they travel or are hunting, and have no other opportunity to prepare their food.
>
> For bread they use maize, or Turkey corn, which the women pound fine into meal (as the Hebrews did their manna in the wilderness), of which they bake cakes, for they know nothing of mills. They also use pounded maize, as we do rice, and samp [cracked hominy], with their boiled meat. Their common food, and for which their meal is generally used, is pap, or mush, which in the New Netherlands is named sapaen. This is so common among the Indians that they seldom pass a day without it, unless they are on a journey or hunting. We seldom visit an Indian lodge at any time of the day, without seeing their sapaen preparing, or seeing them eating the same. It is the common food of all; young and old eat it; and they are so well accustomed to it, and fond of it, that when they visit our people, or each other, they consider themselves neglected unless they are treated with sapaen. Without sapaen they do not eat a satisfactory meal. And when they have an opportunity, they frequently boil fish or meat with it; but seldom when the meat or fish is fresh, but when they have the articles dried hard, and pounded fine. This food they usually prepare at the close of the winter and in the spring, when the hunting season is past, and their stock of provisions is nearly exhausted. They also use many dry beans, which they consider dainties. Those they boil soft with fresh meat. They use for their subsistence every kind of fish and flesh that is fit for food, which the country and the places of their settlements afford, and that they can obtain. . . . On extraordinary occasions, when they wish to entertain any person, then they prepare

beavers' tails, bass heads, with parched corn meal, or very fat meat stewed with shelled chestnuts bruised.[22]

Between these two reports we can make out some intriguing outlines of Indian food in New Netherland. Still, the actual tastes that people experienced in any dish will always be beyond our ken. It is important to understand that our own preferences are useless as a clue to anyone else's. (The cooking of surviving Native American groups now has too many European-derived accretions to be of much help.) What tastes good to us would not necessarily have tasted good to the Lenapes, and vice versa. In fact, the evidence from European accounts—surely reliable on this point, if not on all details of pre-Columbian civilization—firmly points to a certain amount of mutual distaste on the part of both natives and newcomers.

For the indigenous peoples of eastern North America, the largest hurdle in accepting European food was salt. None of them had ever put salt on food, not even for preserving it. This in itself indicates a staggering cultural divide, because salt is, and was in the seventeenth century, virtually the core seasoning of all European cuisines. The colonists on their part found much of the Indians' food rank-tasting, absolutely spoiled, or disgustingly unclean. The only local preservation methods—drying with or without smoke—took a while to halt bacterial action in the absence of salt, so that dried meat or fish would at first begin to rot. And they cheerfully accepted flavors that revolted the Dutch, like those of the guts cooked in an uncleaned fish or deer intestines eaten contents and all.[23]

These preferences represent clashes of taste that well-meaning modern reconstructors never can reconcile. Nor should we suppose that enough other seasonings would paper over the difficulty. Aside from salt—where the evidence is not of use but of nonuse—we know virtually nothing about pre-European flavoring preferences in this or any other region.

Clearly, the wild landscape furnished many potential seasonings, like fragrant sassafras leaves or tart sumac berries, that we can well imagine putting into savory meat stews. But for all we know, stews with such embellishments would have been incomprehensible to the Indians. We cannot even assume that before the Europeans arrived anyone made or used a reputedly age-old ingredient like maple syrup. No people would invest the huge amounts of time and fuel necessary to boil down many gallons of sap to a few quarts of syrup—difficult enough with iron pots and nearly inconceivable with clay vessels—without a very powerful incentive in the form of a sweet tooth, something that our predecessors in this region may or may not have possessed.

There is perhaps one way in which a modern cook could experiment with one pre-European preference or complex of preferences. We have ample evidence that the northeastern Indians loved fat. (One Dutch observer in Mohawk country reported that people would "take a piece of bear's fat as large as two fists, and eat it clear without bread or anything else.")[24] They could not cook in fat, but they could cook with it and had access to many different kinds—from black walnuts, butternuts, hickory nuts, several kinds of acorns, squash seeds, and sunflower seeds; the luscious fat in the heads of striped bass; the heavy deposit of fat over the breast of a turkey cock in fall; the porklike fat of bear; and the various fats of lynx, raccoon, beaver, and virtually all other meat animals. Aside from chunks of fat cut from a carcass, all could be obtained by cooking the source in water until the fat was rendered out and rose to the top in a layer to be removed when the liquid cooled.[25]

Since all these fats were unrefined, they all had individual flavors as distinctive as that of bacon grease or new unfiltered olive oil. The world of unrefined fats is (with one or two exceptions) nearly a closed book to most Americans; for the most part, we are surrounded with vegetable oils and spreads that have had the original characteristic taste refined out of them. But for preindustrial peoples with access to many different sources, fats are among the best and most varied natural flavorings. At least a few of the kinds that were plentiful in Lenape country ought to be reproducible by historically minded cooks willing to track down something like white oak acorns (the most mellow and least bitter) or black walnuts.

We cannot pretend that this gesture would go far toward reconstructing the whole fabric of Lenape foods and techniques. A skilled forager with a knowledge of how to handle wild roots and shoots could travel a little more of the distance. So could anyone with access to a supply of Northern Flint corn and the stamina to turn it into lye-treated meal using pre-European methods. But the real system of foodways died long ago or, more accurately, was destroyed. It depended on both a vast range of interconnected local resources and the ability to move freely throughout a diverse range in order to get to any one of them at the right moment.

Moving freely around miles of terrain was alien to the European concept of real property: measured pieces of ground that owners were entitled to use as they saw fit by, for example, cutting down every tree, pasturing cows, plowing up the soil, and fencing out other people. When enough of these things had been done by enough exercisers of property rights, no means of self-support remained for the bewildered Lenapes, who could conceive of using land or, more precisely, what lived on it, but not owning it.[26]

Exterminating the Lower Hudson Valley habitats meant exterminating the wild food supply. In the not very long run, it also meant exterminating the Indians. No trace of a Lenape "cuisine" remains in or anywhere near Greater New York.

The Dutch and English accomplished this destruction not because they were monsters but because to their understanding, wild plants in unimproved habitats were of no consequence. The food resources that they understood demanded drastic alteration of landscapes—a signal achievement of the dike-building Dutch in their own country—for the purpose of growing domestic crops. We can hardly wonder that they had no special respect for wild plants, much less anything as abstract as primal ecosystems.

The Myth of Exchange

Nonhistorians may easily suppose that northeastern peoples like the Lenapes exchanged foods and expertise with the first European colonists, like housewives swapping recipes and cups of sugar. I doubt that this assumption would hold up well anywhere in the colonial Northeast. It certainly was not true in the Greater New York region. Exchange exists only where two parties give and receive things that both account of comparable value. If such transactions ever took place in the Northeast, they were over in the blink of an eye.

The only real Old World–New World food exchanges occurred thousands of miles south of New York. The crucial places of interchange were in Mexico and Peru. To this day, pre-Hispanic crops native to those regions, from tomatoes and cacao to potatoes and chiles, not only thrive there but are grown and enthusiastically eaten in many parts of the Old World. By contrast, not a single food plant uniquely native to northeastern North America is still a significant source of food in the Northeast or anywhere else.

What made the difference is plain: the peoples of the Aztec and Inca lands had systematically domesticated—and founded cuisines on—a very large range of food plants that the Spanish at once recognized as a token of high civilization. They also knew how to create or improve arable land through engineering feats that awed European beholders.

Domesticated crops, no matter how strange, inspired some respect and thoughts of profit on the part of even very ruthless conquerors. The ability to conduct intensive agriculture with native plants is a crucial reason that large elements of the indigenous population still survive in Latin America. Lacking it, the first peoples of the Northeast—especially those closest to the coast and least given to agriculture—were almost wholly destroyed. All that the Dutch saw in New Netherland was *wilden,* or "savages," hunting, fishing, and collecting all manner of unfamiliar weeds and roots while practicing some limited cultivation of three crops introduced to the Old World by the Spanish and thus already partly known to the newcomers. And by European lights, the natives could not have placed much value on this last activity, since they left it up to the women.

The Europeans did pay some attention to Lenape foods and foodways while they needed the "savages'" help, which was not very long. The Lenapes, for their part, took a much stronger interest in the invaders' food. On both sides, what aroused most admiration was the other's principal grain. Dutch and English settlers benefited at once from the local peoples' prehistoric achievements in breeding and growing corn at such northerly latitudes. They liked the meal and cakes made from it and promptly took to *sapaen,* the Lenape version of cornmeal mush.

Perhaps their favorite Lenape food was the particularly valuable parched corn made by ember-roasting the grains until they acquired a concentrated nutty flavor. The Lenapes in turn developed a great liking for flour from Old World wheat—something that the Dutch were eager to establish as quickly as possible on their newly cleared fields—and the bread and buns made with it.[27]

There was a terrible difference between these two new appetites—a painful illustration of why the exchange was really no exchange. The Indians of New Netherland could no more have grown wheat, ground flour, and baked yeast breads for themselves than they could have distilled rum (another foreign introduction for which they developed an insatiable craving) or made iron kettles. The Europeans, however, swiftly managed to grow corn on such a scale (and on cleared lands taken from the first occupants) that within a few decades the Dutch and the English were selling it to the Indians, having made it impossible for the latter to either forage or farm.[28] The landscape was being progressively denuded of useful wild plants, while the Indians' attempts to cultivate garden plots on ground of their "own" were trampled over by the invaders' livestock and courts of justice.

Already in the first century of Contact, the people had committed themselves to great cultural change for the sake of things that they were utterly powerless to make or supply for themselves. In the early colonies, their desire for gifts like knives and rum would hasten their own destruction. Although within a few generations they would acquire a European taste for salt and sugar (which they had to buy), they never brought about any comparable change in the newcomers' preferences. By the early eighteenth century, the Lower Hudson Valley Lenape peoples had been decimated by disease and pushed out of any nearby land suitable for settlement and farming. From a few short-lived sheltering places, they were almost entirely driven out of the Northeast early in the nineteenth century and forcibly relocated to scattered parts of the young United States. A few Munsees still survive in Oklahoma.

In a strange instance of poetic justice, creatures that the Lenapes hunted for food have now returned to the Greater New York region—themselves hunting for food— in large enough numbers to inconvenience suburbanites and some townspeople. Every county adjacent to New York City is familiar with raccoons dining from garbage pails, tulip-loving deer, and black bears that amble up to promising front doors. For the first peoples of the region, there will be no return.

NOTES

1. My account of local geology, including the land base and formation of the Hudson River, is chiefly drawn from Chet Raymo and Maureen E. Raymo, *Written in Stone: A Geological History of the Northeastern United States* (Chester, Conn.: Globe Pequot Press, 1989); and Christopher J. Schuberth, *The Geology of New York City and Environs* (Garden City, N.Y.: Natural History Press/Doubleday, 1967). For crucial information on local land and water habitats as well as plant and animal species, I have drawn on Elizabeth Barlow, *The Forests and Wetlands of New York City* (Boston: Little, Brown, 1971); Robert H. Boyle, *The Hudson River: A Natural and Unnatural History* (New York: Norton, 1969); John Kieran, *A Natural History of New York City* (Boston: Houghton Mifflin, 1959); and Stephen P. Stanne, Roger G. Panetta, and Brian E. Forist, *The Hudson: An Illustrated Guide to the Living River* (New Brunswick, N.J.: Rutgers University Press, 1996). Like all who write about interactions between people and environments in the Northeast from precolonial times on, I am deeply indebted to William Cronon, *Changes in the Land: Indians, Colonists, and the Ecology of New England* (New York: Hill and Wang, 1983), which contains much that is as applicable to the Greater New York region as to New England.

2. On this subject, the most valuable source is Anne-Marie Cantwell and Diana diZerega Wall, *Unearthing Gotham: The Archaeology of New York City* (New Haven, Conn.: Yale University Press, 2001). In addition, I have drawn on the archaeological and anthropological accounts of Lenape (or Munsee) civilization in Robert S. Grumet, *Historic Contact: In-*

dian People and Colonists in Today's Northeastern United States in the Sixteenth Through Eighteenth Centuries (Norman: University of Oklahoma Press, 1995); Julian Harris Salomon, *Indians of the Lower Hudson Region: The Munsee* (New City, N.Y.: Historical Society of Rockland County, 1982); and John A. Strong, *The Algonquian Peoples of Long Island from Earliest Times to 1700* (Interlaken, N.Y.: Empire State Books, 1997).

3. Many early Dutch and other European descriptions of the region and people are collected (in English translation) in J. Franklin Jameson, ed., *Narratives of New Netherland, 1609–1664* (New York: Scribner, 1909; facsimile repr., Elibron Classics). The accounts I have found most valuable are "Letter of Isaack De Rasieres to Samuel Blommaert," 102–116; David Pietersz De Vries, "Korte Historiael ende Journaels Aenteyckeninge," 186–236; and Adriaen Van der Donck, "The Representation of New Netherland," 293–354. The best single seventeenth-century source is Adriaen Van der Donck, *A Description of the New Netherlands*, ed. Thomas F. O'Donnell (Syracuse, N.Y.: Syracuse University Press, 1968).

4. In this category, the works indispensable to anyone interested in reconstructing precolonial Indian foodways are two studies by early-twentieth-century anthropologists who collected information from the Iroquois: Arthur C. Parker, *Iroquois Uses of Maize and Other Food Plants*, New York State Museum Bulletin 144 (1910; facsimile repr., Ohsweken, Ont.: Iroqrafts, 1994); and F. W. Waugh, *Iroquois Foods and Food Preparations*, Anthropological Series no. 12 (1916; facsimile repr., Ohsweken, Ont.: Iroqrafts, 1991). Although it must be recognized that Parker's and Waugh's informants did not attempt to disentangle aboriginal from Europeanized foods or foodways and enormous differences existed between the precolonial ecologies of the Iroquois Confederacy regions and the Lower Hudson Valley, these two works furnish our best window into actual food preparation and cooking practices. A helpful secondary source of information on native food plants and household technology that has much material also relevant to our region is Howard S. Russell, *Indian New England Before the Mayflower* (Hanover, N.H.: University Press of New England, 1980).

5. Cantwell and Wall, *Unearthing Gotham*, 113.

6. The best early European accounts of the regional fauna are Van der Donck, *Description of the New Netherlands*, 43–54, and "Representation of New Netherland," 296–97; and De Vries, "Korte Historiael ende Journaels Aenteyckeninge," 220–22.

7. Quoted in Johan De Laet, "New World," in Jameson, *Narratives of New Netherland*, 49; also see Cantwell and Wall, *Unearthing Gotham*, 104–9.

8. Van der Donck, *Description of the New Netherlands*, 53.

9. "Letter of Isaack De Rasieres to Samuel Blommaert," 115; De Vries, "Korte Historiael ende Journaels Aenteyckeninge," 221. The best modern description of the bird is A. W. Schorger, *The Wild Turkey: Its History and Domestication* (Norman: University of Oklahoma Press, 1966).

10. Very brief early descriptions of useful native plants can be found in Van der Donck, *Description of the New Netherlands*, 23, 25–29, and "Representation of New Netherland," 295–96, 298–99; and De Vries, "Korte Historiael ende Journaels Aenteyckeninge," 218–19. It is not surprising that seventeenth-century European observers were usually not able to identify and describe the local flora. For surveys of the surviving flora, see Barlow, *Forests and Wetlands*, esp. 29–34; and Kieran, *Natural History*, 165–289. Anyone trying to explore the area today in quest of wild food plants should consult "Wildman" Steven Brill, with Evelyn Dean, *Identifying and Harvesting Edible and Medicinal Plants in Wild (and Not So Wild) Places* (New York: Hearst Books, 1994). For lists of useful plants native to parts of North America and exploited by New York's regional predecessors, see Russell, *Indian New England*, 209–15; and Elizabeth J. Reitz, "Temperate and Arctic North America to 1492," in *The Cambridge World*

History of Food, ed. Kenneth F. Kiple and Kriemhild Coneè Ornelas (Cambridge: Cambridge University Press, 2000), 2:1289.

11. Cantwell and Wall, *Unearthing Gotham*, 112–14; Jared Diamond, *Guns, Germs, and Steel: The Fates of Human Societies* (New York: Norton, 1997), 104–9. For a lucid summary of some issues involved in reconstructing the diffusion of agriculture to precolonial North America, see Bruce D. Smith, *The Emergence of Agriculture* (New York: Scientific American Library, 1999), 184–205.

12. Tom Lewis, "Hudson River," in *The Encyclopedia of New York State*, ed. Peter Eisenstadt (Syracuse, N.Y.: Syracuse University Press, 2005), 739–40; Stanne, Panetta, and Forist, *Hudson*, 2–6.

13. For contemporary descriptions of the Lower Hudson Valley's water, fish, and shellfish, see Van der Donck, *Description of the New Netherlands*, 6–17, 54–56, and "Representation of New Netherland," 297–98; and De Vries, "Korte Historiael ende Journaels Aenteyckeninge," 222–23.

14. Various implications of transitions from hunting and gathering to sedentary farming are well summarized in Cantwell and Wall, *Unearthing Gotham*, 93–95, 112–14; and Diamond, *Guns, Germs, and Steel*, 104–9.

15. The study that for the past thirty years has dominated all discussion of this question as well as the impact of prerecorded Contact on coastal areas is Lynn Ceci, "The Effect of European Contact and Trade on the Settlement Pattern of Indians in Coastal New York, 1524–1665: The Archaeological and Documentary Evidence" (Ph.D. diss., City University of New York, 1977), esp. 93–134, 143–71, 187–90, 277–83.

16. Ibid., 111–12, 118–19.

17. Ibid., 135–37, 143–44; Cronon, *Changes in the Land*, 83–84, 97–108.

18. Ceci, "Effect of European Contact," 122, 277–81.

19. The following description of pre-Contact culinary techniques and equipment draws heavily on the accounts in Parker, *Iroquois Uses of Maize*, esp. 45–61, 66–78, and plates 1–30; and Waugh, *Iroquois Foods*, esp. 54–71, 134–38, and plates xiv–xix, xxii–xxxv, although many of the objects pictured or described (for example, wooden splint baskets) represent post-European technologies. See also Russell, *Indian New England*, 56, 58–65, 72–75. Interested reader-cooks should note that some of the techniques reconstructed by the British archaeologist Jacqui Wood, in *Prehistoric Cooking* (Charleston, S.C.: Tempus, 2001), undoubtedly were practiced as well in Stone Age North America.

20. Cantwell and Wall, *Unearthing Gotham*, 53; Strong, *Algonquian Peoples of Long Island*, 45; Waugh, *Iroquois Foods*, 55.

21. "Narrative of a Journey into the Mohawk and Oneida Country," in Jameson, *Narratives of New Netherland*, 139–62.

22. Van der Donck, *Description of the New Netherlands*, 75–76.

23. Johannes Megapolensis, "A Short Account of the Mohawk Indians," in Jameson, *Narratives of New Netherland*, 176.

24. Ibid., 177.

25. Parker, *Iroquois Uses of Maize*, 100; Russell, *Indian New England*, 91; Waugh, *Iroquois Foods*, 124.

26. For a thoughtful statement of landownership or non-landownership issues in nearby New England, see Cronon, *Changes in the Land*, 54–81.

27. Parker, *Iroquois Uses of Maize*, 76–77; Peter G. Rose, introduction to *The Sensible Cook: Dutch Foodways in the New World, De Verstandige Koek*, trans. Peter G. Rose (Syra-

cuse, N.Y.: Syracuse University Press, 1989), 26–27; Russell, *Indian New England*, 78–79; Van der Donck, *Description of the New Netherlands*, 75–77; Waugh, *Iroquois Foods*, 88–89.

28. Ceci, "Effect of European Contact," 123–25; Cantwell and Wall, *Unearthing Gotham*, 147–48; Grumet, *Historic Contact*, 221, 226–29; Salomon, *Indians of the Lower Hudson Region*, 55–62.

The Food and Drink of New York
from 1624 to 1898

ANDREW F. SMITH

SINCE 1626, food has played an important role in the history of New York City. In the early years, food simply was a means of survival for the small group of colonists from the Netherlands. Later, when their settlement was better established, nearby farmers began to send their crops and products into the city, and food became a major item of commerce. Throughout the eighteenth and early nineteenth centuries, New York produced or processed massive amounts of food, such as flour, sugar, and alcoholic beverages, which were exported to other communities in America and Europe. Then in the nineteenth century, as wealth and immigrants flowed into the city, New York developed an unusually heterogeneous and ever-changing culinary life, which continues to thrive.

New Amsterdam

Beginning in 1624, the Dutch West India Company settled the region around what is today New York City. The early settlers found an abundance of game, particularly deer, bear, wild turkey, migratory fowl, fresh and saltwater fish, shellfish, turtles, and even buffalo. From local Indian tribes, the Dutch also acquired maize, but they were so focused on making money in the fur trade that they neglected to establish the gardens, farms, and orchards they needed to sustain their community. A growing food shortage was not the only problem the Dutch settlers faced, however. Their small, widely separated outposts were ideal targets for marauding Indians, and concern for their safety was the main reason that in 1626 the Dutch decided to concentrate their efforts on a central location at the southern tip of Manhattan. They called their settlement Nieuw Amsterdam (New Amsterdam).

Although the Dutch had begun to develop their agriculture and husbandry, food shortages remained a serious problem in New Amsterdam. In 1628, the Reverend Jonas Michaëlius, the first minister of the Dutch Reformed Church in the settlement, reported that the colonists still had failed to "obtain proper sustenance for want of bread and other necessaries." Butter and milk, he wrote, "cannot here be obtained" except at "very high price," and he urged the Dutch West India Company to send more farmers and dairymen.[1] The Dutch did persuade dairy farmers to settle in New Amsterdam, and as a result, milk, butter, and cheese became staples (as they had been in the old country). Having learned from the Indians how to plant corn, the Dutch ground the kernels and made cakes by mixing the cornmeal with water and baking the dough in hot ashes. They also ate *samp,* a type of hominy, and *suppawn* (or *sapaen*), a thick cornmeal porridge mixed with butter. Other colonists planted Old World grains, such as wheat and barley, and a wide variety of fruits, nuts, and vegetables, such as apples, berries, cherries, grapes, almonds, hazelnuts, onions, peas, and turnips.[2]

Unlike Boston, New Amsterdam never developed a large deep sea–fishing fleet, perhaps because the local waters, both fresh and salt, offered such an abundance of fish and other seafood. According to Adriaen Van der Donck, a Dutch lawyer who arrived in the city in 1644, "All the waters of the New Netherlands are rich with fishes." The Hudson estuary was teeming with bass, shad, carp, pike, trout, suckers, flounder, eels, lampreys, turtles, crabs, clams, mussels, terrapin, and many other fish and shellfish. Lobsters were plentiful, and some were remarkably large: "from five to six feet in length; others again are from a foot to a foot and a half long." In early June, sturgeon were extremely plentiful in the rivers, but Van der Donck noted that they were not much esteemed and were not eaten when large. In fact, he reported that no one took the trouble to catch them for profit, and among those who caught sturgeon for sport, the "roes from which the costly *caviaer* was made" were discarded. Oysters were abundant in the bays and harbors around Manhattan and Long Island—enough to be considered an everyday food rather than a luxury—but Van der Donck observed that "they don't have any pearls in them."[3]

As in the Netherlands, bread was a staple in New Amsterdam, and bakeries were in operation by the 1640s.[4] Wheat was easily grown in the New York hinterlands, and flour was milled in the city. Grain, flour, and bread became major export items, so much so that New York, New Jersey, and Pennsylvania became known as the "bread colonies." Ships leaving New York Harbor stocked up on bread, hardtack, and flour before sailing out to sea. By the 1760s, 75 percent of New York's exports were agricultural products in the form of flour or biscuits. During the following decades, the city became the world's largest merchant and milling center.[5]

The Dutch made their favorite sweets in the new settlement: *olykoeks* (oil cakes), rich, sweet cakes fried in deep fat; and *krullen,* deep-fried twists of dough. Almost a century and a half after the end of Dutch rule, Washington Irving described the former as "balls of sweetened dough, fried in hog's fat, and called doughnuts, or olykoeks."[6] The Dutch also excelled at making wafers using decorative irons and *koekjes* (little cakes), which initially referred only to sweet biscuits flavored with nutmeg or cinnamon. Later the word "cookie" came to include a wide range of small baked goods. Thanks to the availability of affordable sweeteners (the Dutch imported raw sugar and molasses from the Caribbean), all sorts of sweet pastries were common in New Amsterdam.

The Dutch typically breakfasted on bread, butter, cheese, and milk. Dinner, usually served at midday, consisted of one main dish accompanied by a "great salad," which was likely *koolslaa* (cabbage salad). Another common dinner dish was *hutspot* (hotchpot), a New World version of a traditional Dutch casserole, composed of coarsely ground corn mixed with root vegetables and boiled salt meat, preferably pork. Suppers frequently consisted of "bread and butter and bread and milk."[7] Rather than expend their time and effort raising and growing their own food, the Dutch in New Amsterdam bought beef, pork, wheat, and butter from farmers on Long Island; beef, lamb, fish, butter, malt, salt, and cider apples from New England; and beef, pork, and fruit from Virginia.[8]

New York

As the profitability of fur trapping began to diminish, the financial problems of the Dutch West India Company began to mount. Fewer people emigrated from the Netherlands to New Amsterdam, and immigrants from other countries, including Spain and England, were permitted to settle in the colony. By the 1660s, almost half the people living in New Amsterdam were not of Dutch origin. The colony was located between the rapidly expanding English colonies in New England to the north and Virginia to the south, so when the Second Anglo-Dutch War broke out in 1664, the British sent four warships into the harbor. New Amsterdam surrendered before a single shot was fired, and the city was renamed New York in honor of James Stuart, Duke of York, the future King James II.

Under English administration, New York shifted from a small, unprofitable, fur-trapping colony to a major trading center. Agricultural commodities, such as wheat, molasses, and apples, were shipped into the city, where they were converted into marketable products like flour, sugar, rum, and hard cider.

Foreign imports into colonial New York included favorite English beverages, and both coffee and tea were imported from England. In 1696, Lieutenant John Hutchins opened a coffeehouse called the King's Arms, and it became the unofficial headquarters of English émigrés in New York. During the early eighteenth century, many more coffeehouses were opened in New York City, and they served hot chocolate and food as well as coffee and tea.[9]

Most alcoholic beverages, particularly wine, were imported. Other liquor, such as hard cider and rum, were manufactured in the New York area and often exported to other colonies. Drinking alcohol with meals, including breakfast, was common, and residents of the city consumed substantial quantities of beer, ale, spirits, cider, and wine. By the late seventeenth century, Manhattan had several good inns and taverns, some of which served the gentry; Elias Chardavoine's victualing house, for instance, served French food. By the 1730s, the social life of the city revolved around taverns, one of which invited diners to sample "the most Dishes of Meat," in the "best Order," and to "drink the richest Wine." For the lower classes, there were many dram houses, ale houses, and tippling houses.[10]

Revolutionary New York

By the mid-eighteenth century, tea was a staple beverage in the American colonies, all of it imported from India. In May 1773, the British imposed a tax on tea, and seven months later, on December 16, 1773, Bostonians responded with the famous Boston Tea Party. Although this event received wide attention and drew the wrath of the British, a similar "party" was held in New York Harbor when a ship carrying tea came into port on April 22, 1774. Thereafter, many colonies signed nonimportation agreements, refusing to permit the offloading of taxed tea. Dutch smugglers, however, were able to spirit tea into New York, and this untaxed tea remained affordable. But when the War for Independence broke out, many Americans gave up tea to signal their patriotism.

Early in the Revolutionary War, when British forces captured New York City, supporters of the Revolution fled. New York was occupied for the next seven years—longer than any other American city during the war. Thousands of British troops and German mercenaries were garrisoned in the city. But because American soldiers controlled the hinterland and many farmers refused to sell their products to British-controlled New York City, virtually all commodities had to be shipped to the city from England and Ireland. Consequently, the cost of food jumped 800 percent during the war, and when food shipments failed to arrive, the British even considered abandoning the city. Only the arrival of a victualing fleet from Ireland prevented mass starvation.[11]

Samuel Fraunces, a popular tavern owner of French and African descent, remained in the city during the British occupation, although he supported the cause of the patriots. In 1783, when the British occupation ended, General George Washington visited Fraunces's tavern, where he gave his famous farewell speech to the officers of the Continental Army. The following year, New York became the temporary capital of the new nation, and when Washington was inaugurated president at Federal Hall in 1789, he selected Fraunce as his head steward. While in New York, Washington hosted lavish dinners and receptions, much to the shock of some members of the cabinet and of Congress.[12] A guest described one such dinner, given in August 1789: "First was the soup; fish roasted and boiled; meats, gammon, fowls, etc." It was followed by dessert: "apple pies, pudding, etc.; then iced creams, jellies, etc.; then water-melons, musk-melons, apples, peaches, and nuts."[13]

Vendors, Markets, and Grocery Stores

Street vendors, farmers' markets, and grocery stores provided a complex distribution system for New York's wide variety of foodstuffs. Vendors had hawked their wares throughout the city since its earliest days, and by the early nineteenth century, they were selling buns, clams, fish, gingerbread, hot corn, oysters, soda, milk, and tea rusks.[14]

By 1800, vendors were selling roasted peanuts on the streets of New York. Peanuts became even more popular in the city after the Civil War, when Thomas Rowland of Norfolk, Virginia, bought peanuts from farmers and shipped a small batch to New York. This batch found its way to an Italian commission merchant, who sent out Italian peddlers to sell the peanuts. When this system proved successful, the commission merchant recruited more peddlers and this time equipped them with pushcarts and bags of peanuts, which they bought on credit. The peddlers were required to sell a certain quantity of peanuts within a given period of time; if they did not, their carts were taken away, and they were refused further supplies. Successful vendors returned 25 percent of their sales to the commission agents and pocketed the remaining 75 percent.[15] Some vendors then became wholesale dealers themselves, hiring other immigrants. This method worked well, and other foods began to be distributed and sold in the same way.

In 1870, an article in *Harper's* claimed that vendors generated only "a few shillings' worth" of sales, but the author had greatly underestimated the income of peanut vendors, some of whom made small fortunes. In 1887, a house on Mulberry Street was sold at auction to a man who bid more than $24,000. Much to the surprise of those at the auction and other members of New York's elite, the buyer "was a dingy, dwarfish specimen of Italian immigration"—in other words, a street vendor.[16]

Because many first-generation immigrants ended up in the narrow confines of big-city ghettos, street vendors could easily cater to their particular culinary needs. For some groups, street food became an important way of retaining their ethnic identity. Pushcart peddlers selling old-country foods were particularly important to Jewish immigrants in the late nineteenth century. In her book *Hungering for America,* Hasia Diner wrote that "food drew Jewish men and women to the streets. In the immigrant and first American-born generations, Jews lived in relatively compact Jewish neighborhoods. The provision of food to Jews by Jews enhanced the sense of community."[17] Other immigrant groups followed a similar pattern. Some street foods had an almost universal appeal, and by the end of the nineteenth century, the streets of New York were filled with pushcart vendors selling a variety of such foods: sausages, hamburgers, hot dogs, peanuts, popcorn, pretzels, and ice cream.

Since the days of New Amsterdam, farmers' markets had been an important distribution mechanism for food, and the market system expanded when the city became New York. These markets offered a great diversity of products. Pork, beef, lamb, and mutton were plentiful, and butchers were licensed and regulated. Markets also provided New Yorkers with abundant fruits and vegetables. Apples were a major crop in New York State, and hard cider was a widely drunk beverage. By the late eighteenth century, tropical fruits—pineapples, limes, oranges, lemons, and figs—were being imported from the Caribbean and were generally available in season at relatively low cost.[18] The nineteenth century saw the continued expansion of the city's public markets. Fulton Market (later renamed the Fulton Fish Market), on the East River, opened in 1822; Washington Market, across town on the Hudson River at Fulton Street, was established in 1828 and quickly became the city's largest market.[19]

In the second half of the nineteenth century, the importance of the public markets began to decline when the city failed to open new ones to keep pace with the its growth. This created an opportunity for small, family-owned food stores, which sold mainly nonperishable items. In 1859, George F. Gilman, a prosperous New York businessman, and his partner, George H. Hartford, started to sell tea in New York City. Three years later, they named their business the Great American Tea Company. At the time, most grocers bought their stock from distributors; but Gilman and Hartford imported tea from China and sold it directly to their retail customers, lowering the price so dramatically that they were easily able to undersell the competition. By 1865, Gilman and Hartford had five small stores in New York City, thus creating America's first chain grocery store. When the transcontinental railroad was completed in 1869, Gilman and Hartford changed the name of their company to the Great Atlantic and Pacific Tea Company, subsequently shortened to A&P. The firm expanded the number of stores and increased the variety of products they carried. In the 1870s, A&P stores began to sell coffee, and during the following decade, sugar, spices, and canned milk were added to the inventory. Well into the twentieth century, A&P was the largest grocery chain in the United States. Seeing its success, other entrepreneurs emulated the operation. Accordingly, in 1872 the Grand Union Tea Company was founded in New York, and by the early twentieth century, renamed Grand Union, it was the nation's second largest food retailer.

Beverages

By far the most important beverage in New York's early years was water. Until the middle of the nineteenth century, obtaining clean, wholesome drinking water was a constant problem for Manhattanites. Although wells were dug in the settlement early on, epidemics were common throughout the colony because the relationship of drinking water, waste disposal, and disease was only dimly understood. During the eighteenth century, more wells were dug, but the water was brackish and not good for drinking, causing many residents to visit springs just north of the city to collect fresh and safe water.[20] In 1832, the city government decided to resolve the water problem. The Croton River, north of New York, was dammed to create a reservoir, and an aqueduct was built to bring the Croton's clean water into the city. When the project was completed, ten years later, New Yorkers celebrated with parades and fireworks, and it was announced that the Croton Aqueduct would secure the city's water needs for the next century. Within a few years, the city had begun to expand the system to meet the needs of the rapidly increasing population.[21]

Another important beverage was milk, which from the earliest years of the city had been distributed by women and men hauling large wooden pails.[22] As the demand increased, they carried several gallons at a time using a wooden yoke

> three feet long chiseled out and smoothed to fit over the shoulders and the back of the neck, with nicely rounded arms extending over the shoulders. A light chain or a rope was suspended from each arm with a hook at the end. With this yolk across

his shoulders the carrier stood between two pails or other containers, and by stooping forward attached the hooks to the vessels; then straightening up, the weight of the vessels rested on his shoulders.[23]

As the population of New York grew, the demand for milk increased. Beginning in the 1820s, ambitious brewers built stables for cows adjacent to their breweries, and mash or slop ran from the breweries to the mangers through wooden chutes. By the 1830s, eighteen thousand cows living in New York City and Brooklyn were fed almost exclusively on this swill.[24] The milk from these cows was, however, low in butterfat, thin, and bluish. To make it more appealing to customers (and more profitable to themselves), unscrupulous dealers added water for volume, chalk and annatto for coloring, molasses for sweetness, and an occasional egg for creaminess. The brewery dairies were generally badly managed and badly kept. Not surprisingly, therefore, simultaneous with the rise of brewery dairies was the outbreak of cholera among infants, and infant mortality dramatically increased. By 1840, every fifth child in Manhattan died of cholera.[25]

The first person to blame the brewery dairies for the high infant mortality rate was Robert Milham Hartley, a strong temperance advocate. In 1842, he published an exposé pointing to the abuses of the brewery dairies. He called their product "swill milk" or "whisky-milk." Finally, in the late 1850s, *Frank Leslie's Illustrated Newspaper* declared war on the brewery dairies in Manhattan and Brooklyn. The stables surrounding the distilleries were "dilapidated and wretchedly filthy" and "disgusting." They were rude wooden shanties thickly hung with cobwebs. The cows were "arranged in double rows, their heads to the swill troughs and their tails, or rather the remnants of their tails, towards each other: so close that sometimes one cow actually lies on the other." One reporter was killed while developing the exposé, which gave added impetus for reform. One by one, the brewery dairies were closed.[26]

The lack of clean, safe water and milk was one reason for the widespread consumption of alcoholic beverages. In New Amsterdam, one-quarter of the buildings are estimated to have been "grog shops or houses where nothing is to be got but tobacco and beer."[27] A female visitor in 1704 consumed beer, *metheglin* (mead), and cider, and she reported that the locals drank "liquor liberally." Others noted excessive imbibing of alcohol throughout the century.[28] At the time, rum was the prevailing drink in the city's "dram houses." Improved technology in the late eighteenth century made the mass-production of alcohol possible, and liquor flowed freely. In 1819, about fifteen hundred grocery stores and taverns were licensed to sell "strong drink," and this number doubled within eight years. The choice of alcoholic beverages also expanded during this time. By 1837, ale, brandy, cider, gin, ginger-beer, mead, mint julep, porter, and a variety of punches were common beverages in New York.[29]

Many of the Irish immigrants who came to New York beginning in the 1810s opened eating and drinking establishments. Then, after the potato famine began in Ireland in 1845, the initial trickle of immigrants became a massive wave. In 1851, Seamus O'Daoir, owner of a "porter house" on Duane Street, wrote a poem for the *Irish American* promoting his drinking establishment and extolling the connection between the Irish and alcohol.[30] Another enterprising immigrant, John McSorley,

ley's Old Ale House still served beer and its famous liverwurst-and-onion sandwiches.
In *Hungering for America,* Hasia Diner observed that

> alcohol linked the Irish in America to the emotionally satisfying world of past
> memory and ushered them into a comfortable world of friendship with others
> like themselves. Above all, it heightened their Irish identity. In saloons, under the
> influence of alcohol, they declared their unswerving loyalty to Ireland, the place
> they had left but claimed still to serve, while they articulated a deep American
> patriotism.[31]

Similar to the Irish pattern, German immigrants began arriving in New York
during the early nineteenth century, a migration that greatly expanded after the failed
revolution in Germany in 1848. German immigrants introduced lager beer to the city
and opened "beer gardens," particularly on the Lower East Side. Unlike Irish saloons,
which served men almost exclusively (McSorley's did not admit women until 1970),
German beer gardens attracted entire families, thereby playing an important role in
preserving the identity of German immigrants.[32]

Not everyone was in favor of the widespread availability and consumption of
liquor, and to help stem the growing tide of alcoholism, temperance groups formed
in New York. In 1831, New York's temperance societies invited Sylvester Graham to
give lectures in the city, and he drew large crowds. Graham also advocated vegetari-
anism and opposed the use of refined flour, which did not endear him to the city's
bakers. By the mid-1830s, Graham boardinghouses, which espoused his philosophy,
opened in New York. These establishments provided sustenance in accordance with
Graham's strict "no stimulants" regimen: no alcohol, coffee, tea, sugar, meat, or
spices. That left whole-wheat bread, fruit, and gruel.[33]

Oyster Houses and Cheap Eating Establishments

Particularly impressive to visitors was the quality and diversity of the fish and seafood
sold at New York's markets. Live fish were brought to the city in smacks that had a
"fish well" filled with seawater in the center of the vessel. According to the French
West Indian traveler Médéric Moreau de St. Méry, who visited the United States
at the end of the eighteenth century, there were "sixty-three sorts of fish, as well as
oysters, lobsters, sea and fresh-water crabs, crawfish, fresh- and salt-water prawns,
eight other sorts of shellfish, turtles."[34] When the Englishman George Sala visited
New York in 1879, he reported that fish were "amazingly plentiful, delicious, and
inexpensive."[35]

Oysters particularly delighted New Yorkers. Peter Kalm reported in 1748 that
New York had "oysters of such exquisite taste, and of so great a size." Indeed, the
oysters were so numerous that they were "pickled and sent to the *West Indies* and
other places" in great quantity.[36] By the 1770s, oysters were so cheap in New York
that "very many poor families have no other subsistence than oysters and bread."[37]

In 1783, Johann David Schoepf, a German physician assigned to German troops in the British Army during the Revolutionary War, proclaimed that oysters could be "had in more or less quantity everywhere around New York." Oysters were eaten raw, broiled, baked, dried, pickled, or boiled in vinegar. They were so large that "one oyster makes several mouthfuls."[38] In the 1790s, Moreau de St. Méry proclaimed that "Americans have a passion for oysters, which they eat at all hours, even in the streets. They are exposed in open containers in their own liquor, and are sold by dozens and hundreds up to ten o'clock at night in the streets, where they are peddled on barrows to the accompaniment of mournful cries."[39]

Oysters were among the few foods that were avidly consumed by both the lower and upper classes, and as a result, oyster cellars and saloons proliferated throughout the nineteenth century. These establishments permitted customers to eat as many of the bivalves as they wanted for only 6 cents, although it was said that if a patron ate too many, the waiter would slip him a bad one. Charles Dickens, visiting New York in 1842, wrote that he considered such places "pleasant retreats" with "wonderful cookery of oysters, pretty nigh as large as cheese plates."[40] Another British visitor reported that "there is scarcely a square without several oyster-saloons; they are aboveground and underground, in shanties and palaces. They are served in every imaginable style escalloped, steamed, stewed, roasted, 'on the half shell,' eaten raw with pepper and salt, devilled, baked in crumbs, cooked in *patés,* put in delicious sauces on fish and boiled mutton."[41]

In addition to opening saloons and bars, many Irish immigrants worked in the oyster houses that clustered along Canal Street; others found employment in working-class restaurants.[42] In 1846, Daniel Sweeney, the owner of one such eatery on Anna Street, was called the "father of the cheap eating establishment." Sweeney's was a "sixpenny eating house," which permitted working people to buy dishes of meat for 6 cents and vegetables for even less.[43]

Holidays

New Yorkers loved holidays, and national holidays were particularly important in the city, which was the nation's capital until 1790. The Fourth of July was always celebrated, and an Englishman, Frederick Marryat, described the festivities in 1837:

> On each side of the whole length of Broadway, were ranged booths and stands . . . on which were displayed small plates of oysters, with a fork stuck in the board opposite to each plate; clams sweltering in the hot sun; pineapples, boiled hams, pies, puddings, barley-sugar, and many other indescribables. But what was remarkable, Broadway being three miles long, and the booths lining each side of it, in every booth there was a roast pig, large or small, as the centre attraction. Six miles of roast pig![44]

Thanksgiving was another national holiday. Although it had originated in New England, it was quickly adopted in communities throughout New York. Indeed, it was in New York City that President George Washington issued the first presidential thanksgiving proclamation, which set aside Thursday, November 26, 1789, as a day of prayer and thanksgiving. New York was one of the first states outside New England to declare Thanksgiving an official holiday. In 1795, John Jay, the governor of New York, tried to establish a statewide thanksgiving day, and in 1817 it was finally recognized as a state holiday. Thanksgiving was celebrated with what is now considered the traditional meal of turkey, apple pie, mince pie, and cranberries; New Yorkers often added doughnuts and crullers to the menu.[45] Thanksgiving holiday remained an important holiday throughout the nineteenth century. The Ladies Home Missionary Society of the Methodist Episcopal Church opened a mission in the gang-infested Five Points District, and on Thanksgiving Day, under the eyes of their benefactors, the ladies paraded and fed hundreds of Sunday-school students.[46]

The immigrants arriving in New York brought their holidays with them. The Dutch celebrated Christmas in New Amsterdam almost from the founding of the settlement.[47] Many of the Dutch culinary traditions related to Christmas were incorporated into New York festivities, an unusual one being the Christmas turkey shoot. Historian Mary L. Booth reported that in New Amsterdam on Christmas Day, "the young men repaired to the 'commons' or 'Beekman's swamp' to shoot at turkeys which were set up for a target. Each man paid a few stuyvers for a shot, and he who succeeded in hitting the bird took it off as a prize."[48] Whether or not this accurately represents events in New Amsterdam, the "turkey shoot" was an infamous Christmas tradition in nineteenth-century New York. One New Yorker, Henry Bergh, was particularly upset with this part of the celebration. Bergh, the founder of the American Society for the Prevention of Cruelty to Animals (ASPCA), believed that the practice of shooting turkeys was villainous and insisted "on the substitution of a dummy target for the living animal."[49] By the end of the century, Bergh had succeeded, and the turkey shoot was eliminated in the city.

As early as the second decade of the nineteenth century, the Irish began to celebrate St. Patrick's Day with communal banquets. With the massive Irish immigrations during the mid-nineteenth century, St. Patrick's Day communal meals and comradely drinking for men became ways in which some Irish maintained their cultural identity.[50]

Cafés, Restaurants, Gardens, and Soda Fountains

After the French Revolution, many refugees fleeing France came to America, where they shared their great legacy of French cuisine. One of those who came to the United States was the gastronome and author Jean-Anthelme Brillat-Savarin, who lived in New York for three years during the 1790s. He particularly liked to visit Michael Little's Old Bank Street Coffee House, which served turtle soup and Welsh rabbit, which he washed down with ale and cider. He also met a fellow Frenchman, a Captain Collet, of whom he wrote admiringly that he "earned a great deal of money in New York in 1794 and 1795, by making ices and sherbets for the inhabitants of that commercial town. It was the ladies above all, who could not get enough of a pleasure so new to them as frozen food; nothing was more amusing than to watch the little grimaces they made while savoring it."[51]

Ice cream was advertised in New York as early as 1777, and it became a favorite treat in the city during the nineteenth century. One British visitor to New York found ice creams "served in public gardens, in saloons that hold a thousand people, at the confectioners, at the uniform price of sixpence, and generally of excellent quality and flavour."[52] Toward the end of the nineteenth century, the soda fountain, which served soda drinks and many ice cream dishes, became a very important social gathering place for New Yorkers, particularly those who supported the temperance movement.

Although boardinghouses and inns were common in New York, the City Hotel on Broadway in Lower Manhattan, which opened in 1794, was the nation's first real hotel. In the dining room, meals were served family style at long tables that could seat 150 guests. The hotel also had a bar and a good wine cellar. During the next decades, many larger hotels were built in New York, including the palatial Astor, which began construction in 1834. These hotels often employed French chefs to run their dining rooms, and a number of these men became quite famous. An English visitor to the Astor Hotel in 1830s wrote that he had dined there on "excellent" French food.[53]

New York's first stand-alone restaurants appeared during the second and third decades of the nineteenth century. William Niblo, a self-proclaimed gourmet from Ireland, opened the Bank Coffee House at the corner of William and Pine streets in 1814, considered one of the best eating establishments in New York.[54] Fifteen years later, he launched Niblo's Garden at Broadway and Prince Street, in what was then a genuinely rural area. Copied from English models, New York gardens had been established in conjunction with bars and saloons by 1810. To enhance the country atmosphere of his garden, Niblo planted shrubs and trees and built cages for birds. He also constructed a restaurant, which quickly became one of the city's most important eating places.[55]

A sea captain from Switzerland, John Delmonico, opened a wine shop in New York in 1825. Two years later, he enticed his brother Peter to join him in New York, and together they set up a small café and pastry shop that served ices, bonbons, cakes, and coffee. The brothers saved their money with an eye to expansion, and four years later they opened a small *restaurant français*. In 1835, a fire destroyed many structures in Lower Manhattan, including the Delmonicos' restaurant, but the brothers opened a larger establishment the following year, offering a longer menu that included salads and other French dishes.[56] The new and enlarged Delmonico's became very popular, and it remained one of the city's premier restaurants throughout the nineteenth century, moving to new premises every so often as the city expanded northward.

By the middle of the nineteenth century, Delmonico's was an elegant full-service restaurant serving classic French cuisine. In 1862, the French-born Charles Ranhofer was hired as a chef, and he remained at Delmonico's for most of his professional life. Ranhofer flattered the egos of his wealthy patrons by occasionally naming dishes after them, such as lobster à la Wenberg, named after a ship's captain who was a frequent customer. When Ben Wenberg fell out with Delmonico's, the restaurant changed the name of the dish to lobster Newberg. Ranhofer was also among the first

American chefs to achieve international acclaim. British writer George Sala, who dined at Delmonico's in 1879, recorded the following description of Ranhofer's latest novelty, baked Alaska:

> The nucleus or core of the *entremet* is an ice cream. This is surrounded by an envelope of carefully whipped cream, which, just before the dainty dish is served, is popped into the oven, or is brought under the scorching influence of a red hot salamander; so that its surface is covered with a light brown crust. So you go on discussing the warm cream *soufflé* till you come, with somewhat painful suddenness, on the row of ice.[57]

When Ranhofer retired in 1894, he produced his masterwork, *The Epicurean*, the most comprehensive French cookbook published in the United States up to that time.[58]

German and Jewish Food Businesses

In the mid-nineteenth century, German immigrants began making New York City their destination. In 1842, Frederick and Maximilian Schaefer began to brew German lager, which by 1850 had become all the rage in New York; previously, heavier ales had been favored. By 1855, New York boasted fifteen hundred German bakers, at least nine of whom were Jewish. Other Germans became sugar refiners and wholesalers of chocolate, coffee, and mustard. During the 1850s, immigrants from Germany took over many grocery stores, and German cooks found work in restaurants.[59] By 1867, Germans had a near monopoly on the market-garden business supplying New York City.[60]

Some German immigrants opened small restaurants known for serving generous portions of food at low prices. Auguste Ermisch, for instance, opened a restaurant at Nassau and John streets. In 1873, his menu featured a number of traditional German dishes, including a "Hamburger steak," the first located reference to this dish. An article in the *New York Times* described it as "simply a beefsteak redeemed from its original toughness by being mashed into mincemeat and then formed into a conglomerated mass. This is very appetizing, but conscience compels us to state that it is inferior to the genuine article, which can also be had here in a very satisfactory condition of tenderness." Hamburg or hamburger steak was an inexpensive dish made by grinding scraps of beef left over after butchering choicer cuts, such as porterhouse steak or sirloin.[61] Within ten years, this dish had become commonplace throughout the country, and by the 1890s, hamburgers were sold by street vendors who served them in buns for a convenient stand-up meal, thereby creating the hamburger sandwich.

In 1877, August Guido Lüchow, an émigré from Hanover, Germany, went to work in a beer hall on Fourteenth Street, and by 1879 he had saved enough money to buy the place. William Steinway, a manufacturer of pianos, was a fan and frequent patron of the establishment, which became a favorite of New York's musical elite. As

Lüchow's became popular, it grew from a beer garden into one of New York's most fashionable restaurants.[62]

German immigrants also introduced the concept of the delicatessen to New York. The first reportedly opened on Grand Street, on the Lower East Side, around 1868. At that time, the neighborhood had a substantial German immigrant population. Delicatessens served not only German Americans but also others who were enticed by the foreign and fancy foods. During the late nineteenth century, delicatessens filled the gap between butcher shops, which sold mainly uncooked meats, and general grocery stores, which offered primarily generic and packaged goods.[63]

During the 1870s, Jewish immigrants began pouring into New York. Some opened cafés, grocery stores, bakeries, coffee shops, restaurants, and saloons in Jewish neighborhoods. They sold bean soup, borscht, cold fish, bread, and sandwiches.[64] Other Jews opened delicatessens, patterned on the German model. If the delicatessen was kosher, only meat and pareve (neutral) foods were served, which eventually included chicken soup, corned beef, gefilte fish, lox, knishes, pastrami, chopped liver, pickled tongue, and garlic pickles. If kosher laws were not followed, the menu expanded to include bagels, bialys, cream cheese, and Jewish-style cheesecake. Delis also popularized Jewish-style breads, notably rye and pumpernickel.

During the 1880s, New York City received a great influx of immigrants, many of whom went into the food business, opening fruit stands, neighborhood grocery stores, and small restaurants. The number of immigrants from eastern and southern Europe rapidly increased beginning in the 1890s, bringing with them the splendors of Italian, Greek, and Hungarian food (among others) to the polyglot city. Each successive wave of immigrants enriched New York's culinary life, an influence that was felt throughout the twentieth century.

A Greater New York

In 1898, Manhattan was consolidated with four other boroughs (Brooklyn, Queens, Staten Island, and the Bronx) to create what was then called "Greater New York." At the time, the city's streets were filled with pushcarts and vendors selling a tempting variety of foods and beverages. Along the streets were saloons, fruit and vegetable stands, tea and coffee shops, grocery stores, delicatessens, butcher shops, and fish dealers. Farmers' markets dotted the city; elegant restaurants thrived in upper-class precincts, but there were plenty of eateries where a workingman or -woman could get a satisfying meal for a reasonable price. Today, in the most fortunate of New York's neighborhoods, that description still fits, but gentrification and globalization now threaten the variety and individuality of the city's food purveyors.

NOTES

1. "Letter of Reverend Jonas Michaëlius," in *Narratives of New Netherland, 1609–1664,* ed. J. Franklin Jameson (New York: Scribner, 1909), 132.

2. Adriaen Van der Donck, *A Description of the New Netherlands,* ed. Thomas F. O'Donnell (Syracuse, N.Y.: Syracuse University Press, 1968), 23–24, 31.

3. Ibid., 54–56.

4. William G. Panschar, *Baking in America* (Evanston, Ill.: Northwestern University Press, 1956), 25.

5. John Storck and Walter Dorwin Teague, *A History of Milling Flour for Man's Bread* (Minneapolis: University of Minnesota Press, 1952), 149–50.

6. Washington Irving, *History of New-York: From the Beginning of the World to the End of the Dutch Dynasty,* rev. ed. (New York: Putnam, 1861), 90.

7. Richard J. Hooker, *A History of Food and Drink in America* (Indianapolis: Bobbs-Merrill, 1981), 41, 49; Peter Kalm, *Travels into North America,* trans. John Reinhold Forester (Barre, Mass.: Imprint Society, 1972), 335–36.

8. "Description of the Towne of Mannadens," in Jameson, *Narratives of New Netherland,* 423.

9. Edwin G. Burrows and Mike Wallace, *Gotham: A History of New York City to 1898* (New York: Oxford University Press, 1999), 108.

10. Carl Bridenbaugh, *Cities in the Wilderness: The First Century of Urban Life in America, 1625–1742* (New York: Oxford University Press, 1971), 266–67, 427.

11. Burrows and Wallace, *Gotham,* 251.

12. Ibid., 176, 301; Barbara Kuck, program prepared for the exhibition "The First Stomach," Johnson and Wales Archives and Museum, Providence, R.I.

13. *Journal of William Maclay,* ed. Edgar S. Maclay (New York: Boni, 1890), 137–38.

14. Hooker, *History of Food and Drink,* 101, 131.

15. Edward Mott Woolley, "Tom Rowland—Peanuts," *McClure's Magazine,* December 1913, 184; Thomas Rowland, *Note Book,* cited in F. Roy Johnson, *The Peanut Story* (Murfreesboro, N.C.: Johnson, 1964), 13; "Thomas B. Rowland," *Peanut Promoter,* January 1920, 110–11.

16. "Pea-Nuts," *Harper's Weekly,* July 16, 1870, 449; *Harper's Magazine,* November 1888, 938.

17. Hasia R. Diner, *Hungering for America: Italian, Irish, and Jewish Foodways in the Age of Migration* (Cambridge, Mass.: Harvard University Press, 2001), 199.

18. Hooker, *History of Food and Drink,* 60.

19. Burrows and Wallace, *Gotham,* 451.

20. Kalm, *Travels into North America,* 129.

21. *The Diary of Philip Hone, 1828–1851* (New York: Dodd, Mead, 1889), 2:150–51; Burrows and Wallace, *Gotham,* 594–95.

22. Esther Singleton, *Social New York Under the Georges, 1714–1776* (New York: Appleton, 1902), 358.

23. John J. Dillon, *Seven Decades of Milk: A History of New York's Dairy Industry* (New York: Orange Judd, 1941), 1.

24. Ibid., 2.

25. Pauline Arnold and Percival White, *Food: America's Biggest Business* (New York: Holiday House 1959), 174–76; Ralph Selitzer, *The Dairy Industry in America* (New York: Dairy and Ice Cream Field, and Books for Industry, 1976), 35.

26. *Frank Leslie's Illustrated Newspaper,* May 8, 1858; David Marshall Owen, "400 Years of Milk in America," *New York History* 31 (1950): 452.

27. Burrows and Wallace, *Gotham,* 33, 85, 229.

28. *The Private Journal of Sarah Kemble Knight: Being a Journey from Boston to New York in the Year 1704* (Norwich, Conn.: Academy Press, 1901), 63–64; *Gentleman's Progress:*

48   *The Itinerarium of Dr. Alexander Hamilton, 1744,* ed. Carl Bridenbaugh (Pittsburgh: University of Pittsburgh Press, 1992), 177; Jean-Anthelme Brillat-Savarin, *The Physiology of Taste; or, Meditations on Transcendental Gastronomy,* translated by M.F.K. Fisher (Washington, D.C.: Counterpoint, 1986), 272.

    29. Frederick Marryat, *A Diary in America, with Remarks on Its Institutions* (New York: Colyer, 1839), 31–32; Burrows and Wallace, *Gotham,* 285.

    30. Diner, *Hungering for America,* 87.

    31. Ibid., 139.

    32. Ibid., 140.

    33. Sylvester Graham, *Treatise on Bread and Bread-Making* (Boston: Light & Stearns, 1837), 75; Stephen Nissenbaum, *Sex, Diet, and Debility in Jacksonian America* (Westport, Conn.: Greenwood Press, 1980), 14; Burrows and Wallace, *Gotham,* 533.

    34. Hooker, *History of Food and Drink,* 98; *Moreau de St. Méry's American Journey,* ed. Kenneth Roberts and Anna M. Roberts (Garden City, N.Y.: Doubleday, 1947), 155.

    35. George Augustus Sala, *America Revisited: From the Bay of New York to the Gulf of Mexico* (London: Vizetelly, 1883), 94.

    36. Kalm, *Travels into North America,* 124–25.

    37. Harry Carman, ed., *American Husbandry* (New York: Columbia University Press, 1939), 76.

    38. Johann David Schoepf, *Travels in the Confederation (1783–1784),* ed. and trans. Alfred J. Morrison (New York: Burt Franklin, 1968), 13–15.

    39. *Moreau de St. Méry's American Journey,* 266.

    40. Charles Dickens, *American Notes for General Circulation* (London: Chapman and Hall, 1842), 1:208–9.

    41. George Makepeace Towle, *American Society* (London: Chapman and Hall, 1870), 1:272–73.

    42. Thomas Butler Gunn, *The Physiology of New York Boarding-Houses* (New York: Mason Brothers, 1857), 17–18, 33, 38; Chas. H. Haswell, *Reminiscences of an Octogenarian of the City of New York (1816 to 1860)* (New York: Harper, 1896), 235, 379; Diner, *Hungering for America,* 126.

    43. *Picture of New York* (New York: Homans and Ellis, 1846), cited in Diner, *Hungering for America,* 128.

    44. Marryat, *Diary in America,* 31–32.

    45. A.C. Dayton, *Last Days of Knickerbocker Life in New York* (New York: Harlan, 1882), 161.

    46. Burrows and Wallace, *Gotham,* 775.

    47. Mary L. Booth, *History of the City of New York: From Its Earliest Settlement to the Present Time* (New York: Clark, 1860), 192.

    48. Ibid.

    49. "Turkeys and Turkey Raising," *Poultry World,* November 1879, 343.

    50. Diner, *Hungering for America,* 130.

    51. Brillat-Savarin, *Physiology of Taste,* 271, 305.

    52. Thomas Low Nichols, *Forty Years of American Life, 1821–1861* (New York: Stackpole, 1937), 168–69.

    53. Frederick Marryat, *Second Series of a Diary in America, with Remarks on Its Institutions* (Philadelphia: Collins, 1840), 35.

    54. Lately Thomas [Robert V. P. Steele?], *Delmonico's: A Century of Splendor* (Boston: Houghton Mifflin, 1967), 10.

55. Dayton, *Last Days of Knickerbocker Life,* 9; Michael Batterberry and Ariane Batterberry, *On the Town in New York: The Landmark History of Eating, Drinking, and Entertainments from the American Revolution to the Food Revolution* (New York: Routledge, 1999), 49.

56. Thomas, *Delmonico's,* 7–11.

57. Sala, *America Revisited,* 90.

58. Charles Ranhofer, *The Epicurean* (New York: Ranhofer, 1894).

59. Robert Ernst, *Immigrant Life in New York City, 1825–1865* (New York: Kings Crown Press, 1949), 87, 88; Haswell, *Reminiscences of an Octogenarian,* 379; Burrows and Wallace, *Gotham,* 741.

60. "Germany in New York," *Atlantic Monthly,* May 1867, 555–56.

61. "German Restaurants," *New York Times,* January 19, 1873, 5.

62. Batterberry and Batterberry, *On the Town in New York,* 132.

63. Artemas Ward, *The Grocer's Encyclopedia* (New York: Kempster, 1911), 212; Henry T. Finck, *Food and Flavor* (New York: Century, 1913), 341.

64. Diner, *Hungering for America,* 199.

Digging for Food
in Early New York City

NAN A. ROTHSCHILD

FOOD FORMS the core of a person, both physically and metaphorically, in its expression of identity when people of different social classes and ethnic backgrounds select or favor certain items. The concern in this chapter is what New York City's early inhabitants ate. Although our knowledge is fragmentary, at least two stories are involved: what early New Yorkers ate and how we know what they ate. A third question, and one of the most important and interesting topics in food research, is why people eat what they do. Not all people in New York City ate the same food, except perhaps in the very earliest days. In any case, their diet seems to have been particularly heavy in meat and its substitutes, and both archaeological and documentary data indicate social rank in foodways, although sometimes only subtly.

We have some clues about what the early settlers ate and were not able to eat, what innovations they brought to their diets, and what treasured elements of their pre-migration foodways they retained. Some of this information comes from such written sources as travelers' or local diaries and occasional letters home, as well as from descriptions of grand banquets and accounts of oyster cellars from Charles Dickens. More information comes from archaeology, by way of the skeletons of the enslaved Africans buried in the African Burial Ground that were recently excavated and analyzed, and from analysis of the remains of New York City households that have been recovered archaeologically. Using these sources, I will try to create a picture of what early New Yorkers (and New Amsterdammers) ate and how their diet changed over time as the city grew.

We cannot assume that today's eating habits reflect a direct and unmodified line of descent from those of the seventeenth and eighteenth centuries. Indeed, today's foodways are far from stable, although some food habits may be retained amid the ever-changing food fads. It is reasonable to assume, however, that the first settlers from Europe—the Netherlands or United Provinces, France, and England—wanted to eat familiar foods. Accordingly, they brought with them their knowledge of domestic animals and the animals themselves; grains like wheat; vegetables like cucumbers, carrots, salad greens, radishes, and peas; fruit trees like peach, plum, and apple; and their knowledge of how to raise and cook these traditional foods. Sometimes, though, the animals or plants from the Old World did not thrive in the New World. Letters back to the Netherlands complained that many of the cows had died, leaving the Dutch residents without cheese or milk.[1] The smaller English cattle did better in America. The New World had an abundance of both familiar and new foods, and the European settlers arrived with a taste for game and deer and learned to like corn and pumpkin.

People's food choices are influenced by a number of factors. They represent the intersection of foods that are already known and preferred with those that are available from the environment and various provisioners. Although some members of society have more choices in determining their diet than do others, all have some options. Those with the greatest range of choices are influenced by local practices and social customs but also retain inherited, ethnically determined tastes. Some people (often the poorer ones) continued to hunt, gather, and fish and grow some of their own foods, particularly in the early years of settlement. But the availability of particular foods was not consistent over time, owing to changes in the environment, which eliminated some items, or to new trade patterns, which increased or decreased dietary variety.

When the island we know as Manhattan was settled, its new residents obtained their food in three ways: they grew or harvested some of it themselves; they bought some of it from the market near Fort Amsterdam established in 1656;[2] and they were able to import some—usually the more costly and exotic—items. Many people living in New Amsterdam in 1660 kept kitchen gardens, and fish and shellfish were plentiful (oysters littered the shore, clam beds were nearby, and fishing from the shore or a small boat would have been easy).

Food was abundant in the natural environment. As Daniel Denton reported in 1670: "The Island is plentifully stored with all sorts of English Cattle, Horses, Hogs, Sheep, Goats &c. . . . These Rivers are very well furnished with Fish, as Bosse, Sheep-sheads, Place, Pearch, Trouts, Eels, Turtles, and divers others."[3] Some households kept chickens and perhaps pigs or a cow. Meat, both from domestic animals, like cattle and pigs, and from deer and small game, also came to market. Denton also described the variety of birds for sale: "Wild Fowl . . . as Turkies, Heath-Hens, Quailes, Partridges, Pigeons, Cranes, geese of several sorts, Brants, Ducks, Widgeon, Teal, and divers others."[4]

As land became more valuable and was needed for residential use in the growing town, the kitchen gardens shrank and disappeared, although some people continued into the nineteenth century to keep cows, pigs, and chickens. In 1816, Charles Haswell noted that cattle roamed the streets in the city and were stabled at night;[5] he believed[6] that there were ten thousand hogs in New York City in 1817,[6] and Charles Dickens mentioned that pigs were kept domestically even in the mid-nineteenth century: "They are the city scavengers, these pigs . . . they are never attended upon, or

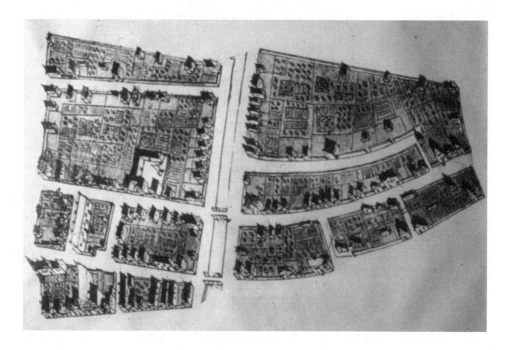

Jacques Cortelyou, Castello Plan, 1660. This early map of what is now Lower Manhattan was created by the surveyor of New Amsterdam.

fed, or driven, or caught, but are thrown upon their own resources in early life. . . . Every pig knows where he lives. . . . At this hour, just as evening is closing in, you will see them running towards bed by scores, eating their way to the last."[7] Pigs would have been useful to minimize the amount of food garbage and, of course, were a food resource themselves.

Archaeological Approaches to Food

Many of the documentary sources for what early New Yorkers ate are both incomplete and biased, tending to focus on the food of the elite or on remarkable meals. Archaeology, however, offers another source of data on food, as faunal material (the bones of animal, fish, chicken, and other species) has been recovered from many sites in the city. In fact, New York's five boroughs contain a wealth of archaeological sites, from the pre-Columbian period on. Sites have been excavated in Staten Island (Conference House), the northern edges of the Bronx (Clason's Point), southern Brooklyn (Ryder's Point),[8] and the northern tip of Manhattan (Fort Tryon Park). These sites contain no information on food, however, either because the excavations took place before faunal analysis was routinely done or because of poor preservation. But we do know, from other sites, that the indigenous inhabitants consumed mostly deer and smaller mammals, shellfish and fish, wild fruits and nuts, and, after 1000 B.C.E., corn.

They had ample food for their needs, although they usually moved with the seasons to exploit a variety of resources.

All of New York's five boroughs also contain sites from the period of European colonization, although most of the analysis of faunal material comes from Manhattan. Some of the colonial sites in other boroughs are farmhouses, like the Bowne House in Flushing and King Manor and several hotels in Jamaica.[9] The Hendrick I. Lott House in Brooklyn was a small farm residence owned by relatively affluent people. One of the dramatic finds there consists of some corncobs and other objects, recovered under the attic's floorboards and thought to have been left by African slaves who lived there. Weeksville, also in Brooklyn, was a community of free, middle-class African Americans who lived there from the late 1830s to the late nineteenth century. Four wood-frame houses from that period were identified in the 1960s because they lay along Hunterfly Road, which had been preserved because it was not aligned with the grid. The houses have been restored, and a community museum, the Society for the Preservation of Weeksville and Bedford-Stuyvesant History, was opened. In 1999, some material from the eighteenth century was recovered from City Hall Park, in an area that at that time lay on the edge of the city, where the poor were housed and noxious activities such as tanning were carried out.

Food Practices Derived from Archaeology

Archaeology provides very specific information about food practices, from the examination of human remains, which especially offers insight into food deprivation, and from food remains left at sites excavated in modern times. Although human remains from the historic period are rarely excavated in North America, in 1991 an amazing discovery was made in New York City. As plans to build a new federal office tower unfolded, an archaeological assessment of the project area revealed the possible presence of a "Negroes Burial Ground." While no one had anticipated that the cemetery could still be intact, it became clear that the original land surface was almost twenty feet below the present surface and thus hundreds, perhaps thousands, of intact human remains were still in the ground. Ultimately, more than four hundred sets of these remains were excavated and studied. The analysis of the skeletal remains has yielded much direct information about the effects of epidemic disease, dietary stress, and the cruel exploitation of bodies for labor, and similar analyses have examined the impact of colonialism on Native Americans.[10]

The new demands associated with disease, dietary stress, and heavy labor had altered these bodies' physical structure. The bones had changed shape (through hypertrophy, or the expanded growth and enlargement of certain muscles and bones) and had been remodeled as a result of the heavy work; rugged muscle attachments had developed in response to the new assigned tasks; and arthritis had appeared in various skeletal parts because of forced labor. The African Burial Ground (ABG) provided data on demography, trauma, nutritional stress, and the effects of malnutrition. Seventy percent of the bodies analyzed had enamel hypoplasias (lines on the teeth that appear in childhood because of insufficient food), suggesting a general dietary inadequacy in childhood. Not surprisingly, children born in colonial New York "within the condition of slavery were more vulnerable to health risks and early death due to nutritional deficiencies and illness than is evident for the childhoods of those who were likely to have been born in Africa."[11] These indicators were common in the ABG population, "regardless of age or sex,"[12] and the children found in the ABG had higher levels of dietary stress than did those from contemporary populations of enslaved people in Maryland or Barbados.[13]

The skeletons of both males and females showed indications of workload, such as arthritis, pressure facets, fracture, and hypertrophy of those places where tendons and ligaments attach.[14] Women had particularly high rates of arthritis in the lower back (around 58 percent of the sixty-nine individuals studied), suggesting the effects of strenuous labor on the vertebral column.[15] There were many examples of the deformation of vertebral elements resulting from carrying loads on the head or performing other tasks that involved heavy weights.[16] The most troubling findings were the indications of violence. The remains revealed a large number of fractures, the most on the cranium or skull (males, 11 percent) or femur (females, 12 percent). Cranial fractures usually indicate violence, although limb fractures also were found among non-African laborers.[17] One young adult female had thirty-two fractures; a fifty-year-old woman had ten, eight of which were inflicted after death on the arms, legs, and pelvis; and a male of the same age had twenty-three fractures.[18] Even adolescents were found to have fractures, some of which—especially cranial fractures—were undoubtedly the cause of death.[19] The most shocking is burial 25, a twenty- to twenty-four-year-old woman who had been shot, had blunt trauma force applied to her face (perhaps by a rifle butt), and had had her arm broken through simultaneous twisting and pulling. She appears to have lived for a few days after the beating.[20] These bodies bear especially compelling witness to the relation between slave and master, and its associated violence. Other colonial contexts demonstrate similar, although perhaps less dramatic, evidence of violence from physical abuse and enforced social and dietary change.

The other form of archaeological evidence regarding diet is derived from the analysis of food remains: bone and plant fragments, especially seeds, which often are well preserved. These remains are basically garbage left from meals that have been disposed of, sometimes neatly and sometimes not. Archaeological food remains provide only limited information. For example, we can identify the kinds of creatures that were consumed—birds, fish, mammals—and the way they were butchered. We may recover some kinds of plant remains, especially fruits—these sites contained many strawberry and raspberry seeds, peach pits, and nutshells—but there were few remnants of vegetables because they do not preserve well. The diets of many immigrants to the New World were made up mainly of meats and fewer vegetables, but the absence of these plants biases our interpretation of their diet. During this period, most people ate at home, and most of these deposits were residential, so we are not missing an important component of food consumed out of the house. In a project that I conducted in 1984, I analyzed food remains from specific blocks in present-day New York City chosen to compare the garbage from households of different socioeconomic levels. The most elite block in that study had almost no bones in its garbage, because residents often dined in restaurants and ate boneless cuts of meat (for example, beef filet or boneless chicken breast). The poorest blocks had the highest bone yield (for example, ribs and chicken wings).[21]

Archaeology projects in New York City have often found large quantities of these important materials.[22] I analyzed three sites in Lower Manhattan, with deposits derived from the seventeenth through the nineteenth century: the Stadt Huys Block, the Seven Hanover Square Block, and the Telco Block,[23] all of which were excavated before the construction of large office towers there. The Stadt Huys Block, which was excavated in 1979, had been established during the first period of Dutch settlement, around 1624.[24] It faced Pearl Street, which was the shoreline before the landfill extended it and was home to several important Dutch families, and it housed a tavern, which became the Dutch town hall (Stadt Huys) in 1642. The Seven Hanover Square Block lay diagonally across from the Stadt Huys Block and was of one of the earliest blocks to be inhabited, beginning in 1687 and completed by 1697.[25] The Telco Block was farther uptown, on Front and Fulton streets, and was filled in the second landfill, beginning in the 1730s.[26] Many of the best-preserved deposits on these blocks were contained in a well, cistern, or privy (called "features" by archaeologists). These were often used for garbage disposal once the active period of their use was over. The first two sites, representing the initial settlement, were located in a relatively affluent area of the city, along the East River. A number of merchants had their homes and warehouses on the Stadt Huys and Hanover Square sites, which contain material from the late seventeenth, eighteenth, and nineteenth centuries. The Telco Block was occupied by more "middle-class" people, such as shopkeepers, artisans, semiskilled workers, and white-collar workers. Telco was in a different ward from Stadt Huys and Hanover Square, and the land there was filled between the 1730s and 1760s.[27] None of these areas had socially or ethnically uniform populations, as early New York City neighborhoods were diverse, populated by artisans, shopkeepers, and construction workers, all living relatively close together. Both the Hanover Square and Telco blocks were built on landfill, which may have led to better preservation of the food bones, since the soil tended to be consistently damp.

When we examined the food remains from these sites, we were interested in answering two questions:

1. Did these sites reveal general trends in eating practices, and, if so, how did they change over time? Can these changes be explained?
2. When faunal deposits could be linked to a specific owner or occupant of a house, how did the deposits differ, and could these differences be tied to either the social status or the ethnicity of the occupants?

In regard to the first question, we could observe that the diet of relatively early New Yorkers generally relied heavily on large mammals (mostly beef, but with substantial amounts of pork and mutton), with lesser amounts of poultry and fish. Around 1760, these eating habits changed. Mammal bones dropped from 72 to 40 percent of all bones, and fish consumption increased from 17 to 40 percent. Fishing fleets thrived in the mid-eighteenth century. The city promoted deep-sea fishing,

The excavation of the Stadt Huys block. (Photograph courtesy of William Duncan Strong Museum of Anthropology, Columbia University)

offering prizes for the biggest catch of fish, especially cod, and the largest fish.[28] The kinds of fish that were eaten also changed over time, as early New Yorkers consumed sheepshead (71 percent of all fish bones), with striped bass second (24 percent). By 1760, only 4 percent of the fish bones came from sheepshead, and a bit more from striped bass; the new leaders were sea bass and scup. The disappearance of sheepshead seems to be tied to the ways in which the landfills changed the contours of the river bottom, as sheepshead live close to shore and feed on mussel beds, preferring uneven bottom surfaces. Scup, however, like smooth river bottoms.[29]

Poultry accounted for about 11 percent of bones before 1760 and rose to nearly 20 percent after that. Chickens became larger and more standardized by the late nineteenth century.[30] In the early period, it seems that wild animals like deer, rabbits, and squirrels were eaten, but their consumption declined thereafter. Some of those disappearances can be connected, I think, to changes that accompanied the increasing growth of the city and the alterations in its landscape. Landfilling began in New York in 1687, when the city sold water-lot grants to individuals who wanted more land and access to the newly emerging waterfront; these sales also provided income to the city.[31] The filling of marshes, clearing of land, and creation of landfill, as well as the increase in population, would have had an impact, reducing the preferred econiches for birds, turtles, small mammals, deer, and shellfish. Peter Kalm reported that all the residents of this area noticed the declining numbers of wild birds and fishes, compared with the great numbers in their youth, and he suggested that this was due to environmental changes caused by the Europeans and their overexploitation of some species.[32]

To answer the second question, regarding differences, we compared eight deposits: two from 1700 to 1760, four from 1760 to 1820, and two from after 1820. The nature of archaeological deposits and the ways that they are connected to specific residents through documentary records mean that only relatively few can be assigned with some confidence to particular households. These function as case studies and provide glimpses into the lives of different families. The earliest site contained faunal material from the Lovelace Tavern, built in 1670 and torn down around 1702 (there were no archaeological contexts that we could definitely connect to the early Dutch period, before 1664), but we did not include the tavern bones because we had no way of connecting the food remains to specific inhabitants.[33] For the second time interval (1700–1760), we had a deposit from a well (Test Cut [TC] CD) in the backyard of a house owned by Lewis Carre, a merchant on the Stadt Huys Block, and material from lot 14 at Hanover Square, where Simeon Soumaine, a silversmith, lived. The material from the third period (1760–1820) came from a privy (TC G) on the Seven Hanover Square Block, on land occupied by Gulien Verplanck, a merchant. Another privy (TC J) on the same block reflects use by either the painter/glazier Daniel Ogilvy or the hatter Stephen Smith.[34] Also from that period is bone from a large deposit related to a ceramic and glass merchant on the Hanover Square Block (TC AO), and material from the Telco Block (TC AX) that was probably left by grocers and a hairdresser. The deposits from after 1820 are from a backyard privy (TC H) on the Stadt Huys Block and a privy (TC AM) associated with a boardinghouse on the Telco Block.[35]

As an experiment, we tried evaluating the cost of food in these deposits, using price lists from each period and comparing the cost of a family's food with an estimate of their wealth, calculated by the taxes they paid. Although the data did not correlate perfectly, we did make some interesting observations. Some families invested their food dollars in expensive cuts of meat (for example, Lewis Carre, a merchant on the Stadt Huys Block [TC CD] from 1700 to 1760), while others seem to have favored more expensive fowl and fish (the ceramic and glass merchant on Hanover Square [TC AO], who lived there between 1760 and 1820). Gulien Verplanck from Hanover Square (TC G), a contemporary of the china and glass retailer, was himself a merchant, assessed at the second-highest tax rate; whereas his overall food costs were relatively low, we found more of the most costly meat cuts in his privy than in any other deposit. Verplanck seems to have had a rather diverse diet, with considerable amounts of fish as well as chicken and meat from domestic animals, even though he lived after 1760, when some foods, such as meat, were generally more expensive than they had been before 1760. The residents of the boardinghouse on the Telco Block (TC AM) ate the least expensive mammals but ate well in regard to birds and fish, probably because two of the boarders were fishermen.[36] In general, the overall cost of food seems to have fallen over time, especially after 1760, perhaps related to the economic slump that Gary Nash described as following the French and Indian War.[37] The residents of the Telco Block also ate less expensive food, as shown in both deposits (TC AX and TC AM), than did the other households we examined. They lived in a ward different from that of the other sites, and they seem to have been less financially successful than their neighbors.[38]

Cisterns unearthed during the excavation of the Courthouse Block in Five Points. (Photograph courtesy of Government Services Administration)

The Five Points project was an archaeological excavation undertaken in 1991, at the same time as the African Burial Ground project and before the construction of the new federal courthouse on Foley Square. This project offers an important contrast to the sites just described because the residents of Five Points were not wealthy. Nineteenth-century accounts describe the neighborhood as a notorious slum,[39] but the reality was more complex and interesting. In the early period, one of the blocks that was excavated (block 160) consisted of "moderately well-off artisans who set up residences and businesses" along Magazine (now Pearl) Street.[40] Although we do not know much about the ethnicity of these first residents, we do know that some of them were free blacks and others native-born blacks.[41] By midcentury, however, the block was home to many immigrants (as much as 75 percent of the block) from Europe— Irish, German and Polish Jews, Italians—and some from China. By 1855, the Five Points neighborhood was crowded with many working-class families. The focus of interpretation for this project was different from that at the sites just described. Since there was little suggestion of class difference, the project's archaeologists analyzed the food remains (faunal material and seeds) with an eye to considering food differences among the ethnic groups.[42]

Once again, a number of deposits were linked to specific individuals. One such case is represented by the Hoffmans, a German family that lived at 474–476 Pearl Street, whose material dates to around 1800. They were fairly well off (as seen in their choice of ceramics and glassware) and kept a bakery next to their home. The Hoffmans ate a lot of meat and seem to have been equally fond of beef, pork and lamb; their meat was purchased from a butcher, probably at one of the city's mar-

kets.[43] They also consumed poultry—chicken, pigeon, turkey, duck, and goose—being unusual in eating more of the latter two species than the more typical chicken and
turkey.[44] They were less fond of fish. After Mrs. Hoffman was widowed in 1812, she
took in a number of boarders, some with families, and lived in the house until her
death in 1836.[45] By the 1830s, the household's diet had altered in a couple of ways.
Pork had become the predominant meat. Mrs. Hoffman may have kept pigs, as suggested by the presence of immature pigs in the assemblage[46] and by the generally less
costly cuts of meat than those eaten when Mr. Hoffman was alive.[47] The amount of
chicken in the diet also increased, although duck and geese still were consumed.[48]

Another faunal assemblage was identified as being connected to a brothel at
10–12 Orange Street in the 1840s. The workers, and perhaps their clients, used elegant china and glassware, ate relatively well, and drank coffee and "fine wines."[49]
Some cuts of meat were expensive, but others were less so; perhaps the clients got
the best cuts. Pork was the dominant meat (the brothel may also have kept pigs), and
the inhabitants ate a fair amount of veal and rather expensive fish (salmon), as well
as a wide range of shellfish: soft-shell clams, oysters, and lobsters.[50] Some of the other
artifacts from the brothel's deposit suggest that the residents ate snacks of imported
brandied fruits, olives, or capers (recognized by their containers) and drank coffee
(identified by beans). These foods were not recovered from any other household at
the Five Points site. Prostitution was one of the few (and most lucrative) occupations
a young woman could enter, although many of those who did so remained in it for
only a short time.[51] The presence of these young women was marked by a number
of objects—perfume bottles, combs, pieces of mirrors, sewing equipment[52]—as well
as the remains of two infants in the privy,[53] although they may have been associated
with other families in the tenement rather than with the residents of the brothel. Some
other artifacts in this deposit were related to health: a syringe, a number of urinals,
and thirty-nine medicine bottles, one of which (Bristol's Extract of Sarsaparilla) was
thought to cure syphilis.[54]

The Goldbergs represented a contemporary household: Mr. Goldberg was a tailor who also was the Polish Jews' local rabbi in charge of an Orthodox synagogue,
Shaarey Zadek, located in a storefront at 472 Pearl Street. Seven young men lived
in his household; they may have been either his students or apprentice tailors.[55] Less
meat was consumed in this household than in most, and it was predominantly beef,
with little mutton and almost no pork. Many of the meat cuts could have been associated with roasts or soup; poultry was not as common as expected; but fish was
significant, perhaps because kosher laws permit fish to be eaten with either meat or
milk.[56]

Another important set of archaeological remains, dating from the late 1840s
to the 1860s, was from a five-story tenement building constructed on the same site
at 472 Pearl Street around 1848,[57] occupied almost entirely by Irish residents who
had come to America to escape the potato famine.[58] Many of these households were
headed by women, although men may have been present even if not officially recorded. These families ate mainly pork, in the form of hams, steaks, hocks, and pigs'
feet.[59] We also found bottles of Lea & Perrins Worcestershire Sauce and pepper sauce,
often used by the Irish.[60] Most cuts of meat were moderate to low in cost (and pork

itself was less expensive than other meats), although 11 to 13 percent of the meat was from beefsteak, and leg of lamb was also a popular cut. There was no evidence that these families kept pigs;[61] their consumption of chicken was low; and they ate less fish than any other group.[62] This is a good example of a culturally defined preference dominating the need to economize. Although less costly than meat, fish and chicken were not desirable foods for Irish immigrants, whereas meat was, and it was sufficiently available in New York City that even working-class households could eat meat two or three times a day.[63]

One of the surprises from this project was the recovery of the remains of expensive fruits from most households in this working-class neighborhood.[64] The Hoffmans consumed a large quantity of blackberries and raspberries and also some figs and grapes,[65] both before and after Mr. Hoffman's death. Tomatoes were not recovered from the earlier component of the household but were eaten after Mr. Hoffman's death, which ties in well with Charles Haswell's comment that until 1823 tomatoes were considered poisonous.[66] The fruit preferences of the brothel's consumers were similar: raspberries, blackberries, strawberries, and figs; they also ate a fair number of tomatoes.[67] The Goldbergs consumed the same kinds of fruit as did their contemporaries in the brothel, although they also ate grapes.[68] Archaeologists also recovered evidence of some condiments (chives, onions, mustard, mint, and poppy seeds)[69] and such imported items as tea, coffee, coconut, peanuts, and Brazil nuts.[70]

In general, the archaeological record from these sites demonstrates a number of things. First, during the earliest periods there seems to have been somewhat more dietary variability and flexibility as immigrants used the resources available to them. As domestic animals adapted to the New World, the diet of New Yorkers evolved to consist of beef, pork, and lamb, modified by additions of fish, fowl, and game. Their diet also was altered by both the disappearance of certain creatures as the environment was modified and the inclusion of foods made available from overseas trade or extension of the market into the hinterland. Second, with the exception of the African slaves whose skeletal remains indicate multiple episodes of inadequate food provided to children, people at all socioeconomic levels seem to have eaten relatively well, having access to a variety of meats and other basics.

While these large sites allowed the examination of major research questions, we also have information from smaller sites about New York's increasingly urban life. The Hendrick I. Lott House in Brooklyn was both a small residence occupied during the mid- to late nineteenth century and a working farm in an area undergoing urbanization. Maura Smaule, who did the faunal analysis, was surprised not to find any remains of wild mammals (such as deer or smaller creatures), even though they presumably would have been available to hunters. There also were no bones from wild birds, only those from chicken. The Lotts appear to have raised cattle and kept females into their middle age, while killing males at a younger age. They seem to have done their own butchering of cattle and sheep and also consumed quite a bit of pork. They ate all cuts of animals, both the most desirable (and costly) and the least, although some of this food may have eaten by servants in the household.[71]

Roselle Henn examined faunal remains from several deposits from Weeksville, the free African American community, dating to the late nineteenth and early twentieth centuries.[72] She found that the working-class residents ate the less expensive cuts of the domestic animals available: pork (the least expensive) was eaten twice as often as beef; moreover, the less costly cuts of pork were selected, as revealed by head and foot bones rather than hams and shoulder bones.[73] Henn cautions, however, that the inhabitants of Weeksville may also have raised some of their own protein (chickens, geese, and goats) and that boneless cuts of meat (also less expensive than bone-in cuts during this period) would not be visible to archaeologists.[74]

The material recovered from City Hall Park is different from that found at any of the other sites because it does not seem to have been associated with houses. That is, the bones may have been the result of dumping activities in the city, as some of the bones consisted of beef heads, which could have been used to produce soup for those in the alms (poor) house, and some (the better cuts of beef) may have come from a nearby military barracks. Quite a bit of pork was consumed, some of it from hams or shoulders, which were likely to have come from butchers outside the neighborhood. The fish eaten were local species, striped bass and porgies. The most distinctive faunal remains were horn cores, left from industrial or craft activities, as horn was a valuable raw material.[75] This assemblage is quite different from the domestic ones just described and suggests that animals were used for food and nonfood purposes in various ways by special categories of people (for example, the poor or the army).

Conclusion

Even though we have only hints of information about eating practices in early New York, we can observe some differences. Only during the early days of New Amsterdam did all the residents eat mostly the same kinds of foods. Meat and other proteins always were plentiful in the seventeenth through the nineteenth century. Both archaeological and documentary data indicate social rank in foodways—that is, in specific dishes, cuts of meat, quantities of food, or the ways in which it was served. Peter Kalm's reports suggest ethnic preferences for foods, as do the prevalence of pigs' feet and pepper sauce in Irish homes and the absence of pork from the Goldbergs' household. The foods available in New York changed rapidly from the Dutch period to the British and American eras as the city's own shape and landscape changed. The evidence of the impact of social and ethnic influence on diet is subtle, however, and hard to derive from historic and archaeological sources, but there is enough to indicate that these factors were just as important then as they are today.

Food habits in contemporary New York are complex and affected by many things, with some elements changing almost from year to year. Social status may vary over a lifetime, and the ways in which food is used to express it may change as well. Nonetheless, some food customs remain stable because they are literally ingested during childhood. These customs emerge at holiday and special meals, which preserve especially well the ethnic heritage of their consumers. New Amsterdam and New York always were diverse, and New York continues to receive new waves of immigration. Food customs are crucial to reflecting and preserving these identities and making the city an exciting place to live—and eat.

Today's archaeologists recognize the value of recovering a range of materials from sites, including food remains (animal and fish bones, shells, pollen, and plant remains). When archaeologists decide to excavate a site, either because it is about to be destroyed or to address a specific research question, they try to retrieve as many kinds of data as possible from the site. Often the best recoveries are found in association with houses or other building remains, because the material recovered can be linked to a specific family or group of individuals. The conditions for preservation need to be amenable to full recovery. The best preservation comes from a consistently wet or dry environment, whereas the alternation between wet and dry, along with the naturally acidic soils of the northeastern United States, are quite destructive of any organic materials.

Faunal material (bones and shells) is recovered during normal excavation. As a unit is removed, layer (stratum) by layer, the dirt is screened, and any fauna are bagged separately from the other artifacts recovered. When brought to the lab, faunal material like bones is normally brushed free of dirt, whereas shells (and artifacts) are usually washed. Material from each context is identified and analyzed separately from other contexts; then the contexts may be compared. Ideally, analysts try to determine the species (or if the bone fragments are too small, some larger animal class, such as bovid or medium mammal), the animal's age at death, and which part of the skeleton is represented. Other important information pertains to butchering—Was the animal chopped up, cut with a saw, or, for small creatures, eaten whole?—and the degree of weathering or gnawing by other animals: rats, dogs, and the like.

Although all this information is important, it is used for different purposes. The types of animals represented are obviously basic to determining diet. When discussing how people lived at a site occupied in the past, it is important to know what they ate. Did they eat only locally available creatures, or were they able to consume more exotic species? Did they keep animals like chickens in the backyard? Did they hunt or fish? If they fished, did they fish from the shore or use boats that could go into deep water? And if the site has different levels, or strata, how consistent were the eating practices over time? If different structures are being excavated, how uniform were food consumption practices from one place on the site to another? Shellfish are identified by species and evaluated according to the relative proportions of different kinds. Oysters used to litter the shores of Manhattan and extended up the Hudson, as they fare especially well in partly salty, or brackish, water. They were much larger than they are today; more frequent harvesting, as well as pollution, has reduced their size.

The counting of bones is not as straightforward as it might seem. One technique is simply counting the number of bones (NISP, or Number of Individual Specimens) of each species (for example, 570 cattle bones, 250 pig bones, 130 chicken bones, 450 salmon bones); another respected method requires analysts to try to calculate how many creatures (MNI, Minimum Number of Individuals) have been found from each species (for example, 24 cattle, 22 pigs, 15 chickens, 3 salmon). When archaeologists examine the remains of a culture in which residents hunted or procured their food

Animal bones. (Photograph courtesy of Telco Block Collection)

from the wild, they can assume that whole animals were consumed and thus MNI is a useful count. But if the residents of a site obtained their food in a market or from a butcher, they might have purchased a segment of an animal (a quarter or side of beef, or a leg of lamb), and thus the MNI count overstates the presence of that animal. Some experts also prefer to estimate the actual yield of animal mass from bones, in terms of food available. Thus, some cattle parts (trunk and upper limbs) yield large amounts of edible meat, while others (head and lower limbs) are less meaty. The specific cuts of meat may be an indicator of the residents' rank or class and offer some information about the relative costs of different animals or fish.[76]

If animals were butchered, the ages at which they were killed provide information about the site occupants' strategic choices. Often, for example, female cattle were kept for several years because they produced milk and calves, but males were slaughtered at the age of one year or so. Sheep, if used as wool producers, would probably be kept for several years, but if they were simply food, some would be killed at an early age. Pigs have no potential value as anything other than food and thus are usually killed around one year of age. In some settings, seasonal weather influences when animals are slaughtered. In a harsh environment where no food is naturally available in winter for domestic animals, a large number of animals are killed as winter approaches. In any case, identifying animals' ages at death provides important information about cultural subsistence strategies.

Butchering practices, as revealed by marks on bones, also are important cultural and chronological markers. The appearance of metal tools, especially saws, offers useful information. And the way that large animals are butchered (how are the units configured?) is relevant as well, as different cultures have different practices. Other kinds of marks on bone show how quickly the bones were incorporated into archaeological deposits. If the bones show evidence of weathering, it means that they were exposed on the ground or other accessible places before being buried. And if there are rat or dog tooth marks on them, similar inferences can be drawn.

Plant remains are recovered differently from faunal material, as they usually are so small that they fall through the normal screening process. A column of soil is taken from each location (either each stratum or specific features such as hearths or wells) and saved. Then the process of flotation is used, in which the samples are placed, one at a time, in a large barrel or tank with circulating water (sometimes a stream can be used). Plant materials are light, especially if they have been burned, and so float on the surface. They are scooped up, dried in a barely warm oven, and then identified under a microscope. Not all plant remains indicate their use as food. Because some reflect what kinds of plants existed in the environment, the analysts must be knowledgeable about the environment in order to be able to make these interpretations. In general, remains of fruits are more likely to be preserved than those of vegetables because seeds (either tiny ones from berries or larger peach pits) are quite sturdy. Although corncobs and kernels are often preserved, wheat and other grains are more delicate. Nuts preserve well, and charcoal is an important plant remain, indicating what woods were used for fuel or construction.

Information about food habits also comes from other kinds of artifacts, especially ceramics. A number of ceramic forms suggest the use of specific foods or beverages. Milk pans were commonly found in Dutch deposits in the New World, with holes in them to cool the milk and separate it from the cream. A small, three-legged pot called a *grapen* was distinctively Dutch and may have been used for various gruels and grains.[77] Colanders also were recovered in European or Euro-American contexts. The size of serving bowls suggests how many people made up the eating unit. Archaeologists have found many kinds of storage and serving containers, mostly for various liquids. In rare circumstances, a deposit is found on the interior of a vessel and may tell us what it contained. The shape of a common ceramic form—a bowl or a plate— provides information about whether it was used for dishes such as soups and stews, in which meat was a relatively minor ingredient, or for roasts and chops, the main component of a meal. Of course, tea services are very distinctive, and most New York families of middle class or higher status had several tea sets in a different patterns. In addition, other containers for drinks—such as posset pots, chocolate pots and cups, and punch bowls—were found in eighteenth-century settings.

NOTES

1. Nan A. Rothschild, "Food," in *Archaeology in New York City*, ed. Anne-Marie Cantwell and Diana diZerega Wall, Special Publication (New York: Professional Archaeologists of New York City, 1992), 1:36.

2. Nan A. Rothschild, *New York City Neighborhoods: The 18th Century* (Clinton Corners, N.Y.: Percheron Press, 2008).

3. Daniel Denton, *A Brief Description of New York: Formerly Called New Netherlands* (Ann Arbor, Mich.: University Microfilms, 1966), 5.

4. Ibid., 6.

5. Chas. H. Haswell, *Reminiscences of an Octogenarian of the City of New York (1816 to 1860)* (New York: Harper, 1896), 60.

6. Ibid., 86.

7. Charles Dickens, *American Notes for General Circulation* (New York: Harper, 1842), 87.

8. Diana diZerega Wall and Anne-Marie Cantwell, *Touring Gotham's Archaeological Past: Eight Self-Guided Walking Tours Through New York City* (New Haven, Conn.: Yale University Press, 2001).

9. Ibid.

10. Nan A. Rothschild, "Colonized Bodies, Personal and Social" (paper presented at the Symposium on Past Bodies, Leverhulme Research Institute and Royal Anthropological Institute, University of Cambridge, January 2006).

11. M. L. Blakey, M. Mack, A. R. Barrett, S. S. Mahoney, and R. A. Goodman, "Childhood Health and Dental Development," in "The New York African Burial Ground Skeletal Biology Final Report," ed. Michael L. Blakey and Lesley M. Rankin-Hill, The African Burial Ground Project, Howard University (General Services Administration Northeastern and Caribbean Region, 2004), 331.

12. C. C. Null, M. L. Blakey, K. L. Shujan, L. Rankin-Hill, and S. H. H. Carrington, "Osteological Indicators of Infectious Disease and Nutritional Inadequacy," in Blakey and Rankin-Hill, "New York African Burial Ground," 398.

13. Blakey, Mack, Barrett, Mahoney, and Goodman, "Childhood Health and Dental Development," 313.

14. C. Wilczak, R. Watkins, C. C. Null, and M. L. Blakey, "Skeletal Indicators of Work: Musculoskeletal, Arthritic, and Traumatic Effects," in Blakey and Rankin-Hill, "New York African Burial Ground," 403.

15. Ibid., 412.

16. Ibid., 442.

17. Meredith Linn, personal communication, 2005.

18. Wilczak, Watkins, Null, and Blakey, "Skeletal Indicators of Work," 450.

19. Ibid., 457.

20. Ibid., 458.

21. Nan A. Rothschild and Shira Birnbaum, "Compliance to Bottle Bill Survey: An Analysis of Garbage from Nine Blocks in New York City" (on file, New York City Department of Sanitation, 1984).

22. Anne-Marie Cantwell and Diana diZerega Wall, *Unearthing Gotham: The Archaeology of New York City* (New Haven, Conn.: Yale University Press, 2001), 91.

23. Rothschild, *New York City Neighborhoods*.

24. Nan A. Rothschild, Diana diZerega Wall, and Eugene Boesch, "The Archaeological Investigation of the Stadt Huys Block: A Final Report" (on file, New York City Landmarks Preservation Commission, 1987).

25. Nan A. Rothschild and Arnold Pickman, "The Archaeological Excavations on the Seven Hanover Square Block" (on file, New York City Landmarks Preservation Commission, 1990).

26. Diana Rockman, Wendy Harris, and Jed Levin, "The Archaeological Investigation of the Telco Block, South St. Seaport Historic District, New York, N.Y." (on file, National Register of Historic Places, 1983).

27. Wendy Harris Sapan, "Landfilling at the Telco Block: Social, Historical and Archaeological Perspectives," *American Archeology* 5 (1985): 170–74.

28. Thomas F. De Voe, *The Market Book, Containing a Historical Account of the Public Markets in the Cities of New York, Boston, Philadelphia and Brooklyn* (1862; repr., New York: Burt Franklin, 1969), 181–83.

29. Darlene Balkwill and Steven Cumbaa, "Faunal Analysis," in Rothschild and Pickman, "Archaeological Excavations on the Seven Hanover Square Block," 155.

30. Ibid., 148.

31. Sapan, "Landfilling at the Telco Block."

32. Peter Kalm, *The America of 1750: Peter Kalm's Travels in North America: The English Version of 1770,* trans. A. B. Benson (New York: Dover, 1960), 152–54.

33. Rothschild and Pickman, "Archaeological Excavations on the Seven Hanover Square Block," 150.

34. Ibid., 152.

35. Ibid.

36. Ibid.,164.

37. Gary B. Nash, *The Urban Crucible: Social Change, Political Consciousness, and the Origins of the American Revolution* (Cambridge, Mass.: Harvard University Press, 1979).

38. Rothschild and Pickman, "Archaeological Excavations on the Seven Hanover Square Block," 166.

39. Rebecca Yamin et al., "The Rediscovery of Five Points," in *Tales of Five Points: Working-Class Life in Nineteenth-Century New York,* vol. 1, *A Narrative History and Archaeology of Block 160,* ed. Rebecca Yamin (West Chester, Pa.: John Milner Associates, 2000), 9.

40. Rebecca Yamin et al., "Construction of Class, Race, and Ethnicity in an Urban Context," in *Tales of Five Points: Working-Class Life in Nineteenth-Century New York,* vol. 2, *An Interpretive Approach to Understanding Working-Class Life,* ed. Rebecca Yamin (West Chester, Pa.: John Milner Associates, 2000), 133.

41. Ibid.

42. Ibid.

43. Ibid., 135.

44. Ibid., 137.

45. Ibid., 198.

46. Ibid., 147.

47. Ibid., 140.

48. Ibid., 142.

49. Ibid., 199.

50. Ibid., 153.

51. Cantwell and Wall, *Unearthing Gotham,* 220.

52. Ibid., 222.

53. Ibid., 335.

54. Ibid., 325.

55. Ibid., 161.

56. Ibid., 167.

57. Ibid., 199.

58. Ibid., 179.

59. Ibid., 180.

60. Ibid., 263.

61. Ibid., 181.

62. Ibid., 182.

63. Ibid., 196.

64. Ibid., 234.

65. Ibid., 210.

66. Haswell, *Reminiscences of an Octogenarian,* 148.

67. Ibid., 212.

68. Ibid.

69. Ibid., 221.

70. Ibid., 220.

71. Maura Smaule, "Rural to Urban Transitions on the Edge of New York City: Nineteenth-Century Foodways at the Lott Homestead, Kings County, New York" (Ph.D. diss., New York University, 2000).

72. Roselle Henn, "Reconstructing the Urban Food Chain: Advances and Problems in Interpreting Faunal Remains Recovered from Household Deposits," *American Archeology* 5 (1985): 202–9.

73. Ibid., 206.

74. Ibid., 207.

75. George Hambrecht and Seth Brewington, "Faunal Remains from City Hall Park," in *Archaeological Investigations in New York City Hall Park,* ed. H. A. Bankoff and A. Loorya (New York: New York City Department of Parks and Recreation, in press).

76. De Voe, *Market Book.*

77. Meta Janowitz, personal communication, 2002.

My Little Town

A Brooklyn Girl's Food Voice

ANNIE HAUCK-LAWSON

My family seems always to have been "food people" grounded in food-centered ac-
tivities. This opened the door to my life, both personally and professionally, a life in
which I saw, felt, and heard ways in which food, keenly and on many levels, functioned,
nourished, sustained, consoled, held and conveyed meaning and identity, and made a
profession.

    The "aha" moment for me in all this came during my dissertation fieldwork. While
studying the roles and meanings of food to Polish American families in New York—
spending time in my participants' kitchens and grocery stores, at their churches and
community events, watching, talking, and working alongside them as they cooked, ate,
commiserated, and celebrated—I understood that through their ways with food, they
spoke clearly, sometimes even without words. Where food served as a vehicle to convey
abundant meaning and aspects of identity, it served as a voice, a food voice.

    This epiphany, this food voice, not only drove my dissertation to completion, but
also opened the door even wider to the food-grounded world. Sharing with family,
friends, and colleagues, the concept has fit people's relationships with food for time im-
memorial. Accordingly, I use this concept of food voice in this book to convey some of
the identities of people and city—that is, what food says about New Yorkers and New
York City.

THAT FIRST DAY, I sent eyeballs to my kid's school in an insulated Russ &
Daughters caviar bag—not that the bag had ever seen caviar; it's the kid's school
lunch bag. A year earlier, while I was visiting the sixth grade's science class, the
teacher described optics, culminating in the dissection of a sheep's eye. When I asked
her, the teacher said she got the specimens "from science supplies." The eyes were
dried, like raisins, and smelled like formaldehyde. Did she know about the sheep's
heads with bright eyes for sale in halal butcher shops all around Brooklyn? No. Could
I send in a sample set? Sure.

I headed for the Pakistani and Bangladeshi grocery stores on Coney Island Avenue, picked a nice sheep's head from a butcher case, and, at home, pried out and packed up the eyes. Handing the bag to my daughter, she asked what was in it. I said, "Sheep eyes." She replied, "Eeeeeeeeek!" and carried the bag as far out as her fingers could reach. But the science teacher was pleased: "Fabulous—lots of vitreous, clear corneas." A Brooklyn tradition had begun.

Every year now when the dissection rolls around, my halal butcher friends step up to supply science, Brooklyn style. During "optics" month, usually celebrated in January, they put aside the sheep's heads with the clearest eyes, enough for a hundred kids. At the various stores on Atlantic and Coney Island avenues, the butchers bring out plastic milk crates from their walk-in refrigerators, and we sort through these crates full of heads, picking out those with the best eyes. They then zip around the sockets with a buzz saw and bag the eyes. I pry them out at the kitchen table. The dean of the fifth grade, a neighbor, fetches the day's supply from our front porch, packed in various bags saved from the city's food and sweet shops: Sahadi's, Zabars, Fairway, Teuscher, and Godiva. The butchers also bag for me any other part of the head that I want to take home and cook, the bonus of leftovers.

This is my Brooklyn, a Brooklyn lived through the lens of food: seeking it, growing it, gathering it, giving it, sharing it, at times selling it, cooking it, eating it, and enjoying it all—including, yes, sheep, pig, and fish heads.

Brooklyn's food history was made by natives and immigrants using the land and waters to feed themselves and others. These foodways were woven bit by bit into the tapestry that is Brooklyn. My Brooklyn of the not too distant and partly gritty past was one filled with food experiences, some that hardly seem possible now that the borough seems to many a bit of heaven on earth. All join in a choir of food voices that tune the uncanny character that is "Brooklyn," and this is one little melody. Listen.

Hauck Family Foodways in the BK (Brooklyn)

I am a Park Slope native, born on Berkeley Place. When I was four years old, our corner brownstone with the big backyard was condemned to make way for the construction of Public School 282. Despite the fires set by bum squatters in the surrounding buildings, which had gradually been vacated by the power of eminent domain, my mother implored the condemnation judge for extra time extensions until she found our next home, which turned out to be on Third Street between Seventh and Eighth avenues, a genteel Park Slope block and a great place to grow up. Ours was the single brownstone that topped a long line of limestones, all with postage stamp–size yards, front and back, and with stoops that invited conversation and games like points and others played as only ten-year-olds can.

Even though they did not get along in the long run as a couple, my parents shared a love for food, everything about it, planting, growing, shopping, cooking, eating— all carried out with sweeping, sure, comfortable gestures. We kids were naturally swept into that embrace: sweeping fish out of the water; sweeping food from a cutting board into a big black cast-iron skillet; moving hunks of bluefish fillet from their peppered flour, egg, and breadcrumb coating into hot oil; sweeping along crowds to sell "healthful" lunches from a hand-built pushcart in Borough Hall. My motions were confident, even if my emotions were not. If other aspects of my young life were jangly, food was not. It was a constant.

My family was passionate about growing things and seeing the food potential in our surroundings. My mother was born and raised on a farm in Poland and lived in Northside near Greenpoint when she first came to this country as a teenager. My father, whose family owned a candy store on Hoyt Street during the Depression, studied on the agricultural track at Newtown High School in Queens. Methods of procuring food were thus part of the Hauck family's implicit mission. For us, raising and gathering were our modus operandi. Connections were important—that is, connections with the land, water, and air for their ability to bear; with people; and with other gatherers, producers, and merchants who understood and respected our needs, ways, styles, and food preferences.

Hence, food was very often in my hands from the water, the soil, bushel baskets, store shelves, the countertop, the stove, the grill, the table: its movement flowed all around my life. We traveled to and through Brooklyn neighborhoods sharply demarcated as ethnic enclaves and shopped for food specialties imported or produced by the locals. From the 1960s through the 1980s, on trips to the "old neighborhood," we stopped by the stores where my mother had shopped for snacks after her evening English-language classes decades earlier at Eastern District High School. Merchants along the route filled my mother's orders for her transition foods to the new country: from Sam Erde's Moishe's Bakery on Whythe Avenue for 100 percent rye bread known as corn bread; to Bedford Avenue or Nassau Avenue for fresh or smoked kielbasa; to the appetizing stores along Havemeyer Street for dairy, bialys, half-sour pickles, baked salmon, smoked whitefish, lox, and pickled herring; and to the area around Kent Avenue near the Schaeffer brewery for some of the fish locally smoked and brined. As a child on these trips, I stared down at the herrings as they sent up a combination salty, fishy smell, much of it embedded in the wood of their barrels. I scanned the bunch to zero in on the biggest ones with silky, salty miltz protruding from chopped heads. My parents filleted them and set them on the table.

I daydreamed through the butcher cases at Pergola Meat Market, one of many small food stores along Seventh Avenue, this one between Garfield Place and First Street, past the cuts of what was situated, artful but immobile, in the front of the cases to watch the butcher's hands deftly cut around the bone and trim sinews from the malleable meat. At the Children's Garden at the Brooklyn Botanic Garden, every Saturday in the spring after Planting Day, my eyes searched the newly seeded soil for protrusions of hardy bean stems and brave radish tops. I remember my very first harvest there in 1965; the assignment on the chalkboard was "Harvest radishes." Wonder, newness, and naïveté guided my first ever white radish harvest as I pulled up the whole line in one fell swoop. Although impressive, it was a bit much. What do you do with 107 peppery white radishes? The next day their stems drooped, and most went to the compost.

At six years old, I would stare out the parlor floor window, waiting for fruit to grow on our one peach and two apple trees in the backyard, saplings that my parents planted for each of us. And for a moment, I believed that the banana strung from the tree on April 1, 1962, was true bounty.

The visuals and the procurement experiences in Brooklyn gave me a sense of place and also food eyes: a view of the world, this world, charged and nourished by food for more than its nutrition, but also for its sense of direction, purpose, cohesion, meaning, history, celebration, and consolation. In and of this world, I was a keen observer.

Ours was a four-story brownstone. We lived on the ground and parlor floors. My German grandfather, his sister Tante Martha, and their friend lived on the top floor. Tenants rented studios with a shared bath in between. The house had its aromas, often perceived as we approached the gate of our ground-floor entry. The fragrance of Friday afternoons had nothing to do with food. My sister's piano teacher was heavy-handed with Avon scents, and I could smell the lesson in progress even before hearing it. A few hours later, when the smells shifted to Friday fish dinner, I would beg for an invitation to my best friend Betsy's house across the street for her Catholic meal of tame buttered noodles. Some Fridays, my mother came home from school downtown with treats from the distinctly aromatic Abraham & Strauss Cheese Shop or from Bohack on Seventh Avenue and Carroll Street with a couple of three-pound lobsters (79 cents a pound). She would set them in the bathtub to wait for dinner. We would then take them out to Third Street and transform them into our latest playthings, hiding them in the prim front yards of our friends. Whoever found one would grab it and chase all the other kids around the block, the flailing lobster held high.

Home aromas, especially of garlic sautéing in olive oil, made us hungry. As kids, we commonly took our baths before dinner, and my mother, cooking within earshot, would serve us a little bit of whatever she was making as an hors d'oeuvre, right on the tub ledge. Our pets occasionally joined us in the tub. One time, my mom set one of the pet ducks to swim there with us, the pet duck that joined us at the dinner table as dinner some time later.

Although compost, another constant at our home, made a bad smell, we knew that would dissipate over time. I remember only one smell so horrendous that it prevented me from even approaching the kitchen. Our freezer, packed with bluefish fillets from my brother's fishing trips, had been accidentally turned off during summer vacation. When we returned to the summer city heat two weeks later, burst six-ounce cans of grape juice concentrate were oozing onto the floor along with the fermented bluefish, creating an indescribable stench. I retched. My mom stoically cleaned it up.

Circa 1961: on Sunday nights, our house would swell with people, food, and aromas. Sunday dinners were ritual: my grandfather, great-aunt, and their friend would clop down the three flights of stairs, two carpeted and one open wood, all creaky. Any other visiting friends or relatives would join around the kitchen or dining-room table. My mom "ran the oven," her version of frat kids piled in a telephone booth. So as not to waste electricity, she would squeeze in as many "oven dishes" as possible:

meat for roasting, some sort of starch dish—creamy scalloped potatoes, potato pudding, macaroni, Yorkshire pudding, fruit-topped cake, fruit-filled pie, whatever—the flavors and textural undertones were rich, brown, crisp, crackly, buttery, seasonal, festive. Bittersweet smells of Sunday's yummy roast beef meant yucky school the next day.

When I was seven, my parents divorced. They ceased their partnership in the family business, although they continued to co-own the brownstone. My mom went back to school to study nursing. My dad moved upstairs (they couldn't live with each other; we couldn't live without them). Despite all the goings-on with this, not the most conventional, family arrangement, our dysfunctional family functioned, and there was food—delicious, intriguing, fun, abundant—in this family where things were sometimes jangly.

Our meal pattern changed in response. We had breakfast upstairs with Dad at 7:30 every weekday morning, accompanied by *Daily News* readings and card games "to sharpen our brains." Norman cooked "breakfasty things" like pancakes and French toast. He also made savory breakfasts like hamburgers with chopped dill pickle kneaded into the freshly ground beef; spaghetti with *ragu* thick with shredded and melted mozzarella, just one of the cheeses he bought in five-pound loaves; freshly caught mackerel with rich dark meat and seared skin that crackled like a potato chip; and different kinds of poultry—crisp roasted chicken with stuffing, succulent turkey tails, also known as *tuchases* or "pope's noses," which my mother and her sister competed for at Thanksgiving dinner downstairs. Weekend breakfasts upstairs were more leisurely, with Sunday morning walks down the block to Herzog's Delicatessen for jumbo eggs displayed in open cartons only on Sunday. Counterman Ritchie checked each for cracks. I then would crack them open at home with anticipation of how many were double yolkers—some dozens had as many as ten. These eggs became an integral part of "eggs in the nest," a ritual Sunday breakfast that we had eaten communally at the kitchen table downstairs before the divorce and had now moved upstairs, served on individual plates at Dad's. A steaming ring of rice, mashed potatoes, or corned beef hash surrounded a center of sunny-side-up eggs, melted cheese on the ring optional. My mother made corned beef hash from scratch. We set up the meat grinder and fed in cooked corned beef, cold from a previous dinner, onions, carrots, and potatoes; shaped it into patties; dipped the patties in bread crumbs; and fried them in bacon fat. They were tasty, but I still loved that canned stuff from Broadcast. My dad ribbed me that it was dog food and cooked it religiously, per my request. To illustrate his point, though, he conspired with my sister to bring him an empty and clean dog-food can from downstairs, transferred the cylindrical corned beef hash into it, and, within my view, slid it out of the dog-food can into the frying pan as if to say, "See? I told you it's dog food."

From Dad's windows, we watched Park Slope life on the street: who was coming up the block carrying what, doing what, in what shape; who was walking to school or to Mass; how early or late they were. My dad, a pigeon fancier who had had a coop full of racing homers at every place he lived except this one, set up a little wooden ledge on the windowsill and fed the birds, some of which we befriended. One

Norman and the pigeons, Berkeley Place rooftop. (Photograph courtesy of Jane Hauck)

we called Anthracite for its color. And so, while we had our breakfast, we looked at the birds. I remember the moment when Norman served us breakfast, announcing it was "Georgia quail." I felt a prompting coming from somewhere within, like "Sit up straight—this is fancy," that imposed a layer of I don't know what onto my consumption of the food. Later I concluded that it was, in fact, pigeon. When I asked my dad, he said, "Yes. But it wasn't Anthracite."

Lunch and dinners were downstairs with Mom. Before we cooked the food, we had to get the food, and there were a lot of ways we did that; raising and gathering were the gold standards, followed by specialty shopping. Food also came to us, sometimes literally on our doorstep. In cold weather, in the tin box right out front, frozen milk would pop the paper lid that had lost its grip over the glass bottle's top. One night, my St. Saviour classmate Raymond, who helped deliver milk in the wee hours, lost his footing on the running board and slipped under the wheels of the milk truck. On Saturdays, Resnick's old blue truck lurched up Third Street. Although the truck looked precariously overloaded to us—with tall, scratched bottles of Hoffman or Yale soda, India ale, Rheingold the dry beer, and blue or clear seltzer bottles in sturdy wooden crates—Resnick rarely broke a bottle. Horse-drawn wagons brought wares up Third Street. In springtime, the vegetable man's wagon carried flowering plants: pansies and wax begonias for the tree pits and yards out front. The junk man's horse clopped up the block, in tune with the clanking bells on the wagon and the junk man's tired song, "Rag man, rag man, any good junk?" which sounded like "Yaig man, yaig man, any good yunk?"

If my mother didn't raise food herself, she would entrust other people to supply it. She engaged and developed a rapport with merchants at individual shops. Once, when she and I were shopping along Fifth Avenue in Brooklyn, the normally friendly owners of Spinner's on Union Street teased me, a three-year-old wearing my mother's red lipstick. I covered my face with my hands as she pushed me along the checkout line in her shopping cart. Home Bakery's éclairs overflowed with freshly whipped cream. For years, my sister and I enjoyed many of them in "Midnight Feasts" we held on weekend nights. At the Merkel Meat Market, a store that may have changed its name to Merck-O after being investigated for selling horsemeat, the butcher would hand me a slice of bologna over the counter while my mother placed her order.

On Third Street, we usually shopped for food on Fridays. Holding the Bohack and A&P circulars, the "specials" already circled, I would watch out the front window for my mother to pull up at 4:20 P.M., home from her shift at the hospital. Jumping into the "heavy Chevy," I would read the sale items to her as we drove. She told me what to buy, and after we had the groceries, we would swing down to Fifth Avenue, to Nappy's on Second Street. Nappy's had its produce bins out front and shelves along the walls of an otherwise hollow interior. We'd pull up in front, and I'd jump out and quickly scan the produce. By this time, my mother was outside the car. I would rattle off the prices and quality, and she would tell me how much of what to buy. Jane would make a point of including "first of the season" whatever—bing cherries, artichokes, asparagus, and the like. Then she would talk to Nappy about larger seasonal, perhaps discounted, purchases: a peck of spinach, curly leaf edges sticking out from the thin wooden lid fastened with wire; a crate of Jersey beefsteak or plum tomatoes; or some slightly bruised or turning produce that had to be used quickly.

Seventh Avenue between President and Fourth streets was loaded with lively little familiar and friendly shops. Punch and Judy, which sold children's clothing, moved across the street to a bigger, two-steps-down, corner shop and is now a coffee shop on First Street. Despite the bigger space, Punch and Judy still overflowed with petticoats, boys' shirts, underwear, and lace-trimmed socks for First Holy Communion outfits. Spotless glass cases and shelves at Ebingers displayed the impressive "blackout cake," pecan-studded coffee rings, hot cross buns, and fruit strudels. The store's pale green–striped cardboard boxes were tied with thin twine dispensed from a suspended globe. Bars like Caulfields, the Eagle, and the Coach were where people our parents' age frequented, sometimes too frequently. When we came of age, we frequented their offshoots: Snooky's, Stack o' Barley ("Stacks"), the original Mooneys, the Gaslight, Minsky's, McFeeley's. We swelled these places to overflowing, especially on Thanksgiving weekend when everyone came home.

Finnegan Brothers Food Store, or Danny's, was near the corner of Fourth Street, and the brothers often scowled as they filled your order. The ever-expanding Al's Candy Store on the corner of Third Street competed for candy customers with Irv's Stationery on the corner of Fourth. Sun K. Louie's Laundry was between them. The younger son, Edward, taught my mother how to seal egg rolls with a dab of peanut butter. Al, of Al's Fish Market between Second and Third streets, offered my brother a nickel a pound for the garbage can full of mackerel he had just caught. In response to the insult, Rob turned around and donated the entire catch to the Methodist Hospital and received a fine thank-you note from its director of dietetics, who, years later, trained me at Middle School 51 on Fifth Avenue when I became a public-school lunch manager.

The Pergola Meat Market, on Seventh Avenue between Garfield Place and First Street, had easily five men behind the counter, all of them busy on a Saturday morning. Noel was our butcher, quiet, kind, benevolent. I knew to go to him, and only him, because he understood our orders. Noel ground the meat fresh, set aside the trimmed bones for soup, and, from the walk-in refrigerator, carried out pounds and pounds of lung, heart, and frozen beef kidneys (29 cents a pound). He then carried out more bones for the dogs (free), all wrapped in yards of brown butcher paper.

These days, there are innumerable permutations of dog-food products. In the 1960s, though, there were hardly more than about three brands of dog food: Alpo, Gaines, and store label. For the most part, we cooked from scratch for Midnight and Trekkan. Lung and heart made a savory broth, to which we added some starch: macaroni, rice, oatmeal, crumbled-up bread, rolls. Sometimes the dog food was so tasty that I ate some, although did not partake when their meal was liver.

We'd bring home all the groceries on Saturdays; it'd be near lunchtime, so we'd start unpacking, ripping open brown paper and lunging in to the contents: cheeses, cold cuts, meat freshly ground. The meat we would form into patties and put into a hot iron skillet, searing the outside while the center stayed rare, a hunk of it salted and eaten raw out of hand. While hamburgers were sizzling on the stove, we would sort the vegetables. Lettuces and curly spinach would go to the backyard for washing and de-sanding. We would fill a basin with water, agitate to loosen sand, drain in a colander, transfer to a linen kitchen towel, bundle and knot, then into the refrigerator, ready to go. We would arrange the fruit and set it on the dining-room table, the ripest positioned to be eaten first. A bowl of nuts sat next to the fruit. One mild Saturday, while we were eating lunch, a squirrel walked in from the backyard, hopped onto the dining-room table, picked out a walnut, put it in its mouth, and hopped out the open ground-floor window while we watched, mouths agape.

We cooked with Mom. Weekdays, cooking was done quickly and mostly on the top of the stove. I would work alongside her, most often as her prep helper—peeling garlic, chopping onions, and trimming bruised tomatoes and roughly chopping and simmering them into a fast, fresh sauce or stuffing them with grated cheese, bread crumbs, olive oil, flat parsley, minced garlic, and paprika and running them under the broiler until they bubbled. My mother's deft hands would skin vegetables with a well-worn, wooden-handle paring knife, closer than with a swivel-bladed peeler, shearing off thin ribbons of potato skin for the compost bucket, wasting as little as possible, and even what was "waste" was dug into our city backyard or by the side of our beach bungalow to decompose into the soil or sand.

My mom embraced any and all cuisines that came her way. At holiday potlucks at work, her fellow nurses' fishcakes and beef patties inspired her to make them at home. She often referred to tips she learned from "Trumpetto," a friend from her days as a young married—the first time, before she was widowed at age twenty-six—who himself had cooked for European royalty and was a kitchen legend to us.

We ate everything our parents put in front of us, even when it was the head, the feet, the tail, and lots in between, mostly willingly. Health was an element in my mom's culinary repertoire, and for some reason, Saturday dinner was often liver. Far too often. Even though liver was not one of our favorite foods, we were obliged to eat it. As a kid, my sister would invariably start a fight at the table and be sent to the laundry room to eat. There, she stood up, her dinner plate resting on the washing machine, and would secretly drop her unwanted food behind the washing machine. Late Saturday afternoons, more typically, she would "run away from home," right down to Steve's, the greasy spoon between Third and Fourth streets. Perched on one of the spin-around metal stools, she would order a hamburger. Or for weekend dietary variety, she would go to Al's Candy Store for a pack of Twinkies. She would eat them in the front yard, in my full view, waving assuredly and merrily to me while I slogged through my serving of beef liver. I used to think that I was obedient and she was rebellious. In retrospect, I admire her pragmatism and smarts.

I recall one particularly endless encounter with liver. I was maybe three years old—we were still living on Berkeley Place—and my parents were having a party that Saturday night. Chew and chew as I might, I couldn't finish the last fibrous mouthful, which must have been from what my friend Celeste called, in later years, "cirrhotic cows." The guests arrived, and I was still chewing. Finally, one came over and said, "Your mother says you can spit it out now." Which I did, right into the napkin that she held open and ready for the catch.

But really, besides that and the fact that my mom always added black pepper to the corn even when we begged her not to, night after night the meals were varied and interesting and ranged from good to simply delicious. She was a maestro. She made a stove sing. Her food voice rocked.

The Joy of Foraging

New Yorkers have gathered food throughout the city's history. Immigrant women foraged in city parks, found mushrooms, and dropped silver coins into the pans to test whether or not the mushrooms were poisonous. If the coins turned black, the mushrooms were not safe to eat. More recently, "Wildman" Steven Brill made his name as an urban forager, leading New Yorkers through parks, seeking edibles.

We gathered as a family, and as a family, we raised and gathered food that punctuated mealtime offerings and were an important adjunct to shopping. With a sense of purpose in growing, seeking, and finding, our efforts accorded these foods a reverence of their own. From the land, from the sea, from the air, the places where we got our food gave me a sense of place, and that place was largely Brooklyn. In the 1960s, we kids from Third Street pulled up chives by tuftfuls in Prospect Park and munched on them through the afternoons, feeling like we had discovered gold. The potential for food was seen subtly and sometimes abruptly around us. To this day, my mother spots fruit trees along the Prospect Expressway or in front of someone's home, gleans the windfalls, or sends us back to specified roadsides or sidewalks to pick up gnarly apples or pears, especially after windy September days. If she spots a strong clump of dandelions somewhere, she pries it up to cook in a pot with garlic and olive oil, as long as the greens aren't from tree pits or other spots where dogs are likely to pee. I do the same with these greens or with gummy purslane, both that crop up, unsolicited, between planted rows at Floyd Bennett Community Gardens at the end of Flatbush Avenue.

Our family foraged on Long Island, too, where my mother's sister, a star mushroom picker, lived. Cioci's adventuresome spirit and expertise radiated on gathering expeditions that she led with game friends and family in various woods and then served up big pots chock full of all sorts of mushrooms of all sorts of amazing shapes and textures. One time, driving home, my mother veered off the Southern State Parkway onto a swath of grass blooming with dandelions. We spilled out of the car for an impromptu pick and brought home bags of the flowers, which my mom simmered to make dandelion wine, a recipe for which she admits she had no previous experience. Two cloudy golden gallons brewed on the kitchen counter by the window. Days later, while in the laundry room, something exploded nearby. I ran into the kitchen to find the unvented wine bottle shattered, both glass and liquid shot all over the room.

Some food gathering was magical. While the Parachute Jump, a transplant to Coney Island from the 1939 World's Fair, was thrilling riders in the background, my family was swimming and gathering food from the saltwater in the foreground. I jumped from rock to jetty rock, found an impressive cluster of mussels, and handed them to my mother, intuitively knowing that she'd figure out something delicious to do with them. She debated—the waters in the Rockaways were cleaner than at Coney—but did decide to cook them: small, dense meat, packed with flavor of the sea, tomatoes, garlic, olive oil, the ocean. In 1973, when walking along the surf's edge in the Rockaways, a little lobster washed up right at my feet. It was a "short," definitely one that our Connecticut lobsterman friend Bob Mitchell today would throw back into Long Island Sound, where he hauls traps and measures each and every lobster's carapace for "keepers." Then, however, I felt that its appearance was a special gift from the sea. I carried it home, and my mother transformed it into a miracle of the loaves and fishes; a lobster salad stretched so far with celery, onions, green pepper, mayonnaise, and lemon juice that there was some for everyone in the family. Like everyone, we loved good food. We ultraloved foods that we gathered.

Growing Food in Brooklyn

Brooklyn has a long and rich agricultural history. Colonists wrote letters to friends and family in Europe describing its lands and waters abundant with food. Early European settlers brought their farming ways; Gravesenders grew food on "planters' lots," triangular swaths of land whose apex rested on the perimeter of the town square. Even before the aqueduct system brought good water to the city, Bushwick Springs supported farming and the brewing industry. Farmers rewarded helpful kids with dippers of milk, and even during the urbanization of places like Troutman Street, neighbors from homes that encroached on Brooklyn farms could still pick bags of vegetables.

Urban decay in the 1960s and 1970s pockmarked the city's complexion with rat-infested vacant lots. But in the early 1970s, community gardens transformed many of them, and they began to bloom. Members of the Green Guerrillas beautified debris-filled lots by throwing seed-filled glass Christmas ornaments over tall fences. When the support of legislators and organizations like the Cornell University Cooperative Extension, New Yorkers accumulated acres of wasteland, some created by arson in the sad and scary days of the city, into food-bearing neighborhood oases. Now, community gardens are even more precious, as every inch of vacant land sits poised to be hungrily scooped up for development.

Once my mother learned that there was such thing as the Children's Garden at the Brooklyn Botanic Garden, we were there weekly for a good part of the year for the long haul, the entire length of time that a kid back then could participate, from age nine to eighteen. Indoor theory and practice classes on late-winter Saturdays meant sitting in the auditorium for meetings called to order by the ancient Ms. Miner or Ms. Douglass and conducted by "the girl and boy presidents." I served in 1974. Among the "honors" research projects was one about Fibonacci numbers, with mathematics and nature relationships illustrated by pinecones. I thought my head was going to explode, but it always stayed with me. The ultimate award at the Children's Garden was the Butler Cup, a trophy given annually to a gardener for outstanding service.

On chilly late-winter Saturdays, we worked in the greenhouses, transplanting seedlings or learning to propagate brilliant coleus by soaking clippings until roots emerged. On slate tables, we mixed humus, potting soil, and sand for planting in pots. And we always brought something home, marigolds or whatever, to shorten the days of winter. In classrooms, we planned for Planting Day by working on paper, scaled to represent our ten- by twenty-foot plots of soil. We carefully figured each row to maintain a proper distance, and I felt my mother's influence in planning the garden most productively. The teachers supported our creative ideas. In 1973, with the idea to plan an organic garden, they directed me to Brooklyn Botanic Garden library books such as *Companion Gardening,* about planting vegetables that help one another; for example, radishes put back in the soil what cabbage takes out, so you don't have to add chemicals to prevent clubroot; marigolds discourage aphids, so plant them near tomatoes even if they aren't organic, as it gives them an advantage.

Planting Day started with a festive march from the greenhouse to the gardens, a small gardener pushed in a wheelbarrow leading the way. Our garden plots looked like an archaeological site with strings stretched across the soil, marking straight lines above the soil on which we were to plant the seeds. Once growing season was under way, we would walk under the garden house transom emblazoned with the words "He is happiest who hath power to gather wisdom from a flower," read the instruction board, gather our tools for the day, and set out to weed, stake, hand cultivate, and ultimately harvest. In the early season, pickings were piecemeal. After that surfeit of radishes, there were tender lettuces and heads of cabbage. In July, gardens exploded with vegetables and weeds. We tied heavy tomato plants to wooden stakes, and zucchini grew like wild. One fellow gardener, Werawanna, nicknamed "Wee Wee," harvested a twenty-three-pound zucchini that kids used as a baseball bat in an impromptu game in the north field. In that same summer before we left for vacation in late July, my mother told me to pick as much as possible, "even the little green

ones." I picked bell peppers so small that they would now be called "baby," a market
form unknown in Brooklyn in 1973. A few days later, my mom cut a few of them into
a small salad that she made for my brother. Rob ate it and responded, "This tastes
good." I was in the adjoining room of our tiny beach bungalow, heard his words, and
experienced that moment when the effort of growing and harvesting, the *terroir* of
the Children's Garden, unknown to him at the same moment, came together simply
in his appreciation of the food's flavor.

From the Sea

Brooklyn is embraced by water with a warm, wet hug. Water as a food source has
had a long history here. Native Americans summered along the coastline, fishing,
hunting shore birds and rabbits, harvesting clams and oysters from Jamaica Bay,
and shucking and sun-drying them for winter use inland. They also fashioned the
shells into wampum at the waterside shell works. The Gerritsen family acquired
this tract of land in the seventeenth century and built a tide-driven mill, where between the seventeenth and nineteenth centuries, grain was ground.

Water is my family's business. Water is my family's passion. From *schmutz* to the sea,
water in the right place and the right condition determines how we approach it. For
work, my father and now my brother make it flow where it previously did not. My
mother owned and operated a sewer-cleaning business when she and my dad married
in the early 1950s, and my dad, then a carpenter by trade, became a sewer cleaner.
He wore denim overalls and drove a Volkswagen van, a trendsetter for hippies of the
1960s and 1970s. Phones were answered and drains unclogged as best as he was able,
24/7, and I sometimes woke in the middle of the night hearing Norman going down
the stairs and into the night to get someone's drains flowing again. This included a
lot of our town's food businesses, like clearing blood and trimmings in the middle of
the night at the Gansevoort Meat Market. At breakfast, he would announce, "I went
to see Harry and Bert last night," meaning customers like Piels Brewery, where he
unstopped the drains clogged with labels, which stopped the bottling line cold. Now
my brother does the same, and Rob's business T-shirts say "Your Sh-t Is My Bread
and Butter!"

But that has to do with fresh, albeit *schmutzy,* water. Between summers in the
Rockaways and days spent at Coney Island and Plumb Beach, the saltwater around
New York has drawn me like a magnet. From 1959 on, family fishing trips took all
types and forms. Some were to Long Island, with the emphasis on clamming. On
those trips, we loaded a rented garvey with gear buckets, burlap bags, fishing poles,
and the killy trap that we filled with chunks of bread that swelled in the saltwater to
lure spearing and other bait. We would fish until the tide was low and then jump out
of the boat and hold on to the side, kneading our feet in the squishy muck until we felt
a rock. We would wiggle it loose with our toes and bend over to pull up a hard clam,
tossing it into the boat. Crawling on our knees along the water's edge, we used the piss
clam rake to dig up steamers. Back in Brooklyn, Mom would cook them in a lemony

broth, and we would slip off their turtle necks and dunk them in melted butter. In our backyard, we would sort all the clams by size, from cherrystones to chowders, and prepare them accordingly: Manhattan and New England clam chowders, clams casino, baked clams, linguine with clam sauce. But I liked them raw on the half shell best, dressed at most with a squeeze of lemon. They tasted like the sea.

Along the Brooklyn coast, we would surf cast on beaches, throw our lines off the Sixty-ninth Street or Coney Island piers, snake along wooden pilings near Tamaqua hoping to net some blue claw crabs, or motor into Jamaica Bay for fish and eels. And we spent the most time fishing out of Sheepshead Bay. In the 1960s and 1970s, the bay definitely had a scruffy, salt-of-the-earth undertone, made a little creepier when my dad's *Saltwater Sportsman* arrived in the mail with an article entitled "Sheepshead Bay: Where Gangsters, Their Feet in Cement, Sway in the Tides." We established our comfort zone by always fishing on the *Glory*, a former World War II subchaser owned by Captain Chubby Martin with Second Captain Harry Rydberg, men with zero tolerance for sleaze or slime. By example, they, in turn, expected pride and proper comportment. When my dad placed a sand shark in a coiled rope on the *Glory*'s deck and the shark bled onto the tight cotton, Captain Harry's admonition, "Norman, you should know better than that," was so stern that it turned us all around with our tails between our legs. For a decade, my brother worked as a mate on the *Glory* on weekends and during summer vacation and went on to know and fish varied saltwaters from Brooklyn to the Rockaways, Montauk, New England, North Carolina, the Gulf of Mexico, and beyond, in all conditions and in all seasons.

For our fishing trips, we prepared the night before by making a boatload of sandwiches, not knowing whether we would be seasick or ravenous, but prepared nonetheless. Despite early bedtimes with the clock set at 4:00 A.M., we had a hard time falling asleep from anticipation. We woke up tired, but we rallied for the day ahead.

On these mornings, Third Street slept, quiet and dark, streetlights simultaneously illuminating and making shadows as we opened the doors of the VW bus, parked in our next-door neighbor's driveway. Even in the 1960s and 1970s, Park Slope was "No Park Slope." We would load the van with fishing poles and reused plastic spackle buckets, cleaned and filled with everything: tackle, hooded sweatshirts, the sandwiches, a thermos, and a moving-van blanket to later wrap and nap in. Whether fishing ourselves or, in the summer, picking up my brother from night fishing trips, we would set off down Ocean Parkway, singing at the top of our lungs to "Mrs. Robinson" and "MacArthur Park" on the radio. When we got to the part about leaving the cake out in the rain, we would crack up, laughing.

Sleepy Brooklyn was replaced by a gently awakening town once we turned onto Emmons Avenue, party boats alight as mates stood curbside, some wearing close-fitting denim jackets snazzily embroidered with the names of their boats: *Elmar, Effort, Betty W, Helen H, Brooklyn, Amberjack*. These guys vied for customers by hawking the party boats' names, older guys relaxedly and the younger ones more aggressively. We would transfer our gear directly onto the *Glory*. At 6:00 A.M., the boats would chug out backward from the piers, righted, and, just past the bend where Kingsborough Community College now stands, gun the engines and pick up speed for the run to wherever fish might be. Once on the fishing grounds, the *Glory* maneu-

On a summer morning in 1981, Rob, Dianne, and Norman goof off while motoring during one of our fishing trips. We rolled up a brown-paper lunch bag into a jaunty hat for our dad and stuck a cigarette in his ear to accompany the ever present one that he smoked. (Photograph courtesy of Annie Hauck)

vered from spot to spot, following the fish by sonar. Captain Martin then would idle the engine and sound a little toot to signal that it was okay to drop our lines.

Someone asked me whether we fished for fun or for food; both, plus my brother fished for spending money all through his school years. Overall, though, we fished most definitely for food. I imagine that my dad's sense of urgency came from growing up during the Depression, even though his family never went hungry. His dad, a professional waiter at the India House/Wall Street Club, was nicknamed "Greasy Pockets" because he always carried leftovers home to his family. Back on the boat, though, even if Norman was in the midst of a relaxed conversation and smoke, when the horn tooted, his eyes would snap to attention as he sprang up and over to his pole and dropped his line in the water, all the while urging us to get going, too, not to lose a second on the possibility of catching fish. We would throw out chum to lure mackerel and bait hooks with chopped clams or bloodsucker worms, with their little hooks that attached and withdrew; even when cut up, they would squirm. Lead sinkers, some made at home from melted lead poured into molds, pulled hooks and lines down into the ocean: halfway for mackerel, to the bottom for fluke and flounder, and to whatever depth the bluefish swam, announced by the first few people who reeled them in. First the wait, then the little shaking pull, a yank of the pole, and a turn of the reel to feel whether you had hooked the fish.

Reeling in caused a buzz. As the mates called, "Walk 'em on down," neighbors pulled their poles up and their bodies back to give way to the one reeling in along the boat's railing. If the fish seemed big, a mate would hurry over with the gaff, a pole with a big hook to spear the fish and hoist it into the boat, bloody and flapping on the wooden deck. More excitement rippled if it looked like a contender for the "pool," the dollar or two that people put in the hat, hoping they'd win with the day's biggest fish. Pulling out the hook was a matter of gripping the fish securely by the gills with the left hand and pushing the hook farther into the body to dislodge and then pull out the capturing barbed wire.

On the trip back, with the "pool" fish determined, purposeful cleaning followed, of both the fish and the boat. En route to the bay, seagulls trailed the boat, swooping down to catch heads and guts that we threw into the air. Once back in the harbor, boats blared their horns. This meant FISH! attracting a crowd of potential customers to the dock. Mates sold their catches, sliding whole fish into thick brown paper bags. They also stashed their earnings in such bags. Once, a mate mistakenly handed the money bag to a customer, who disappeared onto Emmons Avenue with the day's catch in cash. If my brother had any fish unsold, he would come home and fetch my sister, and they would park by the Grand Army Plaza subway station to sell fresh fish to people returning home from a long day's work in Manhattan.

From the Air

Bees were in our Brooklyn picture, going eye and ear level with them. Honeybees connected to heads of clover as we laid our heads on the grass of the Sheep's Meadow in Prospect Park. The Brooklyn Botanic Garden had an observation hive, and I loved watching the bees determinedly cover the surface of the comb. One Park Slope apiarist, Father Lester, from All Saints Episcopal Church on Seventh Avenue, occasionally rescued entire swarms perched atop lampposts along Seventh Avenue. Wearing his net bonnet, he would calmly climb a ladder, shake the bees into a box, and carry them away.

Somehow, when I was in my early twenties, I got a bee in my bonnet to raise bees. I learned of the existence of the Long Island Beekeepers Association and joined the group, traveling by train to monthly meetings in Suffolk County. In the big yard where the meetings were held, hives were lined up in rows. The association's members would cluster around the master beekeeper, Reinhold Meyer, a Charlie Weaver lookalike easily in his late seventies, in shirt sleeves, opening hive after hive and pulling out drawer after drawer with his "hive tool," the tire iron of beekeeping. We listened to his assessments of what he saw on each frame: pollen or nectar packed in cells, brood ready to hatch, capped honey, drones, workers, and an occasional queen bee.

In the cold months, I read beekeeping magazines and kept the apiarist's bible, *The ABC's and XYZ's of Beekeeping* nearby. Finally, I thought, the time to do this is now. I ordered almost everything by mail and built the hive from a kit with new, good-smelling wood; a beeswax foundation comb; and little nails to secure the frames. With the raw materials in place, it was time to populate the hive, with the help of one of the club members, a supplier. A three-pound box of Italian bees with queen arrived in Suffolk, so I traveled on the Long Island Rail Road to a club meeting to pick it up. The bees were neatly contained in a traveling case, a sort of minihive, the size of about half a hive with an air screen at the top but no flight opening. Back on the train, I put the box on the seat beside me and sat with my arm cautiously atop for the ride back to Flatbush Avenue. The conductor came by and asked casually, "What's in the box?" and I replied, equally casually, "Pets." He asked, "What kind of pets?" and I whispered, "If you promise not to tell anyone, bees." "BEES!" he shouted, and everyone on the train car shot their eyes at me: glares, looks of fright, and a few gleams of interest. The conductor shifted into high gear, calling to the car the other conductors, who gathered round and laughingly offered me big bucks to release the bees into a packed, rush-hour train car. Finally, we pulled into the Flatbush Avenue station, and I carried the box home along Prospect Park West.

The bees were docile. My approach to working with them was what I had learned: staying calm, not wearing perfumes or deodorants but wearing light-color cotton clothing, and not blocking their flight path. It was a smooth transition into the permanent hive and the bees were on their way, living on top of my brother's garage roof, their hive set proximal to the Brooklyn Botanic Garden and midway between Prospect Park and Greenwood Cemetery, known for its flowering trees. Foraging as far as a five-mile radius, much of what they pollinated had further food potential in Brooklyn: fruit trees and vines, vegetable plants in backyard and community gardens. My dad would climb a ladder to the top of the garage and, shaded by the big tulip tree and with his jar of coffee and his ever-present cigarettes, just watch the bees' rhythmic sweeps into and out of the hive, much as I had years before at the Botanic Garden.

The bees were healthy and gathered abundantly and differently through the months: lemon yellow linden in early June, golden clover in July and August, and darker maple as autumn approached. Working on the hive sometimes with and sometimes without the netted safari hat was, for the most part, a clear translation of theory to practice.

Then there were the sweating times. Neighbors complained, so I had to move the hive, and my mother volunteered her place for its relocation. Late one night, with most of the bees in the hive, I closed their entrance with a piece of screen. The next morning, we wrapped the hive with rope and slid the whole thing down the sides of the angled ladder off the roof, onto a hand truck, into the work van, and over to my mother's small yard. The bees adjusted easily there and foraged so successfully that they almost outgrew their space. One night in late May 1979, while walking along Prospect Park West, I looked up to see linden trees flowering and came home to find the bees painted in a mass outside the hive, which had quickly grown overcrowded. Brood, pollen, nectar, and honey covered and filled nearly all the cells on the frames, and the bees were poised to swarm to a bigger space. The next day, I quickly assembled and added another drawer, and they marched back in and settled into their expanded space.

That summer, when I hoisted the hive to the top of my mother's garage, using a similar ladder technique, the transition was not as smooth. While sliding one of the wrapped drawers, heavy with honey, up the ladder, it slid off the runners and wedged under the coping. Sweating like crazy from the bee gear and the tension, I was barely able to hold on to, much less sway, the rope to free the box. The bees inside loudly buzzed their upset with all this jostling and commotion. A few that escaped flew directly at me, stinging whatever they could, including my ankles in nine spots, right through the socks. On this day, Pope John Paul II was visiting the United States, and this scene was scored by the sound of someone's radio playing the highlights of his travels.

There was consensus among some of the apiarists that bee venom quelled arthritis pain. Rheumatoid arthritis racks my mother's body with aches and pains, so with good intentions, we started a course of bee-venom therapy with progressive numbers of bee stings. Unfortunately, she developed an allergy to bee venom; moreover, it gave her no relief from her arthritis pain.

The payoff for my efforts was honey. One club member who lived in Marine Park sold me his nearly new stainless-steel extractor. I removed the hive's full frames with the hive tool and uncapped the wax cells with an angled comblike tool, slid the frames into the extractor, and whirred the centrifuge with a hand crank. Honey shot out to the walls. We repeated the other side, and the thick liquid sweetness oozed out of the spout through cheesecloth and a mesh sieve. Jars of Brooklyn honey, some packed with comb, made a handy holiday gift in the early 1980s.

Pets

We had a regular roster of pets: dogs, cats, fish, turtles, reptiles, a snake, parakeets, a canary. Sometimes more colorful additions were made to the menagerie. Children out for walks with their parents or schoolteachers regularly stopped to look at the rabbits in our Berkeley Place yard, visible through a wide-slatted wooden gate. Early one morning, my mother got a phone call from the nearby school custodian, saying, "Mrs. Hauck, your rabbits are here." They had gone under the fence, hopped halfway down the block to the old schoolyard, and huddled by the basement door. In the early 1960s, parts of Canarsie still were designated as farms on the city's real-estate tax rolls. My dad went there one December with the idea of buying a goat and tying antlers to it so we would have a Christmas "reindeer." Although the goat never reached Third Street, one evening my dad walked in and put down a full-grown turkey right on the kitchen floor. He held its wings and body still for us to meet and greet it before heading to the backyard, excitement flying everywhere. My father also brought home a pair of little white ducks and a baby chick that we kept indoors in a tabletop cage with a copper warming light until they were big enough for the backyard. We wondered aloud whether the chick would grow into a laying hen. Early one morning, we heard that we had a rooster. Neighbors in the apartment building next door applauded its morning call with a daily toss of glass bottles into our backyard.

Dianne, Annie, and Nicky the Pig in the backyard of Third Street, Park Slope, Brooklyn, 1961. (Photograph courtesy of Jane Hauck)

Our duck played the role of "bald eagle" at a Cub Scout show at St. Saviour on Sixth Street. As part of the skit, my brother had to pick up the duck onstage. Rob was so afraid that it would poop in front of the audience that he made the den mother (our mother) promise not to feed it until after the show.

On one Sunday outing to the Long Island Farm Fair, my parents bought a piglet, for $14. We sat guard over it in the back of the station wagon for the entire drive home to Brooklyn and then took it out to the backyard. The piglet immediately wiggled its thin body right through the iron fence slats and made a beeline onto Third Street, running up and down the block almost as excitedly as we did, trying to chase it down.

Nicky the Pig and all these other animals were our pets, and we played with, fed, watered, and cleaned up after them. At some point, each of them disappeared from the backyard. When we asked our parents where they had gone, their explanations varied: "The turkey flew away." "The rooster went to Babci's backyard in Bay Ridge, and two talent scouts rang her doorbell, saying they had a part for the rooster in a Hollywood movie." We kids were thrilled that our rooster was a movie star. The pig just disappeared. Meanwhile, we ate whatever was served at mealtime.

Although I do not specifically recall Nicky on the table, I do think that he was named "chicken" at dinner. Years later, while rummaging through a box of family photos, I found some black-and-white shots of my dad in the basement with an ax in one hand, Nicky's front legs in the other, and his hind legs suspended from a rafter.

Livelihood

Pushcart food on city streets is as varied today as it has been for much of New York's street-food history. But this was not so in the mid-1970s, when the offerings were almost as dry as the salted pretzels sold on the carts, along with hot dogs, knishes, and soda. In the bicentennial summer of 1976, a natural-foods pushcart seemed like a refreshing sidewalk alternative. My family, therefore, responded positively to my proposal, and we started on our pushcart. First, we had to get a license. Next, my dad designed a cart and began to build it out of wood. Wheels were a dilemma, and our friend, "the Joey," and I scoured the Hamilton Avenue sanitation dump for wheels. Ultimately, my father configured collapsible wheels affixed with wing nuts. My then boyfriend, and now husband, posted the cart's menu on a painted yellow crate: "healthful" sandwiches, natural cakes, juices, fresh fruit, and dried-fruit-and-nut mixtures. Finding, developing a rapport with, and purchasing from vendors in both Park Slope and Canarsie's Brooklyn Terminal Market—all seemingly straightforward enough.

We read the vendor's rule book and considered where to set up shop, ideally an empty corner with enough foot traffic to attract some customers. If we had followed the rules to the letter, we'd be selling off the coast of Plumb Beach. In any event, on our first day of business, we optimistically headed for the Wall Street area, but that day on the corner of Dutch Street and Maiden Lane, the difficulties—traffic! parking! barely a corner free of hot dog wagons to set up shop!—sent us running back over the Brooklyn Bridge. Where could we sell? We found an empty spot at Remsen and Court streets downtown. As we unloaded the station wagon, another vendor walked over to us, warning us that this was "his" corner. As we argued back that no corner was assigned, a police car pulled up, the bully disappeared, and we turned to face the approaching officer, doing an incredulous double take as Ritchie from Herzog's Deli, now in uniform, recognized us. Big smiles broke out all around as we caught up with mutual "What are you doing here?" His parting words as he got back into the patrol car were, "If anyone gives you trouble, tell them you're my cousin."

Once located, those summer days went like this:

• 8:20 A.M. Mother arrives home after working the midnight to 8:00 A.M. shift at the hospital. I would immediately drive her station wagon down to Atlantic Avenue and buy warm whole wheat pita bread from Damascus Bakery, return home, assemble sandwiches (sliced Muenster cheese and mixed salad), make sauce for the sandwiches, pack chilled juice, fruit, and pastries into cooler.

• 11:00 A.M. With sister's help, load the pushcart into the station wagon and drive to "our" corner. Slide out wagon, attach wheels and canopied awning, and move cooler and crate onto wagon. Leave Dianne with wagon, change apron, and look for parking space. By the time I joined my sister at the cart, she already would have started selling, with more customers on the way. The lunchtime foot traffic and some really nice people—court officers; a college student back home in Brooklyn for the summer from Santa Cruz, where he studied ways to make tomato skins so hard they could be dropped from a six-foot ladder without splattering; an assistant district attorney—formed a small crowd of regulars, and I began to feel a little less vulnerable, a little more secure. My father would make runs out to the Canarsie Market to deliver more supplies as needed. Sometimes he just drove up alongside the cart in the course of his workday to see how we were doing, and one afternoon I looked down Remsen Street to find him parked and in his work clothes, those denim overalls, leaning against his van, protective as always of his kids and watching as always for any trouble that any other vendor might cause his daughters.

These Days in the BK

My parents eventually split their partnership as co-homeowners, and as adults, we dispersed from Park Slope and set up our individual homes in other neighborhoods. I delved more formally into the borough's food history, combing books, clippings, and photos at the Brooklyn Public Library at Grand Army Plaza and the Brooklyn Historical Society, collecting and connecting the stories of native peoples who fished from these waters, immigrants who planted and gathered in ways brought from many homelands, and Brooklynites who made food their business here. I continued visiting different Brooklyn neighborhoods to see what was going on with food and sent my Brooklyn College students out to do the same.

At my brother's house, Dad moved upstairs from him, his wife, and their babies. More homebound now, Norman's cooking largely involved sitting at his worktable and carefully cutting up ingredients with the television providing an incessant backdrop. A pot simmering with a meaty bone—yes, sometimes even a head—some grain, and lots of vegetables was a fixture on the back of the stove. Norman sharpened his paring knife, his chef's knife, and his "pig sticker" on a whetstone for all his cutting, which was slowed by care and age. On the day my father died—in the long hours that we waited in his apartment, first for the paramedics, then for the detectives, and finally for the pair sent by the mortician to carry out his body—assisted by my sister, whose heart was heavier than our dead dad, I started to clear his kitchen of perishables. I emptied the soup pot one last time, a lamb shank and a mass of barley and vegetables. One piece of carrot caught my eye, cut from a stalk that had split while growing. With Norman's slicing, it naturally took the shape of a heart.

I did not inherit my parents' skills or ways with knives. Even though I teach "Introductory Foods" to students at Brooklyn College, I peel far more skin off vegetables than my mother does. I wouldn't know how to stick a live pig swiftly, as my parents and their parents did. Instead, these days, I bring home a roasted pig's head from Sunset Park. My neighbor proudly sings his "food voice" through ribs, which he painstakingly prepares on weekends. He starts in the early morning, making a wood

"We gathered as a family, and as a family, we raised and gathered food." The Haucks at Floyd Bennett Community Gardens, Gateway National Park, at the end of Flatbush Avenue, Brooklyn, 1999. (Photograph courtesy of Annie Hauck)

fire, stoking it periodically, and tending it throughout the day, basting the ribs with a signature sauce on a special mop. Anticipation in the nabe is palpable as I near our homes. With pig's head in tow, I offer some to him in return for his offer of ribs. He recoils in disgust. I remind him that the head of the pig is just a wee bit north of the ribs of the same animal and mention that some people think that the word "barbecue" comes from the phrase *barbe à queue*—"from beard to tail." I set the head on the table. Some people cringe, and others cut off a piece for their plates.

These days, my brother fishes off the coasts of Montauk, New York; Point Judith, Rhode Island; Wells, Maine; North Carolina; and Gloucester and Hyannis, Massachusetts. In 1993, he started an annual "family fishing trip" to Orient Point, near where our dad had taken us fishing, and to duck farms by the Southold Fishing Station and Port of Egypt. Three generations boarded the charter boat, which had never before held a playpen. While driving up my street after one of these trips, I saw some neighbors, pulled over, opened the cooler in the back, held up a fillet, and asked, "Do you want some bluefish that were swimming today?" One neighbor was thrilled. Two others took fillets less than enthusiastically, and as I drove away, I caught their mutual looks askance.

These days, I cook the codfish heads that my brother saves special when he comes back from winter trips to Georges Bank. Selected friends and family sit at the kitchen table. We squeeze lemon into the jellied, chilled broth and feel like we're drinking the ocean.

These days, when Rob and I set out at 5:00 A.M. to join Bob Mitchell for a day of work hauling, cleaning, and baiting traps and measuring, sorting, and banding lobsters, requests to "bring us back some lobster" trail us in the rearview mirror.

These days, my Brooklyn College students in the foods lab know to set aside their onion skins and carrot peels for compost that makes its way farther down Flatbush Avenue to the Floyd Bennett Community Garden at Gateway. Each season, I plant pumpkins and am lucky if a single one can be coaxed out for a Halloween jack-o'-lantern. Strangely, though, during the summers that my children were in utero, the vines produced prolifically. My daughter, born during the heat wave that coincided with Hurricane Andrew, made her first trip to the garden when she was two and a half days old. The vegetable plants were parched and needed watering. Four days later, she helped me settle the foods lab and other classes before I could feel comfortable going on maternity leave. These days, she makes *kapusta* using a wooden circle that her dad formed in his shop to press down the salted cabbage as it ferments. As we three generations of Hauck women hand out sauerkraut samples to hungry New Yorkers on International Pickle Day, she tells how she'd rather have tamped down the cabbage barefoot in a wooden barrel, as both our *babcia*s did in Poland.

These days, my twelve-year-old son asks me to take him fishing off the Coney Island pier. There, we swap recipes with other Brooklynites jigging for herring, different accents, different recipes, identical poles, identical motions, so Brooklyn. We expect to be joined shortly by newer immigrants, many born in other states or boroughs, as the food character continues to emerge in Brooklyn, where all things are possible.

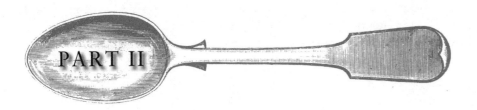

People

EVERY NEW YORKER has a food voice, and together these voices create a chorale—sometimes cacophonous and always interesting. Part II, "People," highlights several of New York's food voices.

Martin F. Manalansan IV, in "The Empire of Food: Place, Memory, and Asian 'Ethnic Cuisines,'" leads us by the nose into the complex cultural food spaces of Queens, New York City's most ethnically diverse borough. He takes us through food stores, into restaurants, and particularly to family kitchens, where we can smell the tension between the deeply rooted re-creation of homeland meals and the perceived stigma of the swirling aromas of other worlds.

The food voice of Jessica B. Harris, a cookbook author, food writer, and anthropologist, uses the metaphor of a calendar in "The Culinary Seasons of My Childhood." Her school year, parents, grandparents, and summers help illustrate the varied and multiple influences on her omnivorous palate.

In "The Chefs, the Entrepreneurs, and Their Patrons: The Avant-Garde Food Scene in New York City," Fabio Parasecoli, of the magazine *Gambero Rosso*, discusses the avant-garde and uniquely American concept of hip in relation to chefs, the heavy hitters of New York's food scene. Parasecoli describes such elements of their creative expression as motivation, philosophy, and forms, and particularly how in New York, they balance public, palate, and business pressures. He shows us the avant-garde and the hip through the chefs' creativity and, of necessity, pursuit of profit.

Harley Spiller, or "Inspector Collector," concludes this section with "Chow Fun City: Three Centuries of Chinese Cuisine in New York City." With the menu from Port Arthur, one artifact in his record-breaking collection of Chinese restaurant menus, as a starting point for an interview with the patriarch of a multigeneration Chinese restaurant family, Spiller follows Chinese food from its early exoticism in the city through its current ubiquity.

The Empire of Food

Place, Memory, and Asian "Ethnic Cuisines"

MARTIN F. MANALANSAN IV

WHILE DRIVING along the Brooklyn-Queens Expressway near the rolling hills of Calvary Cemetery in the New York City borough of Queens, I can see the Manhattan skyline rising on the horizon from beyond the tombstones. From this vista, Manhattan's cosmopolitan modernity seems like Oz, beyond the reach of the inhabitants of Queens. Queens has been seen as Manhattan's "other," its poor cousin, located outside the glare and vigor of sophisticated urban life. Indeed, Queens was historically considered as the best place to bury the city's dead and was often portrayed by the media as socially awkward and colorless. Yet this urban space is filled with an effervescent quality demonstrated by the bright signs, diverse cuisines, honking cars, and number 7 train rumbling overhead in the busy business and residential neighborhoods. Beyond this evidence, Queens offers more sensuous signs of its flourishing urban existence. Nowhere is this more evident than in the food and culinary cultures of its diverse inhabitants. Queens offers a kaleidoscope of aural, aromatic, and gustatory delights. Such is the promise and allure of this borough, which I explore in this chapter.

The following is a series of overlapping gustatory and other sensory narratives about the Asian foods, physical spaces, and cultural habits and rituals in the three Queens neighborhoods of Woodside, Flushing, and Jackson Heights and their complicated ideas of space, selfhood, and the traditional binaries of modernity and tradition. These narratives are not meant to be exhaustive or definitive but are impressionistic vignettes illustrating both micro and macro social structures and rituals. The best way to think of them is as momentary "tastes" of the neighborhoods, highly focused yet open-ended stories perhaps leading to experiences without easy conclusions.

My aim is to locate physical places, foods, and people in New York City's contemporary symbolic and sensory topographies, with Queens as a springboard. To many travelers, Manhattan is the center and final destination, and Queens is merely a conduit between it and the outside world. Even though Queens is the site of two of the city's principal airports, LaGuardia and Kennedy, it is not a mere passageway into a cultural and culinary destination elsewhere. Instead, I would argue, Queens itself is a stopping place for the intriguing sensory experiences of its cuisines, people, and landscapes.

Queens is not, however, an easy terrain to navigate, as it lacks specific landmarks such as Manhattan's Central Park to anchor the space. One Manhattan denizen admitted that he dreaded venturing into the "wild" space of Queens because he could easily get lost in its seeming labyrinth of three- and four-story houses in neighborhoods that appear to follow one another without rhyme or reason. Stories abound of trying to navigate to the corner of Thirty-sixth Street and Thirty-sixth Avenue or among the parallel Sixty-seventh Avenue, Sixty-seventh Road, and Sixty-seventh Drive to deliver a hastily addressed package labeled only "Sixty-seventh." My stories are meant to unravel this seeming "spatial disorder" and create not a neatly arranged set of meanings but a complicated intersection of sensory, biographical, and social experiences.

My ethnographic fieldwork was on Asian American immigrants, with a focus on their cuisine, from 2001 to 2005. Much of my time was spent hanging out in typical culinary spaces like restaurants, cafés, and groceries. I also spent considerable time observing and talking to people in their homes, sharing home-cooked meals, walking around neighborhood streets, and riding the trains and buses that crisscross Queens's urban landscape.

I describe and analyze these experiences from two perspectives. The first is based on the idea that food is a medium for expressing identity, or what Annie Hauck-Lawson calls the "food voice."[1] The other perspective is that of scholars of the senses, who believe that the senses are the building blocks of everyday experiences that eventually become routinized into manageable and domesticated forms like daily habits.[2] While it is easy to understand that food locates people—"You are what you eat"—I submit that, conversely, food can dislocate people, taking them into the terrain of the unfamiliar, the strange, and the absurd. Far from an easy equation of *food equals ontology or being,* food is also about the conflicting and often ambivalent experiences of homelessness, mourning, cultural shock, and confusion.

The terms that I use in the title of this chapter, particularly "empire" and "ethnic," should clarify my argument. I use "empire" for the borough of Queens to denote hierarchies as well as to play on the banal use of this word in many of the names of "ethnic" restaurants. I also use "empire" to indicate the lingering influences of the diminishing and emerging experiences of the "ethnic" and the mainstream. Queens is the ethnic other in relation to Manhattan. Queens is the "over there," the noncosmopolitan alternative space, the poor cousin, and/or the place of abjection. Whereas "ethnic cuisines" are often touted as colorful exotic phenomena coupled with the seemingly contradictory notions of attraction and repulsion, the practices related to "ethnic" foods, especially Asian foods, pertain to negotiating hierarchies of power.

My interest is in how meaning making becomes part of place making or, more specifically, how taste and place are connected in the construction and experience of immigrant life in Queens.

Sensing Queens Through the Number 7 Train

Planes, buses, and cars are the usual vehicles for getting to and from Queens, but the subway—or, more accurately, the elevated train—is the best way to experience the borough and recognize the panoply of "flavors" and other sensual experiences, some of which may not be readily palatable or acceptable to mainstream tastes.

By entering through the turnstile at one of the city's subway stations and boarding a train, one is not merely traveling from one place to another but is experiencing the city in a specific way, through the windows and train cars. Each subway line follows a specific series of points in a fixed itinerary of transit stops. In a way, each subway line, denoted by a single letter or number, is a highly specialized story of the city.[3] Here is one.

The number 7 train is sometimes called the "Orient Express" and, increasingly, the "International Express." Number 7 goes through the old neighborhoods in

Roosevelt Avenue and Forley Street, Elmhurst, Queens, September 18, 2005. (Photograph courtesy of Harley Spiller)

Queens that have the city's highest concentration of Asians. A good part of the line travels on an elevated platform above the busy streets, providing a literal and figurative eagle's-eye view of the borough. At the beginning of my research, I talked to people on the train as a way to get to know the borough and its specific neighborhoods through this indirect means to the food in three sites. In this chapter, I take this "detour" to showcase the myriad ways in which food becomes enmeshed in nongustatory sensory experiences and to show how place making must be part of the discourses regarding ethnic immigrants' food and lives.

Part of the story of the number 7 train is not the sights and sounds of the city, but its smells. Some people talk about how neighborhoods "smell," with most of their discussion about why each neighborhood has a specific odor. While some of the odors may have nothing to do with food, many discussions do concern Queens as an immigrant community, with strong and "strange" aromas emanating from restaurants and residences.

In his remarkable study of urban aromas in Paris at the start of the modern era, Alain Corbin suggests that the creation of boundaries between life and death, between business and domesticity, and between rich and poor becomes the turning point in the transformative "deodorization" of modernizing Western cities.[4] Following Corbin, I propose that the discourses of smells in Queens have much to do with Queens being at the "other" side of these boundaries. Besides being the primary city location for cemeteries, Queens has long been the residential space for working-class people. These ideas of marginality permeate people's statements, loosely linking the neighborhoods with the people who live in them through their smells and aromas of food.

Part of the intersection of space, smell, ethnicity, and food in this study has to do with the fact that Asians have been historically and popularly imagined to be linked to food. Filipinos, Koreans, and Vietnamese have been branded as dog eaters, and Chinese are accused of cooking and eating cats, rats, and every other imaginable animal. Indians are known for creating a fiery, spicy cuisine that defies human capacities. At the same time, economic realities have also rendered true some of the stereotypical conjunctions of Asian Americans and food. The Chinese, particularly, have been associated with the food-service industries as waiters, busboys, and cooks. Furthermore, Chinese food is the most common and "most ethnic" American fast food. But even though studies of Asian Americans' alimentary constructions debase them in American immigration history and culture, these works depend on hegemonic visual and gustatory apparatuses.

Smell, therefore, is another lens through which food and Asian Americans can be understood. Let us take the example of an Indian woman I talked to while riding the number 7. Shilpa was a twenty-year-old student who had come to the United States when she was three.[5] She had created a fascinating map of the neighborhood based on food aromas and ethnic communities.

For Shilpa, the olfactory features of the various stops in the various Queens neighborhoods hinted at a sensory maze of the gustatory experiences of each space. For example, at the Sixty-first Street–Woodside stop is a mixture of garlic, tomato, and vinegar aromas, with peppers and turmeric permeating the Jackson Heights stop, and the faint smell of kimchi and scallions at Flushing—the final stop.

Along with the public spaces, immigrants' kitchens serve as repositories of food aromas. Often, the aromas are inescapable despite attempts to mask them. One notably clean kitchen I visited at a party in Elmhurst was particularly instructive. The hostess was intent on showing me how she had scrubbed the kitchen. The pots, the rice cooker, a couple of clay pots, and other utensils were orderly; the white tiles and kitchen cabinets gleamed. But one guest remarked that she could detect a faint odor of garlic at first and then decided that it was kimchi. The hostess was obviously dismayed, although she admitted later that even after using strong cleaning solutions, the family meals she had cooked for years in that kitchen still haunted it.

Visiting homes in the three- and four-story brick buildings and high-rises in Queens created another means of experiencing the links among aroma, space, and migration. A Jackson Heights apartment building provides an illustration. The simple, undecorated lobby was clean and devoid of trash. Liz, my Filipino American informant, has lived in this building for four years. Most of her neighbors are South Asians, Koreans, and Puerto Ricans. Despite the clean appearance of the lobby, Liz observed that people immediately notice that most of the building's residents are immigrants. She complained that while the superintendent did a great job of maintaining cleanliness, there was nothing to be done about the smells of various cuisines emanating from the cracks, doors, and windows of the apartments, which wafted across the corridors and adhered to the walls. Liz noted that the intensity of this olfactory United Nations reached its crescendo during Christmas, Thanksgiving, and other holidays.

Accordingly, while Shilpa's olfactory and culinary map may seem to be idiosyncratic at best and immigrant kitchens and apartment buildings may seem banal, such ideas and situations echo the experiences and statements of several other informants who linked food, place, ethnicity, and aroma in interesting ways. Here I list three key points that segue to my discussions of the three neighborhoods. First, food is experienced not only at mealtimes or while eating but also during people's mundane daily trips to work or school. Second, food and place can be linked though the sense of taste as well as, most intriguingly, olfaction. Finally, the number 7 train serves as a stage for people's literal and metaphoric travels during their daily lives, travels that evoke the tastes that reside in the neighborhoods.

Woodside: The Search for an Authentic Adobo

According to scholars and residents, Woodside used to be an Italian and Irish enclave, and the symbol of the clover still can be seen in store and pub windows. Now, however, the neighborhood has been transformed by the influx of new immigrants from Korea, China, the Philippines, and Central and Latin America. Restaurants serve a variety of dishes introduced by the new residents. Grills and take-out places illustrate this diversity, from the sharp smell of kimchi to the sweet-sour smell of barbecued meats.

My story of Woodside is highly specific. It is the story of Pete, a second-generation Filipino American, and his search to find an authentic adobo recipe. Adobo is a meat

Mexican corn vendor, Fifty-fourth Street and Roosevelt Avenue, Woodside, Queens, September 2007. (Photograph courtesy of Harley Spiller)

dish made of chicken or pork or a combination of both, cooked with vinegar or sometimes lemon juice, with lots of garlic.

Pete was born and raised in Manhattan. Both his parents were nurses who worked long hours, so he grew up with fast food and takeout until the age of six when his maternal grandmother came to live with them. His grandmother cooked all their meals, and it was only when she arrived that Pete started to learn about his Filipino background. His grandmother cooked only Filipino food, which created some tension with his parents. Pete's father argued that Filipino food was greasy and unhealthy, and his mother complained about the smells that permeated the house when the grandmother fried fish or cooked a dish with fish sauce. His mother worried that the neighbors in their housing complex might not like the food smells emanating from their apartment. Even though no one complained, Pete's grandmother was very cautious about opening the windows when she cooked anything with strong aromas.

When Pete was fourteen, his grandmother became ill. When she recovered, the family decided that she would return to the Philippines to live with her eldest son. Five months after she arrived, she died of pneumonia. Pete and his family, taken by surprise, were devastated.

After his grandmother's death, the pungent dishes that had come out of their kitchen became only faint memories: "Our kitchen suddenly became quiet and clean." The food aromas vanished. Pete noted that the family returned to the fast-food and take-out routine and that he missed his grandmother's cooking. He particularly craved the adobo that had simmered on the stove, its sharp vinegary smell welcoming him home. His own mother refused to prepare the dish, not only because she was not a good cook, but also because she hated how it "reeked."

Once in a while, his parents took Pete and his siblings on a trip to Woodside, where they had cousins. They would meet in a Filipino restaurant, and Pete would order the adobo. But somehow, something was missing from it.

Pete thought that the missing element had to do with authenticity, maintaining that authentic adobo must be cooked with love, as his grandmother's had been. He surmised that the Filipino restaurant cooks prepared the adobo in a perfunctory manner. "They are not cooking for family," Pete argued. "That is why the adobo is too sour. There is no balance between the saltiness and the vinegar." He argued that the entire dish should show the browning that hints at the piquant combination of garlic, vinegar, and sweet caramelized bits of meats.

When Pete visited his relatives' homes in Woodside and New Jersey, he found that there, too, the adobo dishes failed in comparison with his grandmother's. He guessed that the home cooks also prepared them too quickly. He remembered his grandmother saying that adobo cannot be rushed: "My grandmother said that if you boil the vinegar too fast, its sharpness will remain, and in fact it will become stronger and you will end up with an inedible, sour dish."

During our first interview, we walked around Woodside. Although Pete still lives in his old neighborhood on the Lower East Side of Manhattan, he professed a certain affection for Woodside. He said that while his search for the elusive authentic adobo was continuing, he had found other gustatory delights there.

We went to visit two of the five or so Filipino restaurants in the area. At Ihawan, Pete pointed out the big plastic containers of sweet, cool drinks. One was filled with shreds of orange cantaloupe swimming in a faintly orange mix of cantaloupe juice, water, ice, and sugar. Another contained a caramel-color liquid with sago bubbles and gelatin cubes floating in sugar, caramel, water, and banana flavoring. Attracted to the visual appeal of these drinks, Pete ordered one of each. He admitted they were a rare treat, as even his grandmother did not make them. We then ordered the pork and chicken barbecues for which the restaurant was famous: "There is no way we could cook these things back in Manhattan. Our kitchen was too small to have a grill."

Nowadays, for Pete and the other second-generation Filipino Americans he knows, Filipino food is served mostly on special occasions and no longer is part of their daily routine. Pete goes to Woodside only when he can find extra time on the weekend to ride the number 7 train to visit cousins or walk around the neighborhood. He said he enjoys walking around and seeing groups of Filipinos talking in his parents' native tongue, Tagalog, especially near St. Sebastian Catholic Church on Roosevelt Avenue. But he feels more like a tourist than a person who actually belongs there. Interestingly, Pete's moment of estrangement evaporated briefly when we entered the Filipino grocery stores.

We entered the Phil-Am (short for Philippine American) grocery store, an ethnic food store selling Philippine items. Ethnographers of Asian food stores have long

Outside New York Supermarket, Forty-fifth Avenue near Broadway, Elmhurst, Queens, September 28, 2007. (Photograph courtesy of Harley Spiller)

suggested that ethnic food stores offer sensory experiences that welcome "native" ethnic shoppers into its familiar and familial fold.[6] As an illustration, Pete gave a satisfied sigh, as though Phil-Am were a second home. Phil-Am is the size of a narrow-aisled convenience store, and the chatter is mostly in Tagalog or another Filipino language. The store is filled with brightly colored jars of sweet beans, frozen vegetables usually not available elsewhere, nutty snacks in red and yellow packages, canned goods such as sardines and corned beef, and cooked delicacies of fried fish, egg rolls, and various, multihued rice cakes. The store's predominant aromas range from fishy to sweet. Non-Filipinos unfamiliar with such stores often feel out of place or puzzled, if not appalled, by the seeming chaos and strangeness of the sights, sounds, and smells.

For Pete, the smell of the store has a lot to do with memories of his grandmother's cooking, which became forbidden or rare in his and his parents' apartment. Pete now lives in a modern high-rise not too far from his childhood home. He does not cook often, as his job as a Wall Street broker is too hectic and his schedule too erratic. He describes his childhood food world as "schizophrenic," the abundance afforded in his grandmother's too brief presence contrasting sharply with his parents' restricted and dull "noncuisine."

Pete's rare forays into stores like Phil-Am are not to buy food to cook but sometimes just to ogle, to inhale, and to remember. Sometimes he buys the cooked items stacked in plastic containers at the back of the store: fish, vegetable, and meat stews. More often, though, he just buys the cookies, pastries, or rice cakes arranged throughout the front of the store, like the colorful rice cakes wrapped in banana leaves or the candies wrapped in crepe paper festooning the shelves near the cash registers.

During our second interview, Pete and I again visited Phil-Am. This time, he fished out a piece of paper from his pocket, a grocery list. I was curious about what this list contained, as Pete was a Manhattanite who had only juice, coffee, and beer in his refrigerator. He shyly said that it contained the recipe for adobo. Pete had called his uncle the previous day to ask if he knew his grandmother's recipe.

LOLA'S (GRANDMOTHER'S) ADOBO

1 whole chicken, cut into serving pieces
½ cup white vinegar, preferably Datu Put (Filipino brand)
2–3 tablespoons *patis* (fish sauce)
1 whole head of garlic, peeled and chopped
2–3 bay leaves
⅓ cup water
¼ teaspoon oregano

Place all the ingredients in a pot. Bring to a boil, and then reduce heat to a simmer. Cook slowly for forty minutes. When chicken is done, remove it from the cooking liquid. Brown the chicken in cooking oil. Meanwhile, reduce the liquid to a thick syrup. Return the browned chicken pieces to the liquid. Serve with rice.

Pete collected all the items he needed and picked up a cut-up chicken at his neighborhood meat shop. I called him a week later to ask him about the results. He clearly was disappointed. His kitchen smelled of adobo, which was a source of both irritation and nostalgia. Although it smelled like his grandmother's kitchen, the recipe did not produce anything near the adobo of his memory. I asked him what he would do next, and he replied matter-of-factly, "I will do some more research. Read up on the adobo. I plan on going to Woodside in a couple of weeks. In other words, I will continue with my search for my Lola's adobo."

Flushing and Pan-Asian Tastes?

Sunita was born and raised in Flushing and is very proud of her "hometown," as she puts it. She is of Indian descent, and her parents are from Mumbai (formerly Bombay). There are a few Indian restaurants in the area, and Sunita herself would admit that Flushing is better known for other Asian cuisines. Despite her South Asian heritage, Sunita has grown up around kimchi, dim sum, and other East Asian culinary delights. Indeed, for her a Sunday without dim sum is an incomplete or failed weekend.

Sunita took me on what she called the best tour of the neighborhood: Main Street, Flushing's business area. Number 7's last stop, in what had been a predominantly

Jewish and Italian neighborhood, now leads to an Asian haven. In the process of this area's ethnic transformation, interethnic tensions flared for a time, but now with the bustling commercial and entertainment area on Main Street, they have quieted down. Sunita noted that some people did not appreciate that Flushing had become the "other" New York City Chinatown, but she loved Flushing's various Chinese, Korean, Malaysian, Japanese, and other ethnic flavors: "I think that it all is colorful, you know. Vibrant, yes, vibrant—that is the word for the Main Street area."

Sunita drove me around to see the industrial facades of buildings near the waterfront. Business signs in various Asian languages used to be a cause of contention; a former non-Asian councilwoman claimed that she detested the "Asianification" of the neighborhood. But Sunita insisted that now people appreciate the multicultural atmosphere.

Sunita parked in an expansive municipal lot adjacent to several major restaurants. She took me to a huge place that served dim sum, pointing out that one feature of Flushing is that it is not as cramped for space as Manhattan is. Space is a major consideration for a busy and successful dim sum business, space and good turnover of customers.

I asked Sunita whether people found her obsession with dim sum rather odd for an Indian American woman. She looked at me strangely, saying, "If you lived in this area as my friends and I do, you would not think that dim sum is only for Chinese or that curries are only for Indians." She told me that her group of second-generation Asian American friends—which include Koreans, Chinese, Pakistanis, and Filipinos—no longer thought of food only as markers of national ethnic identity but believed that "Asian" food was part of their upbringing.

As Sunita noted, "Our mothers may not have cooked all these dishes in their kitchens, but we grew up going to the various ethnic restaurants. My parents did not think twice about taking us to a Korean restaurant one day and having Malaysian takeout the next. We were pretty open to all cuisines, including non-Asian ones like Mexican."

Such an entanglement of ethnic foods from ethnic identities is an outcome of living and growing up in an ethnically diverse neighborhood with a variety of restaurants. This does not mean, however, that food has been drained of meaning. Instead, what is clear from Sunita and others like her is that New York City's Flushing neighborhood has complicated the relationships between culinary traditions and the generations of each community that consumes them. Yen Le Espiritu was the first to point out the emergence of Asian panethnic sentiments in the past two to three decades.[7] Even though these sentiments have materialized in neither a strong political movement nor a visibly successful multicultural milieu, they clearly have been influential in eroding the cultural borders between Asian consumers of various cuisines. Fusion cuisine notwithstanding, traditional Asian cuisines and the restaurants in Flushing that serve them are finding second- and third-generation Asian Americans who travel within and across various culinary divides.

In the large restaurant where Sunita and I had dim sum, groups of friends and families from various Asian ethnic groups had gathered. On the one hand, Sunita had suggested that dim sum was no longer an exotic dining experience. Although she did admit that once in a while she was stumped by a dim sum item that she had not eaten before, she was as much "at home" in these places as she would be in the "Indopak-bangla" establishments in Jackson Heights, home to a South Asian enclave.

Flushing's stores and restaurants recall the Chinatowns of other cities and times. And yet, as Sunita argued, this is a Chinatown of the present. By this she meant that while Chinatown evokes something mysterious and strange, a highly bounded space in a cultural time warp, Flushing as the "new" Chinatown has a "modern" feel to it. When I appeared unconvinced, Sunita argued further that this new Chinatown included various Asian establishments and was not merely a conglomeration of Chinese ones. At the same time, the cosmopolitan atmosphere of these Asian establishments was able to coexist with American fast-food chains.

Sunita contended that most, if not all, of these establishments know that non-coethnic consumers form a major part of their clientele, so unlike enclave establishments that cater only to their own, these enterprises must appeal to ethnic "outsiders" as well. But Sunita also made a point of saying that the idea of being an ethnic "outsider" no longer applied and that her generation was making this possible. In fact, she plans on opening a restaurant that features various curries from Thailand, Singapore, Malaysia, Japan, China, Pakistan, Bangladesh, and, of course, India.

The juxtaposition of these various traditions is clearly shown in the neighborhood's architecture, aromas, and sights. A Korean electronic shop sits beside a Malaysian restaurant, which is across the street from Macy's, which used to be Stern's. Sunita observed that "Chinatown" is a misleading term for her neighborhood. Rather, the concatenation of different cultural spaces led her to say, "This is not the 'new' Chinatown but the new 'Asiantown.'" She proudly pointed to the street that was no longer the typical "Main Street USA" but now was an emerging culinary space and ethos of pan-Asian ethnic sentiments. Despite her celebratory and optimistic view of this pan-Asian culinary multiculturalism, Sunita was also a bit cautious: "I know I can be too giddy about [the cultural and political possibilities of] the Asian ethnic cuisines here, but I know that this is not the end. It is just a beginning. I know it is easy to like curry and still hate Indians and other South Asians. Look at some of the incidents after September 11 [referring to the violent and ugly racist incidents against South Asians in the city]. But food is a way of coming together. So it is a start. We have to start somewhere. Right?"

Jackson Heights: Lost in Whose Translation?

Jackson Heights is adjacent to Woodside, separated by the Brooklyn-Queens Expressway. Walking along Roosevelt Avenue from Sixty-ninth Street underneath the elevated tracks of the number 7 train and crossing a short bridge where the avenue intersects with the expressway, the transformation is, at first, subtle, with the conglomeration of Filipino and Latino establishments gradually giving way to Korean, Colombian, and then South Asian shops, stores, and restaurants. If Flushing is a "new" Chinatown, then Jackson Heights is a "Little India," with its concentration of Indian and other South Asian restaurants, clothing shops, groceries, and other businesses. This includes those labeled Afghani, Pakistani, Bangladeshi, and the strange neologism "Indopakbangla"—a combination of "Indian," "Pakistani," and "Bangladeshi"—a hybrid umbrella term for the ways in which the typically separate South Asian cuisines and cultures come together in immigrant spaces.

John, a second-generation Korean American in his early twenties, was my "native" informant in this neighborhood. Although informants in classic ethnographies are often "cultural experts," John admits a kind of awkwardness in showing me around the neighborhood where he has lived for eighteen years since coming to America as a young child with his family. John's parents often left him at home with his grandmother, who spoke very little English, or they had him help at their electronics shop in the area. Unlike Sunita, John believes that he was sheltered from the culinary influences of the area and has refrained from going to the Colombian grills and Indopakbangla restaurants near the apartment building where he still lives with his family.

John noted that his family, particularly his parents, was so involved in trying to get their business running that they did not eat out and explore the culinary cultures in the neighborhood. Instead, his grandmother cooked Korean food, which he and the other family members ate every day. When he got older, instead of eating rice for lunch, he bought fast food or cafeteria food. In a strange way, John was as much an outsider as I was. But it was clear from our conversations that he was proud of the neighborhood and was glad that he now had a chance to explore its culinary establishments.

John took me to those restaurants and grocery stores that he thought that I, as an outsider, might want to see. These were the same places that he himself had first visited several years ago when he started his neighborhood "tour." Part of his selection of these establishments had to do with what he thought would be "palatable" to me. Although it was not clear whether this idea was based on his own preferences, it was clear that he was interested in "translating" the neighborhood for me.

We first went to the Jackson Diner, which John said was one of the more popular restaurants in the area, drawing people from other parts of the city. He pointed out that the decor was very modern and that the food was only mildly spicy. While I could not judge how "watered down" the food was for the non-Indian mainstream palate, it still was quite delicious. In any case, my interest had less to do with specific restaurants than with how people like John experienced the translation of the neighborhood's "ethnic cultures" to become legible and acceptable to outsiders.

John agreed that Jackson Heights's "Little India" offered a contemporary version of an ethnic enclave that departed from the bounded and isolated notion of an economic and cultural community.[8] While a majority of local customers were of South Asian origin, it also had a growing clientele from outside the community, and, as a consequence, many business owners were trying to cater to outsiders' tastes. This puzzled me. What happens to people who are not South Asian but who have grown up in the neighborhood? Like Sunita in Flushing, John is one of an equally large number of people from the neighborhood who are not South Asian but who do patronize the local establishments. Is a culinary translation still needed? And, if so, what does it entail?

I talked to several business owners about these issues. At first, the term confused them: What did "culinary translation" mean? One owner insisted that the restaurants cooked their foods as though they were cooking for themselves. Although they understood that spiciness might be a problem for some people and they did give people choices, they did not radically alter their recipes.

The persistent idea that those Jackson Heights restaurants catering to non–South Asian customers had watered down their dishes was problematic. As one of the business owners observed, "If we were trying to suit a mainstream taste, who would we be really trying to please? Who is the mainstream, and do they have particular tastes?" In most cases, this mainstream is "white." Many people believe that the idea of a mainstream is based on the stereotypes of one monolithic white ethnic group with specific cultural traits, tastes, attitudes, and worldviews. But such a contentious idea cannot reconcile the complexity of the so-called white community, assumed to be educated, middle class, and conservative. Despite their initial denials, some of the South Asian business owners did confess that they did agree with this view.

At the heart of the idea of culinary translation is the fact that ethnic food is marginal to a more powerful mainstream. As a process, translation is rarely about two commensurable linguistic, cultural, or culinary systems but, more typically, about unequal power systems. Consequently, an ethnic cuisine must be translated or, more appropriately, "filtered" to make it culturally legible and palatable. Therefore, if culinary translation does occur in Jackson Heights and elsewhere, it would be on the basis of trying to cater to a potential niche outside the "enclave."

Most important, culinary translation is based on the idea that ethnic cuisines are discrete systems of preparing, cooking, and eating different from the ideas and practices of other cuisines. But nothing can be further from the truth. In her historical study of American ethnic food, Donna Gabaccia demonstrates that immigrant households and ethnic cuisines are resilient and open to improvisation and outside influences.[9]

One of John's discoveries about Asian cuisines is that they are products of their specific histories. For example, Korean food has a strong undercurrent of Japanese flavors because Korea was a Japanese colony for a long time. This is true as well for the British influences on South Asian, specifically Indian, food. These seemingly banal discoveries enabled John to understand his neighborhood's culinary cultures better and to be more aware of the cultural "proximity" of his South Asian neighbors. Although cuisine is typically an easy, "multicultural" way to understand other communities, John, who has created strong friendships with his neighbors, went through this process in reverse, with the culinary realm as the last "frontier." John abandoned his initial ideas about "culinary translation" when he realized that ethnic food is not about easy translations based on practical business decisions. I talked to John a few days before I finished writing this chapter and discussed this issue with him. He told me that Jackson Heights still was noisy and smelly and full of restaurants and other businesses. Having made more explorations in the past few years, these unfiltered and untranslated sights, sounds, and aromas had become more familiar and endearing to him.

This chapter presented three stories about food and place in three neighborhoods in Queens. I did not intend to tie together the rather divergent themes in each neighborhood or to have each story represent each neighborhood. Rather, like variations on a theme, I wanted to explore how the experiences and meanings of a place can be linked to experiences and meanings of food. The protagonists of the three stories set the stage for my elaboration of other, related issues, including authenticity, memory, identity, and, particularly, ethnicity.

John discovered in his neighborhood that questions about culinary authenticity are based on specific beliefs about Asian ethnic food, including their essential purity and being, that are impervious to outside influences. In *Dislocating Cultures,* Uma Narayan suggests that the persistent and popular misconception about the "purity" of ethnic food fails to consider that almost all cuisines are hybrids or products of intersecting influences of colonial histories, mass media, and travel.[10] Jackson Heights is a good example of the fluid characteristics of Asian ethnic cuisines. Far from a planned landscape, this neighborhood has brought together cuisines from various parts of the world in sometimes jarring juxtaposition.

"We are what we eat" is an overused and misunderstood dictum about food, as it does not go far enough in acknowledging the complications of identity formation regarding food. Two of my stories in this chapter focused on New Yorkers who were not members of the culinary cultures being discussed. Nevertheless, both Sunita and John talked about the kinds of intimacy and loyalty that food creates among people. Pete, Sunita, and John are, in a sense, learning new ways of living in and interacting with other ethnic communities. They are creating new ideas of home and alternative ways of belonging to their ethnic groups and their city.

Although food is far from an easily understood, multicultural medium, in these neighborhoods, food lends itself to the creation of facile intimacy and affiliation among the inhabitants. It has provided a means for communities to form as well as a pedagogical tool to learn history and culture. Food is also a means for acknowledging and engaging cultural dislocation and displacement. As Sunita's hopeful yet somewhat naive comment suggests, food offers possibilities and some hope but is not an end unto itself.

Despite being faulty and unreliable, memories have long been an important medium for food narratives and explorations of people's histories.[11] Through memories of his grandmother's food, Pete is trying to fill the loss created by her death These memories have led him to Woodside, which has allowed him to engage with other Filipinos. Much like the weekend tourist from another part of the city, Pete travels from Manhattan to seek both the familiar and the strange. Unlike these tourists, though, Pete is on a personal search for the lost tastes and aromas of his grandmother's cooking. Therefore, his food voice is a means of rebuilding the past through the present.

These admittedly unwieldy and disparate stories say more about place than a tightly constructed narrative would. Queens is not built on grids and symmetry. A stranger can get lost in Queens, since it has few monuments or skyscrapers to serve as spatial markers. Queens is a chaos of smells, sounds, and sights that form its panoply

of communities and lives. The unruliness, however, enables it to house several culturally diverse communities and neighborhoods. As I mentioned earlier, this borough
is often seen as a mere conduit or passageway to the world at large. And yet, as my
three stories show, the culinary and cultural worlds of Queens surpass the limits and
boundaries of the culinary worlds elsewhere.

NOTES

Funding for this research was made available through grants from various programs at the
University of Illinois, Urbana–Champaign, including the Asian American Studies Program,
Center for Democracy in a Multiracial Society, and the Faculty Research Board.

1. Annie Hauck-Lawson, "When Food Is the Voice: A Case Study of a Polish-American
Woman," *Journal for the Study of Food and Society* 2 (1998): 21–28.

2. For a broad-ranging and excellent review of the scholarship on the senses in social sciences and critical theory, see David Howes, *Sensual Relations: Engaging the Senses in Culture
and Social Theory* (Ann Arbor: University of Michigan Press, 2003).

3. I explore the cultural politics of smell and immigrant lives in New York City in Martin
Manalansan, "Immigrant Lives and the Politics of Olfaction in the Global City," in *The Smell
Reader,* ed. Jim Drobnick (New York: Berg, 2006), 41–52.

4. Alain Corbin, *Foul and the Fragrant: Odor and the French Social Imagination* (Cambridge, Mass.: Harvard University Press, 1988). For a wonderful historical survey of the sense
of smell, see Constance Classen, David Howes, and Anthony Synott, *Aroma: The Cultural
History of Smell* (New York: Routledge, 1995).

5. All names have been changed to protect the informants' privacy.

6. For ethnographic works on Asian groceries, see Enrique Bonus, *Locating Filipino
Americans: Ethnicity and the Cultural Politics of Space* (Philadelphia: Temple University Press,
2000); and Purnima Mankekar, "India Shopping: Indian Grocery Stores and Transnational
Configuration of Belonging," *Ethnos* 67 (2002): 75–97.

7. Yen Le Espiritu, *Asian American Panethnicity* (Philadelphia: Temple University Press,
1993).

8. For detailed ethnographic studies of Jackson Heights, see Madhulika Khandwewal,
Becoming American, Being Indian: An Immigrant Community in New York City (Ithaca, N.Y.:
Cornell University Press, 2002); and Sandya Shukla, *India Abroad: Diasporic Cultures of Post-
war America and England* (Princeton, N.J.: Princeton University Press, 2003).

9. Donna Gabaccia, *We Are What We Eat: Ethnic Food and the Making of America* (Cambridge, Mass.: Harvard University Press, 1998).

10. Uma Narayan, *Dislocating Cultures: Identities, Traditions and Third World Feminism*
(New York: Routledge, 1997).

11. For the role of Bengali memory in practices and beliefs regarding food, see Krishnendu
Ray, *The Migrant's Table: Meals and Memories in Bengali-American Households* (Philadelphia: Temple University Press, 2004).

The Culinary Seasons
of My Childhood

JESSICA B. HARRIS

FEW CULINARY traditions are as undocumented as those of middle-class African Americans. Scroll back to the 1950s, when segregation was still rampant in the South, and the foodways are even less well known. Although they are briefly mentioned in a few autobiographical narratives and in some fiction, the concern of most African Americans was more with throwing off the shackles of southern segregations that our forebears had come north to escape. This is reflected in our life tales more than in our recollections of meals eaten and foods purchased. The result is that most outsiders believe that ham hocks and hard times are the only remnants of our culinary past. Certainly there were plenty of ham hocks and no shortage of hard times. In fact, my New Jersey–born and –raised mother always claimed that that state could best Mississippi in the racist sweepstakes and that she had the stories to prove it! In North and South alike, middle-class African Americans ate the same cornbread and fried chicken and chitterlings and foods from the traditions of the African diaspora as did our less well-off counterparts, but we also ate differently, foods that expressed our middle classness and reflected our social and political aspirations.

Even though chitterlings might be on the menu, they could equally likely be accompanied by a mason jar of corn liquor or a crystal goblet of champagne. Southern specialties like fried porgies and collard greens show up for dinner, but they might be served along with dishes becoming common in an increasingly omnivorous United States that was just beginning its love affair with food. Nowhere is this more evident than in my own life and in the culinary seasons of my childhood.

A descendant of the enslaved and free Africans who made their way north in the Great Migration, I grew up in a transplanted southern culture that still remains a vibrant region of the African American culinary world. My family, like many others long separated from the South, raised me in ways that continued their eating traditions, so now I can head south and sop biscuits in gravy, suck chewy bits of fat from a pig's foot spattered with hot sauce, and yes'm and no'm with the best of 'em.

But that's not all of me. I also am a postwar baby who was the only child of striving middle-class parents who were old enough to have been young African American adults in the poverty of the Great Depression. They showered me with love and childhood coddling that makes my childhood seem like an African American version of *The Little Princess.* I also am a child at the confluence of two major African American culinary traditions. My mother's family could claim a smidge of black southern aristocracy, as they were descended from free people of color who migrated to Roanoke, Virginia. My father's family was from Tennessee and had upcountry Georgia roots that extended down the Natchez Trace. Both families showed their backgrounds at the table.

My maternal grandmother, Bertha Philpot Jones, was the quintessential African American matriarch presiding over a groaning board filled with savory foods. The role has become a visual cliché in movies like *The Nutty Professor Part II: The Klumps, Soul Food,* and *Dear Departed,* which revel in the dysfunction of African American life. No such dysfunction, however, was tolerated at Grandma Jones's table; she would not allow it. She was the matriarch and absolute sovereign of the Jones family; she ruled with a delicate but steel-boned hand, and the family marched to her tune. Watermelon-rind pickles spiced with fragrant cinnamon and whole cloves and the reassuring warmth of a full oven wafting smells of roasted joints and freshly baked bread are the aromas I most associate with her. She was a Baptist minister's wife and could put a hurtin' on some food. She had to, for as the minister's wife, she had not only her own brood of twelve children plus husband to feed, but the church folks who dropped in to take care of as well. She pickled fruits like Seckel pears, which had a curiously tart-sweet taste that comes back to me even today. The smell of Parker House rolls, the warmth of the kitchen, and the closeness of a large family all were part of the thrill of Grandma Jones's house. I didn't see her often—only on holidays and special occasions when we'd take the Holland Tunnel and head off to Plainfield, New Jersey, to visit and sit around the table.

Ida Irene Harris, my paternal grandmother, was at the other end of the culinary spectrum. I saw her much more often, at least once a week. When I travel in the South, folks are astounded to hear that as a child I had no southern roots, no grandmother to visit by segregated train or bus under the tutelage of kindly porters and with a tag pinned to my coat. Instead, my South was in the North, for Grandma Harris, in her day-to-day existence, re-created the preserved-in-amber South of her nineteenth-century rural youth in the precincts of her small apartment in the South Jamaica projects. I remember her apartment well, particularly the kitchen, with the four-burner stove on which she made lye soap, the refrigerator that always contained a pitcher of grape Kool-Aid with lemons cut up in it, and the sink in which she washed clothes, punching them with a broomstick to make sure they would get clean. Most of all, I remember the taste of the collard greens that she prepared:

verdant, lush, with just enough smoked pig parts and fat for seasoning; they were the culinary embodiment of her love and, along with her silky beaten biscuits, one of the few dishes that she made well.

Grandma Harris lived in a self-created southern world. For years, she maintained a small garden plot at the back of the South Jamaica projects. This was just after the victory gardens of World War II when tenants could plant a small plot of land if they wished. Grandma Harris grew southern staples: collard and mustard greens, peanuts, snap beans, and more. I remember her weeding the peanuts and breaking off a leaf of the greens to test for ripening as the Long Island Rail Road train roared by on the tracks above. She taught me to love the slip of boiled peanuts, to sop biscuits in Alaga syrup with butter cut up in it, and to savor the tart sourness of buttermilk long before there was any romance to things southern.

I didn't understand the education she'd given me until years later, in Senegal's Theatre Daniel Sorano, I heard a griot sing. It was as though Grandma Harris had leaned down from the clouds and touched me. The timbre, the tone, the almost keening wail of the Mandinka singer captured the tuneless songs that Grandma sang as she went about her daily tasks, as much as the tastes of the Senegalese food recalled flavors from my childhood. It was then that I realized that unknown to both of us, Grandma Harris had taught me the ways of the past in her demeanor, her stalwartness, her faith, and her food. Those ways would help me survive. She also taught me to behave. I will never forget the summer day when she administered the only childhood whipping I can recall.

"Whipping" was not a word that was used in my house as I was growing up. I was a Dr. Spock baby through and through, and discipline was more about firm conversation than about Daddy's belt. At Grandma Harris's apartment, though, the rules changed and that one time, I knew I was going to get a whipping for sure.

Grandma Harris was another kind of old-line southern matriarch. It didn't matter that she lived on the third floor of the South Jamaica projects in Queens; her world was deeply rooted in the traditions of her South. She would brook no contradiction about manners. In her home, New Year's was celebrated with a mix of collard, mustard, and turnip greens that she had stewed down to a low gravy to accompany the obligatory hoppin' John and chitterlings. I always passed on the chitterlings and ate the hoppin' John, but the greens were my favorite. I had even more respect for them after they caused my downfall and earned me my only childhood whipping.

It happened on a summer's day when I was about six or seven. My mother worked, so I was sent to Grandma's apartment to spend the day in the traditional, extended-family day-care arrangement. I spent most of those urban summer days of my early childhood in her small one-bedroom apartment reading in a chair and staying out from under her feet in order to avoid going outside to play with the other kids, who invariably made fun of my private-school vowels and bookish ways. She, on the other side, spent her days insisting that I go out and play with the "nice children" who all called her Mother Harris.

On the day in question, when I had managed to avoid the dreaded piss-smelling barrels and rough boys and girls of the playground, she looked up from her sewing and said, "Jessica, come here." I was in for it. I was pleasantly surprised when, instead of ordering me downstairs, she instead went for her purse and gave me some money wrapped in a hankie with instructions to go to Miranda's, the Italian-owned corner market, and get a piece of "streak-a-lean-streak-a-fat" for the greens that she was going to cook.

Thrilled at being sent on an errand and overjoyed at escaping the barrel torture, I headed off. The walk was short, only a scant block through the maze of red-brick buildings that had not yet deteriorated into the breeding ground of hopelessness they were to become. A few small trees were in leaf, and the sounds of other children playing reminded me how grown up I was. *I* was on an errand. Arriving at Miranda's, I went directly to the meat counter, where, as in most African American neighborhoods, there was a vast array of pig parts both identifiable and unknown. Having not a clue about streak-a-lean-streak-a-fat but feeling exceptionally sophisticated in my seven-year-old head, I pointed to the slab bacon that my mother used to season things and asked for the requisite amount. It was brought out for my examination, and I grandly pronounced it fine. Cut off to the desired thickness and wrapped in slick brown paper, it was presented to me with solemnity. I tucked it into the net shopping bag that Grandma had provided and headed back home, proud and pleased.

I pushed open the heavy downstairs door and ran up the concrete steps, heels clanking on the metal treads that lined them. When I got to 3B, I pushed through the door that Grandma always kept open in those kinder times and headed in to present my parcel. To my amazement, when she opened it, she began to mutter and asked me what I had gotten.

"Streak-a-lean-streak-a-fat," I replied.

"Did you ask for it?" she questioned.

"No, I pointed it out to the man," I ventured with increasing timidity.

"Well, this isn't it! I wanted what I asked for, streak-a-lean-streak-a-fat," she countered. "This is slab bacon!"

"It's the same thing, isn't it?" I queried.

"NO! Now you march right back there and get me what I asked for, streak-a-lean-streak-a-fat. Take this back!"

"But?"

"No Buts! Just march back there, young lady! Right Now!"

I trudged back to Miranda's, each step made heavier with the thought of having to tell the butcher that I'd made an error and hoping that he'd take back the offending bacon. The joy of escape of the prior hour had soured into a longing for the nasty boys and the stinky barrels. Luckily, the man took pity on bourgie old me and took back the bacon, replacing it with a fattier piece of streaky pork that was a fraction of the price.

When I got back to the building, Grandma was sitting on the benches out front and waiting for me. She uttered the five words that I'd never heard her say: "Go cut me a switch."

Terrified, I set off and hunted for the smallest branch that I could find in this virtually treeless urban landscape, knowing what was coming next. I returned with a smallish green switch that I had unearthed lord knows where. She took a few halfhearted passes at my legs, solemnly repeating with each one, "Don't think you're smarter than your elders." Tears flowed on both sides: mine because I'd certainly learned my lesson through the humiliation of returning the bacon followed by the public whipping, Grandma's because she adored me and wanted a respectful granddaughter. Despite that childhood trauma, I still love collard greens and never eat my New Year's mess of them without remembering Grandma Harris. I always season them with what I have come to think of as streak-a-lean-streak-a-fat-cut-me-a-switch; savor their smoky, oily splendor; and think of the southern lessons she taught me with every bite.

The other days of my early summers were spent with my working parents. We left New York City for family vacations, and I can remember the ice man delivering big blocks of ice wrapped in burlap to chill the icebox of the small cabin that we rented on Three Mile Harbor Road in East Hampton long before the area attained its current vogue. The year after my whipping, when I was eight, we visited Oak Bluffs, Massachusetts, the African American summer community on Martha's Vineyard that has become much touted these days. It was love at first sight, and my parents bought a summer house there that winter.

From the time I was nine until the present, this house has been a part of every summer. Then we made long trips on the Boston Post Road and the Merritt Parkway up to the Wood's Hole ferry dock. Old habits die hard, and my parents in the 1950s would no more think of hitting the road without a shoebox full of fried chicken, deviled eggs, pound cake, oranges, and raisins and a thermos full of lemonade or some other cool drink than they would leave home without maps and a tank full of gas.

Oak Bluffs was just beginning to grow in popularity among New Yorkers; Bostonians knew about its glories long before we did. Middle-class African Americans from New York and New Jersey summered in Sag Harbor near the Hamptons, but my prescient father did not want to be so close to the city that friends could drop in unannounced on the weekends, so it was Martha's Vineyard for us. We joked that if we lost our way to the Vineyard, we could simply follow the trail of chicken bones left by fellow black New Yorkers and find the ferry pier with no problem. Like us, they were marked by segregated back doors and the lack of on-the-road facilities and also stuck to the old ways. We brought our chicken along for years until the Connecticut Turnpike was completed, and then we gradually left the chicken and deviled eggs at home and settled for the mediocre fare of the rest stops. I was thrilled several years ago when a friend, Alexander Smalls, opened a restaurant in Grand Central Terminal celebrating our traveling ways; it was called the Shoebox Café. While the menu was his own inventive interpretation of the black food of the South, I knew he was also honoring the past that many black Americans share.

My Vineyard summers were where I caught my first fish, a porgy of respectable size, and learned to strip the skin off an eel and find out just how delicious the sweet meat was, once you got over the snake look, and to pick mussels off the docks at Menemsha. The days were punctuated by sharing meals with family and friends, waiting for my father to appear on the Friday night "daddy boat" to spend the weekends, and savoring rainy days because my mother treated us with one of her fantastic blueberry cobblers prepared with berries we had picked before the storm came, from the bushes that grew wild along the roadsides. July folded into August marked by county fairs, cotton candy, Illumination Night, Darling's molasses puff, swordfish at Giordano's restaurant, and movies at the Strand or Islander movie houses, accompanied by hot buttered popcorn served from a copper kettle. Soon it was time to pack the car again and head back to our house in Queens. I never really minded because autumn brought the return to school, and my world expanded one hundredfold. My school saw to that.

The United Nations International School was and is a special place. As the first non-UN-connected child to attend the school and one of very few Americans enrolled in the early years, my playmates were the world. UNIS, as the school is called by the cognoscenti, was small, then so small that it added a grade each year until it finally stretched from prekindergarten through high school. Inside Queens's Parkway Village apartments that had been transformed into classrooms, I made lifelong friends and learned how to function in a world that extended to the globe's four corners. A trip to Vasu's or Shikha's house brought smells of the Indian subcontinent, and on occasions when I was fortunate enough to be invited to birthday parties, there were tastes of rich spices and heady unknown flavors that would never have turned up on the table of my garlic-free household. The rich stews of central Europe were featured at Danuta's, and steak and kidney pie might turn up on the table at Eluned's. I can still feel the rasp of the embossed silver spoon-backs that were used on the table at Jennifer and Susan's house in Great Neck and remember their mother's wonderful way with shortbread with nostalgia that can still make my mouth water more than forty-five years later. The annual round of birthday parties was interrupted by school events like international potluck suppers. Parents brought dishes from around the globe, and students began culinary competitions like eating spaghetti with chopsticks in the days before Asian noodle bowls and the vast array of Italian pastas became common culinary currency.

As more Americans joined the school community, even they displayed amazing culinary inventiveness, and I remember being invited to a formal Coke-tail party at Anne's house, where we were served all manner of multihued nonalcoholic cocktails in delicate stemmed glassware complete with swizzle sticks, umbrella garnishes, and lots of maraschino cherries at a birthday fete that was every young girl's dream. All the class events seemed to center on international households of like-acting folk who proved to me at an early age that no matter what turned up on the table, it was to be savored and eaten with gusto.

During the twelve or so years that I attended UNIS, I grew to understand something about the world's food. My core group of friends spent many of those years together, and we became familiar with one another's households and foods and, with that growing knowledge, came to realize that the table was not only where we held our parties and our class fetes but also where we worked out our problems and got answers to questions about one another. With hindsight, I now realize that we achieved at our birthday tables and communal suppers the same détente and understanding that the parents of many of my friends worked so hard to attain at the tables at which they tried to bring peace to the world.

If my grandmothers' tables gave me a grounding in the African American past that is so much the bedrock of all that I do, and UNIS gave me an understanding of the food of the world, a palate that is open to tasting just about anything, and the knowledge that more friends are made around the table than just about anywhere else, my parents and our daily life completed the picture with the finishing touches.

I have saved my household for last, for it, more than any of the other outside influences, marked the seasons of my childhood eating. While I grew up at the confluence of two African American culinary traditions and lived in an international world at school, at home on Anderson Road in St. Albans, Queens, my surroundings were a wondrous combination of my parents' dueling culinary wills.

Very few African Americans are to the manor born; most of us have a past of want or need, if not for love, then for cash and the opportunities it can bring. My father, Jesse Brown Harris, was such a person. He was a black man and a striking one at that, aubergine-hued with the carriage of an emperor of Songhai. Early photos show him tall and slender, looking very proprietary about his little family of three. Daddy was not a numbers runner. Daddy was not a welfare ducker or an absentee father. Daddy was just Daddy, and the constancy of that statement and my lack of awareness that this was not the norm for all black children made me different.

As a teenager, Daddy had lived over the stables and worked as a Shabbas goy in Williamsburg, Brooklyn. Until the day he died, he was marked by a childhood of grinding poverty during which he had worn flour-bag suits to school and church, cadged coal at the railroad yard for heat, and picked dandelion leaves on the Fisk College campus for dinner. He was torn between the desire to overcome his past and provide differently for his family and the need to remember it with honor.

My father ate southern food whenever he could cajole my mother into preparing the hog maws or chitterlings that he adored. We even put a stove into the basement of our house so that the smell would not taint our living quarters. He would occasionally bring home cartons of buttermilk, which he would savor with squares of the flaky and hot cornbread that my mother baked at the drop of a hat. Sunday breakfast was his special time, and he would proudly sit at the head of the table and sop up his preferred mix of Karo dark with butter cut up in it with the hoecake that was off-limits to anyone else in the household.

He was the only one in his family of man children who did not and could not cook. My Uncle Bill, his older brother, gave me my first taste of rabbit stew, and my Uncle Jim's spaghetti sauce was the stuff of family legend. Actually, my father cared little for food, but he loved restaurants and, with his increasing affluence, dined out with the best of them. In the early years, dining out meant heading to the local silver bullet diner near our house for specials like mashed potatoes with gravy and Salisbury steak or sauerbraten (the neighborhood was German before we moved in). The bakery on Linden Boulevard, the main shopping street, sold flaky butter cookies and gingerbread at Christmas. Later, when St. Albans became blacker, we would head to Sister's Southern Diner after church on Sundays, still dressed in our Sabbath finery, for down-home feasts of smothered pork chops and greens or stewed okra and fried fish in an orgy of southern feasting that Mommy did not have to cook. In later years, restaurants like the Brasserie, La Fonda del Sol, and the Four Seasons were where we celebrated birthdays and anniversaries. There, my father's duality surfaced, and he would order wine for the bucket or "spittoon," as we had baptized it in our family jargon, and crêpes suzette or Caesar salad for the flamboyant tableside service, but we three secretly knew that all the while what he really wanted was a ham hock and some butterbeans to satisfy the tastes of his youth.

My mother, though, truly loved food and had amazing taste buds that could analyze the components of a dish with startling accuracy. She would then reproduce her version of it at home, to the delight of all. Trained as a dietitian, my mother reveled in entertaining and entranced her friends with her culinary inventiveness. Decades later, she revealed that at school, she had been required to sit through classes on how to keep black people out of restaurants and was discouraged from doing anything with food demonstrations that would put her in public view. After a brief stint as a dietitian at Bennett College in North Carolina and an even briefer stay in domestic service as a private dietitian, she found that she did not enjoy the field. Instead, she put her talents to use at the supper table, and I grew up eating homemade applesauce and tea sandwiches of olives and cream cheese when my friends were chowing down Gerber's finest and processed cheese spread. Weeknights featured balanced meals like breaded veal cutlets with carrots and peas and a salad, alternating with sublime fried chicken and mashed potatoes or rice and always a green vegetable and salad, or string beans, potatoes, and ham ends slow cooked into what we called a New England boiled dinner.

Parties were the occasion for pulling out all the stops. My mother would prepare ribbon and pinwheel sandwiches from whole wheat bread, cream cheese, white bread, and strips of red and green bell pepper, long before the spectrum opened up to admit such hues as orange, purple, white, and even yellow! She created cabarets in the basement—persuading her friends to come as babies or in nightclothes, hiring calypso singers, serving drinks with small umbrellas, and devising smoking centerpieces with dry ice and punch bowls—and, each Sunday, presided over tables overflowing with roasts and a multiplicity of vegetables.

My mother created magic in the kitchen and made cooking exciting and fun, with a trick for every dish and a sense of adventure at the stove. As her only child, I got the benefit of this knowledge and accompanied her in the kitchen almost from my birth. In later years, she began to tire of the kitchen, but eventually, she renewed her interest in things culinary and discovered the wonder of ingredients like confit of duck, fresh garlic, pimentos, and arugula. Ever curious, her life was a constant adventure. I did not learn to cook; I simply absorbed it in her kitchen, moving from high chair to small tasks to whole dishes and entire meals.

I am very much the product of all of this, and these seasons of my personal and yet very New York childhood gave me the foods of the world on my plate. For the first years of my life, my fork ranged throughout the world from the simple country food of Grandma Harris to the more elegant Virginia repasts of Grandma Jones and the dishes of the 1950s and 1960s that were, for me, the tastes of home. I also sampled fare from the globe's four corners at the homes of my international classmates and learned that no matter where our origins or our regionalisms, when we eat together and share the commensalism of the table, we make ourselves and our worlds better. It has been said that we are what we eat. I certainly am, and in the many seasons of my New York youth, that included an amazing amount of mighty good food.

The Chefs, the Entrepreneurs, and Their Patrons

The Avant-Garde Food Scene in New York City

FABIO PARASECOLI

FOR MOST Americans, New York City is synonymous with novelty, boldness, and experimentation. Every year, thousands of people from all over the country and the world move to the metropolis to reinvent themselves and enjoy a fresh start. Of course, many try, but very few succeed, making New York synonymous also with defeat and desperation. This scenario repeats itself in all kinds of environments and scenes, the food and restaurant business included. Situated at the crossroads of business, the media, and politics, the city is one of the best places to build a culinary empire. Restaurants open and close at a frantic pace, and social upheaval and economic depression have never been able to stop completely the development of upscale dining.

Money and power are necessary for the development of not only high-end cuisines but also the restaurant businesses in general. Since the birth of the restaurant as a place for the leisurely consumption of food, the upper classes have conferred prestige and financial security on fashionable establishments and renowned cooking artists.[1] Old money, new money, corporate giants, media conglomerates, and all in between have constantly ensured the presence of numerous customers ready to spend money and do business at, take their guests to, or celebrate the achievements of new must-go places. It is not surprising that the restaurant business has always been considered a remunerative, if risky, investment. For these reasons, a few cities like New York have allowed young and daring entrepreneurs and chefs to shine in a unique way, often stimulating their creativity to the point that their work has been defined as "avant-garde." In one way or another, the names of various New York chefs are mentioned in the same breath with the word "avant-garde." Although they share passion for their craft and enthusiasm for research in the kitchen, they embody radically different theoretical and business approaches.

It takes money, and lots of it, for the food and the restaurant business to thrive. In New York, the costs of real estate, staff, and ingredients push chefs to seek the financial backing of investors from outside the industry whose principal concern is monetary gain. This availability of enormous capital for investment is a magnet for many renowned designers and architects, adding prestige and glamour to the food scene. Names such as Adam Tihany and Philippe Starck need little introduction in New York.

Under these circumstances, if creativity in the kitchen produces income, it will be highly praised and valued. But if this creativity becomes excessive, intimidating, or turns away customers, investors will not hesitate to demand a different attitude from the chefs whose salaries they pay. Especially in the case of business meals or important social occasions, patrons do not want to feel uncomfortable. Why, then, should they pay to show that they do not know how to read a menu or are unfamiliar with particular ingredients or culinary techniques? The same attitude holds for the hefty wine lists that require familiarity with a wide range of varieties and obscure foreign producers. In addition, experiments with the usual partition of menus into appetizers, entrées, and desserts, which some chefs justify as an attempt to meet all the possible needs of their customers, have been received with some skepticism.[2] Nevertheless, young talented chefs are often not too worried whether "narrow-minded customers" appreciate their work. They are ready to show off, to shock, and to entertain. Naturally, this means a huge financial risk for investors in the restaurant business. Betting on a new talent is extremely dangerous, especially when his or her work seems to upset reliable customers and influential food critics. The tension between commercial requirements and innovation, as in any other creative field, is not easy to resolve.

Innovative young chefs today often refer to Spain as both an inspiration and a successful economic model, especially Catalonia on the Mediterranean coast and the Basque Country in the north. Many prestigious and groundbreaking chefs, such as Ferran Adrià and Miguel Sánchez Romera near Barcelona and Martín Berasategui near San Sebastián, have created restaurants that have been able to thrive despite the extreme boldness of their culinary choices, the complexity of the menus they propose, the limited number of patrons they are able to seat (Adrià's restaurant, El Bulli, stays closed for many months during the winter season), and the staggering number of employees needed to prepare and serve the food.[3] Some of these chefs buffer these risks with side activities to ensure the financial success of their enterprises. Adrià, for instance, has introduced a sort of high-quality fast food in Madrid and is working with big food companies to develop new products. Sánchez Romera maintained his other professional activity as a neurophysiologist and has patented a cassava-based, gelatin-like substance called Micri, which is receiving attention from chefs all over the world for its gelling versatility, especially at high temperatures.[4] When Sánchez Romera and David Bouley presented the product at the French Culinary Institute in October 2003, they attracted some of the young daring New York chefs like Wylie Dufresne from WD-50 and Sam Mason, now at Tailor.[5] Adrià also exerts a strong influence on young chefs for the simple fact that a period of training

The restaurant WD-50. (Photograph courtesy of WD-50)

in his kitchen or at his *taller* in Barcelona, a sort of creative workshop for culinary arts, has become almost a requirement for anybody in the industry who feels the need to be innovative.

The Spanish business model has been difficult to export to New York, even though the potential audience is much larger and more able and willing to spend. As already mentioned, the high prices of real estate, the prohibitive costs of keeping a large and highly trained staff, and the often huge expenses of public relations and promotion require investments from financial entities that are outside the restaurant business and often are not inclined to risk their capital in excessively creative ventures. It is important to note as well that all these Spanish stars either own or co-own their restaurants. As we will see, though, the situation is different in New York City.

The Akwa Adventures

Let us start with two very creative, often iconoclastic, chefs: the British Paul Liebrandt and the American Will Goldfarb.[6] Liebrandt made his name at Atlas, a restaurant that was located on Central Park South and earned three stars from the *New York Times* restaurant critic, despite an extremely daring menu that included dishes like apple sorbet with banana-infused olive oil, licorice and parsley soup, and beer-flavored mussels. Will Goldfarb, a pastry chef, spent some time at Ferran Adrià's almost mythical Catalan restaurant El Bulli and then worked with Cheong Liew in Hong Kong before moving to New York. Goldfarb is a member of a dynamic international ensemble of young chefs who call themselves "akwa."[7] If their goal is to shock and provoke, they have succeeded on all fronts. Their tactics are impish, shameless, and amusing. So is their cooking, although it is always based on spotless résumés and impeccable technique. They know how to work the media, organizing ad hoc dinners and happenings in various European and American venues, such as a decadent extravaganza at the Quisisana Hotel on the island of Capri, where they provided "shower-hour" room service, during which a selection of three courses was delivered between 4:00 and 6:00 P.M. (after the swimming pool closed and before the dinner was served), with instructions for the guests on how to feed one another.

The professional paths of Liebrandt and akwawarrior Goldfarb (which is how the members of akwa define themselves) crossed at Papillon, a restaurant in Greenwich Village, where a couple of months after September 11, 2001, they organized an event that caused quite a stir. The two chefs worked together to create an interactive dinner, prompting a shocked and bemused review in the *New York Times*. At that meal, the guests were requested to follow the chefs' directions when consuming the several courses. They consequently found themselves feeding one another spoonfuls of green tea–scented lobster tartare while touching silk and sandpaper. Then they were blindfolded and invited to bob, with their hands tied behind their back, for foie gras and urchin–filled ravioli floating in a cold bonito soup. It was all right if they drooled all over themselves. The point for the chefs was to have the guests enjoy a different perspective on etiquette and their relation with food. But that was not all. The increasingly amazed guests were taken into a room hazy with fog from dry ice to slurp banana jelly from the hips of a black latex–clad woman reclining on a table—a playful reference to another sort of underground avant-garde scene, the exclusive and extremely expensive body sushi parties arranged in New York by chefs such as Gary Arabia, known to celebrities in Los Angeles, and by fashionable catering companies like Raw Catering, which in 2002 organized the opening of the Museum of Sex at the Lotus nightclub.[8] These gatherings—the organizers are eager to advertise any angry reactions—are considered to be performance art.[9]

In addition, the guests at Papillon were offered a refreshing cocktail with a small ice cube floating on top. The cube had a strangely soft texture and was, according to the instructions, to be swallowed without chewing. It was onion sorbet, whose aroma was to come back into the guests' mouths to enrich the following dish, cheese served on a mousetrap. Dessert was white chocolate soup and rosewater-infused milk sucked directly from a baby bottle. The whole meal lasted for more than three hours. The reactions to these provocations were at least as intriguing as the dishes. Some guests flatly refused to have their hands tied or their eyes blindfolded, or they felt too embarrassed to be seen sucking from a baby bottle. The chefs had clearly reached their goal to rattle their guests. Moreover, the timing of this event could have not been better; September 11 had deeply shaken all New Yorkers, and this straightforward invitation to share a meal in the most intimate ways, touching and feeding one another, probably affected the guests even more than the chefs had anticipated.

Akwa's similarity to the confrontational style of the Italian futurists is obvious, even if the principles underlying their theories and actions are quite different.[10] The group's explicit goal is to make guests think about their alimentary habits, the use of their senses, and their personal idiosyncrasies regarding food and conviviality while ensuring the highest-quality food—something the futurists never did. But akwa's writing, like that of the futurists, also shows a flair for avant-garde provocation. Its style is quite unusual for an association of chefs: it is oblique, allusive, mind boggling, and, at times, unnerving. In the journal *Gastronomica,* Goldfarb defined the group's five principal axes of creativity as ingredient, technique, philosophy, love, and solitude.[11]

What happened to the Papillon chefs? Goldfarb had been working at Cru in Greenwich Village but left in the winter of 2005, apparently after a bad review by the *New York Times,* which was particularly critical of his pastry creations and accused him of showing "rebelliousness" and "self-conscious showmanship."[12] Goldfarb responded, "At least I got my idea through: they realized my food is idea based, so in some way it was a success." In February 2006, he and a few associates started another enterprise. The place, called Room 4 Dessert and located in Soho, had only a dessert menu, with drinks paired with the different items. Goldfarb offered such interesting creations as "whiskey coca," a new take on the popular drink; "Energy," with lychee sorbet and tea air; and "infance," based on meringue and cotton candy. The focus of the "restaurant" was a long bar where clients could sit and watch the pastry chef and his associates preparing desserts on the spot. Although the interest in experimentation was evident, it was very customer friendly.[13] As of December 2007, chef Goldfarb and entrepreneur Richard Perl inaugurated Dessert Studio at Michel Cluizel's chocolate boutique at ABC Carpet & Home. This is a seven-stool bar open from Thursday through Saturday "with a strong retail component," according to Goldfarb.[14]

Paul Liebrandt went to work at Little West Twelfth in the Village and later at Gilt in the New York Palace Hotel, where Le Cirque 2000 used to be. He has, according to the *New York Times,* chosen a different approach to the restaurant business: "I've learned my lesson, and my food is more approachable now." According to the *New York Times* restaurant critic Frank Bruni, who reviewed his work at Gilt, Liebrandt is heading in the right direction, but not quite mainstream:

> Gilt finds Mr. Liebrandt in a less provocative mood. He's not as intent on gadgetry and eccentric flavor combinations, but he remains too invested in intricate constructions, with so many facets they fatigue. Mr. Liebrandt may use more ingredients per square inch than any chef in Manhattan. While that tendency sometimes works against him, it springs from an admirable thoughtfulness. Mr. Liebrandt, 29, isn't some vacuously flamboyant bad boy, as his detractors have claimed. He's an evolving young artist who needs to draw sharper distinctions between his greater and lesser ideas.[15]

But as of the autumn of 2006, the British chef, nominated as one of the New York's rising stars on an industry Web site, was looking for a more fulfilling venue.[16]

One of Will Goldfarb's desserts. (Photograph courtesy of Peter Pioppo)

Goldfarb's and Liebrandt's careers clearly underscore the tensions between creativity and business constraints in the New York food scene. But are clash and surrender the only viable options?

Avant-Garde on the Lower East Side

Numerous chefs are introducing new ideas and approaches to the New York scene. One of the most successful is Wylie Dufresne, with his new restaurant WD-50, on Manhattan's Lower East Side. As co-owner with two partners, Dufresne has been experimenting in a way that few chefs have been able to do in New York. Born in Providence, Rhode Island, in 1970, he studied at the French Culinary Institute after earning a degree in philosophy. In 1999, after working with Jean-Georges Vongerichten, he became the chef at 71 Clinton Fresh Food, a block from where he opened his own restaurant in 2003 after receiving great praise from critics and the public. Some items on a winter menu? Among the appetizers were pickled beef tongue with fried mayonnaise, foie gras filled with nori caramel and served with a grapefruit-basil crumble, and bay scallops with beet yogurt and *morcilla* flakes. One notable entrée was root-vegetable lasagna with sweet and sour mushroom broth, pork belly, black soybeans, and turnips. The pastry chef, Sam Mason (who has now opened his own restaurant, Tailor, in Soho), sent out such desserts as caramelized apple with miso ice cream and olive *clafoutis* with tangerine sorbet. From the sheer variety of ingredients and their combinations, it is evident that Dufresne believes in the value of research and experimentation in the restaurant kitchen and has very clear ideas about his work: "I do acknowledge that Spanish contemporary cooking has an influence on my work. They might not have been the first to do avant-garde cuisine, but the first ones to get attention and to give legitimacy and credibility to all of us who try to cook creatively, especially with the European market." Dufresne is trying to figure out how to make it work and to bring in additional revenue so that he can continue doing what he does:

> We have noticed a change in the attitude of the diners from the first year to the second year. We have improved our style and our technique, but we have not changed them. We have not deviated from our original spirit, but we have become more legitimized by the fact that the dining public in the U.S. has become more aware that there are people out there being avant-garde. But it is still a struggle, still a fight.

He also believes that culinary professionals now have a better understanding of food science than did their predecessors. Many cooks are taught techniques without any explanation of why they are supposed to do certain things in certain ways and why they work. Dufresne is convinced that the more chefs understand about what happens when they cook, the better they can apply their individual creativity to that understanding. He feels a connection with many chefs, like Heston Blumenthal in England, who embrace the idea of food science inspired by the work of Nicholas Kurti (the father of what is known as molecular gastronomy, or the study of the physical and chemical transformations of food during its preparation for consumption), Hervé This, and Harold McGee, among others. But Dufresne acknowledges that a lot of what he learned was self-taught and tested by trial and error and that he would love to have a food scientist work with him a couple of times a month. But it is hard to find a balance between research and monetary constraints:

> Many European restaurants are run as a labor of love, and not as a corporation, and that allows them to be ahead of us in many ways. Any artistic endeavor that is "corporatized" is going to somewhat reduce its creativity. It's a constant struggle between business and vision. I'm new at this; I still don't have an answer. Many people think that what we do is weird, it's laboratory food, but our food has a lot of heart, a lot of soul, and a lot of taste.

For Dufresne, taste has to be the main focus, while searching to do something different. There is no linear creative process. It is a *process,* during which some dishes can come together in five minutes; others, in five months. Since nobody can decide to make a masterpiece, and inspiration comes and goes, Dufresne believes in team effort:

No modern, innovative food is the work of one person. I like to work with people
that inspire me, that like thinking about things, that are creative, each in a different
way. Sometimes it can come from an idea, from an ingredient that becomes available, from the season. Taste, texture, temperature, visual elements are all ways to
engage the diner, to hold somebody's attention. They keep people connected and
excited.

Dufresne tries every new dish to make sure that it tastes good and that it reflects the
spirit of his restaurant. Only then does he take a chance with the patrons. At any rate,
he never pushes too far; he does not want to serve something just for its shock value.
Rather, he is working to find a balance between his creativity and his desire not to
challenge diners: "Challenge is a negative word. I'm engaging you, I'm asking you
to participate, but I don't want to make you feel inadequate. What kind of business
model would that be? That's upsetting. I'm not trying to be aggressive, I'm not even
trying to be passive aggressive. I'm excited about what I do, and I want to share it."
Dufresne wants to make clear that he does not have any specific client in mind:

> I want anybody who's excited about life. The question is that some people do not
> like this kind of excitement. Right now, the public for my kind of restaurant is still
> limited in New York City. What if there were ten restaurants like mine? Would
> there be enough clients to make them work? As chefs, we don't get the same respect
> as athletes, or musicians, or fashion designers, or painters. Every new movement,
> every new concept, takes time, because people don't have the language to describe
> it, to talk about it. However, people are coming around.[17]

Discreet Avant-Garde

If Wylie Dufresne has no problem playing with the concept of avant-garde and acknowledges his food as being original and cutting edge, Marcus Samuelsson offers a
more moderate appraisal of the issue. Co-owner of the restaurant Aquavit, located
in the heart of Manhattan's business district, many of whose patrons are not very
adventurous, Samuelsson has introduced balanced and nonthreatening innovations
that have made him one of the most successful chefs in the United States. His life
history is quite interesting. A native of Ethiopia, he was adopted by a family from
Sweden, where he grew up and was taught how to cook by his grandmother. After
finishing cooking school in Sweden and apprenticeships in Austria and Switzerland,
he worked at Georges Blanc in Lyon, France. There, in 1994, he was invited to come
to Aquavit to cook Swedish food, and in 1995 he received three stars from the *New
York Times*.

Despite being very imaginative, Samuelsson has developed a business model that
allows him to offer traditional—and outstanding—Swedish food in the café at the
front of his restaurant, while the larger space in the back is dedicated to a more creative (and also often Swedish-inspired) menu. Although Aquavit often changes its

menu, it always is enticing. Among the most interesting appetizers have been oysters with marinated salmon roe and smoked potato cream; lobster roll with apples, trout roe, bacon-egg dressing, and ginger ale granité; and foie gras ganache with duck pastrami, pickled melon, and mint-yogurt sorbet. As entrées, customers were given a choice of brioche-wrapped salmon with salsify fries and porcini mushroom ketchup; black barley risotto with black truffles, chanterelles, coffee foam, and warm tomato salad; and poached lamb loin with smoked lamb tongue and mint *jus* and rutabaga purée. The desserts—including the "arctic circle," a goat cheese parfait with blueberry sorbet and lemon curd, and the apple sorbet with fennel cream, white chocolate, and basil jelly—are amazing in their essentiality.

Recently, Samuelsson has been exploring the culinary heritage of his native Ethiopia and other African areas, an interest that has led him to reflect on the theme of innovation and hybridization:

> Certain pairings come natural to me, like duck tongue and yellow tail tartare. How is it natural? It is about flavor, texture, and how you build different crescendos. Up, and then contrast. People who don't go for these crescendos, they cook meals that you're supposed to eat and that bring other feelings: family, sustenance, and so on. But when they come to restaurants, they expect to be entertained; it is not only a meal they eat when they are hungry.

Because he is from Scandinavia, Samuelsson finds the building blocks of his cooking in that culinary tradition: seafood, game, pickling, and preserving. Starting from that base, he works on aesthetics, texture, and temperature, in addition to flavor. Having grown up in Sweden, he admits, he was used to the aestheticism and homogeneity with which he had been raised. Although he has found new inspiration in Africa and Latin America, Samuelsson feels he is not cooking in an avant-garde fashion but is just using ingredients that have been around forever and mixing them with others:

> I am coming to terms that I am Scandinavian, but I am also from Africa and I am also American. I'm diving into that culture, but I can't do it from there: I have to do it from here. Each time I go, there is something unexpected. I can't do that from a book. My background gives me the opportunity to do that, but every chef can go deeper somewhere. At the same time, I like to stay close to new technology, different regions, and the craft of cooking itself, that changes all the time. I think an evolution is coming because the world is smaller and technology is more accessible. All this will create the new food, but can you define that [as] avant-garde?

Samuelsson acknowledges his interest in new cooking technology, but he is afraid that if he becomes too absorbed in it, it might become tunnel vision:

> I went to Ferran Adrià, I saw what he's doing, but that's it. And it's not that I don't like Ferran, but I want to progress in my own vision. Being in New York helps because you're connected to everything, in a multicultural society. Whoever you are, you have to go through New York. It is true that in this place there is a tension

between business and creativity. I know it, I'm in both positions. Without money there is no creativity, and without creativity there is no money. The Medici in Florence knew that.[18]

Marcus Samuelsson appears slightly annoyed at being labeled as avant-garde, as he is aware that being marked as excessively innovative can harm the business. Consequently, he tries to be creative without being pretentious and with no ideological undertones.

Chefs as Intelligentsia?

A few chefs in New York City are widely perceived as innovative and progressive yet are able to maintain sometimes complex relationships with their patrons and with the business aspects of their profession. Their careers and financial security often are at stake. In such a complicated situation, what is the relevance and the role of avant-garde approaches in New York? More generally, what does "avant-garde" mean? And how can we use the word in regard to cuisine?

According to *Merriam-Webster's Collegiate Dictionary*, "avant-garde" appeared for the first time in English in 1910 to signify "an intelligentsia that develops new or experimental concepts esp. in the arts." The *Oxford English Dictionary*, confirming the 1910 date, defines the term as "the pioneers or innovators in any art in a particular period." The word "avant-garde" was actually created in France at the end of the nineteenth century when the Impressionists defied the status quo of art production by critiquing the conventions and the idealized visions of academic painting. By turning to more mundane subjects and to nature, they also abandoned the traditional rules of composition and introduced technical innovations. In the following decades, many other artistic movements—such as Expressionism, Cubism, and, a few years later, Dadaism—were labeled "avant-garde" or, in English, "vanguard."

Do these movements share any elements with New York's food scene? The term "avant-garde" seems to imply new and experimental concepts, the presence of innovators who can be considered an intelligentsia, and a specific environment: the arts. Can we find the same traits in a totally different kind of creative process, such as cooking?

Most avant-garde movements defined their positions in documents that became known as "manifestos," a word that since the seventeenth century has been used to indicate, according to the *Oxford English Dictionary*, "a public declaration or proclamation, written or spoken; esp. a printed declaration, explanation, or justification of policy issued by a head of state, government, or political party or candidate, or any other individual or body of individuals of public relevance, as a school or movement in the arts." Does any New York chef produce written material whose function and intent can be compared with that of a manifesto? Among the three chefs discussed, only Will Goldfarb did something similar through the akwa group's Web site and other texts. It is not unusual, however, to find written principles and statements on restaurants' menus or advertising materials. For example, Anthony

Mangieri at Una Pizza Napoletana in the East Village has transformed the menus that his patrons may peruse, during the often long waits for his amazing pizzas, into gentle weapons for a cultural battle that extends beyond his actual restaurant, with his pizza making becoming an act of avant-garde guerrilla warfare. Because chefs operate in a commercial environment, they can be expected to use the venues and communication instruments of that environment. Many of them—now referred to as "star chefs"—have become so media savvy, often backed by professionals in public relations, that they can express themselves comfortably in printed or video interviews, blogs, and books. In these contexts, coherent, clearly stated culinary principles help create their "character," a distinguishable brand. For chefs in New York City, creating a desirable image is paramount, especially if they plan to be in business for a reasonable amount of time. But this, of course, does not make them avant-garde.

Because avant-garde artists tend to articulate their ideas in clearly structured manifestos, a common element of the twentieth-century movements was a pervasive intellectualism, even when they were denouncing every form of intellectualism. Can we find the same approach in innovative chefs' media expressions? Sometimes we can. The introductions to their cookbooks, interviews, or Internet profiles often become declarations of their intentions and principles. Among the three chefs discussed, we can recognize different approaches. While Goldfarb does not avoid language and a style that might be perceived as artsy and intellectual, Wylie Dufresne and Marcus Samuelsson are definitely careful to appear more engaging.

Protest and rebellion are other common traits of twentieth-century avant-garde artists, who regarded themselves as the forerunners of new forms of liberated culture. Their discontent with materialism, contemporary society, and its bourgeois sensibility appeared in both their verbal declarations and their work. The most practical aspects of their artistic techniques were often conceived and explained as the physical expression of moral, ethical, social, or political exigencies, which in many ways were perceived as more relevant than the purely aesthetic aspects of the movements. This kind of attitude, however, is not acceptable for innovative chefs, since restaurants developed as a space for bourgeois leisure. Indeed, the personal beliefs and political sympathies of chefs can affect their business activities in a tough environment like that of New York. This might be why they are so cautious about being labeled as avant-garde: the ideological weight of the word is uncomfortable.

Again, the concept of avant-garde usually points to a specific environment: the arts. The food scene of contemporary New York, at least on certain levels, enjoys almost the same prestige and intellectual cachet of other, more historically affirmed, forms of artistic expression. If a restaurant or a chef receives a good review in any of the major newspapers, customers are likely to come in droves for months, just as they do for successful art exhibitions, high-demand concerts, or even exclusive auctions. Some New Yorkers seem to enjoy discussing new restaurants, food trends, and the latest creations of the local star chefs. Of course, the really cool New Yorkers are those who can assert, "I was there *way* before it was reviewed."

Although many wealthy citizens have traditionally patronized the arts by buying works of unknown or upcoming artists or even by giving them pensions and providing them with space to create, the case of food is quite different. After the French Revolution, very few chefs had the luxury of cooking for enlightened and rich families willing to give them free rein in the kitchen, as Antonin Carême did for the Rothschilds, for whom he always preferred to cook, over any noble or crowned head in Europe. At any rate, in New York City, many restaurant goers are interested only in refueling. Although they might first be enticed by the high rating of a restaurant, without bothering to read the actual reviews, when they realize that the food is too unusual or not what they were expecting, they sometimes assume a confrontational, if not belligerent, attitude. Almost every chef has at least one such horror story. Along with eating out are those aspects of cooking as a service-oriented craft, which also depend on the almost nonexistent distance between the meal's producer and the consumer. Even in the most innovative New York establishments, this is an element that no sensible chef can ever neglect, because New Yorkers, compared with the residents of other cities, are often less restrained in voicing their dissatisfaction.

Avant-Garde and Hipness

Are these elements sufficient to define "avant-garde" in a social, cultural, and financial environment like that of New York City? To complete the picture, we also have to refer to a different ingredient, one closely connected to the American historical and social experience: hipness. The word "hip" cannot be translated into any other language, as it lacks any equivalent in other cultures. Nonetheless, New York is synonymous with hipness. According to various references, hip was born from the necessity for African Americans to create their own expression and secret language to affirm their own cultural identity and, sometimes, their agency as human beings, and it was soon imitated by white people looking for ways to express their difference.[19] This interaction became even more complex with the arrival of other ethnic groups and with men and women of different classes, sensibilities, and expectations of their American dream. This rich human landscape reflected its intense dynamics at all levels: highbrow and lowbrow culture, fashion, and social and political habits. This scenario is a precise description of New York City's development as an international crossroads, vibrant with tensions and, at times, destructive energy.

In this fluid and ever-mutating context, hip has often provided forms of rebellion against the materialistic values that America embodies; by being hip, all people can dream to be more than their financial position allows them to be. It is a different kind of status system that does not rely on family connections and financial situation. Hip is not necessarily about money; it is about being an insider, about being one step ahead of the rest of the flock. It is about setting the path for those who can only follow. Although anyone can try to be hip, not everyone actually *is* hip. That is, the more one tries to be hip, the less likely one will succeed, a contradictory rule that determines the intangibility of hipness. Once it entered the mainstream, hip helped strengthen and sell the materialistic and money-driven culture that it had originally tried to undermine. Then, of course, hip had to move to something new, something exciting, something that could create an impression of real freedom.

In a food culture in which new products and trends are created and consumed at a breathtaking pace, particularly in a metropolis that is universally credited as trendsetting and progressive, hipness ensures that certain establishments will have a commercially competitive edge, thereby determining their success and fame. The intellectual climate of New York, one of the world capitals for creativity and novelty—especially for art, fashion, and pop culture—often combines hipness with something special and original: avant-garde and innovation, our main focus. But in regard to food, the connection among hipness, avant-garde, and commercial viability is far from being direct. Food is frequently not very high on the list for young, creative types, often strapped for money, who otherwise could be the most receptive audience, being open to experimentation and even provocation. Businesses, especially those requiring considerable investments, cannot thrive on these patrons, though, as they are unable or unwilling to spend much money. As the result of this contradiction, it is difficult for young, daring chefs to be both hip and avant-garde, despite their efforts at innovation. Since Delmonico's and Sherry's were the places to be at the turn of the twentieth century, hipness has been a constant element in New York City nightlife. For decades, as a result of economic constraints, the most fashionable establishments did not care about hipness per se but instead tried to acquire prestige by catering to the city's upper class.[20]

Beginning in the 1970s, culinary schools were no longer the exclusive breeding grounds of young, successful chefs; now many came from various other backgrounds, working their way up the restaurant ladder in different, often unusual, ways. But they definitely were hip, getting their inspiration from the counterculture and often starting their businesses with very limited financial means but clear ideas about being on the cutting edge, even if in nonconfrontational ways.

Following the example of Alice Waters in Berkeley, California, local produce and cuisines suddenly appeared on the radars of the new generation of young chefs, who soon started to work closely with local farmers to ensure fresh food for their restaurants.[21] They changed their menus according to the season and redesigned their restaurants' decor to better communicate the essence of their work. The interest in local experiences also led many chefs to pay attention to ethnic foods from other parts of the world, especially in a city like New York, where large foreign communities traditionally had their own eateries, markets, and even more formal restaurants. Open to stimuli from California as well as from South Asia, Australia, and Central and South America, these chefs initiated a series of new trends such as fusion, Nuevo Latino, and Chino Latino, just to mention a few. In many ways, they could be considered avant-garde, especially at the highest levels of quality. Although they often lacked a deep social and political consciousness, they introduced new ideas about hybridization and multiculturality, a certain openness to different experiences and ethnicities, and a desire to use new techniques and exotic ingredients. Several of these restaurants surely embodied a certain hipness. Indeed, their patrons often were the same baby boomers who had lived through the counterculture and were enjoying their professional and financial success as adults. When New York City's economy boomed in the 1990s, new generations of professionals joined the cohorts of fashionable restaurant goers, younger than baby boomers and with very different backgrounds but equally sensitive to the allure of the cultural capital provided by hip, avant-garde nightspots. Fully rooted in the capitalistic system of consumption, these new well-off hipsters were after mostly pure fun and the opportunity to socialize with their peers in a stimulating environment. The consequence was that food became just one factor in their overall perception of attractiveness and desirability.

What Future?

To entice a young audience with disposable income, armies of public-relations professionals and popular socialites work with and incessantly lobby opinion makers, the press, and widely recognized hipsters to promote the restaurants they represent to the desirable state of hip, often relying more on looks, ambience, music, and decor than on the food itself. Many "loungey" nightspots have actually started to serve food so anonymous that is often not even worth remembering. But most patrons do not seem to care.

It is evident that many of these fashionable establishments have little interest in stimulating their clientele with creative cuisine or daring menus that actually make sense from a gustatory or culinary perspective. But as we have seen with Wylie Dufresne and Marcus Samuelsson, a few have succeeded in reconciling the financial necessity of counting on a constant and large pool of patrons with their desire to offer something new and different. Hip restaurants often are pricey, accessible only to the few who have the economic means to pay for them and who do not always have the cultural capital necessary to enjoy them. Avant-garde food is appealing and hip to the thirty-somethings and forty-somethings and to all those who want to experience the thrill of walking off the beaten path for a good time while displaying conspicuous consumption. Those in their fifties and older might appear to be less receptive to experimentation and might feel that they should get better value for their money. For these patrons, hip is often a secondary value.

In New York City, as a result, all avant-garde restaurants are hip, but not all hip restaurants are avant-garde. The choices are tough for the young and the restless. New York is full of traps for inventive chefs who are not ready to negotiate their creative autonomy with the financial powers that back many local restaurants by managing food ventures according to the same principles that apply to any other corporate enterprise. However, the competition is so strong, especially in times of economic recession, that many young turks on the food scene have learned to deal with financial constraints and to affirm themselves with skilled tactics that include using public relations, playing the media, and attracting the right crowds. After all, in a place like New York, survival can become an art form in itself.

NOTES

1. Priscilla Parkhurst Ferguson, *Accounting for Taste: The Triumph of French Cuisine* (Chicago: University of Chicago Press, 2004); Rebecca L. Spang, *The Invention of the Restaurant:*

130   *Paris and Modern Gastronomic Culture* (Cambridge, Mass.: Harvard University Press, 2000); Amy B. Trubek, *Haute Cuisine: How the French Invented the Culinary Profession* (Philadelphia: University of Pennsylvania Press, 2000).

2. Frank Bruni, "New York Menus: Read 'Em and Weep," *New York Times,* March 9, 2005, Dining Out section, 1.

3. Fabio Parasecoli, "Deconstructing Soup: Ferran Adrià's Culinary Challenges," *Gastronomica* 1, no. 1 (2001): 61–73.

4. Fabio Parasecoli, review of *La cocina de los sentidos,* by Miguel Sánchez Romera, *Gastronomica* 3, no. 3 (2003): 110–11.

5. The event was discussed at http://www.frenchculinary.com/subpages/events/highlights35 .html.

6. Part of this section appeared in *Gastronomica* 2, no. 3 (2002): 6–7.

7. Although the members of akwa are very young, they already boast extensive experience. Outside the United States, the members so far include the Danish chef Kasper Kurdhal, who works at the Restaurant Scholteshof in Hasselt, Belgium, and the Italian chef Davide Scabin, the chef and owner of Al Combsal in Almese, in northern Italy. A less-involved member of the group is Rubén García, whose smoked chocolate dessert provoked a heated debate in 2001.

8. Bridget Harrison, "Nude Catering Gives New Meaning to 'Naked Lunch,'" *New York Post,* http://www.nypost.com, August 20, 2003.

9. J. Patrick Coolican, "Sushi in the Raw: Restaurant's Displays Get Women's Group Steamed," *Seattle Times,* http://www.seattletimes.com, November 11, 2003.

10. One of the leaders of the movement, Filippo Tommaso Marinetti, actually published a cookbook in 1932. In *La cucina futurista,* he advocated a total revolution of Italian foodways, accusing them of being the cause of the nation's backwardness. The culinary traditions and the past must be forgotten in order to get ready for the modern times. The futurists offered the first incidence of avant-garde in food in the proper sense of the term: a movement with revolutionary aspirations and an intellectual approach that expressed its ideas in a clear and organized way in the form of a manifesto. Furthermore, just as today's innovative chefs do, the futurists played with flavors, textures, visual elements, consumption habits, and even crockery and flatware to stimulate and provoke their audiences. See Carol Helstosky, "Recipe for the Nation: Reading Italian History Through *La scienza in cucina* and *La Cucina futurista,*" *Food and Foodways* 11 (2003): 113–40.

11. Will Goldfarb, "Akwa: Commercializing Creativity," *Gastronomica* 5, no. 4 (2005): 103–5.

12. Frank Bruni, "Where Old Ghosts Fight for a Table," *New York Times,* October 20, 2004, F9.

13. Bill Buford, "The Dessert Lab," *New Yorker,* June 26, 2006, 40–45.

14. Will Goldfarb, personal communication, December 1, 2007.

15. Frank Bruni, "Eye-Opening, Eyebrow-Raising," *New York Times,* February 8, 2006, F10.

16. Paul Liebrandt was profiled at http://www.starchefs.com/chefs/rising_stars/2006/ ny/html/index.shtml.

17. Wylie Dufresne, interview with author, March 24, 2005.

18. Marcus Samuelsson, interview with author, March 11, 2005.

19. John Leland, *Hip: The History* (New York: HarperCollins, 2004); Shelly Eversley, "The Source of Hip," *Minnesota Review,* nos. 55–57 (2002): 257–70.

20. Michael Batterberry and Arian Batterberry, *On the Town in New York: The Landmark History of Eating, Drinking, and Entertainments from the American Revolution to the Food Revolution* (New York: Routledge, 1999).

21. The story of Alice Waters is paradigmatic in this sense. During a trip to France while she was still in her teens, she discovered the pleasures of shopping in open markets where local farmers sold their own freshly picked produce. She never forgot the experience. After completing her degree in French cultural studies at the University of California at Berkeley in 1967, she returned to Europe, first to London and then again to France. By 1971, she had found her way and opened Chez Panisse, offering a five-course, prix-fixe menu that changed every day. Seeking out the best raw ingredients became her priority. She bought directly from farms, usually locally grown seasonal fruit and vegetables, exploiting California's wide range of produce. Waters succeeded in convincing growers to use organic methods, and other restaurateurs in the area followed her example. Inspired by the social and political atmosphere of the day, Waters has always emphasized the importance of the relationship between food growers and consumers in building a sense of community. See Fabio Parasecoli, "San Francisco: Thoughtful Food," *Gambero Rosso Wine Travel Food*, no. 18 (1999): 88. In addition, Jeremiah Tower, a former chef at Chez Panisse, built his skills on passion, travel, and good cookbooks—first solidifying his version of French country cooking and then discovering California as his main source of inspiration.

8

Chow Fun City

Three Centuries of Chinese Cuisine in New York City

HARLEY SPILLER

In the basement of the boyhood home of Harley Spiller, a.k.a. Inspector Collector, there is an office lined with cabinets upon cabinets full of stuff; key chains, bottle openers, ribbons, plastic hands, etc. It is a carnival of fun where his father, an advertising man who produced swag for companies, maintains his office/workshop. The wonderment continues upstairs, where Harley's inspiration for collecting began. As you pass his parent's collection of fine art and artifacts you come to Inspector Collector's first bedroom, where just this year a framed copy of the Guinness Book of World Records for the largest collection of menus was hung with pride.

Harley grew up in Buffalo, New York, with an unexciting palate of brown gravy–covered meat-and-potatoes, but every summer he was off to camp to experience the world through a different lens. There he befriended John Pin, the camp's chef. Every day after canoe outings and such, he would follow exotic smells that coaxed him into his first Chinese kitchen. Thirty years later, now based in New York City, Inspector Collector uses his innate collecting and culinary skills to educate the curious with fascinating programs designed for everyone from kindergarten to college and beyond.

Micki Watanabe

I WAS ONCE a confirmed meat-and-potato eater. Aside from fresh green peas, pizza was about the only "vegetable" I enjoyed. My mom was from Borough Park, and in keeping with the traditions of her Brooklyn upbringing, our family ate Chinese food as a treat on Sunday nights once a month or so. We were not into experimentation and invariably dined on "round-eye" favorites like wonton soup, egg rolls with plenty of duck sauce and mustard, fried rice, and shrimp in lobster sauce. Once, a waiter asked if we would like to share dishes in the traditional Chinese family style, and my dad replied, "No, the *moo goo gai pan* is for me—that's my family style."

In the 1960s, we visited relatives in New York City three or four times a year, but I can recall only one Chinese meal, at Pearl's, a theater-district standby justifiably famous for its lemon chicken. In the early 1970s, though, we were steered to a new place, Hunam, where I tasted my very first hot peppers in what was then a new dish for Americans: chicken with peanuts. Sweat broke out on my brow, but that did not stop me from licking the plate clean. My culinary blinders had been lifted.

I moved to Manhattan in 1981, and my unadventurous ways were shaken up in the proverbial New York minute. Alone in an apartment for the first time in my life, I heard an odd noise at the door. "Oh no," I thought, "here's that New York trouble everyone warned me about." It was not trouble, though. It was the crinkling noise of a Chinese take-out menu sliding under the door. That menu, from the now-defunct Hunan Royal on Ninety-fourth Street and Broadway, was fascinating. I read every word and began to read menus on a daily basis, reveling in foodstuffs like squid, which I had previously thought was good only for bait or biology class. My starting museum worker's salary was in the high one-figures, so luxuries like magazine subscriptions, Q-tips, and restaurant dining had to be crossed off my to-do list. Out of necessity, I began to cook for myself, preferring to procure foodstuffs in the low-priced markets of Chinatown, where, for example, shockingly fresh salmon still sells for one-quarter the price charged uptown.

When I first saw the markets of Mott Street, I was unable to identify even basic ingredients like ginger and scallion. Now, after twenty-five years of hit-and-miss efforts, I've purchased, washed, and cooked dozens of different leafy greens, gourds, melons, squashes, roots, rhizomes, tubers, sprouts, shoots, peas, and beans. Still, there are dozens of dried herbs and roots with Chinese and Latin names that remain unexplored mysteries. I just learned that water chestnuts, like gladiolus, fall into a category of underground stems called "corms." Using texts and, especially, multilingual glossaries has been a big help, but sometimes cooking still boils down to trial and error.

Today there are nearly eighteen thousand food-related objects in my 280-square-foot Manhattan studio apartment. Besides ordinary shelves of cookbooks and drawers of kitchen gear, I have several thousand shopping lists plucked from supermarket carts; more than one hundred types of drinking straws and toothpicks; close to one thousand spoons with different functions (some of which were exhibited at the Cooper-Hewitt, National Design Museum, of the Smithsonian Institution); twenty-eight packs of international chewing gum in flavors unavailable in the United States; a dozen or so funky implements with functions I cannot determine; more than two thousand beer and soda bottle caps; a handful of key-chain bottle openers; eight miniature cast-iron frying pans; seven devices specifically for peeling citrus fruits; seeds from twenty-six unusual fruits and vegetables; hundreds of fact-laden clippings about ice cream, hot dogs, hamburgers, crabs, mustard, corn, pizza, and pickles; an ever-revolving collection of hot pepper sauces; fun food packages like sprats labeled in Cyrillic; coca tea from Peru; an unopened can of Billy Beer; two plastic toy bitter melons; three carved wooden mangoes; and a lemon from a party I attended in 1995 that is so dry it bounces like a Ping-Pong ball.

It is not just for whim that I save such everyday objects, which most people take for granted. "No Menu" signs are fastened to the front doors of thousands of residential buildings in the city, and many New Yorkers compare the incessant flood of advertising in the form of menus with the emergency-locksmith stickers adhered to their front doors: utter nuisances. Despite the protests against menus (Upper West Side police coined a new verb, "menuing"), Chinese restaurants continue to flourish. Without doubt, the public is very interested in my collection of more than ten thousand pieces of international Chinese restaurant memorabilia. They have been exhibited in art and historical museums around the world, from Caracas to Connecticut, and the *New York Times* has covered my work a dozen times. Menus, the mainstay of my archive, were slipped under my door by delivery people or plucked from the counters of take-out shops across the city's five boroughs and beyond. My collection also includes Chinese menus that were pulled out of scrapbooks and donated by family, friends, and strangers. All told, I have Chinese menus from all fifty states and more than one hundred countries.

By nature, restaurants are prone to hyperbole in their self-descriptions, making it difficult to use them to pinpoint historical details. One of the highlights of my collection is a pair of bean-shaped Chinese lacquer boxes from the estate of a San Franciscan who had owned five large homes. Inside the boxes are bits of dried coconut, spiced watermelon seeds, an actual bird's nest for soup, and a menu indicating that these items were "pocketed at a Tiffin (luncheon) by Li Hung Chung, Vice Roy, 1896." Chung was China's first emissary to the United States and has been referred to as the "father of chop suey." While these boxes and their contents appear for all intents and purposes to be genuine antiques, there are dozens of fanciful "histories" of the origin of chop suey, and Renqui Yu's exhaustive study of the dish makes the point that no one true history of the ubiquitous chop suey is likely to emerge from the haze of urban legend.[1]

Nonetheless, one can glean a good deal from menus. Menus are primary documents of their time, artifacts that go well beyond food, opening windows into issues of race, gender, transnational culture, economics, and more. As our high-paced technological world has shrunk over the decades, Chinese food has come to play a more and more central role in the foodways of the twenty-first-century center of internationalism: New York City. Moreover, to some people, even the Shanghai Museum looks like a *ding,* a Chinese Bronze Age cooking vessel.

An integral part of my archive of Chinese restaurant memorabilia is Luc Sante's book *Low Life.*[2] This rarely told history of New York City's underbelly across the centuries informs and confirms what I know about Chinese New York through my menus. The gritty and numerous details that limn Sante's history bring the period to life, and I will try to paraphrase Sante's text and combine it with information from my archive and my quarter century of exploring Chinese foodways.

Relative to other immigrant groups, the Chinese arrived in Gotham late. City records indicate that in 1858 a man named Ah Ken moved into a house on Mott Street and opened a cigar store on Park Row (there is still one there). In 1868, a man named

Wah Kee came to town and opened a store on Pell Street. There he sold vegetables,
dried fruit, and what was referred to in accounts of the time as "curios." He also had
a room upstairs with facilities for gambling and smoking opium. In later years, more
respectable merchants opened businesses like Tuck High, a Mott Street general store,
run for decades by Coon On Lee and Wah On Lee, brothers who eventually turned
over the contents of their store for permanent exhibition at the New York State Museum in Albany. Coon On now lives in Flushing, Queens, where he frequently spikes
his family's oatmeal with ground beef, a simple, little-known, and utterly delicious
Cantonese breakfast staple.

In 1870, census and official estimates recorded from twenty-five to seventy-five
Chinese natives living in New York. It was around this time that Chinatown began to
organize, first with just a few houses on Mott and Pell streets. Over the decade, Chinatown spread in four directions, gradually absorbing the progressively abandoned
ethnic settlements around it. By 1880, there were said to be seven hundred Chinese in
the city, and by 1890, the Chinese population had swelled to thirteen thousand. The
media's reports of the Chinese were notoriously bigoted, and Chinese cuisine initially
struck Europeans as repulsive. Newspapers noted that Chinese people were casual
about smoking, eating, and walking out in the middle of operas, but no one seemed to
acknowledge that American audiences had behaved in exactly that way half a century
earlier. One reporter even went so far as to break down immigrant nationalities by
odor: the French smelled of garlic; the Germans, of sauerkraut and beer; the English,
of roast beef and ale; the Americas, of corn cakes and pork and beans; and the Chinese, of opium, cigars, and dried fish.

In 1896, Congress passed the Chinese Exclusion Act, which permitted only scholars, highly qualified professionals, and the rich to enter the United States. Because
women were denied legal entry, early Chinese settlers lived in bachelor communities.
A poll conducted in 1890 shows a disproportionate number working as laundrymen
and, perhaps following Ah Ken's lead, as cigar vendors hawking outside the major
hotels.

By 1903, there were four Chinese restaurants on Mott Street—the Imperial, Port
Arthur, Tuxedo, and Chinese Quick Lunch—plus the Chatham on Doyers Street, and
the Savoy and Oriental Restaurant on Pell Street. I have a take-out menu from Oriental Restaurant inscribed with the date May 3, 1916, and the names of six people who
presumably dined there that day: W. Simmons, Art. Wells, Chas. Moore, H. Goubert,
D. Edick, and Mrs. Thomas. Checkmarks indicate that the group ate a large portion
of boneless chicken chow mein (75 cents), "chop sooy" with chicken and peppers
(40 cents), almond cakes (10 cents), and "Ly Chee" nuts (15 cents) and sipped the
most expensive tea on the menu, "*Sun Sen Char,* grown on Cloud-Covered Mountain
Heights" ($5 a cup). (They skipped what would be amazing bargains today: steak
and mushrooms for 40 cents and a whole fried chicken for $1.) The exorbitant price
and poetic description of the tea immediately brought opium to my mind, but my
stereotypical Western reaction to Eastern ways was proved wrong when research
revealed that the best teas are grown on mountaintops moistened by clouds and that
$5 was a fair price in New York for a tea that had won the top prize in Taiwan's an-
nual tea competition.

As the nineteenth century turned into the twentieth, dozens of overtly criminal clubs arose, including Jimmy Kelly's Mandarin Club and the Pelham, a Pell Street space that had been home to the country's first Chinese theater. Singing waiters became a fad, and the Pelham's most talented waiter, the young Izzy Baline, soon left the seedy milieu behind, changed his name, and gained enduring fame as Irving Berlin. Chinese restaurants, previously a raffish thrill for sophisticates slumming around Chatham Square, began a new era of popularity when the proprietors of such uptown establishments as the Pekin and the Tokio (apparently a Chinese restaurant despite its name) started hiring jazz bands to play during meals. The combination of Chinese food and dance-band music, as evidenced by a hand-painted sign still visible on a brick wall in Seattle's International District, "Chop Suey and Cha Cha," reached its peak in the 1940s and 1950s and endured until the early 1960s. Chinese dinner-dancing seems to be another Western phenomenon that arose from Eastern exoticism, underscored by the fact that the most common graphic device in my collection of older Chinese menus is a sexy Asian server.

George Washington Connors was a Western factotum of late-nineteenth-century Chinatown. He took the nickname Chuck from his habit of cooking chuck steaks on sticks over fires in the middle of the street. Connors, "the Sage of Doyers Street," was a true character said to have originated many phrases, including "under the table." He grew up loose on Mott Street and was fond of tormenting local Chinese by throwing rocks and pulling their queues (braids; think Martin Scorsese's *Gangs of New York*). Nonetheless, Connors came to appreciate things Chinese, learned the rudiments of Cantonese, and began to sell tours to adventurous visitors looking for cheap thrills. Quite the huckster, Connors would lead patrons through Chinatown, pointing out innocent-looking pedestrians and falsely identifying them as *tong* hatchet men. His tours often ended at Mon Lay Won Company, a restaurant at 24 Pell Street. The expression *mon lay won* can be loosely translated from Cantonese as "gorgeous day," but the eatery also had an English sobriquet, derived from New York's most famous restaurant of the day: the "Chinese Delmonico's." Connors was much in demand and once provided a tour for the tea magnate Sir Thomas Lipton. Always dreaming of striking it rich, Connors imagined his future:

> Me headqua'ters would be da Waldorf, but I would
> Hev a telephone station in Chinatown, so I could git
> A hot chop suey w'en I wanted it quick.

New York's Chinese restaurants have come a long way from their origin in the nineteenth-century Manhattan enclave bordered by Mott and Pell streets, Bowery, and Chatham Square. Chinese food establishments have spread across the island from river to river, as well as in Chinese neighborhoods in Jackson Heights/Elmhurst and Flushing, Queens; Eighth Avenue in Sunset Park, Brooklyn; the secondary Brooklyn Chinatown centered on the Q train stop on Avenue U in Homecrest; and the tertiary enclave now forming in Bensonhurst.

One day I was strolling and snacking on a roast beef sandwich from Brennan and Carr on Gravesend Neck Road, founded in 1938, when I happened upon Richard

Yee's, an old-fashioned Chinese restaurant the likes of which are frequently invoked by members of the Jewish Brooklyn side of my family. Despite all that has been written about the complex sociology of Jews and Chinese food,[3] suffice it for me to say that Sandy Koufax, the Brooklyn Dodgers pitcher who famously refused to play in a crucial game because it coincided with Yom Kippur, loved Richard Yee's special roast pork in wine sauce.[4]

A good deal of New York's ethnic dining history can be seen in the experiences of three generations of the Yee family. In 1952, Joe Yee, a native of Toisan in Guangdong Province who had worked for many years as the chef and then manager of Ding Ho restaurant in Manhattan, opened Joe Yee's restaurant at 650 Flatbush Avenue in Brooklyn. In those days, dining out was a social event that generally meant a trip to Manhattan, which then was less residential than it is today. Patrons regularly spent three or four hours over dinner, conversing with other parties as well as the staff. Yee was an inventive cook and an entertaining host who took the advice of friendly and self-interested customers to transfer the skills he had honed in Midtown to Brooklyn, just a wild pitch away from Ebbets Field. The restaurant flourished, in part because Yee was always ready to honor special requests.

Joe Yee's son Richard grew up in the trade, working his way from dishwasher to head chef to maître d'. In the 1960s, he started to take over the restaurant's day-to-day operations, and in 1967 Richard Yee moved the family business, and most of the original staff, to a location twice as big, at 2617–2619 Avenue U in Marine Park/Sheepshead Bay. The new space was named Richard Yee's, but Joe's portrait remained on the matchbooks. One of the biggest factors in Richard Yee's success was listening to his customers, so it was not uncommon for him to bring raw steaks out of the kitchen so diners could see the marbling. He prided himself on the personal touch and regularly experimented with new dishes by offering free tastes. Customers loved to try dishes before they saw them on the menu, and some of his customers came expressly for his Italian fare.

In the early days, the restaurant on Avenue U frequently was packed; patrons were given tickets; and the staff called out the numbers when tables freed up. The 170-seat hotspot had a swanky bar/lounge and stayed open until 1:00 A.M. on weekdays and 3:00 A.M. on Fridays and Saturdays, accommodating late-night horse-racing fans on the way home from the Yonkers and Roosevelt raceways. The Yees sponsored a lot of Chinese immigrant families so they could have the same chance they had had and cared so much about their clientele that their son's godparents were customers.

Martin Burden often wrote about both Yee establishments in his *New York Post* column "Going Out Tonight," and he reported on April 25, 1956, that "Joe keeps inventing new dishes that are part Cantonese, part Mandarin and part Yee. And we feel it's always worth a trip across the bridge to sample it." Burden suggested the best way to have a fine meal: "Wave away the menu and let Joe take care of you. Joe's new dish, '56 model, is winter melon ding ($3.35) on a big platter heaped with cellophane noodles, chicken, chicken liver, lobster, shrimp, roast pork, bamboo shoots, water chestnuts and winter melon." Crabmeat balls, another Yee innovation, were crusty baseball-size spheres of crabmeat, pork, water chestnuts, and mushrooms so popular that customers would order them by the dozen to freeze, cook, and eat at home. Many such Yee creations catered to the excesses of postwar life in New York: simple wonton soup became "Hong *shu wor* wonton," with loads of extra ingredients like fried wontons, chicken, lobster, pork, shrimp, *bok toy* (bok choy), and a handful of other vegetables in chicken broth. "*Yuen yung* shrimp," another over-the-top amalgam, consisted of "jumbo shrimp pressed with chicken, in a special egg batter, deep fried and topped with shredded crab meat, vegetables, and a rich egg sauce." The ending of Burden's column highlights Yee's advances in the 1950s and 1960s: "Say, whatever happened to chop suey?" After fifty-five years in the business, Richard and Helen Yee turned off the neon one last time and retired. When it shut in early 2007, Richard Yee's was the borough's oldest extant Chinese restaurant. In the mid-twentieth century, Chinese restaurants were a perfect place for a night out on the town, but now, with more than forty thousand Chinese restaurants in the United States, much of the thrill is gone.

Chinese restaurants in Gotham now run the gamut. Tiny bullet-proof store-fronts pushing beef and broccoli dot poor neighborhoods, and downtown is home to ultra-upscale spots like Jean-Georges Vongerichten's 66. Its shrimp and foie gras dumplings with fresh grapefruit dipping sauce may be all the rage, but traditional Chinese foods—like the Beijing-style pork and chive dumplings sold for five for $1 at Vanessa Weng's Eldridge Street Dumpling House—keep true Chinese food aficionados heading back time and again to New York's original and ever-expanding Chinatown.

In New York's less affluent locales, Chinese takeouts are often the only restaurants on the block. The owners are not necessarily professional restaurateurs; rather, many are immigrants who, because of strict federal and industry regulations, cannot practice the professions they engaged in back home. Seeking to quickly establish a financial toehold in their new home, many immigrants follow in the footsteps of friends and relatives who arrived in New York before them. Two centuries ago, Chinese people routinely worked in tobacco stores; if you ask New Yorkers today, chances are they will talk about the Greek-owned coffee shops, Korean-owned green grocers, Senegalese purse vendors, Polish and Jamaican contractors, and other, too easily stereotyped ethnic groups in specific professions.

Chinese restaurants can be found in all five boroughs, in all fifty states, and on every continent save Antarctica (which, although it does not have *any* restaurants, does bring in Chinese products with which to cook). Chinese food has become ubiquitous. There are some thirty-five thousand Chinese restaurants in the United States alone. Western supermarkets routinely offer stir-fries in their buffets, and chain restaurants sell cross-cultural hybrids like Buffalo-style chicken wontons slathered in tomato sauce and Philly cheesesteak egg rolls.

Chinese cooks seem especially skilled at adapting their cuisine to local tastes. For example, to appeal to New York's well-established Puerto Rican and Dominican populations, many of the city's Chinese restaurants serve faux saffron–tinged rice and a choice of fried plantains, *maduros,* or *tostones.* Other Chinese merchants eager to adapt to New York environs deep-fry frozen apple sticks, pizza rolls, French fried potatoes, and a variety of other, distinctly non-Chinese treats. Moreover, whereas fast food is usually subpar, the simpler home-style Chinese dishes can be quite good

at these mom-and-pop shops. Today, for many New Yorkers, Chinese food is everyday fare.

In New York, devotees of Chinese food can now choose from an ever-broadening
array of Chinese cuisines not found in the Cantonese canon, such as Fujianese chicken
wing tips stewed with the red lees left behind in the rice wine–making process; northern Chinese breads; hand-pulled and knife-cut noodles from Lanzhou; and Mao
Zedong's Hunanese favorites like julienne potatoes with vinegar or red-cooked pork
with chestnuts.

To finish our explorations of the origins of New York's fascination with Chinese
food, let us look at a single menu in my collection, dated 1943 from the Port Arthur
Restaurant on Mott Street in the heart of Chinatown. It is printed in red and black
on heavy card stock. The complex cover graphics include the Chinese characters for
Lu Sun, the southern Chinese peninsula better known to many as Port Arthur, site of
the Boxer Rebellion. Two other characters on the cover of the menu reveal what can
be loosely termed a Ho family mission statement: *gung yin* (respectful welcome). The
name Port Arthur in English is printed on the menu in now-cliché brushstroke letters
meant to imitate Chinese calligraphy. Old-fashioned line drawings of clouds, which
can symbolize wealth, run up and down the borders of the menu, alongside a dragon,
two phoenixes, and other mythical creatures.

There is one other Chinese symbol on the cover of the Port Arthur menu, the
symmetrical *fa long* (method of turning), which is repeated four times as a decorative
motif, once in each compass direction. This ancient symbol refers to a principal tenet
of Buddhism, that life is continuous and that even in death there is reincarnation. Chinese people would deduce from it that Port Arthur served vegetarian food befitting
Buddhists. Today this character is used as part of the name of the Chinese religious
group Falun Gong, but most Westerners would not have recognized the symbol until
the 1940s: the swastika.

The dishes served on Port Arthur's second-floor balcony and third floor were as
good as, if not better than, food that was available in China. The head chef was Siu
Tong, and thoughts of his eight-jewel chicken stuffed with sticky rice makes people
pine for a style of regal Cantonese cookery that now has all but vanished. Inside, the
handsome menu lists no fewer than thirty variations of chop suey, including plain
chop suey for 20 cents and less common varieties like mutton and almond chicken
chop suey. "Special Port Arthur duck chop suey, served for two," cost $2. There were
soups, chicken and seafood dishes, omelets, fried rice, cold dishes, sandwiches, and
side dishes. Rice was "5 cents per bowl additional." Tea lovers had a choice of oolong
in five varieties: Loong Sue, Suey Sinn, Lin Som, Loong Jan, and Won Moo.

Port Arthur's drink menu confirms its place in the pantheon of high-class New
York bars. In addition to an international array of brandies, whiskeys, and gins,
Port Arthur's bartenders mixed such fabulously named period drinks as automobile
cocktails, horse's necks, sherry flips, and what must have been a lush's delight, the
morning cocktail. The lengthy wine list is superb and shows that Chinese food had
been paired with fine alcohols for a lot longer than today's haute Chinese spots would
have you believe. Port Arthur offered more than thirty wines, including both red and
white Chinese rice wines; three German Rhine wines: Hochheimer, Laubenheimer,

and Neirstener; but only two Italian wines: Bosca red and Chianti. French grapes are highly prized by Chinese epicures, and Port Arthur had a full complement of cognacs and champagnes.

Even though Chinese cuisine is not well known for its desserts, quite a few are listed on the Port Arthur menu, in small columns labeled "Preserves" (bottled fruits and ice cream), "Crystallized" ("golden limes" and "gingers"), "Cakes and Nuts" ("almond cake, rice cake, li chee nuts"), and "Candies." The last column uses the Latin name for sesame, *Sesamum*, as it then was probably not nearly as common an ingredient as it is today.

I had several extended conversations with the grandson of Port Arthur's owner, Bruce Ho, himself a well-known innovator of Chinese cuisine. We met in Manhattan, at the apartment he shares with his wife, Polly, on East Fifty-seventh Street, just a stone's throw from his erstwhile eponymous establishment, Bruce Ho's Four Seas, on East Fifty-seventh Street near Lexington Avenue. At one time, this address was that of East Horizon, the first Cantonese restaurant on Fifty-seventh Street, but today the original, bronze-mirrored facade fronts a Starbucks.

Ho greeted me at the elevator bank on the tenth floor of the luxury high-rise. His firm handshake and warm smile were a gracious welcome, and I felt at ease as we walked down the hallway to his apartment, chatting about the weather. The spacious Midtown aerie is decorated with bronze, silk, mother-of-pearl, and wooden Chinese antiquities. Not every Chinese restaurant worker has been so successful as to enjoy life from such a vantage, but it was an ideal setting in which to learn about Ho's complicated life: its ups and downs and the names, places, and stories weaving in and out of his nine decades.

Ho likes to say that he has "lived in two worlds." Born in the United States, he was taken back to China as a boy, only to return to America as an adult. Unlike other men in the Ho family, Bruce resisted life's temptations and walked the straight and narrow. "I want people to know me. I have had a tough life. I worked hard. I made myself. I'm still working hard," he explained, easing into the interview. His ocher- and cinnabar-colored apartment features many framed pictures. My host pointed out autographed photographs of his family enjoying themselves at swanky Manhattan restaurants with celebrities like the glamorous Ginger Rogers. From time to time during the interviews, Polly Ho illustrated her husband's tales with photos, menus, and memorabilia pulled from a crowded hall closet.

Ho directed me to his mantelpiece, where, next to porcelain statues of Chinese gods, leans a framed menu. It is another copy of a menu from Port Arthur, his family's long-standing and much-fabled restaurant on Mott Street. Near the menu hang two large frames filled with color reproductions of trading cards and postcards dating back to the late nineteenth century. The old advertisements depict buildings and scenes from the early and formative New York Chinatown. All were enterprises of Bruce Ho's grandfather, Soy Kee, whose name means "nice and peaceful person."

Soy Kee emigrated from China in the 1880s, first to San Francisco's Chinatown and then to New York. Like other pioneering Chinese immigrants of the time, he was attracted by the promise of the "Golden Mountain," mainland China's nickname for the deceptively lucrative New World. Like his compatriots, Soy Kee suffered under government restrictions effectively mandating a bachelor lifestyle.

Almost all early Chinese immigrants to New York were from the city of Toisan in Guangdong Province. In 1965, the federal government passed an act designed to loosen the stringent quotas of Chinese immigrants, which had been established in 1924. In the 1970s, President Richard Nixon reopened relations between the United States and China, and New Yorkers at last got a taste of Sichuanese, Hunanese, and other cuisines from the vast provinces of China. (In fact, Nixon's visit to China in 1972 was directly responsible for the opening of the aforementioned Hunam restaurant in New York. For me and many others, Hunam's spicy chicken with peanuts was a blazing and addictive assault on the senses, not unlike New York City itself. By the mid-1980s, when the East Village restaurant Miraculous Mandarin changed its name to Sizzling Szechuan, New Yorkers were already accustomed to the spicier food that followed the more elegant Cantonese fare they had come to know as Chinese.)

But back to Ho's grandfather, who must have instilled eponymity in Bruce. Early in the twentieth century, Ho's grandfather started Soy Kee Company, an import-export emporium at 36 Pell Street, at the corner of Mott. Later he moved the company to a former horse stable, on the first floor of 7–9 Mott Street—downstairs. It was Bruce's father, Jack, who acquired Port Arthur from its founder, Cho Gum Fai. Eventually, the Hos installed the first escalator in Chinatown, providing easy access to the second- and third-floor Port Arthur Restaurant and Bar (multistoried Chinese restaurants traditionally serve the finer fare on the upper floors). The Ho family was following a practice constant over the centuries: whether Chinese restaurants are fancy or shabby, most are family-run affairs.

Both Port Arthur and Soy Kee were conveniently located near the elevated train at Chatham Square and the subway station at Worth Street. One early-twentieth-century postcard of Soy Kee depicts well-heeled gentlemen in an elegant "reception room" waiting to be shown the Chinese porcelains, silks, woods, and curios that were highly prized in New York City. Around 1923 or 1924, a second Soy Kee Company opened on Fifth Avenue in what is now the Dunhill Building. It stayed in operation for about a decade.

Old postcards show that Port Arthur had partitions in its luxurious main dining room, creating adjustable East and West Halls for banquets and private parties of all sizes. There even was a special room set aside for a bride's traditional change into four different red dresses for various stages of the wedding reception. Port Arthur also had four four-top tables on the second-floor balcony, which overlooked Mott Street. The restaurant's elegant and expensive teak-and-mahogany tables were inlaid with mother-of-pearl and marble. Silk lanterns were festooned with dragons that held red tassels in their fangs. Gorgeous gilded carvings, some with six-inch-deep relief, covered every conceivable surface. Ho's father eventually sold 7–9 Mott Street, but there are rumors that the third-floor Port Arthur dining room is still there, intact. The period staircase between the second and third floors definitely remains, replete with its ornate gilded wood carvings. During the 1980s and 1990s, the building was home

A postcard and menu from the Port Arthur Restaurant. (Collection of Harley Spiller)

to a supermarket, but that closed in 2003. In 2005, "I Love NY" T-shirts and the like were being hawked from folding tables outside the gated doorways.

Grandfather Ho's success allowed him to bring family members from China. First, an older sister moved her family to San Francisco, and then Jack and his bride, Kam Su, came directly to New York. Jack attended business school at New York University and went to work at Soy Kee.

Bruce, the middle of Jack and Kam Su's three children, was born in 1926 in the Suffolk County village of Bayshore, Long Island. His Chinese name, Kai (formal salutation) Hoy (open the door), was surely prescient for the baby maître d' to be. A Catholic sister in his postwar English-language school gave Bruce his Western name. Soon after, Kam See and Jack proudly attached a favorite baby picture of Kai Hoy to Form 430, their son's citizenship papers.

Bruce Ho returned from China to New York on December 8, 1949, to work in the family business. By the end of World War II, "Soy Kee [the store] was already gone." Although his father had returned to China, Bruce and his uncle John stayed to work in the family restaurant on Mott Street. Later, Port Arthur was awarded Chinatown's first liquor license and made good use of it. Ho said that being the first

Chinese restaurant to get a liquor license was nothing special; it just "happened to be the first." The bar was in the back of the restaurant, but in later years, bars were required to be up front and visible from the window to ensure that no illegal operations were taking place.

Along with the bartender Sidney Dung, Uncle John built up the nightlife to the point that the elite of Chinatown society was coming to drink at Port Arthur's second-floor bar every night of the week. It did not hurt that Uncle John's brother-in-law was Shavey Lee, the "mayor of Chinatown."

In the early 1950s, Ho struck out on his own, working in a variety of restaurants in Midtown Manhattan, including Ruby Foo's on Fifty-second Street and Broadway, right in the middle of the Great White Way. Nearly thirty, Ho wanted to "settle down," so he went to work at "a place at 994 Second Avenue at Fifty-second Street by the name of Bill Chan's Gold Coin." The Midtown eatery had opened on September 23, 1953, and catered to an exclusive Western clientele, steadily gaining fame as one of the city's most exclusive Cantonese restaurants. Gorilla-tough Bill Chan had been recruited for St. John's University's basketball team but never attended school because doctors found a problem with his heart. Chan then went into restaurant work, and it was at the legendary second-floor Port Arthur bar, under the Hos' tutelage, that he learned how to tend bar. Even today, there are very few Chinese restaurant schools or classes, and most employees learn their trade from co-workers.

Bruce Ho had worked for Bill Chan for a decade when a new Gold Coin opened on Second Avenue and Forty-fifth Street in 1964, providing the initial spark for the mid-1960s vogue of upscale Chinese and Polynesian restaurants focusing more on drinks and atmosphere than on food. By then, Ho had "become a big boy with a few dollars," so he struck out with a partner to open House of Mah Jong on Jericho Turnpike in Syosset, Long Island. "We did very well. There was a big garden and a couple of acres. We called it House of Mah Jong to make sure they knew it was a Chinese restaurant. We mostly attracted Jewish people [they had "few Chinese customers"], and Jewish people know mah jong has got to be Chinese." On April 30, 1964, Ho opened Bruce Ho's Four Seas, and he got "most of the very good high clientele, very good people." Comedian Alan King, a friend and Long Island regular, followed Ho to Manhattan. King, who wrote the book *Help! I'm a Prisoner in a Chinese Bakery*, succeeded Frank Sinatra as head of the Friars Club, of which Ho became a member and is still a member, as is his daughter.

It was at the Friars Club where Ho developed an amusing chopstick routine to entertain his mainly Western clientele. Burt Bacharach, a newspaper man who loved assorted seafood Cantonese, patronized Four Seas, as did his son Burt Jr., the composer and musician, with his then wife, actress Angie Dickinson (who likes her Chinese food spicy). Dudley Moore and Susan Anton were regulars who unfailingly ordered lobster rolls, spare ribs, and sizzling pork *wor ba*. Gossip columnist Cindy Adams and her husband, comedian Joey Adams, are connoisseurs of Chinese food who regularly opted for dim sum and dishes with black bean sauce. Designer Calvin Klein loved ribs and lobster fried rice. Studio 54 impresario Steve Rubell often rushed in and out for a plate of mixed hot appetizers. Most people, whether or not they are famous, enjoy being recognized. Bruce Ho understands this, and a key to the great success of his "clubby" restaurants was his personalized and friendly greetings of his regulars.

Although Ho did not have a staff photographer, he welcomed independent photographers who wanted to sell souvenir portraits to his patrons. Dignitaries from all walks of life ate at Four Seas: "We even had Roosevelt Jr. come in. Everyone just looked—no one was allowed to talk to him. Also, as you see [he points to a photograph], Donald Trump's father, and when we sit on the table with Holland Steel, the people who did all the big buildings and structures, mixing steel." Ho also is a discreet source of information, such as developer Donald Trump's preference for exceedingly simple food.

Bruce Ho attributes his success in the trade to his training in the 1950s, when he

> was a maître d' at the Gold Coin. I learned the business from there. I already learned the business from Port Arthur, but then I come uptown, and I can come because I'm American born, and I'm a little taller, at that time 5 feet 9 inches, and a little slimmer, not like today with a big belly, and I greet[ed] people accordingly, and I become very good at receiving. You have to know your people. Who's taking out all the beautiful girls? When he comes here, I know he likes to party! Some like to be treated like regal ladies. Then you're talking about the attorney general of the United States who might come with some underworld people. I know where they want to sit. [Ho never had enough capital to build an exclusive private room.] This is something that you have to know. You've got different atmospheres. You've got to know how to sit them. You've got to know how to deal with them.

Although he created a menu of exclusively Cantonese food, he served his customers whatever they asked for. His first chef was Stanley Seid, whom Polly Ho wooed from Trader Vic. Ho noted that Seid was "more or less Jewish." Phyllis Ho, the Hos' only child, remembers how "Uncle" Stanley would cook for her with the "tiniest pinch of salt with the hugest spoon." Seid made a marinated, panfried shrimp like no other. "Even Bill Hong envies the recipe," Ho commented.

Soon after Bruce Ho's Four Seas opened, Ruby Foo's head cook, Lau Wai, a my-way-or-the-highway kind of person from Toisan, asked Ho for a job. Lau Wai had learned cooking in Chinatown, and Ho hired him for his precision. He stayed as the restaurant's second chef until Four Seas closed in 1998. When Four Seas was finally being dismantled, Bruce found some long-forgotten bottles of snake-heart wine. He had given the workers some of the prized and potent tonic as a gift in the 1960s, and gave some again to Stanley. It was an emotional moment for both of them. Stanley observed that he had never worked for anyone longer than six months before he stayed with the Ho family for more than thirty years.

Diners and revelers flocked to Bruce Ho's Four Seas in midtown for both its cuisine and its hospitable ambience. Ho explained the critical factor of "understanding people, greeting people. See what they like and understand them." Patrons might be reluctant to spend a certain amount of money on dinner, but "if they like the service, fine." He also stressed the importance of the maître d' passing this knowledge to the captains and so on, all the way to the bus staff. "Instruct the people next to you, and they're gonna pass it down. Remember what customers like," he said. I interjected that it always feels good when a waiter remembers me and can bring my favorite tea without having to ask. He agreed, "That's right, that's right. Exactly that way and no two ways about it."

I asked why Chinese food, an older and arguably more complex cuisine than French fare, cannot command French-restaurant prices. "It's a way of living," he replied. "When people go for Chinese food or French food, they really don't know what it's all about. Once they taste it a little bit, they say, 'Oh, that's very good.' They're not a connoisseur. They say that just for compromise, 'Oh it's very good, very tasty,'" but the discussion rarely gets deeper than that. "Also, they want to show how intelligent they are." So they have conversations that begin with the food and wander into discussions of other topics, and "then [they] get lost somewhere."

Today, Ho remains a student of the restaurant business and has remembrances and anecdotes about seemingly every Chinese restaurant one can name. I asked whether he was friendly with other restaurateurs of his era, and he replied that he was but that they found him a bit independent. There was no association of restaurant owners, formal or informal, because everyone worked long hours. Of course, he added, "You pay your respects and visit other restaurants and also go out to be seen, perhaps in a Madison Avenue hotel, or at Harry's Bar at the Waldorf."

As attentive to cooking as he is, Ho never trained as a chef and does not cook for himself. Polly Ho often makes a simple family favorite, chicken marinated in soy sauce and panfried. When the couple married in 1959, a traditional banquet was held, of course, at the Port Arthur. Bruce recited the entire wedding menu from memory:

Yu chi tang (shark's fin soup)
Three appetizers: panfried shrimp, lobster rolls, crabs Rangoon
Chicken with broccoli
Pork with broccoli, water chestnuts, and straw mushrooms
Bird's nest soup (a rare and intricate preparation)
Dai buh goo (large black mushrooms in oyster sauce, usually served after bird's
    nest soup to collect any stray feathers that may have been in the bird's nest)
Gua loong gnop (duck skin in wheat buns)
Sautéed hearts of choy sum (the best part of this green vegetable)
Duck meat young chow fried rice (duck is a symbol of fidelity and joy)
Yee mein (very long noodles eaten without biting to symbolically ensure long life)
Sai mai lo (tapioca pearls), which, Phyllis Ho noted, is a dessert akin to today's
    popular "bubble" teas, known by nicknames such as dragon eyes and frog
    eggs

There was even a second seating at the Hos' wedding reception, to accommodate all their colleagues who had to wait for their restaurants to close for the evening before they could celebrate at Port Arthur. After Bruce Ho's recitation of their wedding banquet from a half century earlier, his wife exclaimed wonderingly, "You remember all that?"

Bruce and Polly Ho's wedding reception at the Port Arthur Restaurant. Chinese brides traditionally carried trays of tea to the guests. At the Hos' reception, the two new twists to this tradition were that the men helped and that some of the tea was replaced with whiskey! (Photograph courtesy of Phyllis Ho)

Polly Ho always was an important partner in the business, largely because of the experience she gained in the late 1950s, when she worked in her hometown of Seattle at the Trader Vic's in the Westin Hotel. Trader Vic, or Victor J. Bergeron Jr., a French Jew, was a legendary epicurean and bon vivant. Polly described the "Trader's" first restaurant-bar as a "two-by-four dainty old house." The tiny cabin in Oakland, California, opened in 1934 with the quixotic name Hinky Dinks. Polly advised Vic when he opened branches in cities throughout the world and worked for him from 1954 until the mid-1980s.

In the late 1950s, Vic announced big plans for Polly in Havana, Cuba, but she refused, "No thanks; that's the one place I won't go." She had heard that the Cuban staff was unreliable, and her decision proved to be a wise one: only six months after Trader Vic's Havana opened in 1958, the manager was shot at as he ran for one of the last airplanes evacuating Americans from Cuba. Later that year, Polly accepted Vic's one-way airplane ticket to New York to supervise the opening of Trader Vic's in the Savoy Hilton, at 7 East Fifty-eighth Street and Fifth Avenue (the hotel was eventually razed for the present-day General Motors Building).

Trader Vic's at the Savoy was a huge success. One day, Bruce Ho asked the maître d', "How's business?" and was told, "We're a little over 950 [reservations] for the day." Sugary-sweet Polynesian fare was a draw, but the main attraction for Trader Vic's, and the legions of competitors it spawned, was its tropical drinks. Bruce Ho's restaurants also relied heavily on liquor sales, and the success of Four Seas eventually drew a competitor, Luau 400, farther east on Fifty-seventh Street. The "Polynesian" restaurant trade owed a debt to Polly Ho, who had helped Trader Vic create gaily decorated cocktail menus that featured lurid descriptions of the exotic ingredients and reputed effects of zombies, Samoan fog cutters, mai tais, and the like—drinks that were hugely popular in the 1950s and 1960s before they became tired and worn in the 1970s. These faux-tropical drinks disappeared in the 1980s just as Americans became more sensitive to things foreign, only to reemerge in the 1990s at Manhattan's campy Lucky Cheng's and Otto's Shrunken Head Tiki Bar. The fun that can be swizzled with these off-color cocktails persists even against today's strong waves of political correctness.

"You know what it means?" Polly Ho asked about the "Banana Cow—for butterflies in the opu." "'Opu' means "big"; when you drink it, you be like . . . you know." She laughs about the silly things she wrote years ago on menus: "Suzie Wong—could be wicked. Sailors beware" and "Coolie Collins—It's no lemon. It's kumquat." She admits it had no connection to the famous actor when she created a menu announcing, "Charlie Chan proudly offers these Special Drinks." When customers inquired about the "Tiki Puka Poka—strictly on the kini popo," her servers were instructed to "tell 'em anything and leave 'em" grinning and guessing. Mid-1960s kitsch palaces like Hawaii Kai, in Manhattan's theater district—with their poetic Pacific Island names, "exotic" moon doors, bubbling brooks forded by fake-antique wooden bridges, humongous plastic clamshells with grapefruit-size pearls, and monstrous "Tiki" glasses with eighteen-inch drinking straws—owe their popularity and success to the real-life Trader Vic, with the great help of Polly Ho, a keen observer and reporter of the likes and dislikes of Western patrons of Polynesian restaurant bars.

"Here's our collection of old, old menus," Polly said, pulling out a small stack of well-worn bills of fare from Bruce Ho's Four Seas, Trader Vic's, House of Mah Jong, and a few others. "Look at the price—dollar fifty, dollar twenty-five—ever hear of such a thing?" she marveled. Some are signed by a group of Baltimore Colt football players, including quarterback legend Johnny Unitas. Another is signed by a favorite customer and friend, the Academy Award–winning actor Sidney Poitier.

All of Bruce Ho's restaurants, including the last one to open, in 1969, Bruce Ho's Chateau Gourmet, on Route 9W about ten miles north of the George Washington Bridge, used his own menu design. These short menus reflected his belief that patrons neither wanted nor needed to "spend much time reading a long menu—one page is fine." Although the food and drink offerings changed, the large, distinctive white menu with red and blue lettering stayed fresh-looking for more than five decades. Bruce's clever graphic device, a fake tear in the cover, provided the background for his Chinese calligraphy for *zhong mei,* Mandarin for "Chinese American," a reference to his food and restaurant and himself.

These upscale 1950s Chinese restaurants seem to have taken taglines à la Mon Lay Won. Richard Mei's was "the house of quality food for the epicurean." Bruce's was "Sip, Savour for the Gourmet." Ho always made sure that his menus included the assurance that "any dishes not listed can be prepared upon request." He also helped ensure good service by noting, "Any suggestions or criticisms will be most appreciated to promote a more favorable atmosphere."

From the beginning a student of his customers' preferences and needs, Ho told me that it was customary for postwar diners to make a pit stop at the dirt-cheap Chinese restaurants on Delancey Street for a snack of egg rolls or roast pork and then to come to Port Arthur for chop suey with ambience. New Yorkers' tastes are fickle, and over the decades Ho stayed abreast of foodways, adding and deleting Polynesian, Hunan, or Sichuan dishes as trends waxed and waned. Ho insisted on old-fashioned chow mein: only onions, bean sprouts, chopped chicken, and *gee yow* (brown sauce), all cooked until very soft and tender, with noodles on the bottom. He always consulted with the head chef to create the menu and incorporated the chef's good ideas. In addition, Ho put himself in charge of listing daily specials for captains to recite to patrons. Although the large format of his menus was typical of the period, the actual number of dishes to choose from was smaller than average. But Ho believed that a limited selection meant that patrons "didn't have to keep flipping."

New York is said to have more Jewish residents than does Israel, and in locations where he drew a lot of Jewish customers, Ho knew it was best not only to keep pork offerings to a minimum but also to have a full staff ready on Sundays. When he opened his first restaurant in 1964, Ho knew that he should have a secret specialty to build camaraderie among the regulars. Accordingly, he created mish mosh, a dish that took its name from the Yiddish expression that means "all mixed up," adjusting sizzling *wor ba* platters by substituting Cantonese panfried noodles for the traditional crispy rice-noodle cakes. "Everything else on top," Ho said, "snow pea, lobster, chicken, roast pork, all chopped up with *wor ba* seasonings." At first, the captain did not understand what some regulars were clamoring for, but soon even the waiters learned a little Yiddish. Although mish mosh was never put on the menu, it remained a hit for thirty-five years.

Bruce feeds off New York's internationalism and relishes recounting how he learned about the Italian predilection for pig's knuckles:

> During Prohibition, there was Tony Merenda—had around forty speakeasies in the Bronx—the main one being Tony's Flash Inn, across from Yankee Stadium. They had lots of cash. Tony's son Danny was a real character—liked to challenge you. One day he told me he had very good pig's knuckles at Shun Lee restaurant—asked why can't I make it. Next time he came in with friends—I served him a plate—it hurt a little when he said "just as good as Shun Lee."

The Hos' collection of pretty and evocative menus from a bygone era made my mouth water. I imagined the taste of the specials that had rolled out of Chinese American kitchens when I was still mawing pablum, wondrous-sounding platters like mahi mahi with macadamia sauce. When I asked why shrimp panfried in the shell were listed as "shrimp look-in shell," Ho laughed. When asked about the American side of the menu, he replied that he "had to have American food in those years, you needed American food—steaks—because in compromise you don't want them to go somewhere else." But if they noticed, "Oh, they got American food too; let's go [in]," then he had succeeded.

It became clear during these interviews that I was dealing with a major domo. Bruce Ho has lots of good eating tips, and when we ate take-out dim sum at his home one Sunday, it had been gathered from a number of restaurants to ensure the highest quality of each particular item. During our meal, Ho revealed that he had come out of retirement to moonlight as an actor. When he provided a demonstration of how a sip of Coca-Cola can stop a persistent cough, I knew that I had asked too many questions and rose to leave. Ho graciously escorted me to the door. I could almost feel the 1950s and imagined that I was exiting Say Hoy ("Four Seas" in Cantonese), a head full of Maui Waui, a bellyful of high-class chop suey, and a New York celebrity sighting or two under my belt—in other words, fully sated at the end of another stellar night in Chow Fun City!

In loving memory of Mom

NOTES

1. Renqui Yu, "Chop Suey: From Chinese Food to Chinese American Food," *Chinese America: History and Perspectives* 1 (1987): 87–100.

2. Luc Sante, *Low Life: Lures and Snares of Old New York* (New York: Farrar, Straus and Giroux, 1991).

3. A good place to begin learning about the magnetic attraction of Brooklyn Jews to Chinese food is http://petercherches.blogspot.com/2007/01/chinese-food-early-years.html.

4. While I never tasted the food at Richard Yee's, Helen Yee and Robert Yee, two of Richard and Jane Yee's children, provided the information related here in an interview with me in May 2007.

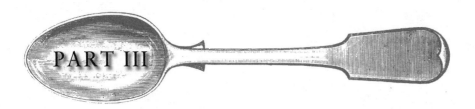

PART III

Trade

IN NEW YORK, food is a business as well as a passion, so part III, "Trade," focuses on the commercial aspects of the city's food world.

Suzanne Wasserman begins, in "Hawkers and Gawkers: Peddling and Markets in New York City," by telling the story of some of the earliest New York food traders, from hot corn girls to pushcart peddlers and through the development of markets. The history of selling food in the city has consistencies and challenges that continue even today.

Joy Santlofer next takes us through an essential but often overlooked side of the city's food commerce: the manufacture of food in all five boroughs. From multigenerational family businesses to start-ups and from highly mechanized manufacturers to handcrafters, food makers face the particular difficulties of operating in a major city, balanced against the special quality of "Asphalt *Terroir*."

In "The Soul of a Store," Mark Russ Federman writes about each of the four generations of the Russ family business, their trials, tribulations, and the atmosphere of their store during each one's reign. The Russ family's dedication to their products, customers, and employees has given their store a soul, tangible to both their customers extending through many generations and the current customers of the new Lower East Side.

Finally, the number 7 train, also called the "International Express," again leads us on a culinary cultural trail. Ramona Lee Pérez and Babette Audant apply sensory ethnography to the concept of *sabor* in "Livin' *la Vida Sabrosa*: Savoring Latino New York." Words on paper are transformed into pulsating sounds, vibrant sights, and captivating flavors and aromas along the commercial district of Roosevelt Avenue, inspiring readers to take out their MetroCards and head to the subway.

Hawkers and Gawkers

Peddling and Markets in New York City

SUZANNE WASSERMAN

NEW YORKERS have spent hundreds of years struggling with the complex and ever-present activity of peddling and vending. Despite its persistence, debates about peddling and open-air markets have consistently caused contention among vendors, merchants, shoppers, and city administrations.

The Early Public Markets

Problems with vendors and their wares date back to colonial times. The first regularly appointed marketplace in New Amsterdam occupied one hundred feet of vacant land between the warehouse of the Dutch West India Company and Fort Amsterdam. Settlers called the area Market Street or Market-field. Here, until 1641, Native Americans and country people (called "strangers" by the Dutch colonizers) sold corn, pelts, and fish each day to the residents of New Amsterdam. The problem was that the sellers arrived neither at a stated time nor on a particular day. In 1641, to help mitigate the chaos created by the haphazard arrival of foodstuffs, officials settled on Monday as the weekly market day.[1]

Because local farmers grew tobacco at the expense of more diverse crops, early European settlers often endured food shortages. Residents, anxious about the availability of foodstuffs, would wait at the landing place, or strand, along the shore of the East River from Whitehall to Broad Street for the farmers and Native American traders to arrive from Brooklyn and Long Island. In 1656, when that trade also became too chaotic, officials established the first public market at the popular location on the strand on the east side of Pearl Street. Saturday became the official market day.

In 1658, officials established the first public meat market in response to charges of corruption at the company store. Called the Broadway Shambles, the meat market stood in front of Fort Amsterdam. Twelve "sworn butchers" were empowered to slaughter all cattle within city limits. Asser Levy, one of the butchers and listed as "a Jew," requested and was granted an exemption from killing hogs. In 1675, the Custom-House Bridge Market replaced the Strand Market.[2]

As the city grew, the public markets flourished. By 1683, market regulations allowed the sale of produce and meat every day but prohibited unauthorized peddlers from selling goods outside the official markets. Although Custom-House Bridge Market remained the primary market until it was razed in 1708, other markets opened as well. Broad Street Market, Coenties Slip Fish Market, and Old Slip Market all were established during the seventeenth century, and at Old Slip, several butchers' slaves conspired to revolt in 1741.[3]

Throughout the seventeenth century, the Common Council made recommendations for market locations. Customs changed with the creation of Fly Market in 1699, as citizens who lived on Pearl Street petitioned for a market there. By the mid-eighteenth century, Fly Market rivaled the other markets because of its location next to the recently established ferry that brought Long Island farmers to Manhattan. It also served as a slave market. But by 1795, Fly Market was overcrowded, filthy, and dilapidated, and it closed in 1823. After Fly Market opened, other communities petitioned for their own markets. Those built in the first half of the eighteenth century included Wall Street Market, Flatten Barrack Market, Broadway Market (where the practice of trading between Native Americans and slaves was outlawed in 1740 for supposedly promoting "disease"), White Hall Slip Market (built on the site of the old Custom-House Bridge Market in 1746), Exchange Market, and Peck Slip Market (the first brick market built by the wealthy community that faced Water Street). Markets built in the second half of the eighteenth century included Bear (or Hudson) Market, Crown Market, Oswego Market, Catherine Market, and Spring Street Market.[4]

In the first half of the nineteenth century, communities built, with the permission of the Common Council, Corlaers Hook (Grand Street) Market, Grand-Market Place, Collect Market, Greenwich Market, Goveneur Market, Washington Market, Fulton Fish Market, Centre Market, Essex Market, Franklin Market, Manhattan Market, Clinton Market, Tompkins Market, Jefferson Market, Monroe Market, Harlem Market, and Fulton Market, which replaced the old Fly Market. Women often brought their foodstuffs to sell at the markets. Some came from New Jersey with butter, pot cheese, curds, and buttermilk; others, like one German immigrant widow, raised garden vegetables on land at Allen and Rivington streets.[5]

Corruption and graft plagued the markets from the beginning. When, for example, yellow fever epidemics ravaged the city periodically in the late eighteenth and early nineteenth centuries, butchers and farmers deserted the markets in the infected districts. "Shirkers," or "shark" butchers, preyed on a vulnerable public. Another corrupt activity was practiced by "forestallers," or speculators taking advantage of desperate farmers who could not find or afford stalls in the markets.[6]

Until 1841, meat and vegetables could be sold only in public markets, which allowed for the control and inspection of meat. Butchers, who wore high hats and long-tailed coats, paid a tax for the exclusive right to sell in the markets and were considered the aristocrats of the early markets. But in 1841, they began to sell meat from shops. Although merchant folklore has it that the first butcher was fined $100, the public preferred the shops, and thus shops came to eclipse the public markets.[7]

Increasingly, itinerant peddlers, or "hucksters," roamed the city streets. Women, African Americans, and children, often the poorest of urban dwellers, survived by selling fruit, vegetables, candies, and hot corn on busy street corners. In fact, women may have been the first peddlers in New York City. One African American woman peddler sang:

Hot Corn, hot corn, here's your lily white corn
Hot Corn all hot, just come out of the boiling pot.[8]

The Emergence of the Stationary Pushcart Market

As New York's population and economy expanded after the Civil War, the city's needs for food supplies exploded as the population rose from 400,000 in 1840 to 2 million in 1880. Farmers close to the city could not meet the huge demand. Perishables arrived by railroad and steamship from all over the country and abroad, but in a totally unregulated manner with no control over demand, quality, or price. Sometimes as many as three hundred carloads of produce arrived in a single day, and oversupply became commonplace. Clearly, the distribution channels had to be expanded, and the pushcart peddler became the middle person, disposing of the surplus by selling in the new stationary pushcart markets.[9]

Officially, a city ordinance forbade peddling in one spot for longer than thirty minutes, but the immense density of immigrant neighborhoods like the Lower East Side convinced vendors that they could defy the law and start selling from a stationary spot. In 1886, four peddlers planted pushcarts on Hester Street. Considered the city's first documented stationary pushcart market, the vendors immediately did a brisk business with local customers. Markets like it soon replaced the earlier weekly markets; in 1887 Paddy's Market opened on Ninth Avenue, followed by the Grand Street Market in 1893 and the Orchard Street Market and Rivington Street Market in 1898.[10]

For the next fifty years, the pushcart, or open-air, markets existed as an integral part of New York City life, especially in the immigrant neighborhoods. Although not all open-air markets are composed of actual pushcarts, open-air markets and pushcart markets have identical functions. In eastern Europe, the pushcart market was a central part of daily Jewish life. Indeed, peddling was an extremely important occupation, especially after the May Laws of 1880/1881 prohibited Jews from owning or renting land. The pushcart market also was a central institution for Italian immigrants. As one observer noted, "The pushcart trade exists only in Jewish and Italian settlements. . . . The pushcart . . . is the bond between the Italians and the Jews." The local market "was an important immigrant institution in ethnic neighborhoods. It provided employment and gave customers a place to shop within the context of their own language and culture."[11]

The Ins and Outs of Peddling

Needing neither a large amount of capital nor a command of English, peddlers worked in a familiar cultural, economic, and social context. Most of them rented carts from a stable, but a minority owned their own carts. In 1880, rentals cost about 10 cents a day, and by 1925 the rent had doubled. The carts were a standard size—eight feet long and four feet wide. When stationary, they had two wheels supported by a stick at one end. Factories outside New York manufactured the wheels, axles, and springs, and blacksmiths and carpenters in the city made the bed and trestle.[12]

Typically, vendors sold surplus fruit and vegetables. Italian shoppers were partial to greens, peppers, cheese, garlic, nuts, and olives; Jewish patrons preferred fish (fresh and preserved), onions, potatoes, cabbage, and carrots. Vendors also sold pickles, sweet potatoes, soda water, halvah, *arbis* (hot chickpeas), knishes, hot corn, chestnuts, fruit, nuts, pretzels, ice cream, and chewing gum. About one-third of the pushcart business was made up of inexpensive and slightly damaged nonfood merchandise: clothing (underwear, hosiery, hats, and shoes), furnishings (enamel ware, pots and pans, curtains, and bedding), as well as handbags, buttons, thread, and beads. Unlicensed women and children sometimes sold shopping bags.[13]

Before 1880, peddlers would haul their carts at dawn to the fish and produce markets on the docks, buy a small quantity, and then push their carts uptown. But this became increasingly difficult as the pushcart markets grew in size. In response, special carting agencies emerged, and peddlers hired trucks or express companies to deliver goods to their carts from the wholesale markets.

At the wholesale markets, the middlemen who collected, graded, shipped, and distributed produce were divided into shippers, commission merchants and wholesalers, jobbers, and retailers. Few regulations governed their practices, and goods often had to pass through several dealers before reaching the retailer. Washington Street Market was the principal wholesale market, extending for a dozen blocks north of Vesey Street to North Moore Street. Secondary wholesale distributing points, or jobbers' markets, were located at Harlem Market and Wallabout Market in Brooklyn.[14]

Groups of peddlers would select a single person, typically a family member, to act as purchasing agent and go to the wholesale market each day to search for bargains. These buyers, or purchasing agents, would arrive as early as 1:00 A.M. in the summer and 4:00 A.M. in the winter to search for the cheapest items, the smallest sizes, the lowest grades, the leftovers, and the odd lots.[15]

Peddlers set up their carts in the streets in the early-morning hours as horses and wagons and trucks arrived from the wholesale markets, driving up to the back of the carts and unloading their goods. The vendors then unpacked and arranged their merchandise. Peddling was backbreaking work. Earlier, while the economy was expanding after the Civil War, some German Jewish peddlers had been able to exchange the rags of the peddler for the riches of the merchant. But after the 1880s, the changing economy tightened the market for peddling, and peddlers increasingly ended up as owners or, more typically, renters of pushcarts. Some peddled as late as 2:30 A.M., selling by lantern light. Only through self-exploitation were some peddlers able to start small businesses in those years. At night, peddlers stored their carts, along with any unsold produce, in nearby cellars. Some peddlers who owned their own carts took their carts home, unloaded the produce, and stored it in their tenement apartments, chaining the carts in the street.[16]

Many families operated on the traditional lines of a family economy, with women and children making up a large percentage of the pushcart workers. "There are many women in the pushcart business, it turns out," wrote an observer from the *New York Evening Post*, "many who rent their own carts . . . just as the men do, but who get them by proxy, it being a law, unwritten but acknowledged, that women should not undertake pushcart trundling."[17]

By 1900, 25,000 immigrants had availed themselves of this option. In her novel *Breadgivers*, Anzia Yezierska captures the experience of peddling with her portrayal of ten-year-old Sara Smolinsky. Sara sells herring on Hester Street to feed her hungry family:

> Herring, Herring! A Bargain in the world! Pick them out yourself. Two cents apiece. . . . I cried out my herring with all the burning fire of my ten old years. . . . Nothing was before me but the hunger in our house, and no bread for the next meal if I didn't sell the herring . . . like a houseful of hungry mouths my heart cried, "Herring-Herring, two cents apiece."[18]

Attempts to Regulate the Markets

The city of New York did little to supervise the markets before the twentieth century, even though public outcries grew in strength and number. A few outdated local statutes governed the regulation of the markets, and the statute that prohibited peddlers from stopping in one place for more than thirty minutes was still in place despite the huge growth of stationary markets. In 1904, for example, 5,124 peddlers were arrested for staying in one place too long. The system encouraged graft and corruption, and the pushcart peddlers were at the mercy of local police. Chaos prevailed. The markets stank, unclean and unsupervised. Hester Street became known as Chazar, or Pig Market. Another contemporary observer noted about the pushcart markets that "the crush and the stench were enough to suffocate one."[19]

During the late nineteenth century, a growing public outcry emerged from middle-class reformers and social investigators that focused on competing visions of the proper use of public space in the city. According to the architectural historian Daniel Bluestone, the reformers increasingly advocated a narrow view of the street as an artery for traffic only and claimed that commerce divorced from the street would "raise the possibility of higher density and [thus] higher real estate values." Finally in 1906, in response, Mayor George McClellan organized the Pushcart Commission. The commissioners discovered that the peddlers were able to survive despite the petty blackmail by police, the extortion by shopkeepers, and the abuses of the padrone system, which allowed one man to own up to 170 carts and to lease them out to peddlers illegally. The peddlers' hard-earned money was used to pay some of the police and licensing officials to ignore an expired license or to secure a particular place on the street. Proclaimed one peddler: "I know them that pays in a quarter or fifty cents occasionally, and keeps out of the muddle, but it has to be done on the sly—slip the money in a pear or plum and offer the fruit to a policeman, on account of its looking so tempting."[20]

The commission recommended establishing official permanent places for the pushcarts in open-air markets and allowing only four to a block in certain restricted districts. The commission saw the pushcart "army" as a "seeming necessity," albeit a nuisance. It did find, however, that not all the peddlers were paupers and newly arrived immigrants, as the press popularly portrayed them. The commission also found that food could be bought more cheaply and at a better quality from pushcarts than in the stores in the same neighborhoods. The peddlers themselves worried about the implications of such a commission. As Harry Plotkin, the president of the Eastside Pushcart Association, wrote: "Dear Mayor McClellan: Please do not forget that we are poor people, that peddling is our ONLY means of earning our bread, and that unless you will grant us this right to peddle, we will fall burdens to the city and to the charitable institutions."[21]

Conditions in the retail markets continued to worsen, and by 1912, there were twice as many peddlers on the streets. But few concrete changes were made until the establishment in 1917 of the Department of Markets, which took over the operation and supervision of the city's wholesale markets, including the Bronx Terminal Market, Wallabout Market in Brooklyn, West Washington Market, Gansevoort Market, and the Fulton Fish Market. By 1925, 31,000 New Yorkers made their livelihood peddling. The vast majority, 72 percent, were Jewish; 22 percent were Italian; and the rest were German, Irish, Russian, Spanish, and American-born. There were fifty-three markets—thirty-four in Manhattan, seventeen in Brooklyn, and two in the Bronx—varying in size from one to fourteen blocks long and from as few as 10 carts to as many as 470.[22]

The Impact of the Great Depression on Peddling

The Depression greatly exacerbated the precarious economic conditions. By 1930, 47,000 family members depended on earnings made from pushcarts, which generated $40 million to $50 million each year. More than 50 percent of all the pushcarts in the city were to be found on the Lower East Side.[23]

The peddler and his 5-cent apples became the classic and ubiquitous folkloric symbol of the economic hardships of the Depression years. Nonetheless, peddling kept unemployed New Yorkers off charity and, later, off relief, both of which many regarded as the ultimate humiliation. The story of a young peddler named Francis Bromberg is a case in point. In the spring of 1928, scribbling in pencil at her pushcart stand, she wrote to Lillian Wald:

I have one of those outside pushcart stands which I [illegible] and sell Ladies' Underwear. When the weather is warm and favorable, my father when he feels well helps me. But he is a sick man with asthma and very frail. . . . My father cannot be outdoors when the weather is the least bit cold . . . he even coughs so that my heart almost breaks watching him . . . so I can't let him down. My mother is very, very ill now, with Diabetes . . . and has Cardiac Heart. . . . I have NO MONEY to move, as I am living a hand to mouth existence sometimes not even that. . . . Please don't refer me to the Jewish Social Service because I don't want charity. I want a loan so I can go on. . . . I myself am anything but well and staying out in the cold with a T.B. hip is no fun.[24]

Another New Yorker, Leopold Patreski, a Polish immigrant, had worked as a kitchen assistant in a hospital for eighteen years. After he lost his job, he refused to go on relief and worked for the next two years as a dock worker, a gardener, a pick-and-shovel man on the Sixth Avenue subway, and a dishwasher at an automat. Finally in 1934, he set up a pushcart selling razor blades. Eventually, he added shoelaces, polish, brushes, and socks to his cart. He was able to avoid charity and keep his four children in school at the same time.[25]

For others, though, even peddling did not provide the basic necessities of life. A woman named Emily Coleman, her husband, and five children were penniless. In late 1930, she wrote to a settlement house, asking for help: "Dear Friends: We are in just need I wish you could help us in some way. Back with our rent, nothing to eat." A few years later, in the depths of the Depression years, her situation deteriorated. "My home is a wreck," she wrote. "I'll tell you the truth that I haven't a bed sheet for my beds and the bed the poor kiddies sleep in, its not fit for a dog to lay in." She continued: "George is really ashamed to face you. You have helped us in time of need a great deal. George had planned to pay you back last summer for the money which you gave him . . . but [he] didn't make nothing at peddling. . . . We sure are up against it. I could write a book of all we are going through."[26]

Itinerant peddling was rampant during these years. A curb market existed on Hester Street where peddlers would try to make enough money for shelter in the Municipal Lodging. "They [cops] move us on a couple of times a day, but we always come back," explained one.[27]

The Fight to Abolish the Pushcart Markets

City merchants did not empathize with the plight of the unemployed; instead, they viewed the influx of peddlers as a nuisance. During these years, the fight to rid the city of open-air pushcart markets began in earnest when city merchants initiated a campaign to wipe them out. One of their primary goals was the "establishment of central public market buildings and the abolition of all curb pushcarts."[28]

Members of several city merchants' associations as well as some reform groups endorsed the anti-pushcart crusade. Together, members of the Queens, Brooklyn, Bronx, Lower East Side, and Harlem Chambers of Commerce; Anti-Litter Bureau of the Merchants Association of New York; Community Councils of New York; New York Board of Trade; and First Avenue Association jointly created the New York Conference on Public Market Research.

In the pushcart districts, store merchants considered the carts unfair competition. Merchants assumed, quite mistakenly as it turned out, that the pushcarts lowered property values and competed unfairly with "legitimate stores" for customers. Merchants also believed that the peddlers were a psychological threat, for little more than a front door and a bit of savings separated them from the pushcarts and their practices. In fact, the peddlers and merchants were tied to each other. Many merchants engaged in the same self-exploitation as the peddlers. They employed their entire families, often lived in the dark backrooms of their stores, and worked from 5:00 A.M. to 11:00 P.M. Their stores were often no more than a "heap of junk," and many were "sweat stores." The merchants were less than a step ahead of the peddlers on the rung of "success."[29]

Sales practices inside the stores and outside at the pushcarts were not very different, but merchants made a great effort to distinguish themselves from the peddlers. While simultaneously trying to rid the streets of peddlers, they also tried to reform members of their own profession. Merchants, they said, must help one another in improving "merchandising methods, general appearance and business management." Reform-minded merchants considered pricing merchandise in stores to be the clearest sign of modernization, and they would not tolerate the immigrants' custom of haggling or bargaining in their stores. Treating customers courteously and promptly were other signs of advancement.[30]

"Pulling-in," or "schlepping," was another custom that the merchants hoped to eradicate. In the shtetl, a store owner would stand "in front of his door calling in and, if need be, pulling potential customers in by their coat sleeves . . . he may even hire a boy to stand in the street and persuade customers, by words reinforced with a persuasive hand on the elbow, to come in." But because of the worsening Depression conditions in the early 1930s, as well as the incompetence and corruption of the administration of Mayor Jimmy Walker, the open-air markets were not reformed. In 1932, with the city on the verge of bankruptcy, "practically all municipal improvement projects [had been] postponed."[31]

Mayor Fiorello LaGuardia's Crusade Against Pushcart Markets

After his election to the mayoralty in 1934, Fiorello LaGuardia took up with a vengeance the issue of the public markets. "As you may know," he wrote to William Fellowes Morgan, the new commissioner of markets, "it is the aim of the present administration to remove all pushcarts now licensed by this department from the streets and enclose them in suitable market buildings." LaGuardia's battle against the pushcarts went hand in hand with his efforts to institute modern politics and efficiency and rid the city of Tammany-style corruption.[32]

LaGuardia pushed through the reforms immediately. Morgan spelled out to the peddlers the administration's intolerance of graft:

I have made it a hard and fast rule that politics is not to play any part in the issuance of licenses or the selection of stands. I realize, that heretofore, it was the practice of pushcart peddlers to apply at their local political clubs for privileges in this department. Anyone has the right to come to my office and make inquiry regarding stands in the market but the practice of coming here with politicians or letters from politicians must stop once and for all.[33]

On one occasion, "it was necessary to eject bodily a politician who DEMANDED THE RIGHT to run the markets in his districts, [but] gradually the peddlers have learned that things are different now, that political leaders have no power."[34]

By 1936, the federal government had poured huge amounts of money directly into New York City, with the aim of creating jobs by promoting municipal improvements. The City Council asked the Board of Estimate to use the city's Works Progress Administration (WPA) funds to create indoor markets, and the first indoor market opened on Park Avenue between 111th and 116th streets. Other indoor markets were opened as well, including the markets on Essex Street, First Avenue and Tenth Street, and Arthur Avenue in the Bronx. But these markets housed only a fraction of the peddlers and also charged more. For example, the new Essex Street Market housed 570 stalls and charged the peddlers $4 week, four times the amount they had paid on the streets.[35]

Peddlers, still acutely feeling the pangs of the Depression, reacted pessimistically to news of the new municipal markets. In 1936, an article in the *New York Post* stated:

THEY MIGHT STARVE FASTER INDOORS:
PUSHCART DEALERS TOO DEPRESSED TO CARE

Indoors, a pushcart woman exclaimed, the peddlers will "just starve faster, that's all . . . Nobody buys, nobody's got the money, everybody's on relief." "Inside it will be worse," claimed another, "but outside it's so bad you can't make a living. Some days I don't make 75 cents. Can you live on that?"[36]

Whether justified or not, there was a fair amount of resistance to the indoor markets. An array of New Yorkers, ranging from the peddlers themselves to newspaper writers, tourists, and housewives, resisted the change in the name of sentiment and/or tradition. While LaGuardia campaigned relentlessly to rid the streets of peddlers and pushcarts, he and the Department of Markets were angered by these voices of resistance.

Documenting the resistance to or support for the indoor markets by the peddlers themselves is difficult, for they left behind little record of their feelings. In the Federal Writers' Project study *The Italians of New York,* the researchers concluded that in general, peddlers were quite conservative, both politically and socially, and that this applied to Jewish as well as Italian peddlers.[37]

The Association of East Side Pushcart Vendors, however, did hold a number of protest meetings against the municipal markets, although nothing is known about their impact. Other vendors resisted the markets with legal action. For example, when the Park Avenue Market was built, some peddlers retained lawyers to fight against their removal from the streets. One photograph depicts a peddler at the Park Avenue site carrying a poster saying, "We paid the Sales Tax," the clear implication being that peddlers should be allowed to sell outside.[38]

Finally, some peddlers engaged in the most basic form of resistance: they simply refused to move. "There are quite a few peddlers who refused to move into the new quarters and preferred their cold, wet, nomadic existence on the streets," wrote one journalist. "They are pushcart peddlers—and they like it."[39]

Two anonymous letters to Mayor LaGuardia suggest that opposition to the push-cart evictions was not limited to the peddlers and attests to a general disapproval of the planned improvements. The first explained that some peddlers were being harassed and that they were not happy about the imminent changes:

> I would like to inform you that a great injustice is being dealt out to the pedlers [sic] of the First Avenue market by your Commissioner of Markets. He is trying to disposes [sic] a number of pedlers [sic] of their places that they have been having in this market for at least 10 to 15 yrs. (pushcart stands) These poor men have been making their humble but honest living in this market for many years. . . . There is no reason for this act except that all the men concerned are hebrews [sic]. It seems to me that your commissioner does not approve of jews [sic] making their living in a market where the Italian people have a majority.[40]

The second, signed "a citizen of the United States for the last 30 years—not a Tammany Politician but an honest Republican who likes to see justice dealt to all rich and poor alike," warned the city that the mistreatment of the peddlers would have political ramifications:

> The Peddlers deserve the maltreatment they are receiving at the hands of the supervisors because they had asked for it themselves when they had elected a mayor with undemocratic principles who gave orders to the affect [sic] that the peddlers should be chased and hounded the way they are being. . . . I beg you . . . to remedy the aforementioned evil if you do not want to lose the support of your staunchest voters, the Italian and Jewish peddlers of Ave. "C" and 1st Ave. markets.[41]

For the most part, the mayor and the Department of Markets reacted callously to the protests against the open-air markets. Sidewalk obstructions were rampant, the supervisor complained, and fights occurred daily, in which "the peddler is nearly always to blame." The Department of Markets did acknowledge that the peddlers in the open-air markets, "with a minimum of overhead expenses, carry fresh produce into the poorer districts at prices to suit the low income consumers."[42] Despite this admission, there was little else the mayor saw worthwhile about the pushcarts.

LaGuardia and Morgan could not completely ignore these various voices of protest. LaGuardia explicitly acknowledged the peddlers' resistance in a memo he sent to Commissioner Morgan, on September 2, 1939: "Proceed to discontinue the markets

. . . slowly but surely. I suggest that you start the elimination where there is the least resistance." In an effort to deal with resistance, a circular issued by the Department of Markets on December 10, 1936, was plastered on city streets in English, Italian, and Yiddish. In it, Morgan stated that "many false rumors and statements have been circulated by politicians and other interests opposed to our plan for enclosed markets." Ultimately, though, the peddlers' opposition did little to deter the erection of the municipal markets.[43]

With the creation of the indoor markets, LaGuardia had been able to accomplish what the merchants could not. With the help of the New Deal's unprecedented aid to cities, through the WPA, LaGuardia achieved his goal in about five years. Peddlers were now "forbidden" to sell merchandise on the streets, and those who could not afford an indoor stand were simply out of luck.[44]

Once the municipal markets opened, LaGuardia continued to attack the pushcart peddlers. In fact, his opposition to the peddlers became an obsession. Because LaGuardia's mother was Jewish and his father Italian, LaGuardia's colleague and supporter City Council President Newbold Morris suggested that his background influenced his attitude toward the peddlers. According to Morris, "Due to the fact, perhaps, that [LaGuardia] was of Italian descent, and because so many pushcart peddlers . . . were Italians, he was especially sensitive to the problems of these peddlers and the spectacle they created."[45]

LaGuardia singled out organ grinders—whom he considered "simply licensed beggars"—flower vendors, and even the Good Humor man. In response, the Good Humor Company accused the mayor of destroying its business, and LaGuardia threatened to cancel the company's license if it took the city to court. He wanted them to sell in stores, not on the street. LaGuardia wanted to rid the city of the peddlers' existence by making them "merchants." One observer at the opening of an indoor market noted that "the peddlers were attired in neat white coats." He continued:

Each stood by his indoor stand, his wares in orderly array. LaGuardia launched into his address, and, suddenly, in the middle of it, stooped and picked up an apple from one of the stands. "There will be no more of this," he said as he pretended to spit on the apple. . . . Pointing to his listeners in their crisp white coats, he concluded, "I found you pushcart peddlers. . . . I have made you MERCHANTS![46]

LaGuardia praised peddlers like Isadore Suranowitz, who had been a peddler on the same corner since 1913. "Tomorrow," Suranowitz predicted, referring to the opening of the market on First Avenue, "You'll see me in a clean shirt. No more like a peddler, I'll be a merchant." Unfortunately, peddlers like fifty-three-year-old Giuseppe Sallemi would never make the move from peddler to merchant. He made $1 a day selling lemons and could not possibly afford a stall indoors. Instead, he would join the ranks of the unemployed.[47]

Peddling no longer was a viable alternative to welfare or unemployment. The indoor markets put the poorest peddlers out of work permanently. Junk peddlers, many of them unemployed garment workers, mechanics, bakers, and workers in the building trades, could no longer choose to hawk their wares on the streets rather than go on the relief rolls. The city now seemed more concerned about impressing visitors to the 1939 World's Fair than about the fate of the peddlers:

> The city fathers are very much concerned with the health and beauty of the city, particularly at this time, when preparations are being made to spruce up New York for the World's Fair . . . they have decided to clean up the debris, both human and material . . . and to whitewash as prettily as possible the ugly facade of city slum life . . . is it any wonder then why some pushcart merchants . . . look more than usually worried these . . . days when so much humanity and concern is being expended on their account by the well meaning city fathers?[48]

This reality did not seem to deter LaGuardia. He claimed that the appellation "pushcart man" was an expression of contempt, and at the opening of one of the indoor markets he announced coldly that he would intensify his drive to rid the street of unlicensed peddlers.[49]

The indoor markets opened with rules and reflected LaGuardia's determination to "professionalize" the peddlers. The rules stated that no used or second-hand merchandise could be sold, a change that threatened the basis of pushcart business, since much of its merchandise was in this category. Just as important, the rules explicitly spelled out acceptable and unacceptable codes of behavior that sought to domesticate decorum, transforming the ambience of pushcarts to that of stores. The commissioner reserved the right to approve or remove signs. Rule 21, for example, stated that "permittees or their authorized helpers must remain behind their counters when transacting business and keep aisles free for the use of patrons"; rule 22 mandated that the peddlers "must, at all times, be courteous"; and rule 23 declared that there was to be "no shouting or hawking by vendors nor abusive and lewd language." An amendment further hardened the administration's position. Now, all vendors had to be citizens, which cut at the very heart of the peddler.

Resistance to Change

After three years of peddling, the Department of Markets informed Leopold Patreski that peddlers' licenses would now be granted only to citizens or holders of first papers. Although Patreski had immigrated almost a quarter of a century earlier, he was not a citizen. He worked from sunrise to sunset and had never had the chance or need to learn the English required for citizenship.[50]

Even for the peddlers who could afford stalls in the new markets, all was not rosy. Many could not adjust to the new regimen in the indoor markets and "preferred the old outdoor system . . . , the idea of supervision of their method of merchandising by the Department of Markets was contrary to their idea of individual independence, as precarious as that independence might have been." Now disputes between customer and peddler would be handled in one market by one of the ten on-site supervisors "behind the closed doors of their offices."[51]

Certainly, for the elder peddlers, set in their ways, these changes were the most difficult. Some of them "resent the change to order, cleanliness and regulations; they insist that shoppers believe that bargains can only be found on pushcarts; a market is like a store—so why go to the market?" The older peddlers also found it difficult to compete in such close quarters with younger peddlers in the market, one of whom provided his customers with "service-music on [his] midget radio and red-hot base-ball scores on [his] slate."[52]

New Yorkers were saddened by the elimination of the pushcarts. Journalist Jane Kirk Huntley "found our tiny apartment near the East Side pushcart section an exciting adventure; and I am sorry that the picturesque pushcarts are now being replaced by modern municipal markets. To me the pushcarts are typical of this great metropolis." Another observer wrote, "New York has suddenly taken on autumnal splendor—not so much on the part of its trees as on the part of its outdoor markets. . . . [They] seem surprisingly fresh and attractive . . . to one previously scornful of pushcarts and curb markets."[53]

LaGuardia found this particularly infuriating, resenting "sentimental people [who] argued that the peddler with his rusty scales hanging from the side of his cart . . . was one of the quaint sights of New York City." He did not "want to hear any more gushing sentimentality about the elimination of the picturesque pushcarts" from the "penthouse slummers." Not just the observers of city scenes but the shoppers themselves missed the pushcart markets. A policeman explained that the indoor markets would not attract shoppers: "The peddlers won't go there. The old women won't walk so far. They want pushcarts right in front of their houses or at least a block away. They want to be able to handle the stuff, pick it up, smell it, choose the best part of the lot. You take that bakery store down on the corner. Sells the same kind of bread as the pushcart fellows. Will the women buy it there? No, they won't."[54] A newspaper article, "New York Women Liked Pushcart Tony's Good Onions and Squashes and Regret the Abolition This Week of the Picturesque Markets," concurred. Women shoppers in the pushcart districts preferred the old way of doing things:

> It is with considerable regret that New Yorkers witness the passing of the city's largest open-air market, which has been a colorful feature of the Lower East Side for many years. No longer will Orchard Street resound to the raucous cries of pushcart peddlers nor will housewives bargain over curbstone barrows: The opening of the Essex Street Municipal market will replace scenes like this with more prosaic enclosed stalls.[55]

A sociological study in a predominantly Sicilian neighborhood confirmed this attachment to the old markets. The author lambasted the community's preference for the pushcart market—an "old established institution on Tyler Street [a pseudonym]." On "Tyler Street," Italian and Jewish peddlers' carts lined its stoops and gutters. Three-quarters of the peddlers were middle-aged men; the rest were even older men and women. The buyers were Jewish, Italian, and Greek. Women shoppers rarely left the block for purchases. The author described one woman on "Tyler Street" as having a "dull mentality" because she told him that she did not have to go to the country to see green vegetables and bright fruit; all she had to do was look out her window at the pushcart stands. The idea of indoor markets for this community "did not make much headway, however, due to sharp protest of neighborhood associations."[56]

Max, of Max and Louise's Botánica and Flowers, one of the three remaining original stands in the indoor Essex Street Market during the late 1980s, explained: "I moved to Essex Street Market when it opened because they took the pushcarts away. People didn't come around like they used to. . . . I figured once they take away the pushcarts they wouldn't bring the customers as much as they did before. . . . Once the pushcarts went away the business died out."[57]

The Impact of Change

Ironically by 1940, the business community, which had fought for ten years to eliminate the embarrassing pushcarts, now complained that their removal had irreparably damaged their trade. Much to their shock and chagrin, the merchants soon realized that once the pushcarts disappeared, they immediately experienced a drastic decline in trade. Within weeks of the new indoor markets opening on the East Side, some merchants requested a 50 percent reduction in rent from the city. A changed caption under a photograph of the pushcart market reflected the merchants' radically altered attitude. In 1929, when the photograph was published in a trade newspaper, the caption read, "This is the disgraceful type of public market we seek to abolish and recommend as its successor sanitary, indoor central markets." The newspaper published the same picture in 1940 with a new caption: "When these pushcarts left old Orchard Street last January, high land value went with them."[58]

The merchants had severely miscalculated the extent to which their business depended on that of the pushcarts outside their doors. Not only were customers local neighbors, but they were citizens and tourists as well. By late 1941, the merchants on Orchard Street had found that "the removal of the pushcarts . . . has reduced gross sales . . . approximately 60 percent. . . . Streets such as Orchard Street enjoyed an international reputation as 'The Street of Great Bargains.' . . . The removal of the pushcarts altered conditions considerably."[59]

The fight over stoop-line stands the same year proved to the merchants that they had been out-crusaded by LaGuardia. Stoop-line stands displayed store merchandise outdoors. LaGuardia considered the merchants in the old market districts to be as much a part of the "old world" as the peddlers and pushcarts. The merchants were convinced that now that the pushcarts were gone, the stoop-line stands in front of their stores were their only defense against complete financial ruin. They understood, but only too late, the attraction of the outdoor carts and displays.

But LaGuardia and the Department of Markets saw the stoop-line stands simply as glorified pushcarts. Several writers mourned the passing of the pushcarts but noted happily that at least "sidewalk stalls still manage to retain much of the color of the old pushcarts" and that the "sidewalk bazaars . . . in colorful profusion . . . still attract Jewish shoppers from all metropolitan districts"; therefore, the Lower East Side still retained "the charm of the tradition-soaked neighborhood for city residents and visiting tourists."[60]

The merchants not only had misinterpreted and mistaken the needs and the character of their own neighborhoods, but also had come to realize that the city government regarded them as part of the problem and not as a part of the solution. The LaGuardia administration had nothing but contempt for the merchants, and the city ordered the stoop-line stalls that did not conform to new standards to be dismantled:

> Two by fours are rent apart, nails are torn squealing out of the flesh of wood, and down tumble neat stacks of merchandise festooning street fronts. This isn't an invasion. It's the law carrying out the last act of a heartbreaking drama. . . . Goods hanging anywhere outdoors, before shop fronts, in cellar openings, on stairs, fire escapes . . . wherever selling seems to have a defiant yet failing air to it, that's a stoopstand. They're the last retreat of five-and-dime rugged individualism and an abomination to city authorities, who have vowed their extermination. . . . No matter what the toll in sentiment, the pull at heart hews, out they go . . . vestigial hangovers, quaint illegalities, or what have you. . . . Stoopstands are out.[61]

Long advocates of renovation and renewal, many merchants had themselves become its victims. Now before the City Council appeared an amendment to the administrative code that prohibited any peddling, vending, hawking, or selling of any wares or merchandise on city streets, including stoop-line stands.[62]

Fifteen thousand peddlers lined the streets of the city when LaGuardia came to power. By 1945, a little more than ten years later, only 1,200 still stood. As early as 1939, LaGuardia had reduced the number of licensed peddlers from 6,000 to about 2,700 and the number of open-air markets from sixty to thirty-six. LaGuardia had succeeded where the merchants had not. But with the new vending restrictions, his success was at the merchants' expense. While the campaign taken up by Lower East Side merchants in 1929 had been stymied, the LaGuardia administration virtually completed it by 1941.[63]

Ironically, by the time of World War II, even the Department of Markets referred to the pushcart markets nostalgically. In the Victory edition of *New York Advancing,* Henry M. Brundage, the commissioner of markets, noted that pushcarts had been "one of the picturesque and distinctive features of New York . . . the visitor would find the sidewalks on both sides of a street for several blocks lined with wagons and pushcarts . . . stacked with attractive produce of fruits and vegetables, being sold . . . to hundreds of residents in the neighborhood."[64] No mention was made of the recently built indoor markets.

The indoor markets never really flourished. The stall rentals were too high, and customers soon abandoned the markets for the convenience of bodegas and supermarkets. Refrigeration also reduced the need for daily shopping.

In 1967, the Hunt's Point Market in the South Bronx replaced the Washington Wholesale Market as the central wholesale market for the city. Today, it is the largest produce market in the world, selling more than $2 billion worth of produce yearly. The market handles 50 to 60 percent of nearly 4 billion pounds of fruit and vegetables consumed annually in greater New York. The 329-acre parcel of land that juts out into the East River includes a terminal market, where fruits, vegetables, and some meat are sold to retailers; a meat market cooperative; and several warehouses owned by private chain supermarkets. In November 2005, the Fish Market, opened on Fulton Street in 1822, relocated to Hunt's Point. In 1976, a farmers' market, sponsored by the nonprofit Council on the Environment of New York City, returned to Manhattan at Union Square. Thirty years later, twenty thousand New Yorkers shop regularly at the Union Square market each year, and forty-six farmers' markets operate in the five boroughs of New York.[65]

LaGuardia never succeeded in eliminating itinerant peddlers. Today, peddling offers growing numbers of new immigrants a way to earn a living. Once again, battles over issues of peddling abound in many predominantly immigrant neighborhoods. In recent years, debates have swirled around vendors clogging the streets of Harlem, Washington Heights, and the Lower East Side. Questions persist about the fate of poor and primarily immigrant people dependent on the marginal economy of peddling, as well as about the place of peddling in the urban environment. Some view the dilemma angrily, others regard it nostalgically, and still others argue that peddling contributes to the vibrancy of city life.

The battles over vending remain remarkably familiar and filled with historical ironies. In the mid-1990s, Mayor Rudolph Giuliani, who fancied himself a LaGuardia-style reformer, proposed banishing all peddlers from New York street corners and relocating them in open-air markets.[66] Mayor Fiorello LaGuardia probably spun in his grave at the very mention of reviving open-air markets.

One example illustrates the continued conflict over uses of the street. With the influx of immigrants from Africa in the 1990s, 125th Street became crowded with as many as a thousand illegal vendors hawking teak trinkets, mud cloth, scented ointments, beads, and services such as African hair weaving. Giuliani granted special licenses for illegal vendors as long as they moved to an empty lot set aside on 116th Street. On October 18, 1994, police descended on 125th Street in order to carry out the mayor's plan and arrested twenty-two people. Vendors promoted a boycott of non-black-owned stores, even though some black merchants sided with the city. The debate generated passions not seen in years. Some praised Giuliani because the vendors did not pay taxes, contributed to congestion, and damaged legitimate businesses. But others called the action misguided because it deprived vendors of meager incomes that kept them off welfare.[67]

Not surprisingly, as soon as the vendors were banished, some merchants began to complain that the removal of the pushcarts and the crowds they had attracted hurt their business. "Do you think that these buses come all the way uptown just so tourists can drive past McDonald's?" asked Richard Bartee, a poet and community activist.[68] One year later, at least some members of the community could claim success. The key resided in the fact that the city asked the Malcolm Shabazz Mosque to sponsor the new market, and many vendors were members of the congregation. Others, though, insisted that they would "wait until this quiets down and—perhaps, perhaps—slip back."[69]

One bright note in recent years is the success of Essex Street Market. Long dormant and a blight on the neighborhood, the indoor market is "thriving today as it never did, making available both the world of the bodega and the universe of the gourmand."[70] The New York City Economic Development Corporation poured $1.5 million into its renovation. In a city increasing segregated into the very rich and the very poor, the Essex Street Market ironically stands as an example of a successful commercial space that caters to local residents and visitors alike.

NOTES

1. Thomas F. De Voe, *The Market Book: A History of the Public Markets of the City of New York* (1862; repr., New York: Kelly, 1970), 15, 28–29.

2. Ibid., 31, 34, 36, 44–45, 70.

3. Ibid., 73, 77–124.

4. Ibid., 125–27, 132, 241, 242–383.

5. Ibid., 387–576.

6. Ibid., 206, 222, 425.

7. Harry Morton Goldberg, "Early History of the Markets in New York City—Continued," *East Side Chamber News,* July 1929, 13; De Voe, *Market Book,* 532.

8. Christine Stansell, *City of Women: Sex and Class in New York, 1789–1860* (Urbana: University of Illinois Press, 1987), 14.

9. Earl R. French, "Push Cart Markets in New York City: A Preliminary Report" (Washington, D.C.: Department of Agriculture, 1925), 6; New York City Department of Markets, *Annual Report, 1940,* 9, Markets file, Municipal Reference Library, New York.

10. Daniel Bluestone, "The Pushcart Evil," in *The Landscape of Modernity: New York City, 1900–1940,* ed. David Ward and Olivier Zunz (Baltimore: Johns Hopkins University Press, 1992), 290; Harry Morton Goldberg, "What Will Become of the Curb Pushcarts?" *East Side Chamber News,* June 1929, 7.

11. French, "Push Cart Markets in New York City," 4; Konrad Bercovici, "The Greatest Jewish City in the World," *The Nation,* September 12, 1923, 260–61; Elizabeth Ewen, *Immigrant Women in the Land of Dollars: Life and Culture on the Lower East Side, 1890–1925* (Atlantic City, N.J.: Monthly Review Press, 1985), 171.

12. Irving Howe, *World of Our Fathers* (New York: Harcourt Brace Jovanovitch, 1976), 77; French, "Push Cart Markets in New York City," 26.

13. French, "Push Cart Markets in New York City," 20, 7, 17; "Street Vendors," in *Feeding the City,* box 3611, folder 6, "Street Vendors—What They Sell," Federal Writers' Project Papers, Municipal Archives, New York.

14. De Voe, *Market Book,* 501.

15. French, "Push Cart Markets in New York City," 41–42.

16. Bernard Postal, *Jewish Landmarks in New York: An Informal History and Guide* (New York: Hill and Nash, 1964), 68; Olive Gunby, "The Pushcart Peddlers, the Swarms in

and about Hester Street—Enormous Growth of the Trade—The Proposed Market Place—Views of a Veteran—What Some Men Have Earned—The Police and the Vendors," *New York Evening Post,* August 20, 1898, in *New York City Folklore: Legends, Tall Tales, Anecdotes, Stories, Sagas, Heroes and Characters, Customs, Traditions, and Sayings,* ed. Benjamin Albert Botkin (New York: Random House, 1956), 204–6; French, "Push Cart Markets in New York City," 28–29.

17. Gunby, "Pushcart Peddlers," 204–6.

18. Anzia Yezierska, *Bread Givers* (New York: Venture, 1975).

19. Goldberg, "What Will Become of the Curb Pushcarts?" 7; Lillian D. Wald, *The House on Henry Street* (New York: Holt, 1915), 4–5; Postal, *Jewish Landmarks in New York,* 65–66, 64.

20. Bluestone, "Pushcart Evil," 294; Rupert Hughes, *The Real New York* (New York: Hutchinson, 1906).

21. "New York Pushcart Army Exceeds 4000," *New York Daily Tribune,* September 16, 1906, box 30, Lillian Wald Collection, Rare Book and Manuscript Library, Butler Library, Columbia University, New York; exhibition text and photograph list for "Hawkers and Gawkers: The Battle over the Pushcard Markets," November 29, 1990, 1, Lower East Side Tenement Museum, New York.

22. Goldberg, "What Will Become of the Curb Pushcarts?" 7. The open-air markets came under the jurisdiction of the Department of Markets in 1920, but no records were kept on peddlers until 1924. See *New York Sun,* October 17, 1930, 1–3.

23. *East Side Chamber News,* March 1930, 7–8. Mary Simkovitch of the Greenwich House Settlement was one of the few reformers who realized that covered markets were "expensive and unnecessary and [will not] tend to cheapen the price of food." She spoke out against the indoor markets as well as the licensing of peddlers as early as 1914. See Mary Simkovitch to Lillian Wald, April 29, 1914, box 30, Wald Collection.

24. "Case of Francis Bromberg of 25 Suffolk Street," box 42, Wald Collection.

25. "Our Alien Neighbors—Case Study," 21–22, Helen Hall Papers, Rare Book and Manuscript Library, Butler Library, Columbia University, New York.

26. Emily Coleman to Karl Hesley, box 43, Wald Collection.

27. A. J. Liebling, "Short Selling Is Paralyzing the Hester Street Curb," *New York World Telegram,* April 4, 1932, 2–5.

28. *East Side Chamber News,* June 1929.

29. Albert Henry Aronson, "The Ramifications of Our Marketing Problem," *East Side Chamber News,* November 1929, 17. See also Rebecca B. Rankin, *New York Advancing: The Result of Five Years of Progressive Administration in the City of New York,* World's Fair ed. (New York: Municipal Reference Library, 1939), 105; and Mark Soliterman, "The Small Retailer on the East Side," *East Side Chamber News,* December 1929, 17.

30. Harry Morton Goldberg, editorial, *East Side Chamber News,* February 1930, 8; Colwin Lahm [vice president of the Citizen's Savings Bank], "How to Put the Lower East Side Again on the Map," *East Side Chamber News,* July 1929, 8, and December 1929, 11. Lahm stated that much like the pushcarts, the stores conducted most of their business on Sundays and in the evenings.

31. Mark Zborowski and Elizabeth Herzog, *Life Is with People: The Culture of the Shtetl* (New York: Schocken Books, 1973), 63–64. The term "schleppers" is used in Federal Writers' Project, *WPA Guide to New York City: The Federal Writers' Project Guide to 1930s New York* (New York: Pantheon, 1982), 117; Joseph Platzker, "The Lower East Side in 1932," *East Side Chamber News,* March 1931, cover.

32. Benjamin Koenigsberg, "Essex Street Market Location," Commissioner William Fellowes Morgan to *East Side Chamber News,* December 9, 1936, *East Side Chamber News,* December 1936, 8; Bluestone, "Pushcart Evil," 305.

33. Commissioner William Fellowes Morgan to Congressman James Joseph Lanzetta, January 26, 1934, box 3638, Fiorello H. LaGuardia Papers, Municipal Archives, New York.

34. Rebecca B. Rankin, *New York Advancing: A Scientific Approach to Municipal Government, 1934–1935* (New York: Municipal Reference Library, 1936), 277.

35. Harry B. Brainard, "City Plans Four Public Market Buildings on Essex Street," *East Side Chamber News,* September 1936, cover.

36. Ruth McKenny, "They Might Starve Faster Indoors: Pushcart Peddlers Too Depressed to Care," *New York Post,* July 11, 1936, sec. 2, 3–6.

37. Federal Writers' Project, *The Italians of New York* (New York: Random House, 1938), 72.

38. Harry I. Baron, "Leisure-Time Interests, Preferences and Activities of Children on the Lower East Side of New York" (master's thesis, Graduate School of Jewish Social Work, 1935), 102–3, Jewish Division, New York Public Library; Mayor's Office to Mr. Joseph Olshansky, May 14, 1936, and photograph, May 25, 1937, both in box 3638, LaGuardia Papers. The man in the photo is identified as a peddler named Wolf Goldstein.

39. "East Side Pushcart Market About to Vanish—Moving Indoors After Picturesque Century," *New York Times,* January 5, 1940, 6.

40. Letter to Fiorello LaGuardia, September 4, 1936, box 3638, LaGuardia Papers.

41. Letter to Fiorello LaGuardia, October 25, 1937, box 3638, LaGuardia Papers.

42. Department of Markets, *Annual Report, 1940,* 9.

43. Fiorello LaGuardia, memorandum to William Morgan, September 2, 1939, box 3638; "Notice to Pushcart Peddlers on Enclosed Markets," December 10, 1936, box 3225, both in LaGuardia Papers.

44. *East Side Chamber News,* December 1937, 8; April 1937, 7; and July 1937, cover.

45. Newbold Morris, *Let the Chips Fall: My Battle Against Corruption* (New York: Appleton-Century-Crofts, 1955), 119–20.

46. Exhibition text and photograph list for "Hawkers and Gawkers," 13. Robert Caro writes that LaGuardia was "sensitive about his Italian immigrant ancestry" and banned organ grinders because of it (*The Power Broker: Robert Moses and the Fall of New York* [New York: Vintage Books, 1975], 447). Protesting a summons given to a flower vendor, Katherine Morse received a reply from the mayor: "It would be rather difficult if the city were required to supply a flower pushcart for every husband who forgets that his wife has all the emotions and romance she had when he was courting her" (April 6, 1939, LaGuardia Papers); Morris, *Let the Chips Fall,* 119–20.

47. Editorial, *New York Herald Tribune,* December 1, 1938, 3–5. Isadore Suranowitz was the president of the Lower First Avenue Indoor Market Association, formerly the First Avenue Peddlers Association. He handed out placards reading, "All for one, one for all," which, according to the article, was sneered at by the peddlers. Anthony Sidoti had been on the same corner for thirty-two years and was not pleased about the change.

48. Nathan Ausubel, "Hold Up the Sun! A Kaleidoscope of Jewish Life in New York," manuscript for Federal Writers' Project, *Jews of New York,* chapter "DeProfundis: Junk," 28–33, box 3633, Federal Writers' Project Papers.

49. Editorial, *New York Herald Tribune,* January 10, 1940, East Side files, Markets and Pushcarts, Seward Park Branch Library, New York Public Library; "War on Pushcarts Pressed by Mayor," *New York Times,* January 10, 1940, 1.

50. "Our Alien Neighbors," 21–22.

51. Elita Lenz, "Feeding the City—Color at Essex Street Retail Market," August 19, 1940, 1, box 3611, folder 5, "Municipal Markets, Research, First Avenue," Federal Writers' Project Papers. Lenz interviewed Mr. Parisi, president of the Merchants' Association, First Avenue Retail Market, and Mr. C. Siegal, secretary of the Merchants' Association, as well as Mr. Peter Diliberto at booth 87½.

52. Nathaniel L. Shapiro, "Feeding the City," August 28, 1940, 2–3, box 3611, folder 5, "Municipal Markets, Essex Street," Federal Writers' Project Papers. Shapiro interviewed Mr. Regina, an official of the Department of Markets stationed at Essex Street.

53. Jane Kirk Huntley, "New York Women Liked Pushcart Tony's Good Onions and Squashes and Regret the Abolition This Week of the Picturesque Markets," *Christian Science Monitor,* January 5, 1940, 9; F. Smith, "Autumn Brings Color and Variety to Our Curb Markets," October 9, 1939, box 3571, Oddities—Market file, Federal Writers' Project Papers.

54. Editorial, *New York Daily News,* January 10, 1940, 30; Morris, *Let the Chips Fall,* 119–20; Caro, *Power Broker,* 447; "51 Pushcart Stables," *New York Sun,* n.d., clipping in East Side files, Markets and Pushcarts, Seward Park Branch Library.

55. Huntley, "New York Women," 9.

56. Harry Manuel Shulman, *The Slums of New York* (New York: Boni, 1938), 107, 24–25, 97–99.

57. Max, interview with Kathleen Condon for City Lore, March 18, 1988.

58. "$350,000 First Avenue Market at 10th Street Approved," *East Side Chamber News,* July 1937, cover; "Essex Street Market Opens" [editorial], *East Side Chamber News,* January 1940, 9; "Tax Commission Hears Chamber Delegation on 'Orchard Street Values'" [editorial], *East Side Chamber News,* March 1940, 3.

59. "Chamber Director Wins Stoop-Stand License Fight Against License Commissioner" [editorial], *East Side Chamber News,* October 1941, 4.

60. Weed Dickinson, "The Jews of New York," chap. 3, p. 2, in Federal Writers' Project, *Jews of New York,* first draft, January 1942, box 3632, folder, "Jewish Communities"; Elita Lenz, "Delancey District Jews," 1–2, box 3633, folder, "Jewish Communities," both in Federal Writers' Project Papers.

61. John Mitchell, "Last Stand," 1, box 3611, folder 6, "Pushcart Trading Areas—Open Air Markets," Federal Writers' Project Papers.

62. Ibid., 8.

63. Rebecca B. Rankin, *New York Advancing: Seven More Years of Progressive Administration in the City of New York, 1939–1945,* Victory ed. (New York: Municipal Reference Library, 1945), 208, and *New York Advancing: Five Years of Progressive Administration,* 105.

64. Rankin, *New York Advancing: Seven More Years of Progressive Administration,* 208.

65. Markets circular files, Municipal Reference Library; Council on the Environment of New York City, "Annual Report," 2000, 4, http://www.cenyc.org.

66. Jonathan P. Hicks, "Giuliani Broadens Crackdown to Banish All Illegal Vendors," *New York Times,* May 9, 1994, sec. B, 1.

67. Jonathan P. Hicks, "Vendors' Ouster and Boycott Divide Harlem," *New York Times,* October 23, 1994, sec. A, 42.

68. Jonathan P. Hicks, "Amid Calm, Anger Lingers on 125th St.," *New York Times,* October 31, 1994, sec. B, 1; Guy Trebay, "A Market Drive," *Village Voice,* November 1, 1994, 33–34.

69. Jennifer Kingson Bloom, "Neighborhood Report: Harlem; Old 125th St. Warriors   173
Find Peace at 116th St. Market," *New York Times*, August 27, 1995, 1; Trebay, "Market
Drive," 33.

70. Ginia Bellafante, "A Market Grows on the Lower East Side," *New York Times*, December 6, 2006, F1.

Asphalt *Terroir*

JOY SANTLOFER

MIDBLOCK ON a quiet street in Long Island City, where aluminum-clad homes and small apartment buildings intermingle with nondescript factories, the air suddenly comes alive with the heady aromas of wine and spices. There are few pedestrians on the street to enjoy the fragrance wafting from the corner building or the breathtaking views of Manhattan just across the East River. Unless you are lucky enough to pass by as the baking smells invade the air or an unmarked door opens to reveal the activities within, there is no way to know that inside these walls, wine biscuits are being handcrafted by skilled artisans. The building is indistinguishable from its neighbors, except for a small bunch of purple grapes painted on its yellow walls. In similar commonplace buildings throughout New York's five boroughs, a vast and growing array of foods are quietly being produced in a little-known industry.

The city's breadth of products, ranging from chocolates to tortillas to pork rinds, are made not only in small factories but in divisions of global corporations; multigenerational, family-owned businesses; and recently begun, single-producer, shoestring operations. Who are these manufacturers producing this spectrum of foods that includes novel inventions and century-old traditional tastes, along with mainstream staples found in every supermarket across the country? What compels this diverse group of businesspeople who serve the city's disparate populations, encompassing those who embrace expensively handcrafted products to recently arrived immigrants who crave familiar foodstuffs, plus all the varying economic levels and consumer tastes in between? What are the ties that bind these widely varied companies in the city's lively and creative food industry, which is deeply rooted in New York's history and tied to its future?

Although New York is no longer the major food producer it once was—that era ended in the early 1980s, when most of the huge food factories departed for the suburbs—a substantial amount of food is still made in the city, which offers unique advantages for food producers. Foods best eaten freshly made have ready access to the city's large population and thousands of restaurants; New York's sophisticated food environment provides a cachet for products marketed worldwide; and the city has a unique diversity, which one manufacturer described as the only place "in the country where you can get a deep penetration of different ethnic groups in a small geographic area."[1] Together, these factors have created a varied industry, the most vibrant segment of a rapidly dwindling manufacturing base and, in the last few years, its only growth sector, which is expected to expand in the near future.[2]

Producing food in the close confines of a city, however, has become increasingly more challenging in recent years. As neighborhoods gentrify, industrial areas shrink, causing rents and property values to escalate, resulting in skyrocketing start-up costs and difficulties for expansion. Along with the struggle for adequate space, the pressure to comply with countless city regulations and restrictions makes day-to-day operations arduous. In a clogged and heavily populated city, with the needs of many more lucrative industries at the top of the agenda, some food manufacturers have come to believe that the city's government is "indifferent to their needs."[3] Yet despite the numerous obstacles, many producers choose to remain in New York.

This chapter, using the stories of several of the city's food producers as illustrations, examines why some manufacturers refuse to move to the greener pastures of the suburbs. While their situations differ, most feel that it is worth overcoming any obstacle to remain in the city; in describing their ties to New York, there is a consistency of emotional tone in the language they use. Underlying their explanations and beyond the more concrete, professional reasons (all are first and foremost businesspeople), these food producers describe a more ineffable bond that links them to New York, which I suggest is, in a contradictory phrase, an "asphalt *terroir.*"

The French have used the word *terroir,* the concept of a specific territory, for several centuries, altering its meaning over time. In contemporary France, the term is used both in the wine industry and for regionally produced foods to describe the somewhat mystical combination of the uniqueness of place, climate, and the producer's skill merging to create distinctive tastes and products rooted to a locale. The notion of *terroir* also is employed as a marketing device, implying a guarantee of authenticity, traditional characteristics, and high quality. The geographical mystique also includes the people and cultures within these regional spaces, drawing on the interconnectedness of the region's "human–historical aspects" and its "know-how memory, historical and social heritages" to create products with a distinct personality.[4]

The American use of the word *terroir* began in the 1990s, but because there was no translatable equivalent in English, a less nuanced meaning evolved.[5] Initially used solely to describe wine from a particular locale or specific producer, more recently *terroir* has begun to imply a sense of quality in products as diverse as chocolates, coffee, and cheeses.[6] Whereas the American meaning is always attached to a consumable product, the French use incorporates a much broader view.

ASPHALT *TERROIR*

To describe New York's food producers, I use the more complex French definition, which Amy Trubek defines in a discussion of cultural misinterpretations as incorporating "culture, in the form of a group's identity, tradition, and heritage in relation to place."[7] I also include the role of the producer, which geographer Daniel W. Gade defines as the "unique human factors," involving the "skills and practices passed on from one generation to the next."[8] However, I am removing the classic French meaning of *terroir* far from its agricultural roots and situating it in an urban setting. When translating Michel de Certeau's *Practice of Everyday Living* into English, Timothy J. Tomasik describes the considerable "mobility" of "the terrain in which *terroir* is supposedly so firmly rooted." No single meaning can be ascribed to this fluid concept, and Certeau uproots *terroir,* relocating what he calls "the soil from which narratives grow," to the "asphalt" of a city.[9]

The food manufacturers believe that their identity as New Yorkers is intertwined with their products and that their bonds with the city have a profound influence on the uniqueness of foods they produce. Although many of their products are sold throughout the world, the producers visualize their customers as being especially discerning New Yorkers who will accept nothing but the best, adding layers of quality to foods produced in the city. In addition, a vast majority of the food manufacturers both live and work in New York (many for several generations), thereby incorporating both their lives and their products into the traditions of the geographical site.[10] This symbiotic relationship plays a significant role in their commitment to continue making food products in the "asphalt *terroir*" of New York. While *terroir* is most often used to describe the unique tastes of a specific place, this important aspect is not a major aspect of my discussion of the city's food manufacturers. That is, a food's identification with a geographic place is generally assigned by those who buy or consume a product,[11] but in this case, it is the manufacturers who have linked their product to the city. Most New Yorkers are not aware that many of the products mentioned in this chapter are even made in the city. Only two of the products refer to their place of production in their name, and just one, Fox's U-bet chocolate syrup, has a local identity as an "iconic food." Again, it is the producers who believe that their products are enhanced by their locale and, conversely, that they add to the cultural fabric of the city, which is one of the factors that motivates them to remain in New York.[12]

While all these companies face a variety of difficulties, only three of the twenty-one manufacturers I interviewed are considering relocating, and two would remain if it were economically feasible. New York is home, and the companies have a sense of loyalty to both the city and their employees, many of whom have worked for them for at least a decade and some for considerably longer. The companies also have a feeling of pride that if they can make it in New York, they must be the best. The third-generation J. Freirich Company, a manufacturer of smoked pork butts, describes the city as "one of the most discriminating retail markets in the country,"[13] which makes success in this demanding setting seem even sweeter than any additional profits that might be gained in an anonymous suburb.

Today's food manufacturers are part of a tradition that stretches back to the seventeenth century. Since the city's earliest days, the history of New York has been entwined with the production of commercially made foods that fed the population of America's largest city and supplied the export trade from the country's largest port. The wheat grown on "Golden Hill," the area today around the corner of William and John streets in the heart of the financial district, was considered the best grain available (an early association of the city's products with quality), and its sale helped increase trade. By the mid-eighteenth century, locally grown wheat, beef, flour, pork, and bread were being shipped to markets in Europe, the West Indies, and the southern colonies.[14]

During the mid-eighteenth century, New York's flourishing food industry included five large sugar refineries, seventeen breweries and distilleries,[15] plus multiple cracker bakers who supplied the biscuits vital to the shipping industry. By 1826, within a year of the completion of the Erie Canal, the flow of foodstuffs into the city included barges carrying "221,000 barrels of flour, . . . and 562,000 bushels of wheat,"[16] which was then milled, baked, and dispatched around the world. The same year, "an estimated two hundred thousand head of cattle," along with "pigs, horses and bleating spring lambs,"[17] were driven through the streets of the city to numerous slaughterhouses. In 1830, the largest sugar refinery in the country, employing three hundred workers, was built on Greenwich Street.[18]

By the 1850s, New York's food production industry was at its height, an era that lasted for the next one hundred years. Steam power, combined with innovations in mechanization, began the industrialization of food production, which was manned by the masses of unskilled, low-paid immigrants who were streaming into the city. By 1860, the city contained 46 breweries,[19] and the Hudson and East rivers were lined with 206 slaughterhouses that butchered 375,000 animals a year.[20] The Havemeyer family built a $1 million, state-of-the-art sugar refinery on the Brooklyn waterfront, and additional refineries congregated in the area. By 1872, sugar refining was New York's most important manufacturing industry.[21]

The nation's first food conglomerate was formed at the end of the 1880s when seven of the city's cracker bakers established the New York Baking Company, which built the most modern bakery of its time at Fifteenth Street and Ninth Avenue. Nine years later, a merger created the National Biscuit Company, which soon filled the blocks between Fifteenth and Sixteenth streets and Ninth and Tenth avenues, making it the "largest cracker bakery in the world" (today housing the Chelsea Market).

In 1889, when Brooklyn was incorporated into New York City, the city's biscuit-baking, meat-processing, and sugar-refining industries became the world's largest centers of their kind; in 1903, an article in the *New York Times* proclaimed that New York was "pre-eminently the candy city of the world," with more "establishments engaged in its manufacture . . . than any other city on earth."[22] As food production further industrialized, its scale expanded, and during the first two decades of the twentieth century, enormous food factories appeared in all the boroughs, particularly Brooklyn and Queens.

Loose-Wiles, later called Sunshine Biscuits, constructed an enormous baking facility, the largest under one roof, in Long Island City (now part of LaGuardia Community College). Once production began in 1914, it took the New York plant only one year to become profitable, whereas the company's factories in other parts of the country had taken up to three years to reach the same level,[23] illustrating the skills, or "unique human qualities" of the city's workforce.

In 1922, at the height of New York's industrial food age, the industry employed 824,000 workers, a 70 percent increase from 1900.[24] However, during this period, the riverside sugar refineries began to consolidate outside New York, and cities closer to western cattle ranches began to capture much of the large-scale meat-processing business. But the large food factories continued to flourish, even during the Depression, when many small businesses also opened, some of which are still in operation.

When the United States entered World War II, the city's food manufacturers began to produce huge quantities of rations in addition to their regular production. During this period, food became the largest industry in Queens.[25] After the war ended, new technologies demanded larger horizontal spaces that were easier to build elsewhere, and a slow but steady exodus of the large New York food producers began. National Biscuit Company left Manhattan in 1958; Queens lost Sunshine Biscuit in 1963; Silvercup Bread, in 1975; Bond Bread, in 1976; American Chicle, in 1982; Hebrew National, in 1986, and Taystee Bread, in 1992. Sugar's diminishing presence ended when the last refiner in New York, Domino Sugar, closed its Williamsburg, Brooklyn, facility in 2004, although its neon sign continued to shine as a landmark.

But food production in the city did not end. The void created by the departing factories allowed many smaller firms to prosper. By the 1980s, consumers, responding to new ideas about foods, demanded higher-quality handcrafted products, creating new opportunities for innovative companies. Artisanal bread makers created a resurgence of small baking companies,[26] becoming a "crucial component" of the city's food-manufacturing sector.[27] Today, the New York–made components of any meal can be purchased in supermarkets and food shops throughout the city: breakfast granola; luncheon cold cuts; peanut butter and jelly, plus the bread or pita to encase them; a side of pickles; a pork shoulder dinner entrée, with the spices to season it; bread, key lime pie, cheesecake, and after-dinner chocolates; along with soda, beer, or powdered iced tea to wash them down. Both newly minted firms introducing original items and those whose products are deeply rooted in the city's way of life are now producing all types and varieties of food in the city.

Social and Historical Heritages

The concept of *terroir* is used to distinguish unique, regional foods with a distinct personality created through the accumulated knowledge of successive generations rooted to the locale. Many French products—Roquefort, Champagne, Brie—use their regional identification to authenticate and distinguish them in the larger marketplace.[28]

Louis Passaro (*right*), pictured in the early 1930s, son of the founder and grandfather of the current owners of Manhattan Special Bottling Corporation, stands in front of the original wooden building on Manhattan Avenue in Williamsburg, Brooklyn. In the same building, rebuilt in brick in the early 1960s, the company continues to produce a variety of sodas, including Manhattan Special Espresso Soda, which is advertised in the photograph. (Photograph courtesy of Manhattan Special Bottling Corporation)

This notion can be transferred to the sidewalks of New York. One local product, Manhattan Special Espresso Coffee Soda, has survived through four generations in the same location, rooted to its community. Originally produced for the local tastes of consumers in the confined neighborhood of an ethnic enclave, today it uses its distinctive name as a marketing tool, a symbol of its regional origins crossing ethnically based local boundaries to enter the wider international marketplace (although its name refers not to the borough across the river but to the street, Manhattan Avenue, where the factory is located in Williamsburg, Brooklyn).

The coffee-flavored soda was created in 1895 when Dr. Theresa Cimino (an osteopath in her native Italy) and a partner capitalized on the espresso-drinking tradition of her close-knit community by creating a cold substitute beverage to drink in New York's stifling summers. During the early twentieth century, new products in Italian immigrant communities typically developed in a progression, according to historian Donna Gabaccia: "Even the humblest of urban immigrants could parley production for family consumption into small businesses, often organized and initially run from a hard-working woman's kitchen," and eventually "many homes and groceries were turned into small-time factories."[29] Following this trajectory, Manhattan Special was soon being bottled for the local neighborhood.

During the third generation, Cimino's grandson, Albert Passaro, became the company's sole owner, and although there are few written records of the company's past, its oral history has been passed down through his children, the current own-ers.[30] From the late 1950s to the early 1980s, Manhattan Special built a following in Italian neighborhoods throughout the New York metropolitan area, producing a product that satisfied a cultural taste but was not available through mainstream food corporations.[31]

After Passaro's death in 1983, his daughter, Aurora, soon joined by her brother, Louis, assumed management of the company. As fourth-generation owners, they con-tinue to use the recipe devised by their great-grandmother, a labor-intensive process that includes grinding coffee beans to extract the espresso flavor for their soda. Still in its original location, in one of New York's typical, small factories, the plant blends into the surrounding neighborhood of aluminum-clad homes and former industrial buildings now being transformed into condominiums. Unless the huge garage doors are open on a warm day or the smell of roasting coffee beans seeps into the air, there is little to suggest the activities inside the brick walls.

Running a food business in New York is filled with complex regulatory difficul-ties, recounts Aurora Passaro, but as long as they "play by the rules," filing all the necessary permits, they are rooted to their location. "This is what we know," says Passaro, and they "love the wonderful location" of their factory, which is "home," a vital part of their family and identity and a mainstay in the fading cultural traditions of their changing environment. Both Aurora and Louis Passaro continue to live in the rapidly gentrifying neighborhood, close to the corner that has housed their family's business since its inception, taking pride in continuing to uphold a culinary tradition on the original site.

Because the popularity of coffee drinks has increased over the past decade, Man-hattan Special Espresso Soda has expanded far from its local origins into national markets and beyond, to Japan, Hong Kong, England, Greece, and the Middle East, where its name clearly identifies its origins. In the factory's immediate neighborhood, every corner deli stocks the soda; during the summer, Passaro proudly watches new residents of the area, many young, upscale Manhattan-bound office workers, walking toward the subway and drinking a bottle of her family's hundred-year-old product, tasting their "local delicacy" infused with sense of history and place.

Part of the elusive mystique of *terroir* is the sense of the history of generations of families and workers entrenched in a specific locale producing a time-honored product. Be it wine or cheese, the meaning of the place is bound together with the food, each helping create a context for the other. Three of New York's family-owned candy companies, two in Brooklyn and one on Staten Island, also embody this sense of heritage. All were established during the era when New York was dubbed the "candy capital of the world"[32] and are part of the city's current confectionery boom, in which long-time manufacturers coexist with new candy makers that produce hand-made sweets in trendy, unusual flavors. Whether stratospherically expensive or mass-produced, candy is a growing segment of New York's food production landscape, and every borough has manufacturers making candy either behind a storefront shop or on a factory assembly line.

The Joyva Corporation in East Williamsburg, Brooklyn, the largest halvah (con-fection made of a paste of crushed roasted sesame seeds and sweeteners) producer in the United States, was begun ninety-eight years ago by an immigrant from Kiev, Ukraine. Richard Radutzky, a third-generation member of the family, describes the "sense of familiarity and of coming home" that customers from around the world experience when eating the company's products, and he regards the confection as "something tangible" that connects the Joyva Corporation to New York.[33] The other Brooklyn-based company, the 104-year-old, fifth-generation syrup producer H. Fox & Company, in Brownsville, has, according to David Fox, the great-grandson of the founder, a "very strong emotional tie to this city and to Brooklyn in general."[34] Beyond being emotionally bound to its location, the company is linked to the city as a culinary icon. An egg cream is a classic New York drink that combines seltzer water (preferably made with New York water),[35] milk, and chocolate syrup. It is considered to be authentic only when it contains the essential, local ingredient, Fox's U-bet chocolate syrup, giving it the taste of the *terroir*.[36]

On Staten Island, Supreme Chocolatiers mass-produces candy in a new industrial park beside the West Shore Expressway. Hidden behind the Hilton Garden Inn Hotel and surrounded by a vast, barren parking lot, its huge retail shop gives little indication of the cavernous factory, built in 2002, behind the storefront. In the factory, only two women are needed to feed colored papers into one of two huge automated machines that can fabricate 5,500 foil-covered chocolate Easter rabbits (or Christmas Santas or Valentine's Day hearts) every forty-five minutes. After the molded and wrapped bunnies are deposited at the far end of the machine, they are bound for the shelves of Target and Wal-Mart stores across the country (although some varieties also sit anonymously in the finest chocolate shops). The third-generation, family-owned business makes three national brands: Superior Confections, House of Bauer, and a 150-year-old California classic, Blum's of San Francisco (now made in New York!). In 1998, on the verge of relocating after being courted by several other states, the Katsoris family made an offer on a North Carolina factory. During the unsuccessful bidding process, the Katsorises, lifelong New Yorkers, discovered how deeply their roots were planted on Staten Island, surrounded by family, customers, and business associates, and realized that they did not relish the idea of moving.

Local politicians, with whom they had long relationships, helped them locate a new space for their factory. Although construction costs were expensive in New York, and it took more than four years to complete the new building, the Katsorises are pleased that they remained on Staten Island, which has been home to both the family and the company since its beginnings as a candy shop in Port Richmond Square in 1911. Mike Katsoris, grandson of the founder, believes that there is "enough business in New York" for any company and that his family's long history and friendly relationships on Staten Island are assets that cannot be easily duplicated. They are happy to have their business in their "own backyard," where their chocolate roses, vanilla pecan fudge, and peanut brittle play an essential part in the celebrations and traditions of their Staten Island neighbors.[37]

Hoping to create a new tradition, along with being part of the redevelopment of the downtown financial community after September 11, 2001, impelled John Down and Joe Guiliano, the two partners who own Christopher Norman Chocolates, to move to their current location in November 2003. The move was "more difficult than they could have imagined," having no idea that delivery trucks would have to negotiate three separate checkpoints in tiny New Street, which is completely blocked by large metal stanchions and guarded by gun-toting security guards. One of the first of more than a dozen Manhattan chocolatiers to have opened retail shops with small factories located in the rear since 2000,[38] Christopher Norman distributes its chocolates through Whole Foods and fancy food shops and in Japan, where the cachet of their New York origin (used as part of the company's name) is a marketing bonus. In the thirteen years that the company has been handmaking and painting chocolates, it has grown from a home kitchen to a Bowery loft (originally Down's painting studio) to the current space amid Manhattan's skyscrapers. Chosen, in part, because it is Down's and Guiliano's home and they wanted to work where they lived, they have also made a commitment to participate in the revitalization of the downtown neighborhood, along with being part of the larger community of the city. Their savory candies contain herbs bought in season at the local Greenmarket, and the matzos they coat with chocolate are supplied by Streit's, a fifth-generation family company and, at the time of this writing, the last matzo maker left on the Lower East Side. The two men believe that they—along with their skilled, tightly knit group of employees, each trained in the factory—are "all in it together, creating an opportunity" to build not only a company, but, along with their customers, a community.[39]

Translating Identity

New York's successive waves of immigrant populations have often clustered in neighborhoods where they have transplanted the food practices of their former homes as a way to preserve their identities. In *The Practice of Everyday Living,* Michel de Certeau describes this as "reterritorialization," as neighborhoods rapidly assimilate new immigrants, who reconfigure the site and make it their own by transplanting their *terroir.*[40] Historically, New York's immigrants have created food businesses in their new geographies to maintain traditional foodways, and, according to sociologist Krishnendu Ray, they sell "a way of being and a way of knowing the world that is embedded in their culture."[41] Although immigrants differ in the importance they attach to maintaining culinary traditions, when they consider a food to be indispensable, it offers a unique opportunity for new businesses, which at the same time helps establish a sense of place in the new environment.

When Mexicans, many from the state of Puebla, began to migrate to New York in the late 1980s and early 1990s, they settled in several Brooklyn neighborhoods where they also transplanted their food traditions. As one manufacturer explained, "If there are no tortillas on the table, you just don't eat."[42] Since this essential part of a Mexican's meal is best eaten freshly made, tortilla factories soon followed. One of the earliest factories, Tortilleria Piaxtla, began producing about 4,000 tortillas a week in 1986. By 1997, its sales had expanded to 400,000 tortillas weekly.[43] As the local Mexican population grew, one of the firm's employees explained, there was "so much business" at the time "that even though the competition is great, all of us sell plenty."[44] By 2001, six tortilla factories, each with roots in a specific Mexican town,

The computerized machinery at the Tortilleria Chinantla factory, in the Bushwick section of Brooklyn, produces 520 tortillas a minute, the most technologically advanced of the six *tortillerias* in the neighborhood. Each of the factories has roots in, and often is named after, a town in Puebla, Mexico, the home of many Mexican New Yorkers. The hot, just-baked tortillas are then packed in plastic bags directly from the conveyor belt to be sold throughout the five boroughs. (Photograph courtesy of Annie Powers)

were clustered in the area around Flushing Avenue near Bushwick and East Williamsburg, producing approximately 10 million tortillas a week.[45]

Today, the competition is fierce, and one brand, Tortilleria Chinantla, begun in 1992, now controls approximately 60 percent of the restaurant, supermarket, and bodega business, according to owner Erasmo Ponce. In its two round-the-clock production facilities, automated machinery flattens and shapes the dough and adjusts the oven temperature when needed to produce almost 1 million tortillas daily.[46] But the even smaller, three-year-old Tortilleria Buena Vista, which hires employees only from the town of the same name, has also become part of New York's food-manufacturing landscape. Although it is struggling to compete with its larger and more technologically advanced rivals, it still has found a local audience. While tortillas help maintain the cultural identity of the Mexican population, the *tortillerias* also offer jobs for newly arriving immigrants, a function that the city's food businesses have served for hundreds of years.

The food industry is often the first point of entry for those at the lowest levels of the city's workforce, today including those from Latin America, the Caribbean, and Asia.[47] New York's abundant labor pool is an asset that all the manufacturers recognize, and they repeatedly express a respect for their employees' abilities. Daniel

The Sweet'n Low factory packages its sweetener with a variety of machines, including those pictured here, from the 1950s, that can wrap seventy packets per minute. The company also has high-tech equipment with the capacity to wrap almost fifty times that amount in the same time, but the older, more labor-intensive machinery preserves jobs for a greater number of workers. This is the goal of the Eisenstadt family, whose factory has been in the Brooklyn Navy Yard for three generations. (Photograph courtesy of Annie Powers)

W. Gade describes the workers' contribution to French winemaking as the "unique human factors" in the *terrior,* the learned human touch that adds the "character of the place."[48] New York's manufacturers clearly acknowledge their workers' contribution to the success of their businesses, and many feel that their workers' long-term involvement adds a sense of history to their products. Indeed, the commitment of some firms to their employees is a major factor in their choosing to remain in New York, as strong bonds have formed between them over ten, twenty, or thirty years of working together.

This is the principal reason that Marvin Eisenstadt has kept the Cumberland Packing Corporation factory in Brooklyn: he wants to keep the staff employed. Although the once mighty sugar-refining industry no longer has a presence in the city, its substitute, Sweet'n Low, has been made in Brooklyn since 1957. Eisenstadt's father founded the company as a tea-bag factory in 1947, soon using the concept to fill packets with sugar, ketchup, and soy sauce. In the late 1950s, the Eisenstadts were approached by a drug company to develop a granulated sugar substitute, but as soon as they developed the formula, the drug company backed out. Cumberland went forward alone with its new product, Sweet'n Low. Today, 33 million pink packets, sold in supermarkets around the United States and in forty-two other countries, are produced daily on assembly lines that also make Butter Buds and Nu-Salt in a conglomeration of factory buildings opposite and inside the Brooklyn Navy Yard.

The company could probably produce many more packets and less expensively if it thoroughly modernized its plant, but the Eisenstadts (the company is now led by the third generation) are unwilling to upgrade all the equipment because of the many jobs that would be lost. The factory's machinery includes both the clanging cast-iron machines from the 1950s that fill seventy packets a minute and the completely automated, roaring, high-tech behemoths that fill three thousand packets in the same amount of time. The reason the company has stayed in New York is the same, to provide jobs for its more than four hundred, mainly low-skilled, ethnically diverse employees, more than one hundred of whom have been with the company for more than ten years and thirty whose tenure exceeds thirty years. "These people who work for me feel like family,"[49] says Eisenstadt, and he and his two sons are committed to remaining in the city they love.[50] More than one hundred of Cumberland's employees either walk or bicycle to work from the surrounding neighborhoods, and their jobs at the factory translate, according to business writer Rhonda Abrams, into "two hundred people [who] spend money in that neighborhood," which in turn "helps keep the neighborhood together."[51] The jobs then benefit the local economy. In a study of immigrant entrepreneurs in Los Angeles, Linda J. Wong found that the economic contribution of workers in small factories was often overlooked and that each worker helped "develop and maintain regional economies in more complex and dynamic ways than most casual observers realize."[52] The relationship among the factory, its employees, and the neighborhood illustrates the integration of people and place in the concept of *terroir*.

New York's neighborhoods also change, however. When Cibao Meat Products moved into the Mott Haven section of the Bronx in 1994, it was surrounded by vacant lots with few residential buildings in the vicinity. Recently, though, apartment buildings have encroached on the factory, particularly a three-story brick building on an adjacent lot where the sausage company had hoped to expand. To coexist peacefully with its neighbors, which the company strives to do, since it does not want to leave the area, it has to make concessions. When residents complained of smells, Cibao moved the location of its garbage containers to a less convenient spot, and during the summer, when refrigerated trucks awakened sleeping neighbors early in the morning, the engines were shut off.

Cibao was founded in the 1960s, in a small shop in Washington Heights, by Siegfried Vieluf. After leaving his native Germany, Vieluf first settled in the Dominican Republic and then moved to New York, along with a large influx of immigrants from the island. Vieluf's traditional Dominican sausages were so successful that by 1970, ten employees worked around the clock to meet the demand. Today, in larger quarters in the Bronx, Cibao employs thirty-five workers, all but two of whom are from the Dominican Republic and only five of whom speak English. They grind, spice, stuff, smoke, and pack a wide variety of Latin-flavored sausages and salamis in the one-story factory.

Lutzi Vieluf, a member of the second generation in the family business, expects that the problems will increase in the changing neighborhood, but the company has no intention of moving. Not only will the third generation soon join the company, but the bulk of its business is in New York. In addition, Cibao has long-standing ties to local businesses and intertwined relationships with many social groups in the transplanted Dominican community who depend on the company not only for jobs but also for the tastes of home.[53]

Reterritorialization

Part of New York's unique character is the diversity of its population, which offers food manufacturers multiple customers for their products. Cibao Meat Products now makes Mexican-flavored sausages, and the multigenerational Gordon family's Coffee Holding Company of Brooklyn, the largest coffee roaster in the five boroughs, targets its leading retail brand, Café Caribe, to the Hispanic market. Since it is essential for a new company to reach a large enough audience that can identify with its product, New York offers many opportunities for those opening a new business.

Ramon Acevedo, who originally launched his frozen mini-empanada company, Rasol Food Corporation, in Georgia, did not have a sufficient mass of local customers, so he returned to New York, where, with his wife and four Mexican workers, he now produces sixty thousand corn empanadas a week in a nonprofit incubator facility in the Bronx, a kitchen where small producers can share space and equipment until they are sufficiently capitalized to go out on their own. Unlike Georgia, New York offers a unique situation, as its many grocery stores are generally independently owned and managers are free to cater to local tastes, which is almost impossible to do in large supermarket chains with regional purchasing offices. This helped Acevedo reach the Colombian and Ecuadorian customers who are his target market, and the greater volume translated into lower operating expenses. Although rent and labor costs are higher in New York than in Georgia, Acevedo believes that the city offers the greatest opportunities for his future, which he projects will include doubling his workforce and operating his own production facility in either the Bronx or Brooklyn.[54]

The economic mobility of immigrant groups is tied to their ability to open businesses, hire coethnic employees, and become a part of the larger economy. According to Roger Waldinger in *Ethnic Entrepreneurs*,[55] the involvement of New York's earlier immigrant groups—Jews, Italians, and Greeks—as "owner/operators" or entrepreneurs "played an important role in their economic progress" while keeping their cultural heritage alive through the traditional foods they produced. Many factors can influence the success of a small business, but when an immigrant entrepreneur meets the needs of an underserved market in a concentrated urban environment, his chances of success are greater,[56] as both Ramon Acevedo and New York's tortillas manufacturers have found to be the case.

New York's diverse populations also provide opportunities for products to cross ethnic boundaries and enter the mainstream, as exemplified by Manhattan Special Espresso Coffee Soda. Products once regarded as exotic become more familiar when served in restaurants and sold in supermarkets that cater to a wide variety of consumers, as geographic proximity creates interconnections.[57] The blurring of borders is illustrated by Twin Marquis, opened as a small noodle factory in Manhattan's Chinatown by brothers Terry and Joseph Tang in 1989. Expanding four years later

into a space fifteen times larger in East Williamsburg, Brooklyn, they added dumpling
wrappers and dim sum to their repertoire. Although all their employees, with the
exception of a few executives, are from China, Hong Kong, Vietnam, and Taiwan,
the Tangs increased their business by creating products for a seemingly unusual new
group of customers. The idea for their new venture originated with requests from
local customers, as well as from buyers at national trade shows, to produce kosher
versions of their foods. After discovering that New York had the largest Jewish population in the country, they decided to enter this market. Since Twin Marquis's products can easily be adapted to adhere to kosher guidelines, the Tangs began to offer
a variety of dumplings and spring rolls. Terry Tang believes that theirs is the only
Asian-owned factory in the city that employs a rabbi to certify its products.[58] The
intersection of these two ethnic groups is not as strange as it may appear, however, as
Jewish patrons have been frequenting New York's Chinese restaurants since the early
twentieth century.[59] Even though Twin Marquis serves two groups of customers, one
Asian and the other Jewish, both are specialized markets in New York's distinctive,
multifaceted populace.

The Best Place in the World

Uniqueness is part of the allure of *terroir.* Not only do the food manufacturers consider New York to be special, but several of them have remained in the city because
they consider it to be the best (or possibly the only) city in the world. The majority
of food producers also live in New York and therefore have located their companies
in their hometown. One of the reasons that Mike Katsoris resisted moving Supreme
Chocolatiers to North Carolina was that "after life in New York, everything else
is so boring." He also believes that for "every con there is a pro," and others agree
that New York is not just the only city in which to live, but also a wonderful place in
which to do business.

In 2000, when Sarabeth's Kitchen had to expand the factory that makes its jams,
William Levine, the president of the company, never considered relocating. One of
the reasons that he believes its current location on a desolate stretch of road in the
Hunt's Point section of the Bronx is an ideal site is because of its close proximity to
the Hunt's Point Market, "where every type of available produce comes into New
York," including those in the company's jams. Levine also considers New York to
be an economical location because he has mastered the intricacies of multiple city
and state programs, securing tax abatements, relocation assistance, preferred utility
rates, and subsidized salaries for some of his employees. He cannot imagine why a
food company would not want to be in the city, since there are "so many prospective
customers," and he agrees with Mike Katsoris that there is "enough business in New
York to keep any business going."[60]

New York is "the greatest city in the world," said John S. Wilcha, the Bronx-
educated former chairman of Old London Foods, interviewed while he was still with
the company in early 2005. The company was more than happy to remain in its
Bronx factory, where it bakes 98 percent of all the melba toast sold in supermarkets

across the country. Constructed in 1968, the factory is a sleek, white-brick building in the middle of an eight-acre parking lot in the Morris Park section of the Bronx, almost adjacent to the Hutchinson River Parkway, which offers good transportation. But, more important, is its "skilled, loyal workforce."

Melba toast was created at the Devon Bakery in the Starrett-Leigh Building in Manhattan in 1932 when Marjorie Weil devised a method to re-create crackers sampled at Delmonico's by flattening thin slices of toasted bread with a clothes iron. Her husband, Bert, then invented mechanical ovens for mass-production.[61] Renamed Devonsheer Melba in the 1940s, the company licensed the rights to Old London Foods, also founded in the 1930s. Today, six huge silos, each holding 100,000 pounds of wheat, tower over the two-story factory where squat, black compressing irons, similar to the original invention, flatten sliced and toasted bread, which is transported by conveyor belts to automatic packaging machines. The company's ownership has changed several times over the years, hitting a low point in 1997, when Bronx officials scrambled to keep two hundred long-term jobs in the borough.[62] When the company was bought by Dubilier and Partners, the workforce was expanded to 250 mainly female union workers, under Wilcha's reign. The company was sold again in February 2005, for $70 million, to Chicago-based Nonni's Food Company, and the new owners have vowed to keep the factory operating and to "add significant numbers of jobs to the Bronx plant."[63] The Bronx is also home to Stella D'Oro, founded by Italian immigrants, also in 1932, and once the nation's largest family-owned cookie maker. It is now part of the global Kraft Foods Corporation.

The Unique Human Factor

An asset repeatedly mentioned by the city's food manufacturers is New York's skilled and loyal workers. Today, slightly more than "5 percent of all the manufacturing employment"[64] is in the food industry, which has steadily employed more than fourteen thousand employees.[65] Cumberland Packing, Old London Foods, and Christopher Norman Chocolates credit their workers' contribution to their success, and they are part of the human history of the city's *terroir*.

American Vintage Wine Biscuits, the small artisanal company mentioned at the beginning of this chapter, was started sixteen years ago by Mary-Lynn Modich, who had moved to New York as a young chef. Adapting an old family recipe to produce handmade savory crackers, she was soon packaging them for distribution. The company has moved through various stages of evolution while retaining a craftsman-like atmosphere. In a small, industrial kitchen, a closely knit group of six women hand-roll dough into long tubes, slice it, and then pack the baked, slightly irregularly shaped crackers in hand-labeled packages. The employees' tenure ranges from ten to sixteen years, and the head baker, who has been with American Vintage since its inception, keeps the company's baking secrets and recipes in her head, a matchless human skill that Daniel W. Gade describes as a component of *terroir*. Although not a native New Yorker, Monich considers the city to be her home, the only place where she believes her small team can produce her unique biscuits, which, if transplanted elsewhere, would lose their "soul," as she derisively describes a competitor's products after relocation.[66]

Moving Elsewhere

Some manufacturers do consider relocation when expansion is necessary or, in the case of one company, when the environment becomes too hostile. Gillies Coffee Company, one of the oldest coffee merchants in the country and doing business in New York since 1841, is now owned by the second and third generations of the Schoenfelt family. The roaster moved from Greenwich Village to Sunset Park in early 1991 and, because it had installed high-tech roasting equipment, was astounded in April 2003 when an anonymous complaint to the Department of Environmental Protection resulted in charges against the company for "fugitive odors": the smell of coffee. Believing that the charges were false, Gillies began a $40,000 battle over a $400 fine. Although owner Donald Schoenfelt hopes he can survive in the city he loves, where he has "great customers" and a long history, he finds doing business in New York "so difficult to cross every 't' and dot every 'i' in the myriad of city regulations." He has come to believe that the city government has a "hidden agenda," in which "all little businesses [would] be ground out." He is in a fragile position in which the city holds the upper hand, and he fears that the company may be forced to move elsewhere.[67]

For Damascus Bread, simple finances may be what will tip the scales, forcing it to leave the city, according to owner Edward Mafoud, the third-generation producer of pita and flat bread. The noisy, crowded factory's computerized machinery can speed ten thousand dough balls an hour through high-temperature ovens, which create the hollow center of six-inch pitas. But the company has just about outgrown its small one-story bakery in Vinegar Hill, Brooklyn, as the neighborhood rapidly gentrifies (a new apartment building is within half a block of its corner lot, and several old buildings are rapidly converting into condominiums). The land under the bakery may be too valuable not to be converted into residential property. Projecting that constructing a new factory in the city would be too expensive, Damascus Bread is contemplating leaving New York within a year or two, when expansion becomes crucial.[68]

Any small business, particularly one with little capital or a small labor force, faces tremendous challenges, and the odds can be particularly daunting in New York. In a rented commercial kitchen, Pat Lindsay, with one part-time employee, personally makes every batch of the bottled natural juices—including tamarind, papaya, and sour sop flavors—of six-year-old Pat's Exotic Beverages. Although she would prefer to stay in the Bronx, close to her Caribbean customers, she needs more space to expand, and the high rents in New York are beyond her reach. Coupled with Lindsay's numerous and expensive parking tickets acquired while making deliveries, Pat's Exotic Beverages, unlike Ramon Acevedo's Rasol Food Corporation, cannot afford to remain in the city and also, reluctantly, may have to relocate.[69]

Although some food companies leave New York to expand or operate in more modern or less expensive facilities, many find ways to work successfully within the city's constraints. Despite the many hurdles, New York's food manufacturers continue to produce a banquet of foods. City government initiatives, proposed to create and maintain industrial neighborhoods, may help manufacturers in the future, and clearly this would be worthwhile, because eating locally produced foods generates benefits beyond satisfying hunger. As the layers of sediment that create the soil impart the unique tastes in the traditional sense of *terroir,* local food producers have long been a part of the history of New York. Moreover, preserving the fragile food traditions of previous generations enhances the heritage and cultural traditions of the city, strengthening the "sense of place."[70] Emerging ethnic entrepreneurs foster a sense of group identity through the foods they manufacture while creating jobs for those at the lowest rung of the economy. In addition, the new products developed in New York's cutting-edge food environment introduce varied new fare that can help counter the "flattening out of taste"[71] that occurs when foods are mass-produced by global corporations far from the flavors of local communities. Collectively, these factors add to the diversified flavors available in New York that make it such a vibrant and cosmopolitan food city.

Although some manufacturers in New York make foods that are best eaten when fresh, many produce foods packaged to last on the shelf, tasting the same whether purchased in one of the city's neighborhood markets or halfway across the world, and many have no distinctive New York identity. Why, then, should one make an effort to buy the products made in one's hometown? Donna Gabaccia explains, "If our food tastes good, gives us pleasure, and connects us—if only commercially or sentimentally—to our neighbors, why not embrace those ties and the multi-ethnic identities they create?"[72]

Locally made foods, either a hundred-year-old syrup or a five-year-old empanada, have "a unique and important story behind [their] creation," remarks Brian Halweil in *Eat Here,*[73] one that has a "face" in the anonymity of mass-produced foods. The narratives of New York's food producers are part of the saga of the city's past and the continuing, sometimes unfamiliar, tale of its present. Although the taste of the "asphalt *terroir*" or "place" is not easily discernable in many New York–produced foods, they are an interconnected part of the geographical and emotionally imagined place that is New York. These varied tastes are woven into the city's identity, the place that locally produced foods have had in New York since its earliest days, and the position that they should have in its future.

NOTES

I would like to thank Jonathan Deutsch and Annie Hauck-Lawson for their insightful guidance, patience, and unwavering support, and Amy Bentley for gently guiding me toward the ideas that formed this chapter. The manufacturers interviewed in this chapter were selected from several sources. Some were recommended by the Brooklyn Chamber of Commerce, New York Industrial Retention Network, New York State Department of Agriculture and Markets, and the manufacturers themselves. Additional companies were also chosen from NYIRN's Web site (http://www.madeinnyc.org), from newspaper articles, and by inspecting products on the shelves of New York City supermarkets. Because most of the companies discussed have taken advantage of available marketing programs or have a presence in supermarkets and gourmet shops, the selection process may have biased the responses. Although New York also has a large segment of manufacturers supplying the food-service industry, this chapter focuses primarily on retail producers.

1. Becky Aikman, "Food Choices Abound in New York as Consumers Demand Highest-Quality Selections," *Newsday,* November 17, 2003, 1.

2. Janny Scott, "Enjoy That Danish: It's Lifting the City's Employment Rate," *New York Times,* July 31, 2003, B1.

3. New York Industrial Retention Network (NYIRN), *Food from New York: An Analysis of New York City's Food Manufacturing Industry* (New York: New York Industrial Retention Network, 1997), 7.

4. Emmanuelle Vaudour, "The Quality of Grapes and Wine in Relation to Geography: Notions of *Terroir* at Various Scales," *Journal of Wine Research* 13 (2003): 117–41.

5. Daniel W. Gade, "Tradition, Territory, and *Terroir* in French Viniculture: Cassis, France, and *Appellation Controlée*," *Annals of the Association of American Geographers* 94 (2004): 866.

6. Kate Washington, "Singles Bars," *Sunset,* February 2005, 26; Emily Schwab, "Coffee for the Connoisseur," *Boston Globe,* August 4, 2004, E2; Janice Schindeler, "Think Taste, Texture and 'Terroir,'" *Houston Chronicle,* June 23, 2004, 1; Marie Valla and Christopher Dickey, "A Cuisine Crisis: France's Famed Food Industry Is in Decline. Blame Globalization as Well as the French Government," *Newsweek,* May 24, 2004, 40; Patrick Martins, "Set That Apricot Free," *New York Times,* April 24, 2004, A17.

7. Amy B. Trubek, "Incorporating *Terroir*: L'Affaire Mondavi Reconsidered," *Gastronomica* 4, no. 3 (2004): 90.

8. Gade, "Tradition, Territory, and *Terroir*," 849.

9. Timothy J. Tomaski, "Certeau à la Carte: Translating Discursive *Terroir* in the Practice of Everyday Life: Living and Cooking," *South Atlantic Quarterly* 100 (2001): 519–37.

10. Ibid.

11. Barbara G. Shortridge and James R. Shortridge, "Food and American Culture," 7; Stephen Frenkel, "A Pound of Kenya, Please, or a Single Short Skinny Mocha," 61; George H. Lewis, "The Maine Lobster as Regional Icon: Competing Images over Time and Social Class," 66; and Cary W. de Wit, "Food-Place Associations on American Product Labels," 101, all in *The Taste of American Place: A Reader on Regional and Ethnic Foods,* ed. Barbara G. Shortridge and James R. Shortridge (Lanham, Md.: Rowman & Littlefield, 1998).

12. NYIRT, *Food from New York;* manufacturers, interviews with author.

13. J. Freirich Company, http://www.freirich.com/index.asp (accessed April 8, 2005).

14. Virginia Draper Harrington, *The New York Merchant on the Eve of the Revolution* (New York: Columbia University Press, 1935), 88, 206–8.

15. Ibid., 147–48.

16. Edwin G. Burrows and Mike Wallace, *Gotham: A History of New York City to 1898* (New York: Oxford University Press, 1999), 431.

17. Ibid., 475.

18. "Biographical Sketch of Robert L. and Alexander Stuart," in *Encyclopaedia of Contemporary Biography of New York,* vol. 2 (New York: Atlantic Publishing and Engraving, 1882).

19. Burrows and Wallace, *Gotham,* 740–41.

20. Ibid., 786.

21. Alfred S. Eichner, *The Emergence of Oligopoly: Sugar Refining as a Case Study* (Baltimore: Johns Hopkins University Press, 1969), 43.

22. "Candy Trade's Growth," *New York Times,* December 20, 1903, 18.

23. "Loose-Wiles Biscuit Co.," *Wall Street Journal,* June 12, 1915.

24. Faith Moors Williams, *The Food Manufacturing Industries in New York and Its Environs: Present Trends and Probable Future Developments* (New York: Regional Plan of New York and Its Environs, 1924).

25. "Queens Attracts More Industries," *New York Times,* February 1, 1942.

26. Sarah Kershaw, "Baking School Offers Job Skills in an Old Specialty," *New York Times,* July 18, 2002, B1.

27. New York Industrial Retention Network, *Baked in New York: Special Report to the Consortium for Worker Education and the Artisan Baking Center* (New York: New York Industrial Retention Network, 2002), 1.

28. Kolleen M. Guy, *When Champagne Became French: Wine and the Making of a National Identity* (Baltimore: Johns Hopkins University Press, 2003), 44.

29. Donna R. Gabaccia, *We Are What We Eat: Ethnic Food and the Making of Americans* (Cambridge, Mass.: Harvard University Press, 1998), 68.

30. Aurora Passaro, interview with author, January 20, 2005.

31. Gabaccia, *We Are What We Eat,* 91.

32. "Candy Trade's Growth."

33. Charles Delafuente, "A Longtime Brooklyn Company That's Known for Its Sesame Sweet," *New York Times,* November 8, 2004, B1.

34. David Fox, e-mail interview with author, April 12, 2005.

35. Some New York food manufacturers consider the city's water to be an essential ingredient in their products. Water is more closely connected to the traditional meaning of *terroir,* and determining whether its effects on manufactured products are related to its high quality and neutral taste or to the elusive mythic status it has gained over the years would warrant an additional study. However, there are those, particularly bakers, who believe that New York City water creates especially fine products. Indeed, New York bagel maker Steve Ross insisted on using city water trucked to Washington, D.C., for a demonstration at the Smithsonian Folklife Festival in 2001. He "tried to make a few bagels and bialys with Washington water and we couldn't get a rise out of the dough. I can't pinpoint what it is—the chemicals in the water, the filtration process, or what—but New York water's the best water around" ("Born to Make Bagels," http://www.nyc24.org/2002/issue01/story02/page02.asp). A similar sentiment was expressed by Damascus Bakery's quality-control manager, Irene Jonata, in an interview with me in 2005. When discussing the company's possible relocation, Jonata expressed concern that if the bakery did not have access to New York water, which she considered the best for baking purposes, the taste of its products would be negatively altered, and all the company's recipes would have to be reformulated to replicate their original flavor.

36. Arthur Schwartz, *Arthur Schwartz's New York City Food* (New York: Stewart, Tabori & Chang, 2004), 132–33.

37. Mike Katsoris, interview with author, January 7, 2005.

38. Julia Moskin, "Hints of Wine? Chocolate Enters the Tasting Room," *New York Times,* December 3, 2003, F1.

39. John Down, interview with author, November 9 2005; Joe Guiliano, interview with author, November 9, 2005.

40. Tomasik, "Certeau à La Carte," 527.

41. Krishnendu Ray, "Ethnic Succession: A Review Essay," *Food, Culture and Society: An International Journal of Multidisciplinary Research* 8 (2005): 132.

42. Seth Kugel, "How Brooklyn Became New York's Tortilla Basket," *New York Times,* February 25, 2001, 14.

43. Joel Millman, "New Blood: How Mexicans Revived the Economy in a Corner of Brooklyn," *Wall Street Journal,* July 10, 1997, A12.

44. Carolina Gonzalez, "Family Fosters Flour Power: Tortillas Grind Out a Big Business," *New York Daily News,* April 13, 1997, Suburban section, 1.

45. Kugel, "How Brooklyn Became New York's Tortilla Basket."

46. Erasmo Ponce, interview with author, May 15, 2005.

47. Ewa Morawska, "Immigrant Transnational Entrepreneurs in New York: Three Varieties and Their Correlates," *International Journal of Entrepreneurial Behavior and Research* 10 (2004): 325–48.

48. Gade, "Tradition, Territory, and *Terroir,*" 849.

49. Tom Fredrickson, "There Is No Substitute," *Crain's New York Business,* July 2–8, 2001, 1.

50. Marvin Eisenstadt, interview with author, October 26, 2005.

51. Rhonda Abrams, *Wear Clean Underwear: Business Wisdom from Mom, Timeless Advice from the Ultimate CEO* (New York: Dell, 2000); Eisenstadt interview.

52. Linda J. Wong, "The Role of the Immigrant Entrepreneurs in Urban Economic Development," *Stanford Law & Policy Review* 7 (1996): 75–87.

53. Lutzie Vieluf, interview with author, April 28, 2005.

54. Acevedo Ramon, telephone interview with author, February 15, 2005.

55. Roger David Waldinger, Robin Ward, and Howard Aldrich, *Ethnic Entrepreneurs: Immigrant Business in Industrial Societies* (Newbury Park, Calif.: Sage, 1990).

56. Kugel, "How Brooklyn Became New York's Tortilla Basket."

57. David Bell, "Fragments for a New Urban Culinary Geography," *Journal for the Study of Food and Society* 6 (2002): 10–21.

58. Terry Tang, telephone interview with author, February 2, 2005.

59. Gaye Tuchman and Harry Gene Levine, "New York Jews and Chinese Food: The Social Construction of an Ethnic Pattern," *Journal of Contemporary Ethnography* 22 (1993): 382–407.

60. John Wilcha, interview with author, November 22, 2004.

61. Obituary of Marjorie Weil, *Washington Post,* April 24, 1990, B6.

62. David W. Chen, "Layoffs Stun Bakery Staff at Melba Toast Company," *New York Times,* April 4, 1997, B5.

63. Lore Croghan, "New Owner Plans to Keep Melba Toast Plant Open," *Knight Ridder Tribune Business News,* February 18, 2005, 1.

64. NYIRN, *Food from New York,* 1.

65. New York State Department of Labor, http://madeinnyc.org/about.cfm (accessed January 15, 2004).

66. Mary-Lynn Mondich, interview with author, November 12, 2004.

67. Donald Schoenfelt, interview with author, November 19, 2004.

194

68. Edward Mafoud, interview with author, September 14, 2005.

69. Pat Lindsay, telephone interview with author, February 14, 2005.

70. Gade, "Tradition, Territory, and *Terroir*," 862.

71. Bell, "Fragments for a New Urban Culinary Geography."

72. Gabaccia, *We Are What We Eat,* 231.

73. Brian Halweil, *Eat Here: Reclaiming Homegrown Pleasures in a Global Supermarket* (New York: Norton, 2004), 123.

The Soul of a Store

MARK RUSS FEDERMAN

THE YIDDISH word that comes to mind is *yichus*. It means "pedigree" or "lineage" and usually refers to royalty or religion, lords or rabbis, the mantle passed down from generation to generation, always along the male line. Since Yiddish is a language that adapts its meanings to local usages, *yichus* has been used loosely on the Lower East Side of New York to describe any family business with the rare good fortune of having survived the generational transfer from father to son. Our family, though, has no royalty or rabbis. We are clearly from peasant stock, and the business being passed on is neither royal nor religious, but fish: smoked, cured, and pickled. I also should note that the business was originally passed down not from father to son, but from father to daughters. We are the Russ family, and our business is called Russ & Daughters. The sign over the door proclaims: Russ & Daughters, Appetizers.

The Memory of Smell

Old-fashioned appetizing stores like Russ & Daughters have a smell that is unique among all specialty food shops. It is the first sensation as you open the door, and it is easily recognizable if you are over the age of forty-five and have grown up in a mostly ethnic Jewish area in one of the five boroughs of New York City, where the concept of the "appetizing store" originated and, for the most part, has remained. This special smell is a combination of particular odors that together become less intense but at the same time more pleasing than any one of its individual parts. It is the combination of smoke, salt, pickle, and sweet. This combination is derived from the various products sold in the store: smoked whitefish, sturgeon, and salmon; salt-cured lox and herring;

The interior of Russ & Daughters. (Photograph courtesy of Russ & Daughters)

pickled cucumbers and tomatoes; and halvah, rugelach, and chocolate jelly rings—on the "candy side" of the traditional appetizing store.

One of the great perks for me, as the third-generation owner of Russ & Daughters, is to see the immediate sense of joy experienced by those who enter our store and are taken back by the aroma. How many times have customers said, with a humor suffused with nostalgia, "If only you could bottle this smell."

These smells connect my past to my present each time I enter the store. As a child, it never bothered me to have been born into a world of smoked fish and herring, even though we smelled different from everyone else. Maybe it was because there were so many of us—grandparents and parents, aunts and uncles—who smelled the same way: fishy and smoky. It never bothered me that my friends' parents went to work in office buildings and worked only five days a week (never on weekends), wore suits, and smelled like soap or deodorant or cologne. It never bothered me because while we were different, we were special.

These smells now bring back memories of a father's taking his son to work in a big, red truck that was more high, square, and boxy than long and sleek. Its logo, in Old English typeface—somewhat incongruous, given that it was used for transporting smoked fish and herring—read:

Russ & Daughters
Queens of Lake Sturgeon

(It wasn't until much later in life that it was explained to me that the title "Sturgeon King" had already been co-opted by an uptown rival.)

Occasionally, I got to ride with my father in the cab of that red truck as he made his rounds from home—then in Far Rockaway—first to the smokehouses in Brooklyn, then to Ratners on Delancey Street for a breakfast of onion rolls and salt sticks, and finally to the store. The first stops were to one or several smokehouses, depending on how many it took before Russ & Daughters was satisfied with the quality and amount for that day's needs. Entering the world of the smokehouse is not a normal experience for a boy of nine or ten years. Everything is different, and it all assaults at once: the sights, smells, and tastes. It is a sensory experience that either leaves you nauseated and totally disgusted or is imprinted on your sensory memory in such a way that reexperiencing those sights, smells, and tastes twenty, thirty, forty, and, now, more than fifty years later feels a lot like coming home after a long trip.

The memories flood back: cavernous rooms with soot- and smoke-blackened walls; intense smells, some sweet and others acrid; and the sight of fish, all manner of fish, submerged in briny baths in huge steel vats, suspended from wooden hooks threaded through their tails, splayed on racks going into or coming out of smoke-filled oven rooms, and finally packed into boxes, hundreds and hundreds of them lining the walls and ready for the "jobbers" who delivered them to stores or for the merchants, like Russ & Daughters, who had to see, smell, and taste each fish before buying it.

The actual fish tasting was a show in and of itself that followed pretty much the same script each time I accompanied my father or uncle to the smokehouses. (Although the store was named Russ & Daughters and its success was largely due to the presence and hard work of the Russ daughters, not one of them ever went to the smokehouse. That was a man's job.) After carefully turning the fish skin side up and pricking a small hole through the center so as not to damage its look and ultimate sale, extracting a small sample, mouthing it, and then spitting it out, my father opened the topic of whether this particular batch of fish was good enough to be sold at Russ & Daughters. The conversation seemed more like a verbal brawl than a serious business negotiation. Particular catchphrases were always used: "This fish is uglier than you"; "If you knew anything about fish, you wouldn't have to sell it to make a living." Shouting and cursing were the accepted forms of communication, and there was no attempt to tone it down even in the presence of a ten-year-old boy. Looking back now, I suspect that part of the show was for my benefit, with the underlying message: "Look, kid, every day is a battle. We enjoy our battles; it's all we know, but you don't have to do this for a living. . . . When you grow up, get a good education and you won't have to sell fish."

After finishing at the smokehouses and loading the truck, we would cross the Williamsburg Bridge. There was always a traffic cop at the anchorage of the bridge on the Manhattan side, and invariably he would recognize our truck and my father and would wave with a big smile and a "Hi, Herbie." If there was enough time before the light changed, he might add, "Teaching your kid the business?" This ritual always impressed me. Cops were important people in those days, and for them to know and seemingly treat my father with respect felt good to me. I may not have expected or even wanted to sell fish when I grew up, but I knew that I did want to become someone important and recognized like Herbie.

The Family

For my grandfather Joel Russ, getting his daughters into the business was not a matter of gentle persuasion. It was a matter of *parnosa*, surviving and making a living. *Vi nemptmen parnosa?* was the refrain most often heard from Joel Russ: "From where do we take our living?" All other questions or issues were of lesser concern. So for these female offspring of Jewish immigrants to the Lower East Side, higher education was not an entitlement, not even an option.

Hattie, Ida, and Anne were the three daughters for whom Joel Russ eventually named his store. It was not, as some might think, that he was an early feminist ahead of his time. It was, rather, that he recognized two things: it was indeed his daughters who had helped him grow and keep his store, and the name Russ & Daughters would be a good marketing tool, since of the twenty or so appetizing shops in the Lower East Side, many had "& Sons" hanging over their doors, but none had "& Daughters."

The store was not always called Russ & Daughters; indeed, it was not always a store. It began as a pushcart that was traded up for a horse and wagon, both of which predated the births of the three Russ daughters. The first store was opened in 1914 on Orchard Street, and in the early 1920s it was moved to its present location on East Houston Street. But it was always on the Lower East Side.

Hattie, the oldest daughter, was the most willing and comfortable in her role in the store and in pleasing her father. Ida, the middle child and the most contentious, spent several years locked in battle with her father about matters both business and personal, and she and her husband ultimately "left" the store. (They either were thrown out by my grandfather or left by their own design, depending on which side of the family is telling the story.) Anne, the youngest daughter and my mother, came in most reluctantly and harbored a quiet resentment about "giving up her youth" until she left the business in 1978, forty years later.

Although Joel Russ did not "arrange" the marriages of his three daughters, he did make sure to retain what would be called in business today "the right of first refusal." He would size up each potential suitor, and there were many for the three young, pretty, and hard-working girls whose father owned a store, not just a pushcart. His evaluation was based solely on whether these future sons-in-law would make "good workers."

After World War II, with his three daughters married and his three sons-in-law ensconced in the store, Joel Russ retired from actively running the business. But for him, retirement meant coming into the store four or five days a week instead of six. Instead of putting on a white "behind-the-counter" apron, he wore one of his meticulously tailored suits. He also moved his red leather chair, cracked with age and stained with fish oils, from his tiny office in the back of the store to a strategic location in the front, facing the fish counter. He could then observe and direct all activities simply by pointing his gold-handled cane at an employee, usually a member of the family, and saying *Nicht a zoy* (Not like that).

When you enter the store today and look up to the right, you see a very large portrait of Joel Russ covering much of the wall space between the shelves and the ceiling. For those of us who work in the store, his portrait faces us as we work on the fish side. Curiously, the eyes of the portrait, though seemingly focused on the cash register, seem to follow us, especially family members, as we walk to either end of the counter. Fortunately, there is the very faintest of smiles on his face, which we take to mean that he is proud of his store and of us, those Russes who keep it surviving and thriving.

I am the only one of the seven Russ grandchildren who chose to go into the business. I had been a lawyer at a fancy, uptown law firm. There was absolutely no expectation that I would take over the business. In fact, the expectation was that all the grandchildren would find a better way to make a living. They all kvelled over me, the only lawyer and the very first "professional man" in the family.

The Customers

While I chose to leave the practice of law and take over the store, the transition from lex to lox was not easy. I had come in with the inflated ego of a trial attorney. I would be the one who turned this mom-and-pop fish store into a "real business." There would be operations manuals, spreadsheets, computers, lots and lots of computers. Ultimately, I would franchise; I would turn this neighborhood shop into "McHerrings." But I learned quickly, on my very first day on the counter, that I would need to park my ego at the door.

I was completely full of myself. After all, I was more educated, accomplished, and cultured than any of the other employees or, indeed, anyone else in my family, current or previous generations. Then a giant limousine pulled up in front of the store, one of those that occupies three parking meters' worth of space. Out of that limo came a rather matronly woman wearing a double or triple mink coat that could have been made only from seventeen identical mink siblings and was affordable only to those who had a brother-in-law in the fur trade. She marched into the store and immediately demanded to see Anne: "Anne always waits on me and knows just what kind of sturgeon to give me and how to cut it." "Well, I am Anne's son, and I'm sure that I can help you," I offered. She said nothing else as I reached into the counter to where the sturgeon was displayed. "Aaaaaach!!" This was the first shriek of disapproval from a middle-aged, wealthy Jewish matron that I heard in the store, though there would be many more in the years to come. "Your mother gets me the 'private stock sturgeon.'"

"Private stock" is a term of art in the smoked fish world. It describes a particular piece of sturgeon, the crème de la crème of all smoked fish, that has been selected from the batch because of its particular fattiness, taste, and texture. (To fish cognoscenti, "fatty" fish are considered better because of their richer taste and, as it turns out, their omega-3 fatty acids, which reduce the body's bad cholesterol.) So private

The smoked fish case at Russ & Daughters. (Photograph courtesy of Russ & Daughters)

stock sturgeon was reserved for those who would appreciate the difference and could pay the higher price it commanded.

At that moment, I surely wanted to let this lady know who I was: not a mere counter person, not just the son of one of the owners, but a lawyer with a substantial curriculum vitae. But pleasing the customer was always the family mantra, and so I reached below the counter to the hidden refrigerator in which the "private stock" sturgeon was kept. I brought it up to the cutting board and with a bit of fanfare proceeded to slice. "Aaaach!" she screeched again, but this time it was not so much the sound that pierced but the look of total disdain that only a woman originally from the Lower East Side and recently made wealthy (probably with a husband in the *shmata* trade) could muster up and deliver to someone who she believed was unfortunate enough to be stuck on the Lower East Side and who had no obvious exit plan. (At that time and for that generation, it was all about "getting out" of the Lower East Side.) Well, I had to disabuse her of this notion of superiority and set her straight— customer or not. As I looked up to deliver my rebuttal in my most lawyerly style, I committed what I would learn was the first and most important rule of smoked fish safety: never look up with a knife in your hand! Needless to say, the cut was deep and bloody. But before the shrew realized what was happening, I excused myself and said that I would get someone else who would cut the sturgeon according to her wishes. With that, I went to the back of the store, got a replacement counter person, wrapped a towel around my bleeding hand, slipped out unnoticed, and went straight to the emergency room of Beth Israel Hospital. Thirty years later, the scar from the cut and ensuing sixteen stitches reminds me that for all my fancy, schmancy résumé, I am and will always be a counter person at Russ & Daughters, there to serve the customers. Forgetting that and still trying to be the lawyer can be dangerous to my health.

Now, thirty years later, I also realize that it has always been about the customers, and sometimes I think I have stayed in the business this long just to hear their stories. Very often we are part of those stories. With our food, we share the customers' celebrations and their tribulations, their *nochis* and their *tsouris*. We have grown to know them and their families over the years and even the generations. What a joy to prepare platters for the wedding of a customer whose bris and bar mitzvah we had catered. What a heartache to prepare the shiva platters for the death of someone who was, for so many years, as much a friend as a customer. What pleasure it is for us to know that when friends and family gather, they want to mark the occasion with food from Russ & Daughters. It often has been said that New York has a love affair with Russ & Daughters. It should also be said that Russ & Daughters has a love affair with New York and New Yorkers.

Of course, we get our fair share of those who kvetch and are just plain difficult: "You sure it's fresh?" "Don't give me that one; I want one from underneath." "Make sure it's a 'nice one.'" But more often than not, we hear things like "This store speaks to my soul." Perhaps the ultimate compliment was paid to us by being included in the eulogy delivered by her granddaughter on the death of one of our old and dear customers:

> I have traveled all over the country, but I don't believe that there is any place other than New York City that boasts so many family businesses who operate "family style." In the age of Target and Wal-Mart, it's nice to know you can still walk into a store, find the owner, and share with him a little bit about your own family. Growing up, I always knew the name, Russ & Daughters, and that my grandmother, Ann Revits, loved the smoked salmon from there. No matter where my grandmother was, in Brooklyn, in Battery Park, or in Miami, we always managed to get her a smoked salmon fix from her favorite store on the Lower East Side. . . .
>
> Food was the primary motivator, discussion point, activity, and obsession. How it was bought, delivered, prepared, eaten, wrapped, and stored. It wasn't just that we discussed what we were having for dinner while we were having lunch. It was the constant striving for perfection in all meals at all times in all locations, no matter what. Of course, the classic example of this is her ability to barter for, appreciate, and consume *smoked salmon*.
>
> Once when I was in my twenties I was sent on a mission to the Lower East Side emporium that was good enough to satisfy Ann Revits's discerning palate: Russ & Daughters. Maybe my grandmother was one of the renegade daughters who never got the chance to have her way with a lox behind the counter. Her request was simple enough: a half pound of salmon. But it was the way she executed this request that made it totally Grandma: she handed me a note to give to the counter man: "Slice it thin for my granddaughter, and you better make sure it's from the belly. Don't send her out of that store unless it's from the belly!"

You can't imagine how happy it made me to successfully perform a salmon run. Her reaction if it was good: "Oh, darling, this is like diamonds!" Her reserved expression for something that was beyond all expectations.

There are, of course, general themes that seem to course through many of the stories of customers, but there is always something unique, something special about each story that keeps me listening. Then there are those stories that seem to sum up the entire Lower East Side, Russ & Daughters experience.

It happened every year in the exact same way. You could mark your calendar by its recurrence. She called herself "Mrs. Manny." That's the only name I knew her by and called her by, even though she had been a customer for many years. I also knew something about her children—this from her kvelling. There were five children, four were boys, and three of them had gone to Harvard Law School and were very successful. She and her late husband had raised these children somewhere on the Lower East Side. Now her grandchildren were attending Ivy League schools.

It would be seven days before *erev* Rosh Hashanah, the eve of the Jewish New Year. The store always would be exceptionally busy for this holiday period. It would be between 6:30 and 6:40 P.M.; the store closed at 7:00. She would emerge from the subway on the corner, pushing her little shopping cart. There would be just enough time at the front door to be spotted by the counter staff who would, as though on cue, let out a collective groan. They would then flee to the kitchen area in the back or put their current sale into slow motion so as not to have to wait on her. She was sweet but demanding in a way that came from making a living the hard way. She demanded quality, she demanded value, and she demanded service. Every year it fell to me, the owner, to wait on Mrs. Manny.

Mrs. Manny was at Russ & Daughters with only one mission: to purchase eighteen herrings that she would schlep home and then pickle. The number eighteen was significant to her: in Hebrew, the word for "eighteen" is *chai,* which also means "life." This number allowed her to give three herrings each to her five children as gifts for the New Year and save three herrings for herself, which she would share with certain, anointed, neighbors.

For some time, Mrs. Manny had been relegated to buying her herrings from the display case in the front of the store. But that ended when she had somehow found out that Mimi Sheraton, the former eminent restaurant critic for the *New York Times,* had been allowed to pick her herrings right from the barrels in the back of the store. Mrs. Manny would accept nothing less when buying herrings for her family. Thereafter, Mrs. Manny and Mimi Sheraton were the only two customers ever allowed to go to the back of the store to select their herrings right from the barrels. Of the two, Mimi Sheraton, known for her sharp eye and discerning palate, was the easier to please; this was taken as a compliment by Mrs. Manny, as it would have been by a generation of Jewish women who regarded shopping for food to be both a fine art and an act of war.

The actual process of choosing which of the approximately 250 herrings in a barrel would go home with her to be pickled was treated with the same degree of gravitas as deciding which of the many young women from the neighborhood she would allow her sons to "court" or which college they would attend. So the battle, or rather the sale, would begin and end in the same way each year. If I was lucky, it would take a half hour. But more often than not, it would take forty-five minutes, fifteen minutes past closing time; when we emerged from the "walk-in," most of the store lights would be off, and the staff would be dressed to go home and in over-time mode.

The process would start with my removing several layers of herring from the top of a barrel and dumping them into an empty bucket. It was understood, without ever having to be said, that Mrs. Manny would never buy a herring from the top of the barrel. The inspection would continue with my fishing the herrings from the barrel one by one, holding each up, and then turning it over and over in my hand for Mrs. Manny's examination. It was as thorough an exam as any doctor would ever perform when attempting to diagnose a member of his own family. Even though every barrel of herring that Russ & Daughters bought contained only top-quality herrings, Mrs. Manny was determined to find "diamonds" in those barrels. And, I must admit, she knew what to look for: clear, shiny, steel-blue skin; plump but firm flesh on the back; and no blemishes, marks, or bruises. Mrs. Manny was a true maven.

One year, she did not come. She never appeared at the store again. There was no way of knowing what had happened. Did she buy a bad herring the year before? Did she find a better place to buy herring? Did her doctor tell her not to expend her strength any longer preparing herrings or not to eat herring anymore? Or did she die?

Some years later, my wife and I were having dinner with new friends, a couple from our home neighborhood. At some point, the husband and I began to recount our Lower East Side roots. He had been raised in a tenement above the shoe store owned by his father. There were four other children, all successful, and three of the boys had attended Harvard Law School. He understood my daily life as a retailer because he and his siblings had been required to work in their father's store on weekends and after school. The name of the shoe store, after his father, was Manny's.

He went on to tell of his familiarity with Russ & Daughters. It seems that every year his mother would go to the store before the Jewish holidays in order to buy herrings from the barrel that she would pickle and give to her children as gifts. Each year, she presented a jar of those herrings, interlaced with onions, to her children as though they were the greatest treasure in the world. None of the children really liked the herring, my friend said, but no one would dare tell her; it was an absolute, un-breakable tradition. Now they miss the herrings pickled by their mother. And I miss Mrs. Manny, too.

The Help

Hiring, firing, human resources, medical benefits, pension benefits, vacations, sick pay—these were concepts that had no meaning for most of the early years at Russ & Daughters. Who needed employees or issues of employment? The family was the workforce, and cheap labor at that. Joel Russ had three daughters, who in turn had three husbands, and that was enough; at times, because the store was so small, it was more than enough. Aunt Hattie remembers that in the 1930s, she and her husband, Murray, were paid $25 for a six-day week, for both of them. Joel Russ paid each of his daughters and their husbands just enough to leave the Lower East Side, move to the suburbs, and buy a house and a car.

We kids, seven cousins in all, also were required to work in the store. From age thirteen (post–bar/bat mitzvah) to age eighteen (off to college), we would rotate shifts on weekends. We would work behind the candy counter, never the fish counter, where there were very sharp knives. The job was to wait on the customers by scooping candy, dried fruit, or nuts into a large stainless-steel basin that was on the right-hand tray of an old balance scale. On the left tray, we would put an appropriate disk-shaped weight or weights in one-, two-, or five-pound increments. In the middle of this scale—which now sits prominently as a display piece in the store, its former location occupied by a scale with no counterbalancing weights, but a digital readout—was a glass-enclosed viewer that had a movable arrow and several hatch marks, the largest and darkest in the center of the viewer. Obviously, when the arrow and the center marker were aligned, the weight was correct. To get that alignment on the first attempt seemed to us kids like hitting a home run, except that no customer was satisfied unless the arrow was at least a tad over on the heavy side, which meant that he or she got "good weight."

There was some sensitivity to the fact that we were not willing workers and would rather be home on a Saturday or Sunday, playing with our friends. So we were paid very well: $1.10 an hour. For a ten-hour day, we got $11 in cash, which was a huge bankroll for a young kid. It kept me in baseball cards, pizza, and Saturday-afternoon movies—assuming there was a Saturday when I did not have to work.

Besides the sense of wealth I had from working in the store, there was a sense of learning, an education about real life and real people and what it meant to "earn a buck" that I was not getting in school. So after my children reached the age of bar/bat mitzvah and before they went off to college, they were working in the store on weekends and holidays. And, as expected, they were not always willing workers.

My wife, too, became part of our cheap labor force. She had had a professional career but had left her position to raise our children. When they grew older and less demanding, she found her free time being spent in the store "helping out" with the books and ordering, as well as adding that feminine presence and flair that the store had not had since my mother—the last of the Russ daughters—had retired. After a while, she found herself putting in as much time and energy as any Russ did, and she then became my partner in the store as she was at home.

Recently, in discussing the store with my mother and Aunt Hattie, the two remaining Russ daughters, they remembered one very odd employee in the early days of the store. And then I also recalled this strange and scary presence from my earliest trips to the store.

Ivan was old. It is difficult to know how old because he definitely had been beaten up by a hard life. He was a drunkard from the Bowery when the Bowery was in the heyday of its infamy. He had been "saved" by my grandfather, who allowed him to sleep in the back of the store and paid him a wage—not much, I suspect—in return for doing all the schlepping and kitchen work: peeling onions, filleting herrings, washing pots and pans. Each morning, he would drag three two-hundred-pound barrels of herring from the back of the store to the front and then outside, where they would stay for the day so passersby could purchase herrings from one of the Russ girls. Ivan had not given up totally on life: for most of the day, he kept up a running monologue/argument with some form of deity. He would look up at the ceiling and shake his fist and say something in Polish that no one understood, not even my grandfather, who spoke Polish. It was clear to all that Ivan was not happy with his life and that he was holding God responsible for his plight. Curiously, Anne and Hattie remembered something else about Ivan. When it was mealtime at the store, he would carefully wash his hands, sit at a tiny table in the kitchen, and meticulously arrange for himself a plate with herring and smoked fish and bread and butter, which he would eat with knife and fork in an impeccable style that they could only describe as "the manners of nobility."

When I took over Russ & Daughters twenty-eight years ago, my mother and father were then running the store but were not in good health. With all the other family members out of the business, they had to rely on employees, and I inherited that rogues' gallery. The one thing this motley crew did have in common was their dislike of me or at least the idea of my taking over the business. After all, I was the owner's son and had had a fancy education. What could I possibly know about the world of smoked fish and herring, a subject in which they believed themselves to be expert. They were determined to see me fail. They were not smart enough to realize that if indeed I "killed" the business, they would be out of work. Of course, my parents would always say, "If they were that smart, you'd be working for them."

With my parents gone, Sidney, the store manager, quickly let it be known that I was working for him. He kept most of the daily tasks a secret and did his job with a certain severe theatricality. The message to me was that he was indispensable; he also delivered this message to each and every customer as often as he could. The best description of Sidney is the Yiddish word *farbissener*, someone dour and bitter who figures he got the short end of the stick and would make everyone around him suffer as well. Steinie was a roly-poly, good-natured incompetent whose primary function was as whipping boy for Sidney. When he left, Louie took over that position. On weekends, there were assorted characters, mostly retired Jewish appetizing-store owners whose own businesses had failed but who had not yet made the final exodus to Florida.

José and Herman were my first hires; they were the kitchen help. They were cousins, young Dominicans, and part of the new wave of immigration to the Lower East Side and, therefore, part of the new labor force. Their job consisted primarily of peeling onions, pickling herrings, and washing dishes—clearly not what they had come to America for, but they did their job very well and with great attitude and spirit. It was about two years into my regime when I finally figured out that it was either Sidney or me. The problem: Sidney was a union man and could not be summarily fired, no matter how bad his attitude. The solution: move José and Herman from the kitchen to the counter and put them in the union. The bigger problem: the concept of placing Latinos behind the smoked-fish counter in a traditional Jewish appetizing store

Mark, Josh, Niki, and Herman in front of Russ & Daughters. (Photograph courtesy of Russ & Daughters)

to serve the traditional Jewish customer had never been tried and was unthinkable. Fortunately for me, these two have talents I had not realized.

José has hands of gold, and watching him slice salmon is like watching the skill of a great surgeon. I have been known to quip, "I have had José's hands insured by Lloyds of London." Herman has the personality and charm of a great salesman, plus an uncanny ear for languages. It was not long before those customers who would normally demand a Jewish counter man were lined up waiting for Herman to fillet their herring and slice their lox while conducting a running commentary in Yiddish. With respect to Herman I have often said, "He was born in the Dominican Republic with the name Vargas, but he has become a Russ."

The Legacy

When I was approached to write a chapter for this book, I immediately refused. In this town, after all, I am known as "The Herring Maven," "The Lox Slicer," and "Mr.

Smoked Fish." I am certainly not a writer, nor do I have any pretensions to be. Indeed,
I have learned in this process that writing is even harder than retail. But when the editors suggested a title for my chapter, "The Soul of a Store," I agreed for two reasons. First, while on a daily basis I was buying and selling food, I always had a sense that there was something deeper going on at Russ & Daughters, something other than the exchange of money for food across a counter. It is, after all, a special kind of food, sold in a very special way, and it has been going on like this for a very long time.

Second, at age sixty-two I have somehow, and what seems to me suddenly, turned into the "old man" of the appetizing world. Like my grandfather Joel Russ, I am now ready to pass on the business to the next generation and move my chair from my tiny office in the back of the store to a strategic location in the front, facing the fish counter. But before I can do this, I feel obliged to give some thought to what I am really passing on. Will it be a blessing or a burden? For me, it was both.

There is an old saying: "The first generation founds the business, the second generation builds the business, and the third generation kills the business." At Russ & Daughters for the past thirty years, I have been the third generation. From the beginning of my stewardship of the store, fear has been my motivator. Failure was not an option. It is the fear that I could be the one Russ who put the store out of business. In my recurring nightmare, the food critic of the *New York Times* enters the store and finds litter on the floor, dust on the shelves, salads dried out, little end pieces of fish in the showcase, and employees inattentive and rude. The only way for me to sleep at night is to make sure that during the day I am on constant alert so that not one of these visions materializes.

The greatest fear, though, was and is the fear of violating traditions. If I changed some product, some manner of display, or some way of doing business, I might incur the eternal wrath of my ancestors: the first- and second-generation Russes. Even more catastrophic would be the disappointment to and probable loss of customers who had grown to expect things to be done as they had been done by my parents, aunts and uncles, and grandparents. If the way the earlier generations of Russes had conducted business had indeed worked before I took over, then what right did I have to change it?

But some changes are necessary, forced on us by factors outside our control. And some traditions can be traps, tethering us to practices that no longer work. Making those changes that are necessary to stay in business and jettisoning those traditions that would turn us into a museum rather than a vibrant place to conduct business will be the burden of the next generation as well. No doubt, they too will have to make changes and will be fearful to do so.

Maintaining those traditions that reflect the soul of our store will ultimately be the blessing of my successors. They will be distinguished from the rest of the world of food commerce: big-box stores, prepackaged products, and impersonal service or none at all. The most important tradition of the Russ family—a dedication to and passion for their products and their customers—will continue to keep Russ & Daughters a "jewel" in this city. It is a jewel worth preserving.

As I now get ready to pass this business on to the fourth generation—both a male, my nephew, and a female, my daughter—I am as proud as the Grand Rebbe who has just anointed his successors. Still, what words of wisdom can I impart? What direction can I provide as a path to success? How can they benefit from my experience when their own will bring different challenges: a neighborhood that has gone from pushcart to posh; a customer base that has changed from older affluent Jews to younger, more urbane, and ethnically mixed New Yorkers; a labor force that reflects a whole different immigrant influx; and products that change or disappear because of the effects of nature and the heavy hand of humans.

It is clear to me that I must teach the next generation how to slice lox and fillet herring, how to ring the register and make change, and, of course, how to tell a good fish from a bad fish. But if I cannot help them find the soul of our store, there will be no success; it will be the end of our *yichus*. Like all generations of the Russ family, their journey must start with an understanding of the question *Vi nemptmen parnosa?*—"From where do we take our living?"

Livin' *la Vida Sabrosa*

Savoring Latino New York

RAMONA LEE PÉREZ AND BABETTE AUDANT

¡SABOR! Of all the possible Spanish translations of the verb "to taste," *saborear* is most specific to encounters with food.[1] Meaning "to savor" or "to enjoy the flavor of," *saborear* is equivalent to neither the impassive, scientific sampling of *probar* nor the declaration of individual preference expressed by *gustar*. Rather, *saborear* communicates a reflexive gustation, a critical pleasure derived from devoting time and attention to appreciating the quality of edible experience. Yet the verb *saborear* and the noun *sabor* encompass more than just the literal tastes of individual foodstuffs. While exceptional and, at times, excessive flavor is the basis of *sabor* as an aesthetic principle, it also implies a multisensory saturation and satiation. Foods stimulate the taste buds, but they also possess tactile, olfactory, visual, and even auditory flavors. Thus *saborear* has the potential for active engagement with all the organs of perception. Simultaneously evoking taste, flavor, and savor, *sabor* encapsulates the notion of multisensation and its potential for excess, key elements of a food-based phenomenology of indulgence. We propose that such sensory hyperbole is integral to a distinctive Latino social aesthetic.

We explore the concept of *sabor* through a sensory ethnography of Roosevelt Avenue, the major commercial thoroughfare in Jackson Heights, Queens. We argue that the intense smells, tastes, sights, and sounds that characterize food and eating in this public setting constitute a powerful yet ephemeral set of place-making practices that inscribe a specifically Latino social space. Restaurants, bakeries, grocery stores, lunch trucks, snack counters, street vendors, bodegas, and corner stores offer an abundance of nostalgic edibles, imported products, and specialty foods. A close examination of these sites reveals a diverse set of people united by language, histories of colonialism and immigration, and, most important, a preference for exceptionally flavorful food. We obtained our data from preliminary ethnographic fieldwork conducted in Latino-dominant neighborhoods located in Queens, Brooklyn, and Manhattan during the spring and summer of 2005, as well as from our earlier experiences as avid consumers of Latino food specialties, both on Roosevelt Avenue and in myriad other places. Our research consisted of an initial survey and photographic documentation of Latino commercial districts in general and Latino food businesses in particular.[2] Through an analysis of the availability and representation of ethnically specific foodstuffs and the places in which they are sold, we articulate *sabor* as an explicitly Latino social aesthetic: a tendency toward an amplified, multisensory savory-ness.[3]

On Roosevelt Avenue, the simultaneity of sensory saturation is doubly productive. First, the simultaneous presence of so many food businesses with complementary menus and visual styles anchors the specificity of place and contributes to the production of a Latino public space by combining different groups and their culinary cultures in a sort of pan–Latin American mosaic. Second, this convergence amplifies the intensity of any visitor's experience, enticing patrons and passersby to indulge their cravings and discover new ones. Unacclimated consumers, however, may quickly reach their tolerance threshold, succumbing to phenomenological overload. For those with more receptive palates, even *sabor* may not be enough to adequately convey the extent of their gratification. We suggest that the visceral pleasures of sensory saturation are best encapsulated by the term *sabrosísimo,* a superlative form of *sabor* construed as "so very delicious" yet containing all the possibilities of reflexive, synesthetic gustation.[4] Finally, *sabor* is not just a culturally cogent analytical framework for understanding sensory data, but also an entire life philosophy. Join us in livin' *la vida sabrosa.*

Sabor of Place

At first, visitors to Jackson Heights, Queens, may be overwhelmed when confronted with the raucous sensuousness that characterizes the Latino commercial district of Roosevelt Avenue.[5] Initial impressions begin with the press of bodies and intermingling of languages on board the number 7 train. Upon arriving at the Seventy-fourth Street–Broadway stop, a heady brew of smells accosts the nostrils. Air fragrant with delectable scents emanating from shop doors intertwines with the perfume of the city—exhaust fumes, human sweat, refuse—composing an odiferous symphony that both enchants and repulses. On the street below, the deafening roar of the train drowns out casual conversation and all semblance of concentrated thought until it passes and the relative quiet of car traffic, blaring music, and street-corner chatter resumes under the steel beams supporting the train tracks. Shops are resplendent in their decoration, a glittering mélange of nationalist iconography and recuperative kitsch. Pictures and hand-lettered signs announce menus and sale items while a dizzying array of merchandise beckons from windows and pushcarts, enticing passersby with their abundance.

Choose fresh fried snapper, simultaneously crispy and moist; roast suckling pig, browned until delectably tender; or marinated skirt steak, grilled to mouth-watering perfection. Sudden cravings may be satisfied by handheld snacks conveniently available from sidewalk vendors: savory tacos, warm empanadas, or mangoes carved into juicy blossoms and flavored with a dash of chile powder and salt. For dessert, cream-filled pastries and luscious tropical fruits entice tongue and imagination alike.

A crossroads of culture within New York City's most international borough, Roosevelt Avenue must be experienced to be understood.[6] How, then, can the rich complexity and intense immediacy of places such as Jackson Heights be conveyed in words? This chapter attempts such a task with the research and writing method of "sensory ethnography."[7] Beginning with Clifford Geertz's "thick description" and Maurice Merleau-Ponty's "pure description," which equally excludes both analytical reflection and scientific explanation, sensory ethnography goes one step further in its attention to the ephemera of everyday experience, as well as the spontaneous social interactions and atmosphere of the places surrounding them.[8]

Located just south of LaGuardia Airport, between the Brooklyn-Queens Expressway to the west and Flushing Meadow Park to the east, the Queens neighborhood of Jackson Heights exemplifies New York City's cultural panorama.[9] Although Latinos dominate numerically, they share space with vibrant Chinese and Indian communities, each with its own residential zones and bustling commercial scenes. Roosevelt Avenue, running west–east underneath the tracks of the elevated train, is the primary business district serving Latinos in Jackson Heights and the contiguous neighborhoods of Elmhurst and Corona,[10] along with destination shoppers from other neighborhoods around the city.

An initial survey of Roosevelt Avenue reveals a heavily trafficked commercial district of twenty-five blocks lined with more than four hundred street-level storefronts.[11] We find multiple representatives of national and international commerce—five major banks,[12] along with McDonald's and Dunkin' Donut franchises, a Blockbuster video store, Voicestream and T-Mobile wireless outlets, an Exxon gas station, and a Rent-a-Center home-furnishings store—yet most businesses along Roosevelt Avenue are local operations owned by Latino entrepreneurs.[13] Among them, more than one hundred food stores and eateries—often more than five such establishments in one block—offer imported merchandise and specialty dishes.

Roosevelt Avenue burgeons with street-corner sociality. Pedestrians stroll under the shadow of the elevated train tracks, skirting car traffic and the press of other bodies. Pamphleteers hand out announcements of special offers as neon signs and competing musical themes clamor for attention. Spanish is the preferred language for informal talk and business transactions. Groups of women, often with children in tow, go from store to store, searching for the best prices. Families stock up on hard-to-find grocery items and stagger away bearing bags heavy with imported foods. Men lean into sidewalk taco counters chatting with servers or cluster in groups in front of favorite hangouts. Potential customers take in the riot of colors, sounds, and smells, stepping closer to read menus posted in the windows or to study the patrons seated inside.

We propose that the experiences and meanings of Roosevelt Avenue's food scene rest on the aesthetic of *sabor,* a distinctly Latino principle of multisensory excess. To do so, we have divided the remainder of this chapter into two parts. Both analyze the tendency toward excess manifested in Latino food establishments. Focusing on the overwhelming variety of foods, both raw and cooked, available for consumption, we begin by exploring *sabor* as a set of material practices that inform the social construction of space and inscribe the cultural distinctiveness of particular places.[14] Then we mobilize *sabor* as an analytical framework to examine visual data—storefront and interior design—and explore the use of exaggerated decor as both patriotic and marketing strategy. Such culinary extravagance and its optical embellishment are vital to the constitution of Roosevelt Avenue as a unique yet culturally representative site among New York City's distinctly Latino public spaces.

Edible *Sabor:* Flavors of Abundance

The merchants of Roosevelt Avenue offer an enticing cornucopia of edibles. We captured abundant data by strolling, tasting, caving in to temptation, and noting the seasonal shifts of availability and variety of single types of goods like chiles or pastries. Simple maps of the area that record the names and addresses of eateries, including the location of taco trucks and mobile fruit vendors, provided useful references, but it was the smells, sounds, and material evidence of field trips—a bag of *pan dulce* or a packet of dried epazote—that enlivened our field notes and were the impetus for this study. Please share with us the pleasures of a gastronomic tour. Meat lovers will find an array of choices: *pollo a la brasa* and *hornado* (marinated grilled chicken and slow-roasted suckling pig); *churrasco* and *carne asada* (thin slices of beef marinated in vinegar, garlic, salt, pepper, and sometimes cilantro and jalapeños); and a succulent dish of *entraña* (skirt steak) or *barbacoa.*[15] You may prefer paella or *asopado de mariscos,* two versions of the ever-popular seafood and rice stew. Better yet, indulge in a plate of piquant *chiles rellenos.* Literally translated as "stuffed chiles," *chiles rellenos* go far beyond their stereotypical white-cheese filling and fried egg batter. They can be made with ground beef, sautéed vegetables, walnuts, and dozens of other ingredients.

Those with a heartier appetite may prefer a bowl of *sancocho.* Roughly translated as "stew," sancocho is a one-pot dish of meat (beef, chicken, pork, goat, or all of them together), along with starchy tubers (yucca, taro root, potatoes, sweet potatoes, plantains) and vegetables (butternut squash, corn, peppers, onion, garlic). Along with many other dishes, this is claimed by many Latino groups, each with its own ingredients and preparation methods. After savoring a main course, join the crowd at one of several bakeries for a piece of sugar-dusted, feather-light Mexican *pan dulce* or a luscious serving of *pastel de tres leches. Pan dulce* (sweet bread) is a category of small pastries, including sugary cinnamon rolls, doughnuts, cream puffs, and gingerbread cookies with fantastic names like "big ear," "shell," and "pig" in reference to their eponymous contours. *Pastel de tres leches* (cake of three milks) combines whole, evaporated, and condensed milk in a creamy dessert popular among Central Americans.

Flame-broiled rotisserie chicken and tacos are two particularly popular items with several eateries dedicated to each.[16] Whatever the declared specialty, we always find an abundance of choice even within a single establishment. Gusty Chicken is one of eight eateries specializing in chicken rubbed with a signature formula of herbs and spices—a blend of cumin, salt, garlic, tomato, cilantro, oregano, black pepper, dried or smoked red chiles and vinegar—and flame-broiled on a rotisserie until the skin turns a crispy golden yellow.[17] Despite its neon declaration of CRAZY CHICKEN — POLLOS A LA BRASA and the pervasive aroma of chicken fat and caramelized marinade emanating from the front door, Gusty's menu goes far beyond poultry. Other house specialties include seafood stew, paella with lobster tail, sautéed *churrasco*, marinated red snapper, *entraña*, spaghetti, marinated fish filet, and crawfish.

At Pollos Gus, a popular Ecuadorian franchise, customers can enjoy the chicken specialty or choose from fish, breaded and panfried meat, or seafood soup. The fried-fish dinner special is served with salad, potatoes, soup of the day, and the diner's choice of beverage: *chicha* (fermented corn beer) or *morocho* (an Ecuadorian term for both whole white corn and a sweet beverage derived from it).[18] Seasoned with vanilla, orange rind, and whole spices like cinnamon, sassafras, and allspice fruit, the milky *morocho* is served warm, with bits of corn fiber and raisins thickening the mixture to a gruel-like consistency. Its soothing fragrance promises a moment of calm to those with the patience to savor its delicate flavor and distinctive mouthfeel.

Taco stands offer a range of street foods popular for their rapid preparation and handheld convenience. Taco Veloz (Fast Taco) serves an assortment of burritos, tacos, and *tortas*. Burritos, at $4 each, are filled with grilled chicken, *carne asada, carnitas,* or beans and rice; tacos, sold for $2, are available with the same fillings plus goat, *pastor,* chorizo (spicy pork sausage), and *suadero* (rehydrated dried meat), as well as tongue, brains, tripe, and *chicharrón*.[19] Taco Veloz also sells $4 *tortas,* sandwiches made with lettuce, tomato, sour cream, and avocado on a soft roll loaded with *milanesa* (breaded chicken breast), oven-roasted pork, steak, sausage, or cheese. Other stands offer their own menu variations: Tacos Rodriguez and Tacolandia (Tacoland) replace burritos with *huaraches,* a fried shell of corn and wheat flour, shaped like the handwoven leather sandals for which they are named and heaped with a choice of fillings. These, along with sweet drinks like imported sodas in tropical flavors and *horchata* (rice milk sweetened and laced with cinnamon), round out the menu.

Bravo Comida Rápida (Bravo Fast Food) presents a unique multicultural selection of fast-food options. In addition to tacos, customers can also buy HOT DOGS, EMPANADAS, CHORIZOS, CHICKEN WINGS, AND GYROS. Hot dogs can also be found at Cositas Ricas (Little Tasty Things), along with an extensive dessert menu. Street vendors cater to demand for handheld foods by offering a plethora of snacks; variations on fresh fruit are omnipresent. Shaved ice and milkshakes come in tropical flavors, as do the *cholados* sold at the stand in front of Tulcingo Café.[20] Other vendors offer sliced mango, pineapple, or coconut served with a squeeze of lime and a dash of red chile powder.

Featuring both a sidewalk counter and a sit-down restaurant, Suaderos Tacos is home to a more sophisticated cuisine than its name implies. The neon image of plate, fork, and knife balanced amid wavy outlines suggesting various foods plus the word PLATILLOS (main dishes) promise more hearty fare such as stews, *pozole* and *pipían*, *cemitas* and *mole*.[21] Hailing from central Mexico, *cemitas* are sandwiches served on a toasted, hollowed-out sesame roll filled with avocado, *panela* and *quesillo* cheeses, caramelized onions, bitter herbs, and a choice of meat. *Mole* refers to an array of sauces whose elaboration is central to Mexican culinary nationalism.[22]

Its awning declaring TYPICAL ECUADORIAN AND INTERNATIONAL FOOD, Hornado Ecuatoriano offers an extensive array of regional favorites, including *hornado, bandera, churrasco,* and *ceviche.*[23] Cuenca Restaurant and El Rincón de J. Jaramillo (Jaramillo's Corner) serve competing versions of *morocho* and *humitas,* delicacies whose places of origin are variously claimed in Ecuadorian, Peruvian, and Chilean folklore.[24] Cuenca adds *sancocho* to the menu, and pictures of fried red snapper, *carne asada, bandera,* chicken salad, *hornado* with *mote,* flame-broiled chicken, fresh *batidos,* and assorted sweets entice passersby.[25] El Rincón de J. Jaramillo uses a hodgepodge of individual handwritten signs to announce its house specialties: *caldo de salchicha* (sausage soup) and *encebollado mixto* (seafood cocktail of fish, shrimp, and onions).

Located at the corner of Eighty-eighth Street, Mexicana Bakery is a multipurpose market that sells a variety of food and housewares. Although the name and storefront advertisements proclaim its specialty as *pan dulce,* it also offers herbs and spices, whole dried chiles, candy, imported sodas and canned products (for example, *escabeche* and salsas, beans, bottled *mole* and *pipían* sauces, and *atole*), a variety of fruits and seeds, and Brooklyn-made corn tortillas, along with cooking utensils and household accessories.[26]

Just one block away, we find Mi Bello Mexico, a full-fledged market selling a vast array of dried foods, prepared foods, and household items. Hand-lettered signs blanket the front window advertising merchandise. Customers can buy piñatas and piggy banks, *molcajetes* and *tortilleras.*[27] Purchase tomatillos, lard, *crema,* farmer's cheese, and chocolate-infused *mole* and add premixed rum punch or a gallon of milk for $2.99.[28] A sign bearing a sombrero-clad dog pitches head cheese and *chicharrón, barbacoa de chivo,* chile-marinated beef, and various sausages (*longaniza, chorizo, rellena*). Another sombrero decorates a sign listing available varieties of fresh and dried chile: *guajillo, pasilla,* ancho, *mulatto, de árbol, meco,* chipotle, jalapeño, serrano.

Perhaps most indicative of the neighborhood's diverse Latino population is the food market Los Paisanos Importadores, located between Seventy-ninth and Eightieth streets. The awning reads IMPORTERS OF TYPICAL ECUADORIAN, MEXICAN, PERUVIAN, COLOMBIAN, AND CENTRAL AMERICAN PRODUCTS, and signs advertise more than a dozen fresh tropical fruits (including papaya, coconut, pineapple, guava, cherimoya, mango, tamarind, mamey, and *curuba*) and frozen and dried merchandise (including dehydrated corn, yellow peppers, *melloco,* and dried *caigua,* a variety of Peruvian cucumber coveted for its medicinal uses).[29] Canned whole chiles, prepared salsas,

Pier 90 Fish Market. (Photograph courtesy of Babette Audant)

powdered chocolate, corn flour, Inca Cola, and tropical-flavored sodas are stacked in the front window.

All along Roosevelt Avenue, seafood is especially popular as both a menu item and raw merchandise. The entrance to Pier 90 Fish Market, specializing in prepared seafood dishes, is graced with the neon form of a large fish swimming above the words PESCADO FRITO. Customers can indulge in that option or may choose from steamed or grilled fish, clams with lemon juice, or fish soup. Specials include breaded shrimp with potatoes for $4.99 or fish ceviche for $6.99. Down the avenue at Seatide Fish Market, the neon outline of a lobster is suspended above large hand-lettered signs announcing a plethora of fresh and imported seafood. Nestled in beds of clean ice, the merchandise is clearly visible through the front window: live crab, Ecuadorian swordfish, black conch, dried cod, and *bagre* (sea catfish). Buy fresh tuna for $3.99, corvina (white sea bass) for $2.99, porgie for $1.99, and live mussels for only 99 cents a pound. Catering to its seafood-loving customers, the snack truck El Guayaquileño offers fried corvina, conch and shrimp ceviche, fish tamales, *encebollado de pescado* (spicy fish cocktail made with tuna, yucca, and onions), alongside such popular red-meat dishes as *carne asada* and *guatita,* an Ecuadorian stew of beef tripe and potatoes in peanut sauce.

Visual *Sabor:* Embellishing the Latino Food Scene

While advocating a multisensory model for analyzing the *sabor* of New York City's Latino food scene, this section focuses on its optical aspect. Digital photography allows us to capture and magnify images, making visual data one of the easiest entry points for ethnographic analysis. This approach is appropriate to the setting, as most businesses that cater to the city's Latino population, including and especially Roosevelt Avenue's small enterprises, strive to be hypervisible, screaming out for attention with their naming and design practices. Flamboyant decor produces an ocular flavor that is integral to an encompassing Latino social aesthetic.[30] Photographic evidence reveals that this baroque decorating style is favored by Roosevelt Avenue entrepreneurs from throughout Latin America. The following analysis addresses two major aspects of visual *sabor:* storefront nationalism and gastronomic iconicity.

Storefront Nationalism

Elaborate displays of national identity are vital to the food scene along Roosevelt Avenue.[31] Owners announce their origins and the provenance of available merchandise with a combination of naming practices and exterior design. Storefront nationalism is not, however, simply a display of ethnic pride. Rather, it is a marketing tool for attracting clientele, both compatriots and culinary tourists, without having to indicate exactly what is on the menu.

Nationalist naming practices fall into two categories: literal and symbolic. Literalists avoid identity confusion by inserting their country of origin into the name of the business.[32] Literalism is, by far, the more common choice among Latino food businesses on Roosevelt Avenue and is most popular among Mexican establishments. This can be attributed to Mexicans' need to announce their presence and clearly demarcate their territory. As the most recent Latino immigrant group to arrive in the city, primarily during the 1990s, Mexicans find themselves in competition with "older," more established Latin American immigrants.

Some establishments eschew country names in favor of specific places and symbols meaningful only to those knowledgeable about that country's geography and cultural history. For example, Cuenca Restaurant and MiraCali Panadería-Pastelería[33] honor cities in Ecuador and Colombia, respectively, while Laureles Restaurant is named for a popular neighborhood of Medellín, Colombia. Indexing the strong presence of immigrants from central Mexico, Puebla Food and Tulcingo Café, Cholula Bakery, and Taquería Coatzingo refer to places in the state of Puebla, and Plaza Garibaldi Restaurant pays its respects to a famous square in Mexico City. Several businesses are named for the native populations of their home countries. Chibcha Restaurant acknowledges the indigenous people of the Colombian Andes; El Sol Azteca and Central Azteca Grocery honor the dominant civilization of ancient Mexico; and Quisqueya Restaurant pays tribute to the indigenous language of the Dominican Republic. Likewise, Colombia's cowboys are the inspiration for Los Arrieros Restaurant. Finally, a few restaurateurs lend their own names to the business, as with Pollos a la Brasa Mario and Jose Fish Market, Pollos Mario, Tacos Rodriguez, and Angelos Restaurant Pollos a la Brasa. However, the majority of Latino food businesses along Roosevelt Avenue openly declare their origins with place-specific names.[34] Regardless of their naming practices, nearly all the markets and eateries practice storefront nationalism in their elaborate interior and exterior design. Ornate displays incorporate flags, patriotic colors and emblems, and other symbols of national popular culture. This creative embellishment indexes and amplifies the visual aspect of the *sabor* aesthetic.

As if declaring COMIDA TIPICA ECUATORIANA (typical Ecuadorian food) on the awning were not enough, letters spelling out the name El Rincón de J. Jaramillo are filled with ribbons of yellow, blue, and red. A large Ecuadorian flag, complete with condor coat of arms, hangs over the restaurant's front door. Los Paisanos Importadores market is notable, as its signage recognizes multiple Latin American countries in order to emphasize its comprehensive merchandise. Advertising Ecuadorian, Mexican, Colombian, Peruvian, and Central American products, lettering for each country is appropriately color-coded to correspond to the national flags printed on the store's awning.[35]

In many establishments, ocular patriotism is more abstract. Rather than waving a flag in the front window, the majority of food businesses on Roosevelt Avenue are swathed in patriotic colors and symbols. Awnings over Tacolandia and Tacos al Suadero are divided into broad vertical stripes of green, white, and red, whereas the signs for El Poblano Taquería, Taquería Coatzingo, and Tacos Mexico scream out in tricolor neon, all to signify Mexico's flag. Also with green, white, and red awnings, Fonda Restaurant Corporation and Viva Zapata Restaurante Mexicano add the coat of arms that lies at the center of the Mexican flag: an eagle, perched atop a flowering cactus, with a serpent in its beak. Suaderos Tacos features not one but two eagles, while Mexicana Bakery displays the coat of arms on its green, white, and red awning and uses neon of the same colors to reiterate its name in the front window.

Visual declaration of national origins becomes problematic, however, when countries share patriotic colors. For example, the Ecuadorian and Venezuelan flags have the same basic design as their Colombian counterpart: a broad stripe of yellow along the top, blue in the center, and red on the bottom. The former two are distinguished only by their respective national coats of arms. Eateries along Roosevelt Avenue address the problem of patriotic color confusion by layering symbols of national identity. The outline of Colombia's borders is stenciled on a window of Laureles Restaurant, and the awning features the country's silhouette filled with yellow, blue, and red stripes. Next door, the letters spelling out MiraCali Panadería-Pastelería sport horizontal stripes of the same colors.

While announcing their national identity with linguistic literalism, both Lechón Hornado Ecuatoriano and Carciofini Restaurant Ecuatoriano feature the national coats of arms in their front windows. Cuenca Restaurant, offering PLATOS TIPICOS

Taquería Coatzingo. (Photograph courtesy of Babette Audant)

ECUATORIANOS Y COLOMBIANOS (typical Ecuadorian and Colombian dishes), infuses the letters of its name with patriotic colors but refrains from such nationalist decor as flags and coats of arms.

Three Peruvian eateries offering take-out chicken present a comparatively simple exterior design. Awnings announce the name, address, and telephone number with white letters on a red awning—colors of the Peruvian flag—but other nationalist iconography is subdued or otherwise absent. Both La Casa del Pollo Peruano (House of Peruvian Chicken) and La Casa del Pollo Peruano II use a simple logo of a chicken standing next to a stylized rooftop, but otherwise their awnings and large plate-glass windows remain unadorned. Restaurante Lima El Pollito Dorado (Golden Chick Restaurant) uses a touch of neon to add LIMA to the store name and announce that it is open, and a small paper flag sits in the lower-right corner. With few concessions to nationalist iconography, Peruvian storefronts are remarkably uncluttered in comparison with their Mexican, Ecuadorian, and Colombian counterparts. We posit that further patriotic display is unnecessary because (1) all three establishments nationalities found in Jackson Heights, Peru is the only country represented by red and white.

Most restaurants and food shops on Roosevelt Avenue, however, favor extravagant tableaux, layering decorative elements to fill all available space, if not with explicitly nationalist symbols, then with icons of popular culture. Los Arrieros Restaurant exemplifies this trend with a six-foot-tall cartoon of a cowboy to match its name and a poster of Café de Colombia, alongside a plastic-laminated menu, signs, and a chalkboard with specials, the words WE DELIVER, and a telephone number—all framed by icicle lights draped around the main window. Not to be ignored is Lechón Hornado Ecuatoriano, which juxtaposes on its awning the image of a plaza with an imposing cathedral and luxuriant palm trees, and a close-up of a pig wearing a red-checkered bib. These seemingly incongruous images conjure the riches of Ecuador: the elegance of its colonial-era architecture and the heartiness of its cuisine.

Mexican establishments are replete with this sort of visual hyperbole. To the national coat of arms, color-fill lettering, and neon signage discussed earlier, Viva Zapata Restaurante Mexicano adds a picture of Emiliano Zapata to its awning, the neon outline of a sombrero in its window, and plastic pennants advertising Mexican beers. Vallecito Bakery, just off Roosevelt Avenue at Ninety-first Street, also utilizes the popular culture icon of the sombrero to signify Mexico. The awning features a heavyset man fast asleep in the shade of a cactus and his oversized sombrero. Tacos Mexico has a large banner hanging over its neon-encrusted front window while a chile pepper labeled MEXICO RESTAURANT wears a ribbon-festooned hat with the word TACOS emblazoned on its brim.[36]

Beyond literal and symbolic forms of storefront nationalism, some establishments chart spaces of postnational community. Rincón Sabroso (Tasty Corner) and Fun City restaurants suggest this, and the idea is best illustrated by a popular lunch counter that surpasses the specificity of place to proclaim an independent Tacolandia located at the corner of Roosevelt Avenue and Seventy-seventh Street.

Eateries on Roosevelt Avenue layer patriotic colors, flags or coats of arms, and other images of national popular culture in order to proclaim their origins. Instances of excessive self-referencing evidence the pervasiveness of a patriotic baroque aesthetic as nationalist iconography identifies each space and its owners, welcoming compatriots as insiders who can interpret the complex symbolism. Outsiders, conversely, are enticed with the sights and smells of "exotic" foods and colorful locales. In either case, individual establishments declare themselves as nationally specific Latino sanctuaries within the encompassing urban landscape.

The widespread use of nationalist iconography is not, however, sheer territorialism. As Suzanne Oboler might argue, the Latino food scene of Roosevelt Avenue is more than the sum of its country-specific restaurants and markets.[37] This visual exercise in self-referentiality takes place within and contributes to the mutual constitution of a historically and geographically specific Latino public space. In other words, the purveyors of storefront nationalism engage their patrons and neighbors in conversation about what it means to be Latino in New York City.

Roosevelt Avenue's visual *sabor* extends beyond simulacra of national identity to the representation of edibles. To attract passersby, many eateries post their menus in their front windows, and several illustrate their lists with storefront imagery in the form of popular specialties. Some include pictures on their signs and awnings, and others prefer window decoration. The latter are equally divided between neon icons or posters and photographs of actual menu items.

The iconic reiteration of many businesses' names illustrates repetitive self-referentiality that characterizes the identificatory practices of Roosevelt Avenue's Latino eateries. Along with its patriotic mise-en-scène, the sign for MiraCali Panadería-Pastelería features the black-and-white outlines of an elaborately decorated three-tiered cake and an oblong loaf of bread, indicating the availability of both sweet pastries and savory breads.

Several restaurants feature representations of swine, both raw and cooked, in signs and window displays. Perched atop the awning of Hornado Ecuatoriano is an illuminated sign emblazoned with the silhouette of a round-bellied animal with a flattened snout and corkscrew tail. Other eateries favor more detailed illustrations. The image of a whole pig impaled on a spit and suspended over licking flames adorns the sign of Broadway Sandwich Shop Lechonera No. 6; Lechón Hornado Ecuatoriano's full-color sign depicts a pig, with a hint of a smile, wearing a red-checkered bib.

Neon molded to the contours of menu items is another mode of representation. For example, Cuenca Restaurant boasts red neon shaped into porcine proportions to advertise roast suckling pig, the yellow outline of a whole cooked chicken complete with protruding drumsticks, and a steaming coffee cup in blue. Piqueteadero Bakery features the forms of a hot dog, a hamburger, and an ice cream cone to advise customers that the menu extends beyond baked goods, whereas El Pollito Dorado outlines its baby-chicken logo in appropriately gold-color neon.

Store logos also play a significant role in the aesthetic of excess that constitutes Roosevelt Avenue's visual tastiness. Centered in the front window of El Pollito Dorado is the cartoon image of a headband- and kerchief-wearing pullet winking and holding one feathered wing aloft in an okay sign; likewise, the menu of Piqueteadero Bakery is announced by the smiling twin of the Pillsbury dough boy. But the most elaborate and entertaining logo of Roosevelt Avenue eateries is found at Taco Veloz, a local mini-chain.

The awnings of all three Taco Veloz locations feature the logo of a taco-chariot: a bow tie–wearing taco perched on its end with wheels at the bottom, complete with limbs and a face. Like an efficient waiter, the taco holds aloft a tray of hot food with its right arm; a folded towel is draped over the left. Smiling and giving the thumbs-up sign, the taco trails particles of meat, cheese, and shredded lettuce out the back of its hard shell. Like the upbeat logos of El Pollito Dorado and Piqueteadero Bakery, this happy-go-lucky taco suggests the revelry associated with eating. Furthermore, with ingredients escaping from its shell, the taco-chariot embodies the notion of excess, showing that tasty food is neither perfectly sanitized nor completely contained.[38] The

Taco Veloz. (Photograph courtesy of Babette Audant)

Taco Veloz logo can be extrapolated as a mascot for Roosevelt Avenue as a whole and perhaps New York City's entire Latino foodscape: superlative *sabor* in action.

Existential *Sabor*

Implicit here is an argument for the concept of "sensing" as an entrée into a theory and method of phenomenological social science. Sensing is a dual process: (1) the sensation(s) of a particular experience and (2) "making sense" or developing an understanding of that experience. Both aspects take place in the context of daily life and our ideas about it. Any theory of sensory perception, therefore, must also incorporate social, cultural, and spatial dimensions. Ethnographic method lends itself to this sort of endeavor, as the researcher is immersed in the particulars of a given setting and can build an embodied repository of experiential knowledge.[39] As an epistemological intervention, sensory ethnography destabilizes knowledge as rational and fixed and relocates it as social, contested, and dynamic: temporally and geographically grounded but collectively fashioned. The selection of the research site, then, determines the kinds of experiences the ethnographer will have and will affect the shape of any theoretical conclusions.[40] The bustling commercial district of a cosmopolitan, urban Latino, international migrant, multiethnic neighborhood anchors this particular ethnography and theorizing. Despite or, perhaps, because of its internal diversity, this setting constitutes a socially, linguistically, and aesthetically unified context. From that empirical location, we argue that *sabor*—a way of knowing predicated on direct, intense, sensual experience—informs the performance of place in city life, shapes the contours of national origins and the limits of cultural commonality, and marks zones of difference within the global city.

Sabor is a food-based aesthetic completely contrary to the high-culture codification of cuisine as a closed system of iconic dishes and regulated cooking techniques. It celebrates multiplicity; there is no question of "either/or," but a pervasive "and." Characterized by undisciplined excess in a generous and inclusive way, *sabor* fosters a feasting atmosphere, an all-you-can-eat buffet, everything laid out on the table just in case you develop an appetite for it. Furthermore, *sabor* is not simply a culturally cogent analytical framework appropriate to understanding Latino food practices. Instead, it is a comprehensive, antiminimalist life philosophy. Rejecting the mind–body split of the distanced, rational, judging self, *sabor* is ultimately about reveling in the present presence. *Sabor* demands the complete absorption in and cultivation of our embodied subjectivity; devotees of *sabor* abhor a sensory vacuum and will go to great lengths to fill any perceived void. Finally, because of its acknowledgment of historical and geographic specificity, the *sabor* model avoids debates over authenticity. There is no false historicization, no location of an imagined past, but the current moment as absolute and all-consuming. As for imagining a *sabor*-centric future, picture the entire city as one big fiesta of flavor, or perhaps it is enough to have space for alternative tastes of reality.

Standing on the tenuous ground between description and theory, this chapter makes documentary, methodological, and conceptual contributions to food studies, multiethnic and immigrant Latino studies, and the anthropology of space and place. It suggests the contours of New York City's Latino foodscape, but only begins to document a fragment of this diverse culinary cartography. We have suggested an approach to mapping urban Latino culinary culture as a set of dynamic spatial practices and have proposed the notion of *sabor* as a unique Latino social aesthetic that advocates savoring the richness of experience. Since *sabor* has the potential for the active engagement of all senses, capturing the specificity of place on which sensorial ethnography is grounded becomes an exercise in deliberately isolating perceptions while cultivating an embodied awareness. Therefore, we have attempted to portray the intense immediacy of a particular cultural setting through a thick description of the public cuisine of Roosevelt Avenue and to posit an emerging model for analyzing the presence of edibles and their representations in public space. It remains for the reader to judge whether this venture into tasteful ethnography has succeeded.

NOTES

Thank you to Jonathan Deutsch and Annie Hauck-Lawson for inviting us to contribute to the writing of *Gastropolis,* to the anonymous reviewers for their generous comments, to all the

1. The verb "to taste" is variously translated as *gustar, probar,* and *saborear*—all with
multiple shades of meaning. *Gustar* can mean "to try, or to test," but more common is the
connotation of giving pleasure, as in *Me gusta chocolate* ("I like chocolate" or, more precisely,
"Chocolate is pleasing to me"). *Probar* has a broader scope of meaning that suggests a rather
impassive interaction with ideas, things, or activities. It can be used to discuss the logic of
argumentation (to prove), engagement with an object (to sample), or the practice of a pursuit
(to attempt).

2. After using census maps to identify zones with large Latino populations, we conducted
our initial surveys and photographic documentation of commercial districts in select neighborhoods throughout the city. Major Latino-dominant neighborhoods include Mott Haven in the
Bronx; Corona and Jackson Heights in Queens; Washington Heights, East Harlem, and parts
of the Lower East Side in Manhattan; and Bushwick and Sunset Park in Brooklyn. Staten Island
has both the smallest total population and the smallest percentage of Latinos among the New
York City boroughs (less than 15%). There is, however, ample opportunity for future research
on this topic as Puerto Ricans, Mexican immigrants, and other Latinos are becoming an increasing presence in northern Staten Island. Each of these neighborhoods could be explored
through sensory ethnography, thereby mapping Latino inscriptions of space and place across
the five boroughs of New York.

3. Our conclusions in this chapter consider data from four neighborhoods: Washington
Heights, East Harlem, Sunset Park, and Jackson Heights. Because this study is still in progress,
surveys for all neighborhoods are not yet complete. Washington Heights, a neighborhood
located in northern Manhattan between the Hudson and Harlem rivers, is home to the city's
largest concentration of Dominicans, many of whom migrated during the 1960s. See Jorge
Duany, *Quisqueya on the Hudson: The Transnational Identity of Dominicans in Washington
Heights* (New York: City University of New York, Dominican Studies Institute, 1994). The
first wave of Puerto Ricans began to settle in East Harlem in the 1930s, with large numbers
arriving after World War II. See Virginia Sanchez Korrol, *From Colonia to Community: The
History of Puerto Ricans in New York City, 1917–1948* (Westport, Conn.: Greenwood, 1983).
East Harlem is home to the city's largest concentration of Puerto Ricans, as well as significant
numbers of Mexicans and Dominicans. In comparison with neighborhoods where more recent
Latino immigrants predominate, like Sunset Park and Jackson Heights, the Latino dominance
evident in the census data is not emphatically staked on East Harlem's landscape, raising
questions about the interplay of processes like assimilation and gentrification that demand
closer attention. Sunset Park, in eastern Brooklyn, is home to a rapidly increasing population
of Mexican immigrants who have joined recent Chinese immigrants in a neighborhood once
inhabited by Scandinavians. Amid chain stores and faded storefronts, Latino businesses have
added to a shifting landscape that tells the story of ethnic succession and entrepreneurship. See
Nancy Foner, *From Ellis Island to JFK: New York's Two Great Waves of Immigration* (New
Haven, Conn.: Yale University Press, 2002).

4. David E. Sutton, *Remembrance of Repasts: An Anthropology of Food and Memory*
(Oxford: Berg, 2001).

5. One-quarter of its residents being Latinos, Queens is perhaps most interesting for the
broad spectrum of its inhabitants' national origins. Unlike in other parts of the city, no single
nationality dominates in the borough. Whereas Puerto Ricans and Dominicans continue to be
significant, neither comprises more than 20 percent of the 550,000 Latinos who live in Queens.
Colombians, Ecuadorians, and Mexicans constitute substantial communities, and thousands

of Peruvians, Cubans, Salvadorans, Guatemalans, Hondurans, Argentines, Panamanians, Chileans, Venezuelans, and Bolivians reside in the borough.

6. Bureau of the Census, *Census 2000*: QT-P9, "Hispanic or Latino by Type," Summary File 1; QT-P17, "Ability to Speak English"; QT-P14, "Nativity, Citizenship, Year of Entry and Region of Birth"; QT-P22, "Place of Birth and Residence in 1995"; and DP-2, "Profile of Selected Social Characteristics," Summary File 3, all at http://factfinder.census.gov/servlet/Dataset MainPageServlet?_ds_name = DEC_2000_SF1_U&_program = DEC&_lang = en (accessed January 18, 2005). Data from the 2000 census reveal the dynamic, multinational composition and distribution of Latino communities across the city's five boroughs. Home to more than 8 million people from all over the world, New York City presents a complex cultural cartography. One-third of the city's total population was born outside the United States. More than half of them, about 1.5 million, came from Latin America. In fact, immigration from Latin America accounts for most of the city's recent population growth. From 1990 to 2000, the official population of New York City grew by approximately 700,000 people, with 600,000 from Latin America. Put differently, more than 20 percent of the urban population was born either south of the United States–Mexico border or in the Spanish-speaking Caribbean. When second and third generations are included, more than 25 percent of the city's residents are Latinos. Of these, most are either Puerto Rican (37%) or Dominican (19%), but more than twenty Latino nationalities were reported for New York City in the 2000 census. See Gabriel Haslip-Viera and Sherrie L. Bayer, eds., *Latinos in New York: Communities in Transition* (South Bend, Ind.: University of Notre Dame Press, 1996).

7. Ramona Lee Pérez, "Learning Cooking in Greater Mexico: A Sensory Ethnography of Apricots and Chile," n.d.; C. Nadia Seremetakis, "The Memory of the Senses, Parts 1 and 2," in *The Senses Still: Perception and Memory as Material Culture in Modernity* (Boulder, Colo.: Westview Press, 1994), 1–43; Paul Stoller, *The Taste of Ethnographic Things: The Senses in Anthropology* (Philadelphia: University of Pennsylvania Press, 1989), and *Sensuous Scholarship* (Philadelphia: University of Pennsylvania Press, 1997).

8. Clifford Geertz, "Thick Description: Towards and Interpretive Theory of Culture," in *The Interpretation of Cultures* (London: Hutchinson, 1973), 3–30; Maurice Merleau-Ponty, *Phenomenology of Perception,* trans. Colin Smith (1963; repr., London: Routledge, 2002).

9. The highest level of population growth in the city was in Jackson Heights and North Corona in Queens. Growth in the 1990s is particularly striking, given that the population of these neighborhoods had been relatively stable since 1970. See New York City Department of City Planning, "Community District Profiles," December 2004, http://www.nyc.gov/html/dcp/ html/lucds/cdstart.shtml (accessed August 20, 2005). Most of this higher population density is attributed to a massive influx of Latino immigrants, especially Mexicans, whose numbers tripled during the 1990s. See "A Changing Nueva York" [editorial], *New York Times,* May 28, 2001. Geographically the largest of the five boroughs, Queens has long been a popular destination for immigrants from around the globe. With 54 percent of its population born outside the United States, Queens is considered New York's most ethnically diverse borough and one of the most diverse counties in the nation. See New York City Department of City Planning, Population Division, "Population Growth and Race/Hispanic Composition," New York City 2000 Census Briefs, DCP 01–11, http://www.nyc.gov/html/dcp/pdf/census/ nyc2001. pdf (accessed November 10, 2005); and Angela Montefinise, "Census Behind the Numbers: Counting Queens Diversity and Loving Every Minute," *Queens Tribune Online,* June 6, 2002, http://www.queenstribune.com/archives/featurearchive/feature2002/0606/feature_story.html (accessed November 15, 2005). Most recently, historic settlements of Europeans—Italian, Irish, and German—are becoming home to people from the Caribbean, East and Southeast

Asia, and, increasingly, countries throughout Latin America. See New York City Department of City Planning, Population Division, "Population Growth and Race/Hispanic Composition"; "Total Population, 1970–2000, and Factors Affecting Population Growth, 1990–2000," 2000 Census Community District Summary, http://www.nyc.gov/html/dcp/pdf/census/cdsnar.pdf (accessed April 12, 2005); and "The Newest New Yorkers 2000: Immigrant New York in the New Millennium," Newest New Yorkers' Briefing Booklet, DCP 04–09, http://www.nyc .gov/html/dcp/pdf/census/nny_briefing_booklet.pdf (accessed September 18, 2005).

Jackson Heights offers the best display of the diversity of Queens, as two-thirds of its 70,000 inhabitants are foreign born. One of just two neighborhoods in the borough with a majority Latino population, Jackson Heights is home to 40,000 Latinos, three-quarters of whom are immigrants. The only other Latino-dominant neighborhood in Queens is Corona, adjacent to Jackson Heights and sharing its major commercial strip. See New York City Department of City Planning, "Community District Profiles." In contrast to other areas of the city and the borough as a whole, migrants from the Spanish-speaking Caribbean do not dominate the local Latino population. Rather, Jackson Heights is a locus of settlement for people from Latin America. Thousands of Colombians, Ecuadorians, Mexicans, Dominicans, Puerto Ricans, Peruvians, and Cubans live alongside their Asian, Caribbean, European, and African American neighbors.

10. Elmhurst lies immediately to the south of Roosevelt Avenue. Although our initial survey covered Roosevelt Avenue from Seventy-fourth to 103rd streets, Jackson Heights ends at Junction Boulevard, which intersects in place of Ninety-sixth Street. While the businesses between Junction Boulevard and 103rd Street are technically in Corona, they are included here because these blocks are a continuation of the main Roosevelt Avenue commercial district, which begins to show signs of decline around Ninety-ninth Street.

Roosevelt Avenue is primarily residential from Ninety-ninth to 114th streets. We suggest that the shift from commercial to residential properties is a dual effect of city planning and public transportation routes. After Ninety-ninth Street, numbered streets do not regularly intersect Roosevelt Avenue. While addresses mark the missing streets, actual intersections are found only at 103rd, 104th, 108th, 111th, and 112th streets. This creates long blocks more suitable for private homes. Furthermore, the number 7 train runs above the entire stretch of Roosevelt Avenue from Seventy-fourth Street to Junction Boulevard, offering easy transportation and a physical structure for the commercial district below. At Junction Boulevard, the train veers northward toward Shea Stadium. Likewise, pedestrian traffic shifts away, taking with it the cash that keeps Roosevelt Avenue so profitable. For more information about Jackson Heights, Corona, Elmhurst, and Queens, see Hsiang-shui Chen, *Chinatown No More: Taiwan Immigrants in Contemporary New York* (Ithaca, N.Y.: Cornell University Press, 1992); Steven Gregory, *Black Corona: Race and the Politics of Place in an Urban Community* (Princeton, N.J.: Princeton University Press, 1998); Madhulika Khandelwal, *Becoming American, Being Indian: South Asian Immigrants in Multicultural New York* (Ithaca, N.Y.: Cornell University Press, 2002); Milagros Ricourt and Ruby Danta, *Hispanas de Queens: Latino Panethnicity in a New York City Neighborhood* (Ithaca, N.Y.: Cornell University Press, 2003); Kyeyoung Park, *The Korean American Dream: Immigrants and Small Business in New York City* (Ithaca, N.Y.: Cornell University Press, 1997); Roger Sanjek, *The Future of Us All: Race and Neighborhood Politics in New York City* (Ithaca, N.Y.: Cornell University Press, 1998); and Roger Sanjek, ed., *Worship and Community: Christianity and Hinduism in Contemporary Queens* (Flushing: Asian/American Center, Queens College, City University of New York, 1989).

11. Professional offices, such as for physicians and accountants, are usually found on the second and third floors, and occasionally in the basements, of multistory buildings or inside

mini-malls. Because most food-related establishments have street-level storefronts, our initial survey documented only these locales.

12. Between Seventy-fifth and Eighty-third streets are Chase Manhattan Bank (Seventy-fifth Street), Nara Bank (Seventy-eighth Street), Citibank (Eightieth Street), Washington Mutual (Eighty-first Street), and Independence Bank (Eighty-third Street), yet there are no banks whatsoever between Eighty-fourth and 103rd streets.

13. There are few major franchises and chains on Roosevelt Avenue. Among four hundred storefronts, including more than one hundred eateries, there is one each of McDonald's and Dunkin' Donuts, plus Broadway Bakery and Kennedy Fried Chicken—two New York–based food chains, the latter owned and operated largely by Afghan immigrants. See Steven Kurtz, "Chicken Little," *New York Times,* August 15, 2004, sec. 14, p. 1. All eateries and markets are small operations, and for most of them, Roosevelt is their only address. The local mini-chain Taco Veloz presents an interesting example of this phenomenon, with three separate Roosevelt Avenue locations. Latino variants of fast food are sold at fourteen taco shops, a snack truck (parked on a side street), and seven establishments selling take-out rotisserie chicken. Aside from fast food, Roosevelt offers thirty-seven restaurants and cafés, a coffee bar, four fish markets selling fresh and prepared seafood, and, on one hot day, three street vendors hawking ices and fresh tropical fruits from their pushcarts. With no major supermarkets in the area, groceries are available from twenty-four small markets and corner stores, including two Asian stores, and fresh breads and pastries are sold at ten bakeries. These Roosevelt Avenue restaurants, taco shops, bakeries, lunch counters, markets, fruit stands, and snack trucks contribute to an abundant local food scene. Roosevelt also offers a plethora of bars and nightclubs, but we leave the study of liquid sociality for scholars skilled in such analysis, such as Thomas M. Wilson, *Drinking Cultures: Alcohol and Identity* (Oxford: Berg, 2005).

14. Miles Richardson, "Being-in-the-Market Versus Being-in-the-Plaza," in *The Anthropology of Space and Place,* ed. Setha M. Low and Denise Lawrence-Zuñiga (Malden: Blackwell, 2003), 88.

15. *Churrasco* is typically made from shell steak and can be sautéed or grilled; *carne asada* refers to grilled flank or skirt steak. *Barbacoa,* more like southern barbecue than American-style charcoal grilling, refers to a process of slowly steaming seasoned meat in a tightly sealed container—traditionally a clay jar buried under hot coals—and leaving it to literally stew in its own juices. After cooking for several hours, the meat is tender enough to fall away from the bone. Goat and sheep are commonly prepared as *barbacoa,* and both are offered in markets and eateries on Roosevelt Avenue.

16. Rotisserie chicken can be found at Gusty Chicken (Seventy-eighth Street), Pollo Gus Sabor Ecuatoriano (Eightieth Street), Pollos a la Brasa Mario (Eighty-first Street), Pollos Mario (Eighty-sixth Street), La Casa del Pollo Peruano (Eighty-seventh Street) and II (Eighty-first Street), Restaurante Lima El Pollito Dorado (Ninety-fifth Street), and Angelos Restaurant Pollos a la Brasa (Ninety-sixth Street); tacos are sold at several Mexican restaurants and are the main fare at numerous taco shops, including Taqueria Coatzingo (Seventy-sixth Street), Tacolandia (Seventy-seventh Street), Taco Veloz (Eighty-fifth, Ninetieth, and Ninety-fifth streets), Tacos al Suadero (Eighty-seventh and Ninety-seventh streets), Tacos Mexico (Eighty-eighth Street), Tacos Rodriguez (Eighty-eighth Street), Suaderos Tacos (Ninety-fourth Street), and La Nueva Espiga (Ninety-sixth Street). As with other Mexican restaurants, taco vendors appear in clusters, yet rarely is there more than one shop on a single block.

17. Some establishments rely on the all-purpose *adobo.* Used as a marinade or sauce, *adobo* can be made from various permutations of chile ancho, vinegar, white wine, onion, garlic, and cloves.

18. *Chicha* has been brewed by the indigenous peoples of the Andes since the times of the Incan Empire.

19. Literally "little meat," *carnitas* is chunks of pork, seasoned and braised until tender on the inside and crispy on the outside. The spicy barbecued pork for tacos *al pastor* is marinated for a day or two in chile *guajillo*, garlic, onions, cinnamon, and other spices until it is infused with these flavors and takes on a deep brick-red hue. *Suadero* is beef shoulder marinated in lime juice and then charbroiled. *Chicharrón* is deep-fried pork skin, similar to southern cracklings. It can be eaten plain, folded into a warm corn tortilla with fresh salsa, crumbled over finished dishes, or cooked in a variety of sauces.

20. A cold beverages common in Colombia, *cholado* is made from crushed ice, fruit and/or fruit syrup, and sweetened condensed milk. It often is topped with whipped cream.

21. *Pozole* is pork and hominy stew flavored with red chile. *Pipían* is a thick sauce of chile and pumpkin seed used for stewing meats, usually poultry.

22. The origin of the word *mole* is variously attributed to Mexico's indigenous or colonial roots. From Nahuatl, the language of the ancient Aztecs, comes *mulli,* which means "sauce" or "potage"; the Spanish verb *moler* means "to grind," as in grinding together a variety of spices.

23. Not a formal dish per se, *bandera* refers to an interchangeable combination of specialties served with rice, beans, and a selection of accompaniments and sauces. Decorating specialty dishes with patriotic colors is a popular mode of presentation perfected in the Mexican dish of *chiles en nogada* (stuffed chiles in walnut sauce). Pomegranate seeds and walnut-cream sauces are carefully spooned over a stuffed green chile to form the pattern of the Mexican flag.

24. *Humita* is a long *tamal* of sweet corn stuffing dotted with fresh kernels, wrapped in corn husks, and steamed. It sometimes is filled with a mild white cheese.

25. *Mote* is an Ecuadorian version of hominy grits. *Batidos* are fresh-fruit smoothies made with milk, vanilla ice cream, and honey.

26. *Escabeche* is a spicy condiment made of jalapeños sliced crosswise and pickled with carrots, onions, garlic, bay leaves, oregano, marjoram, and thyme. *Atole* is a thin corn gruel usually drunk as a breakfast beverage.

27. A *molcajete* is a mortar and pestle set, usually made of porous volcanic rock, used for grinding and blending spices, herbs, and other dry ingredients. A *tortillera* is a hand-operated tortilla press.

28. Although it resembles a small green tomato covered in a paper-thin husk, *tomatillo* is a relative of the ground cherry. American-style sour cream is a poor imitation of *crema,* a rich dairy topping with a slightly more acidic taste than crème fraiche.

29. Mamey is a berry, approximately three to eight inches long and weighing anywhere from three-quarters of a pound to six pounds. Covered by a thick, brown, slightly woody skin, ripe mameys are salmon pink, orange, red, or reddish brown and have a smooth or fine-grained texture. Their flavor is sweet and almond-like. See C. F. Balerdi, J. H. Crane, and C. W. Campbell, "The Mamey Sapote," FC-30, 1979 (Gainsville: Horticultural Sciences Department, Florida Cooperative Extension Service, Institute of Food and Agricultural Sciences, University of Florida, 1996), http://edis.ifas.ufl.edu/MG331 (accessed October 3, 2005). *Curuba* is oblong, approximately two to five inches by one and one-half inches. Covered with fine hairs, the thick, dark green skin gradually turns yellow as the fruit matures. Its highly aromatic pulp is dark orange flecked with small dark seeds. See Elides González and Pedro Baustista, "El cultivo de la curuba," N59, Republica Bolivariana de Venezuela, Ministerio de Ciencia y Tecnología, Instituto Nacional de Investigaciones Agrícolas, http://www.fonaiap .gov.ve/publica/divulga/fd59/curuba.html (accessed October 10, 2005). A starchy tuber indigenous

to the Andes, *melloco* comes in a variety of colors and sizes. See Carlos Vimos N., Carlos Nieto C., and Marco Rivera M., "El melloco: Características, técnicas de cultivo y potencial en Ecuador," 1997, Centro Internacional de Investigaciones para el Desarrollo, http://archive.idrc.ca/library/document/096951/index_s.html (accessed October 15, 2005).

30. According to Anna Indych, "In an otherwise unyielding technological cityscape, saturation and excess afford a certain amount of visibility, or self-imaging, in a society where their image is determined from above or from the outside" ("Nuyorican Baroque: Pepon Osorio's *Chucherias," Art Journal* 60 [2002]: 75). See also Coco Fusco, "Vernacular Memories," in *English Is Broken Here: Notes on Cultural Fusion in the Americas* (New York: New Press, 1995), 89–95; Amalia Mesa-Bains, *Domesticana:* The Sensibility of Chicana *Rasquache,"* http://www.csupomona.edu/~plin/ews410/rasquache.html (accessed October 12, 2005); and Tomás Ybarra-Frausto, "Rasquachismo: A Chicano Sensibility," in *CARA: Chicano Art, Resistance and Affirmation, 1965–1985,* ed. Richard Griswold del Castillo, Teresa McKenna, and Yvonne Yarbro-Bejarano (Los Angeles: Wight Art Gallery, University of California, 1991), 155–62.

31. The majority of food businesses along Roosevelt Avenue are defined by the national provenance of their merchandise. Of the sixty-odd establishments that openly declare their origins most (33) offer Mexican food. Of these, nearly half (14) serve tacos, the epitome of Mexican street food. Colombian and Ecuadorian locales also are important, with ten and eight establishments, respectively. Other countries represented among the Latino food businesses are Peru (4), the Dominican Republic (2), Venezuela (1), and Argentina (1). There also are four Chinese restaurants and a pizza parlor.

At first glance, Mexican restaurants appear to dominate the entire Roosevelt Avenue shopping district. For example, between Eighty-eighth and Ninetieth streets are two taco shops, four sit-down restaurants, two bakeries, a doughnut shop, and a market. Of these ten food businesses, seven sell Mexican food. Closer examination reveals that much like the people who frequent them, the eateries are clustered according to their national origins. This is particularly noticeable with Colombian establishments. Between Seventy-sixth and Seventy-seventh streets, a Colombian restaurant sits next to a Colombian bakery. An Ecuadorian restaurant is located down the block, while across the street are a corner store, a taco shop, and another Colombian restaurant. Between Eighty-second and Eighty-fourth streets, there are three more Colombian eateries, along with a Mexican restaurant, an Asian produce vendor, and a Broadway Bakery. Other blocks better illustrate the cultural kaleidoscope that is Jackson Heights. An exemplary case is the block from Eighty-seventh to Eighty-eighth Street, where diners can choose from six eateries: an Ecuadorian restaurant, a Mexican taco shop, a Peruvian take-out, a pizzeria, and a Mexican market selling, among other things, *barbacoa de chivo* (goat meat barbecue).

32. The literal tendency in naming practices is exemplified in Fiesta Mexicana Restaurant (Seventy-fifth Street), Lechón Hornado Ecuatoriano (Seventy-sixth Street), Viva Zapata Restaurante Mexicano Bar (Eightieth Street), Pollo Gus Sabor Ecuatoriano (Eightieth Street), Meson Colombiano and Tierras Colombianas (Eighty-second Street), La Pequena Colombia (Eighty-third Street), Cositas Ricas Ecuatorianas Corporation and Casa Colombia Restaurant & Bar (Eighty-sixth Street), Carciofini Restaurant Ecuatoriano, La Casa del Pollo Peruano, and Mi Bello Mexico (Eighty-seventh Street), Mexicana Bakery and Tacos Mexico (Eighty-eighth Street), Las Palomas Mexican Restaurant (Eighty-ninth Street), El Azteca Mexican Restaurant (Ninety-second Street), Esquina Tierras Comida Mexicana (Ninety-third Street), El Pollito Dorado Peruvian Restaurant (Ninety-fifth Street), Steakhouse la Cabana Argentina (Ninety-sixth Street), Mexican Restaurant Tenampa (Ninety-sixth Street), and Café con Leche Panadería Ecuatoriana (102nd Street).

33. Selling breads (*panes*) and pastries (*pasteles*), a *panadería-pastelería* is roughly translated as "bakery."

34. Grocery stores along Roosevelt Avenue do not evidence the nostalgic naming found in bakeries and eateries, although they do house flags and other nationalist icons. Instead, markets tend to be named for the local terrain. Examples include the Roosevelt Candy & Grocery (Eighty-fifth Street), Eighty-ninth Street Grocery, Roosevelt Deli Grocery (Ninety-fourth Street), and New York Food Market (Ninety-fifth Street).

35. Notably, the only flags fluttering above taco shops are plastic pennants advertising Corona, Modelo, and Tecate beers.

36. Suaderos Tacos and Fonda Restaurant Corporation utilize another popular cultural artifact to symbolize Mexico: the serape. Both restaurants hang the brightly colored blankets so they are clearly visible from the street. The latter uses them to create a shield of privacy by covering the front window, and the former hangs them on an interior wall as a backdrop for vining plants, signs advertising house specialties, a hunting trophy, and "Viva Mexico" stenciled in the front window.

37. According to Suzanne Oboler, "Latinos are not and should not be seen as a mere sum-total of the Chicano/a, Puerto Rican, Cuban, Dominican, Central and South American national-origin populations: rather 'Latino/a' is a created identity, forged by the interaction among all these groups" ("*Bienvenidos*/Welcome to the First Issue of Latino Studies," *Latino Studies* 1 [2003]: 2).

38. Whether this aesthetic is particular to pan–Latin American urban settings or is an expression of nostalgia is one of the many questions suggested by this initial study.

39. For philosopher Merleau-Ponty, human existence is not reducible to a Cartesian mind–body split, nor is the acquisition of knowledge a grasping of ideal truths or an ultimate reality. We are, first and foremost, beings *in the world,* perpetually in action and interaction with our surroundings. Our ways of knowing are fundamentally inseparable from our situated, physical, bodily selves. Seeing, hearing, smelling, touching, and tasting are not simple windows of awareness onto a concrete, knowable reality. Rather, sensation involves the mutual constitution of person and world. See Merleau-Ponty, *Phenomenology of Perception;* and Maurice Merleau-Ponty, *The Visible and the Invisible,* ed. Claude Lefort, trans. Alphonso Lingis (Evanston, Ill.: Northwestern University Press, 1968).

40. In fact, according to Edward W. Soja, the "ontological spatiality" of particular places "situate[s] the human subject in a formative geography once and for all, provok[ing] the need for a radical reconceptualization of epistemology, theory construction and empirical analysis" (*Postmodern Geographies: The Reassertion of Space in Critical Social Theory* [London: Verso, 1989], 8).

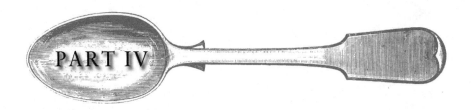

PART IV

Symbols

THE FOOD of New York City is more than the substance; it has iconic status, recognized worldwide. Part IV, "Symbols," considers the symbols, icons, and meanings of food in the city.

"*Cosa Mangia Oggi*," Annie Rachelle Lanzillotto's food voice narrative, viscerally chronicles her family's codes, rules, ways, trials, trauma, and redemption through food in her Italian Bronx household off Arthur Avenue.

Following a generational pattern familiar among many immigrant groups, Jennifer Berg traces the histories of some twentieth-century New York iconic foods in "From the Big Bagel to the Big Roti? The Evolution of New York City's Jewish Food Icons." Beginning as the fare of poor Jewish immigrants, they became iconic symbols of the city and now are found in the frozen-food sections of mainstream American supermarkets.

In "Cooking Up Heritage in Harlem," Damian M. Mosley considers an iconic neighborhood, Harlem, and the tensions there among nostalgia, gentrification, and economic development. Heritage tourism is supporting a Harlem culinary experience that, while attracting visitors, belies much of the culinary diversity of its past and present.

A Manhattan-based restaurant critic, Mitchell Davis, takes us to the white-tableclothed, signature restaurants of Manhattan to explore the role of the restaurant critic, an iconic figure of the New York City dining scene. In "Eating Out, Eating American: New York Restaurant Dining and Identity," he looks not just at the food but also at the images and discourse surrounding these establishments.

On the other end of the dining spectrum, Janet Poppendieck and JC Dwyer write about another important symbol of food in New York City: hunger and food scarcity. In "Hungry City," they consider the disconnect between the need for food and the system designed to help fill that need.

I3

Cosa Mangia Oggi

ANNIE RACHELLE LANZILLOTTO

HUNGRY, I WAS. In search of an honorable lunch. I threw my hand at the sky for strolling clouds to answer: "Where, oh where, can an Italian girl find a lunch in the city she can admit to her ancestors?" I got the tip to go to La Foccaceria on First Avenue just below St. Mark's Place. It was the days just before polenta became chic. Steaming bitter greens, good oil, young garlic, a crusty end of bread to soak up vital juices—was that too much to ask of New York City? I was hungry for the old New York described by my mother—"The boys would start a fire in the lot, we'd each steal a potato and get a stick, and we'd be there for hours"—but those days of the Hot Mickey were scores gone from the Lower East Side streets I walked. One thing remains the same: ancestral accountability. Everything that passes my lips, enters my gut, and becomes my soul has to pass my Grandma Rose's daily unforgiving Eh COsa MANgia eeOGGE! *Cosa mangia oggi!* Thing you eat today! Whad you eat today? Worded in the imperative; the conjugation of orders, *il imperativo;* a whole verb tense for issuing commands, the only tense in which Grandma Rose spoke, and now, o' rest her soul, how she speaks inside me daily. I have to answer. What did I eat today? What if my mind ain't on it? Grandma's life revolved around it. Did I feed sweet tooth or soul? I respond as if in confession. For me, French fries have always been the consummate *F* word. My friends' families would ask them: Where you been? Who with? What d'you do? D'you finish all your homework? All Grandma Rose, ah, little Rosina, born in 1900 in Acquaviva delle Fonte (Living Water of the Fountains), provincia da Bari, the outer heel of the boot of the young unified Italia; all she ever wanted to know was what I ate and if I made any money. The two go hand in hand. To this, all my family elders agreed, even the ones who detested each other: you can't accomplish much on an empty stomach, and all you can accomplish is garbage on

Grandma Rose demonstrating "How to Make *Cavateel*" with actress Valerie Vitale, Arthur Avenue Market, 1996. (Photograph courtesy of Andrew Perret)

a stomach full of garbage. I took solace secretly knowing that there were things on which my warring parents agreed. Hunger beats *acida* (from *acidare* [to make acid] or *agitare* [to agitate], depending on to whom and how and when you say it in response to what and with what level of provocation.) Empty stomachs, empty pockets can kill you. Foods from the outside, like people, were automatically held suspect. Anything grown on fire escapes and in backyards passed. Items from stores were triply inspected with the coordination of eye, hand, and nose. Foods and people had to pass inspection to come into Grandma Rose's kitchen. Every walnut had to be *giovane* (young), and it's an art form to be able to peg the age of a walnut, as Grandma could. Grandma Rosa Marsico Pettruzzelli didn't let my mother or me touch her dough. She yelled, refusing to teach my fingers to make *cavateel* jump like grasshoppers off the fingertips on her rolling board. She mocked my mother's know-nothing attempts, scoffing at the misshapen pasta, poking fun at our AmeriCAHN know-nothing hands. Handling dough is like handling a horse; the dough can scare just as easily and, being a living thing, needs the right balance of handling and solitude to find its full rising. A few stores were implicitly trusted: Frank-n-Joe's down the block on Zerega Avenue and anything from Arthur Avenue, a short pilgrimage from our neighborhood of Westchester Square, the northeastern end of the South Bronx.

To know my grandmother, you had to take her shopping, see her maneuvering up and down the aisles, muttering with arugula, commanding respect from the merchants who believed that Italy had not become a world power because Mussolini ate standing, merchants who handpicked her tomatoes as if giving her diamonds, holding each up to the light, weighing the bags of vegetables on their scales that she would reweigh on her own scale back home. The daily preparation of fresh greens, the companionship of fruit ripened to perfection in brown bags in the bottom drawer of her fridge and along the windowsills, her fire-escape tomatoes and *basilico*, August fried zucchini flowers—Grandma lived with this medicine only. Eating was not taken lightly. Eating was not to be done without thinking. Eating was communion. Transmogrification. When you eat the foods of your ancestors, all the blood comes rushing down through the ages. When I sit down to eat, I wipe the bowl clean with the gratitude of a *campesino* who has the rarity of a herring on which to rub his daily crust of bread; I stare into the light over the dining-room table, mindlessly stirring my coffee with the hundred-yard stare of a survivalist shell-shocked marine; I swallow wine with the stem of the glass straight up, with an epicurean conviction waiting for the last drop of grape to instill *corragio,* from the Latin *cor*: heart, take heart! I pocket garlic without knowing it at the supermarket, and later finding it reminds me where I come from: people of the earth, people who could coax life from rock-hard terrain. I eat second and third helpings with the Depression-era wolf-at-the-door fear of who knows where the next meal will come from. And when I am done, I wash my dishes slowly, wiping in circles with the temporary respite at the sink of Bronx-battered wives and children for whom the hot water hitting the porcelain sink is the site of ablution and transformation from the kitchen violence where commonplace utensils are weaponry. As a kid, I positioned teaspoons like soldiers behind each of the heat pipes; when my father beat my mother, I would hack the heat pipes as a signal to the upstairs neighbors to call the cops. As an adult, I went back and forth each Saturday and Sunday between my parents' abodes and eating habits. At my father's, I'd sit on an overturned bucket in the boiler room of the mental home where he lived out his last decade, drinking coffee he made by unscrewing copper tubing on the furnace to divert boiling water straight from the furnace into my cup. My father, Joseph Rocco, kept a World War II marine K-ration mentality: "The body doesn't need much to survive," and, above all, "Eat with guys you can trust," which generally didn't include civilians. My mother's apartment kitchen was a few feet shorter than a cell block but produced more food than a cafeteria, and over the years she fed just about everyone I ever met on this continent or who passed through New York, which is—just about everyone. My mother, Rachel Claire Pettruzzelli Lanzillotto: even my dog cries for her meatballs. Scaramooch, the shepherd–collie whose name means "little skirmisher," from Scaramouche (Scaramuccia, Scaramuzza)—the Neapolitan Commedia delle Arte, swashbuckling, sword-carrying, long-nosed lover of wine and women— Scaramooch licks my mother's empty hands with faith, like rubbing Aladdin's lamp, knowing that if he licks ten times, her empty hands will procure more meatballs.

Grandma Rose stood at four feet, eight inches, posed no questions, and lived to be one hundred and a half, eating plenty off her neighbors' trees. As Bronx oldtimers say, "In these backyards there's more figs than all of California," and I believe it. In Acquaviva delle Fonte, I heard told contentions with Californian fruits that paralleled an assessment of the American dream: all look, no sweetness. In the Mezzogiorno, fruits are small and unpretty on the outside, but when broken open, gorgeous sweetness pours out of them. You bite into the life force when you bite into a dented pear that's been nipped on the tree by the birds, which are the sweetest because the birds know which to peck. California fruits—polished, huge, and uniform—to a *campesino* seem all appearance, bloated, the taste watered down. I made this pilgrimage to Acquaviva delle Fonte as an adult; I found my relatives, ate their foods, basked my face and neck and arms in their homemade olive oils, bit into their tomatoes yellow, red, green, and full of life, and learned for the first time what should have been obvious all along: foods are living things! By the act of eating, you add life force to your body! I can hear my grandmother laughing at me and my AmeriCAHN realizations that come as such a surprise and so late in life. Yellow, red, green, I could feel the pulse from the vine entering my bloodstream. Eating in Italy feels like breast-feeding straight from the earth. Foods are the answers from the gods. I could feel the surge of life energy biting into the green stalks of the lush deep-purple *brocco* flower. In Acquaviva delle Fonte, my aunts never stop prepping for the next meal. A few days before my departure, they began to cook presents for Grandma Rose that I would carry back to America. I followed my Zia Isabella from her house through the streets and alleyways, each of us carrying a tray wider than a sewer cap full of raw *biscotti di mandorle* (almond biscotti), which she'd been making for days, from her own almonds, of course—these were Grandma Rose's favorite. Where were we walking to in this procession of raw biscotti through the old town square? Our communicating was a game of mime and laughter sprinkled with Acquavivese, or you could have fun saying Acquavivese delle Fontese expressions, hands in the air, no English, and my grasp of Italian, which was kinda useless in the *paese,* which had a living language tree all its own, laden with expressions of multiple entendres. *TENZione*! (Attention!), Zia Isabella instructed me to follow her putting the trays on the stone ground in line behind other large trays in what felt like a cave, guarded by a huge sweating man with a hairy chest who was holding a twenty-foot wooden pole, on the end of which was a flat head that pushed the trays into a stone oven. I looked inside, and the heat hit me. The oven was big enough to cremate a Cadillac. The man adeptly shuffled the many trays around to perfection and ate a bit from each for payment, or tips. I never saw my aunt hand him money. This was the community oven. When I left for the train, my aunts filled my backpacks with a five-liter container of their homemade olive oil; a five-liter container of my uncle's vino, figs, and almonds from their trees; a focaccia made by a neighbor; and a wheel of sheep's cheese requested by my grandma. They sent me off to America with their blessings, foods they had grown, prepared, and alchemically transformed through the miracle of their hands and fire. Grandma must have left this way, I thought, definitely not so abundantly, or she wouldn't have had to leave at all, but with some of these valuables: *i couloumb*—dark black figs, gold and pink on the inside—and thirty-six hands like a flock of birds on the train platform, the wind from their hands sending the train on its way.

To learn to love to eat bitter greens is like learning another language; it took me years. My mom's signature dishes were pasta broccoli with fried bread crumbs, stuffed mushroom caps, and stuffed Italian peppers. When my mom and I ate something quick, uncareful, and American like hotdogs, Grandma would come in from outside, where she had found some roadside *chicorria* (dandelions), and take out a tiny aluminum pot to boil them for herself. The word "dandelion" comes from *dente di lione* (lion's teeth), and Grandma's little pot had the power of the teeth of lions. She said, "It cleansa da blood." One day during our championship softball game, Grandma was picking *chicorria* in left center field. The umpire stood up behind me, whistling and yelling, "Interference!" I was the catcher, so I yelled from home plate, "Grandma, get off the field!" She was quick, already with two full shopping bags. While she cleaned her blood, we opened the windows and stuffed our stomachs. While she peeled a pear, we'd down soup bowls of ice cream. She'd look scornfully at what went into our mouths as she ate alone by the kitchen window.

"BoLENT!" she'd laugh at me in disapproval, pronouncing "polenta" with a *b* instead of a *p* and dropping the last *a*, as happens to words as they migrate south. BoLENT, poor peasant survival food, corn mush, she called me, when a pathetic state would seize me for hours on my mother's couch in front of the television, "Ay BoLENT, whatsamatta?"

By the time I found La Foccaceria, polenta was about to skyrocket in New York City as an Upper East Side gourmet side dish with garnishes. Garnishing polenta is like bow-tying Ferragamo shoes on a *campesino* bending over zucchini in a muddy field. And what of peasants and peasants' descendants? We could all starve while the upper classes appropriated, exoticized, and garnished our mush. Our mush, which our ancestors ate because their ancestors overtaxed our donkey and diverted water from our great-grandfather itinerant farmers who, starving, eating anchovies and sardines instead of salt (my great-grandfather was known as Mangiasard [eats sardines]), huddled on ships that crossed into unknown lands rather than stay home with the destiny of their families. Once in L'America, they wanted to forget BoLENT and other foods from La Miseria. Ahh! My grandmothers' hands could make a *zuppa* out of stones, but in L'America they didn't have to. "We didn't think of ourselves as poor," my mom reports, "because nobody had nothing."

Broccoli rabe sauté, $4.95, was handwritten in black marker on white board reassuring the facts of my world. White board filled two walls of La Foccaceria with names of foods in syllabic New York southern Italianese I understood, at prices that didn't give a young artist *agida*. 'Scarole and spinach were written $2 cheaper than broccoli rabe, stating a hierarchy of greens I didn't understand. *Vesteddi* sandwiches were the cheapest, at $1.95, which suited my pocket but I didn't know what they were, and when I asked, I thought, well, I didn't grow up eating spleen. I never saw eels in my bathtub, never spread bone marrow on toast or marinated a head of any kind, never saw the goat's eyes cry. My Bronx was the flat earth. Paved by our concrete thoughts. I fell off the flat, flat earth. I dreamed of what my life might have been had Grandma Rose not taken her sister's place on the boat, her sister Maria, who was slated to come but the Great War interrupted the plan. At the war's end, Maria was twenty-one and considered too old to start a new life, so she stayed in Acquaviva delle Fonte, as my great-grandmother Rachele casually turned to little Rosina and said, "You, you, go instead," thereby reversing our fates—my cousins living on one side of the Atlantic and us on the other. The ocean was the beveled mirror in which we imagined one another's lives and had distorted vision of our own. We were Italians and thought of those born in Italy as Italian Italians.

Endless baskets of bread were automatically brought to my table by a lanky, dispassionate guy in a white apron who intermittently stood outside the glass doors, slowly blowing smoke out onto First Avenue while protecting the owner's shimmering oyster-pink Cadillac parked at the meter close to the door. I put details together quickly. The waiter was the owner's son-in-law who walked around heavily as if working off a penance for something he never did. Lenticche soup, past'n'fazool, 'scarole, *carciofi*; here were the foods of my youth that would prepare me for the Grandma Rose inquisition even if I were eating on the run between jobs. Finally I could eat out and have answers.

Maybe it was the way I said, "Ayy!" rather than the content of my question, "So why's the broccoli rabe two bucks more than spinach 'n 'scarole, huh!?" The son-in-law looked down over my glass of swaying water and basket of bread with cold, gold foil–wrapped butter squares and dished me the fact as if he were reciting the number of the soldiers killed in combat that day: "It's a labor-intensive vegetable." I stuck a hunk of the soft bread in my mouth. I learned over the years to choose when to shut up instead of mouthing off, especially to men. The bread was doughy and took up the whole inside of my mouth, kneading all the words that were on their way ready to fly out of it back into the dough. I breathed through my nose and kept chewing as he walked to the back table nearest the kitchen and picked up his short knife. I swallowed, thinking of Grandma cutting crosses in the bottom of each broccoli rabe stem as he resumed his seat, cleaning string beans. That was the most conversation I got out of that guy in the next twenty years of eating there. I'd eat efficiently, stand up to meet the owner at the cash register, and then leave, facing First Avenue better equipped to handle whatever situation the city would toss me that day, making my way up to DeRoberti's for an espresso and a *pastaciotta* to top off the meal. Sated. Readied. I'd call her from the corner pay phone, TA 2–7487, and she'd deliver her fastball.

"Hi Grandma, it's Annie."

"Annie!" Then the reinforcement of the Italian greeting with the southern Italian Bronx lilt, "GOOma sta?"

"BEHnay," I would sing proudly from the time I was two, "BEHnay!"

"Brrrava," she would say, and I would repeat her inquiry, "GOOma sta?"

"Menza menz. No complain, honey. I'ma cooking a stringabeans and a lambachop." Then the zing, "*Cosa mangia oggi!*" Boom. Never in English. Foods we confessed in Italian. It was a sacred discussion.

"*Scarol'agli'olio!*" (escarole with garlic and oil).

"Brrava!" she'd have to say, "brrrava. Smarta gherl."

Escarole aced her test every time. "*Un poco di vino.*"

"That's okay."

"I'm thinking of when I could get up to see you."

"That's okay, honey, stay where you are, make the money."

"Make the money? But I want to visit you, Granma!"

"Ehhh! Back ena forth, back ena forth. *Stai tranquilo.* Make the money."

We had codes for eating. (1) *If you were born in America, you had to learn how to eat.* My sister Rosemarie bought herself *The Culinary Arts Institute Encyclopedic Cookbook* when she got engaged, and we lay in bed laughing to the point of losing our breath at night as we read over and over the recipe for headcheese on page 384—". . . scrape the hog's head . . . wash and trim the tongue . . . let stand three days"—imagining the head jumping out of the pot to attack the whole family. Thirty years later, I taught her daughter, my goddaughter Melissa, how to make a gravy, and she wrote down each word I said with Grandma's voice inside me, including "When you sauté garlic, don't let it burn," to which her fiancé, Rob, said, "Yeah, but it's only words on paper," hitting on the dilemma of the generations embodied through Grandma and me—the legacy of an inverse relationship of literacy and the knowledge of the hands.

There's a *sistemazione*, an order in which things can be eaten, and a *sfragganize*, a peasant wisdom saying for the many *sistemazione*. One night, I sat with concentration on peeling an orange with Grandma's old shoemaker's knife, a tool truly made for the hand; its green wooden handle and a scythe-like blade for cutting leather heels fit in your hand so well, and Grandma's thumb would guide provolone into the blade. I was sitting with my orange unpeeling in one long curled strip of skin at night before going to bed, when Grandma gave me her shrill "Eeeee," with arm straight up, indicating that I had broken a code again: *L'arancia di mattina e oro puro; nel pomeriggio argento, di sera piombo* (An orange in the morning is pure gold; in the afternoon, silver; in the evening, lead). Oranges are not to be eaten at night! (2) *Eat until you sweat.* Eating is an intercourse of living things. If you're not sweating, you're not really doing it. Raw garlic and *pepperonici* will get you there. Garlic in one hand, handkerchief in the other. My Zio Francesco listens to my phlegm and says, "Stay with me a coupla days, I'll fix you right up. Garlic is essential. Garlic is the essence of life. Learn how to bite into it so it opens your valves." I began sticking pieces in my ears for earaches, wrapping slices around my neck for swollen glands. Garlic can push an ocean through your aorta. I began to carry it wherever I go. My idea of a SANGwich is garlic folded in bread. (3) *Don't pay for garlic or parsley.* Some things in life you shouldn't pay money for. (4) *If you're not growing your own food, then knowing how to shop is the first step of the art of cooking and eating. A spezzia!* To shop! Shopping is the art of scrutiny. When you get home and cut the eggplant open, it better not be full of seeds; it better be good inside if you're going to work with it for four hours making eggplant parmagiano; you want each eggplant to be good. (5) *Don't pay for what you're not going to eat.* Break off the white ends of the asparagus before they weigh it on the scale. (6) *Open the refrigerator only when you have to and when you do, take several things out at once to conserve energy.* Even announce it to the family: "I'm opening the fridge, anyone need anything?" (7) *Let water run.* Water is meant to run. The kitchen faucet always ran while my grandmother or mother cooked and runs when I cook, to the dismay of my conservation-conscious friends. Running water recalls the fountains in the piazza for the *passeggiata* (after-dinner stroll). Acquaviva delle Fonte. Living water of the fountains. Italy is fountains. Water runs and lets your heart open in the piazza, where you can bend into a kiss or fresh drink of *l'acqua,* elaborate fountains with gaping mouths of horses and simple open pipes all keep the flow. Water talks and tells you where you come from. (8) *Cook in crisis.* Cook when you need to cope with tragedy. Cook to heal. Cook to transform. When JFK got shot, my mother picked me up off the kitchen counter and ran down the block to buy some dough and came home and made focaccia. When my brother was drafted was the first and only time we made homemade ravioli. (9) *Focaccia \fiGATZ\ is cut with a big pair of scissors, never with a knife.* You get underneath it, lift one corner from the pan and revel in how perfectly brown and oily it is, take a big fabric scissor, and snip squares. (10) *Eat foods before they make it to the table.* It's the opposite of natural selection. The meatballs that look the best in our estimation don't make it to the gravy; the next tier gets forked out of the gravy before it's brought to the table. When carrying an Italian bread home in its white paper sleeve from the corner store after Mass, bite off one end of the bread before you make it up the stoop and into the house. At the table, anyone can vie for the other end, but usually someone gets preference; in our family it became Vivian, my brother Charlie's girlfriend; we all knew she had a passion for the crusty end, and we wanted her in our family, so we'd automatically pass it down the table to her. (11) *Savor the end. Savor life.* Perform *a'schapett, la scarpetta,* the little shoe, wiping the juices on the plate and pan with the heel of the bread, acknowledging that the end of the meal is the best part and that not a drop will be wasted. (12) *When grating Parmagiano Reggiano for the Sunday pasta, grate the hunk down to the rind.* If you're not sure if you've grated down to absolutely nothing but the rind, keep grinding until you skin the tips of your fingers and knuckles to little pricks of blood. (13) *Being overweight is a sign of good health.* The highest compliment is if someone says of you, "She's a good eater." If you were depressed, they'd ask, "How's your appetite?" If you were heartbroken, you'd be told, "Eat a little something, you'll feel better." (14) *No matter how you fight with your family, always come back to sit together around the dinner table.* A fight could combust between any two of us at any time, yet we always returned to the table. (15) *Never buy or eat anything from where you don't have total trust,* or where you're getting ripped off, or the quality was bad, or you could just as well cook it at home. (16) *If you ever, for any reason, have to eat out, order something you don't make at home. Don't pay for pasta!* At La Foccaceria, a side of pasta was only $1 with an entrée. I think that for $1, it's allowed. (17) *The codes change as you age.* After a lifetime of eating steak and putting his Lucky Strikes out in the dried waxy meat fat on his dinner plate, my father's last food philosophy was, "Eat what grows in the ground, not what walks on the ground." And Grandma Rose regaled the quality of good Bronx water, but in her nineties, finally scoffed if you tried to pour water into her glass with dinner, saying, "Only drinka d'wine. Water sinksa d'ships." Peaches swimming in a tall glass of deep dark Chianti is the way to go. (18) *Visiting one another's homes is akin to food shopping.* On your way out the door, you will be interviewed about what groceries you're lacking at home, and two bags will be filled for you and placed by the door. My mother packs plastic containers whenever I leave her house. Some plastic containers are from my trip to the homes of Zia Isabella and Zia Rose in Acquaviva delle Fonte. These containers make their sacred rounds. You can't leave a relative's house empty-handed. Not even after they're dead. When my mother's only sister, Lucia, died, we went to her opulent house in the suburbs and retrieved cannelini beans, about six cans; anchovies, the same; a gallon and a half of olive oil; assorted canned goods; a desktop Saint Anthony; and a box of old papers that Grandma Rose had collected over the years, things she had written down. What I didn't know was that this box held her handwritten recipes from her Bronx neighbors and the journey I would take with these recipes. (19) *Always carry food with you when you leave the house.* After one museum excursion in New York City, my mom, niece, girlfriend, and I walked around the Upper East Side hungry. We saw a sign that said EAT. Sounded humble enough. We sat down, looked at the menu, and got our sensibilities KO'd. Every sandwich was $18.95. Coffee was $6.95. This broke code 16 and would change our public eating patterns for life. Too tired to leave, we ordered one lamb sandwich and one coffee, which came in a silver tureen, the four of us sharing. From that lunch on, my mother carried a frittata whenever she hopped the bus to meet me downtown. Rachele's Pocketbook Frittata: "Whatever you have in the bottom drawer of the refrigerator thrown into a frying pan with eggs." Then hustle to catch the bus. Italian women carry big pocketbooks; they're either carrying food or pocketing it. Traditionally, asparagus is laid crosswise in the pan for structure, like steel rods in concrete. (20) *Be open to new foods and spices.* In her eighties, Grandma was the first in the family to try what she called the Chinese mozzarell— tofu. (21) *Cook.* You don't have to know who for. It will always be eaten. (22) *The Lasagna is the king of foods.* In our Bronx Italian household, it was made to celebrate men: Christ's birth, Charlie's coming home alive from Vietnam, things like that.

As a youth, I feared The Lasagna. There was so much in there all at once, layer after layer, stratification of muzzaRRELL, grating cheese, pasta, chopped meat, garlic, parsley, sausage, basil, riGUTH. I couldn't get my mouth around it. The inside squeezed out like lava and could scorch your throat. A tall, sharp knife cut it into heaping squares like city blocks; a spatula carefully craned it toward you, plopping a whole steaming city block onto your plate; and you were expected to eat it. Adults had a passion for it. Good thing the dining-room table doubled as a cave for Penny, our Belgian shepherd. Her reassuring warm tongue licked the lasagna down to the palm of my wet hand. No food took center stage, the center of the table, like The Lasagna. The Lasagna was ceremonial. It came out for holidays and was the only dish that never shared your plate with anything else. You'd never put anything on your plate next to The Lasagna. Holding the respect of the whole plate is no small feat. On Holy Days, before The Lasagna, we'd cover our plates with elaborate antipast, then a meat—say, turkey or a roast—roasted potatoes, and broccoli. Then, after we had finished eating, out came The Lasagna. My mother would lean over the oval maple table to set it in the center as everyone's hands cleared the center space and trivets were lined up by my sister to hold the great pan's heat from the maple table. My mom would lean over to divvy it up. After that came Grandma's brick-heavy calzone filled with provolone and ham, then her *pizzadolce*. When Charlie went to Nam, he was sent off and welcomed home with The Lasagna, and the two years he was away we didn't eat it at all. My mother had made a vow. To her saints. To her son. With the whole neighborhood as witness.

Charlie was in Da Nang when all the women got into action to make ravioli for him. My mother went to Ralph's Butcher Shop and asked for ground sirloin and some pork. "When you went to a butcher and they knew you, you knew what you were getting," my mother says, "and he knew just what you wanted. He only had top-grade stuff." I watched the butcher's wet hand push the meat into a silver grinder and catch it at the other end as it came out in strands, like out of a shower head, swirling onto white paper he wrapped tightly like a diaper, dropped it on the scale, and wrote the price in thick black pencil, as my mother nodded in approval. Charlie's girlfriend Vivian's house in Throgs Neck became a ravioli factory for a day. She lived with her parents and grandmother across the street from Saint Raymond's Cemetery, where all our relatives this side of the Atlantic were buried and we all supposed we would be. With the gray marble headstones in the distance, the women opened three tables and pushed them together in one long rectangle in the basement kitchen. I was five. I remember the women with short sleeves and aprons, their bare arms diving in to churn the giant pot of riGUTH mixture with egg and parsley; the gravy bubbling on the stove with green-gold olive oil, garlic, bay leaf, parsley, and basil in a giant silver pot, the steam reaching the ceiling, and the tallest wooden spoons reddened all the way up the handles; and the table covered with flour and rolled out with pasta by adeptly handled rolling pins. Deep silver spoons ladling mounds of the riguth, a wheelie knife cruising down the table and making long strips of scalloped edges, many soft and strong fingers pressing the edges so each square held its pouch—little semolina raviolis pregnant with riguth. They let me help press the edges together. Clear glass mason jars and lids were boiled and then filled to the brim with fat ravioli in gravy. Others with meatballs. Two grand cardboard boxes packed tight with jars of ravioli and gravy and meatballs. My brother was in the jungle, not a barracks, but still my mother knew how to get him ravioli; she wrote a lot of numbers on the box. This was our women's war effort, to pull my brother's soul back with a long trail of creamy riguth ravioli. Although the ravioli arrived with some green mold in the jars, Charlie fed all the marines he could. I hope the smell alone when those sealed jars were opened made them momentarily forget where they were. The women wept for him but not when they cooked. Vivian's white T-shirt was marked with the Italian women's stigmata: gravy stains over the chest. And these stigmata appear on Sundays to this day.

My mother vowed, "I'm not making lasagna till my son comes home." For two years, The Lasagna didn't make its appearance. My mother couldn't make it. It was Charlie's favorite. He was her oldest child. She made a sacred pact. As soon as Charlie flew overseas, my mother placed her order for his homecoming—everything for two great pans of The Lasagna: two tins of riguth, a dozen eggs, two fresh muzzarell, six cans of tomatoes, hot and sweet sausage, parsley, garlic, the pasta, and the good grating cheese. And all the things for the antipast—salami, *soppressata,* prosciutto, roasted peppers, olives, artichokes, finocchio, everything that goes into an Italian antipast—and, of course, don't forget the big loaf of Italian bread, and you could take ginger ale and milk. My mother's order was akin to a petition you tuck at the feet of a saint at a grotto. Frank-n-Joe's was on notice; she told the guys, "When you get the emergency phone call from me, stop everything and fill my delivery." My mother doesn't remember when she started to make lasagna or how she learned. She is sure

of one thing. "My mother never made lasagna," she says, thinking back. "Maybe 243
Ronzoni reintroduced it; somehow it caught on. It had a resurgence." Although The
Lasagna can be traced to ancient Rome, it was definitely lost in the transition from
the La Miseria *cafone* to the relative opulence in the working-class Bronx, where it
reemerged, at least in my family. The Lasagna rose in status on the table, and eventually after fifty years of performance had outlasted my family's ability to sit with one
another at the table.

Two years later, when Charlie called early in the morning to say that he was on
his way, already out of Vietnam, she made the call to Frank-n-Joe's and started to
cook. A couple of dozen of the extended family came over. I made a "Welcome home,
Charlie" sign with a blue glitter star, and we hung it in the front window. It took two
strong adults to pull the table apart; then two leaves were put in the middle to extend
the table. "Where's all my teaspoons?" she asked, and I ran around the house and
collected them from the heat pipe stations. For now, maybe the fighting was over,
even the kitchen trauma drama. I helped prepare the antipast, hours of rolling pink
and red meats and yellow cheeses and arranging them on a platter like an homage
to a sun goddess, alternating colors, and, the center of the plate, a mound of black
olives. Charlie came home skinny and with a shaved head and big arms. He stood on
his knees and playfully put his arm like a tree trunk around my neck, and I couldn't
breathe. I was seven. To even the fight, I needed a weapon as big as his fist. I ran to
the refrigerator and opened the freezer, grabbing a ten-ounce, frozen-like-a-brick can
of orange juice. I ran back, and as he shadowboxed me, I slammed the frozen can
into his jaw, and one of his teeth fell out, bloody. The women circled the table course
after course, cookies and pastries, it was like a never-ending thing. I don't remember
any big meat like roast beef or anything that day, just *bragiole,* wrapped in long
white thread that the adults had to unwind to eat it. In retrospect, my mother says,
"I remember him standing outside staring, but I'm sure he ate something. It was too
much, the transition." The Lasagna was too much even for Charlie that day, and he
loved it.

Kitchen, kitchen, the kitchen, the portal of creation and destruction, where
our cribs were kept; where our mothers kept their post over the hot stove, *sopre
il forno caldo,* dipping cigarettes into the gas-blue ring of flames with their teeth;
where our ancestors entered in the dark hours when we couldn't sleep through the
white light of the great open 'frigerator while we stacked SANGwiches, and in the
arm of early sunlight reaching through the kitchen window into a well of semolina
dusting up into the light, in the running of the faucet waters calling, in all kitchen
trauma drama; throwing eggplant parmagiano at my brother Johnny and its splattering the ceiling; the kitchen was where we summoned life and took up swords with
death.

My mother was making a pasta for my twenty-ninth birthday when death came
knocking. Water boiling, there was a pounding on the door, and instinctively she
ripped open a second bag of penne, for whoever it was would surely stay and eat.
In that moment, pasta midair, her aorta split, and she called my name as if I were at
a great distance and fell backward with force into my arms as if she'd been shot in
the chest. "I'm okay," she said, so I knew something was mortally wrong. She had

internal bleeding in the regions of the heart. One of many miracles in her life, my mother survived. After she had convalesced for half a year, I threw the wheelchair in the car and said, "Let's go. Wherever you want." It was time she left the house for something other than a doctor. "Arthur Avenue," she said, "let's go to the market." That's where she knew she could refuel her soul. Eating in the market brought out in us a brazen way of interacting and performing our Bronx selves for one another.

At thirty, I moved back downtown, to a room over Chumleys, a Manhattan Prohibition-era speakeasy on Bedford and Barrow streets. Every day at 5:00 A.M., a glass-recycling truck stopped under my window, and two men hurled bags of glass bottles from Chumleys into the truck's gaping back jaw. The sound of glass crushing hit me as if getting punched in the gut, and I jackknifed in bed in my sleep. My journals were filled with metaphoric descriptions of the sound of broken glass: glass tripping down fire escapes like rain, glass like bells lingering, dropping, sparking, and the magnificent glitter of it all. I asked my mother if something had happened in my childhood with glass that I wouldn't remember and she told me:

> Yes, you had your own whatchamacallit—Kristallnacht (Night of Glass Breaking). The crib was in the kitchen. He'd come home all hours. If he saw two pots on the stove, he'd announce, "I'm going out to eat." If there were no pots on the stove, he'd yell, "Where's my dinner?" So I got wise to him. I'd set empty pots on the stove. The bigger the pots, the quicker he'd leave. I'd eat with the kids early. Who knew when he was likely to walk in? Then one night he uncovered the pots. You were in there with him. He blocks me out of the kitchen with the refrigerator and breaks every dish, every cup. You were one and a half. I was screaming, "My baby! My baby!" and you weren't even crying. I didn't hear you cry. I can remember that. When the cops came, he had everything swept up and the bags of glass hidden. He must have hidden them in the garage. No, the basement. He was cunning, your father. I opened the cupboards. I said to the cops, "I have four children! Don't you see the cupboards are empty?"

In their divorce papers, my father's counterclaim states, "Plaintiff failed to prepare meals . . . and on many occasions when defendant came home from work, he would find that supper had not been prepared. . . . In June 1973, at the home of the parties, the plaintiff hit the defendant in the head with a frying pain, causing him to sustain contusions and abrasions."

After contemplating my mother's near death, I began to create performance art. The impulse to hand food to the audience soon joined the work. I typed and adhered paper strips of text on hard-boiled eggs: *forse sogniamo quasi abbastanza / perhaps we dream nearly enough;* and on garlic: *as if skin can hold you.* I handed these out to audiences. One show was called "Pocketing Garlic"; another, "How to Cook a Heart"; and another "a'Schapett." I went back to Arthur Avenue, continuing to bond with my mother and grandmother, and began to perform oral history–based performances about the history of pushcart peddling with the merchants in the Arthur Avenue Retail Market. I became obsessed with what I heard as the street opera of pushcart

Annie with salami, *parmigiano reggiano,* and provolone from Mike's Deli for "a'Schapett" at *Dancing in the Streets: Insights into Onsite* evening in the Guggenheim Works and Process Series, 1996. (Photograph courtesy of Andrew Perret)

peddlers calling up to the windows in the early-morning light. I interviewed senior citizen shoppers to find out what chants they remembered. Out of these, I composed and sang a chant based on shopper Al Paoletta's memory of the Hughes Avenue fish peddler who would call, *Chi mangi pesce mai morite* (Who eats fish will never die). In the late 1990s, when the first fast-food restaurant opened on Arthur Avenue, a neighborhood protest was organized. Once one fast-food restaurant opens, other chains follow; that's the pattern and how New York neighborhoods become palimpsests in old-timers' imaginations. New York neon and hand-painted signs are relegated to our memories of pork stores, *salumerias,* and bakeries. Mike's Deli called me in; they were providing SANGwiches and thought that we artists could add some drama to the protest. The protesters included many old shoppers, even Grandma Rose. Seeing her behind a police barricade was fantastic. In that moment, I came up with "Viva Broccoli Rabe!" for the crowd to chant. The fast-food joint lasted less than a decade on Arthur Avenue. "Viva Broccoli Rabe!"

In 1999, at ninety-nine years old, on Christmas Day, a branch of Grandma's small intestine got twisted, when on top of an entire feast she apparently ate six jelly doughnuts and twelve figs. "She and Mr. Bernadone kept drinking black coffee. No one was counting how much they ate," my mother reported later. "But then when I went to take a jelly doughnut home, there were none left." My mother telephoned me; when she said everything was okay, I drove immediately up there. I walked into the apartment and asked, "What's that smell?"

"Lysol," my mother said. "She's been vomiting, and I've been disinfecting."

"No, that other smell, underneath what you've been covering by cleaning." I smelled Grandma's mouth and knew right away what had happened. Her intestines were completely blocked and backing up. I carried Grandma to the car and drove to the emergency room. That evening, she underwent emergency surgery. I rushed into the post-op recovery unit before she was awake. I touched her hand to make the connection, as if to ground her spirit back into the conscious body. All went fine until a week later, after we had pasta and peas, she shouted at the table, "My leg! *E come 'na pietro!*" It's like a stone! She was in enormous pain, screaming to Saint Anthony and the Virgin Mary: "MaDONE! MaDONE! Sant'AntoNEE! Sant'AntoNEE! My leg! My leg! *E come 'na pietro.* Sant'AntoNEE!! Sant'AntoNEE!!" In intensive care with a blood clot for three weeks, she developed a bed sore on the heel of her left foot. Over months it became cavernous, deep like a bullet hole, exactly marking the part of the heel where Acquaviva delle Fonte is on the archipelago. The leg turned blue and ice cold from below the knee to the toes. The cardiovascular surgeon offered amputation as the best option, to which the men in the family nodded assent. "It's a piece of meat," Charlie said. "Cut it off." This time I had no bread to stuff in my mouth, and I was angry with their willingness to mutilate her. I held my cool. "Give me eight days," I said. "If nothing gets better, then you can amputate." I had no idea what I would do in those eight days. Some voice inside me said, partly as a joke, partly as a last resort. and partly as a test of faith: "If all else fails, get the garlic out." Did I really believe in garlic? For eight days and nights, I smothered Granma's leg in crushed garlic mixed with olive oil. We prayed the Ave Maria, holding the heat of our hands over the leg. All the family put their hands in. We were from the south. We did believe in garlic. The arteries in the blue leg were like arroyos; we could see the sudden infusion of blood make them swell. Grandma pointed to the spot on the leg where we should concentrate the garlic and the heat. Grandma walked out of there. When she died, she died with two legs on.

At her funeral a year and a half later, I handed out artichokes and garlic and peppers, so everyone in church had some vegetable to hold. I tried to collect money to plant a tree in her name. Before anyone gave me any money, a peach tree sprouted right outside my mother's living-room window where Grandma Rose had tossed her peach pits. Again, she had put me to shame with her peasant wisdom, as if to say, "Useless AmERreeCAHN . . . I'll do it myself." On her 101st, 102nd, 103rd, 104th, 105th, and 106th birthdays, I've picked more and more peaches from her tree, and I stand under its leaves in remembrance. When I prune the branches in the fall and clip the ones prone to twist around other branches, I think of how Grandma used to ask me to pull her toes straight and press flat the second toe, which had the proclivity to twist on top of the big toe.

It was the Christmas after September 11, 2001, when The Lasagna sat alone. Too much work for my mother by then, my brother Johnny took on the ritual and made The Lasagna. Never needing anything to argue about, we just got down to it. Holy Days are strewn with arguments around the table, our verbal sparring ring. Bronx alleyways always rang with arguments, and although we were used to knowing one another's business—all our laundry hanging proudly out—we were taught to mind our own business and not be like *betruZZEEN in tutta la minestra* (parsley in everyone's soup). The Lasagna would outlast us. No matter how many times we had left the table shouting behind slammed doors over the years, we always eventually returned to *la tavola,* the table. But not this day. We walked out of Johnny's house and drove around, wondering where to go on Christmas Day while The Lasagna sat out the afternoon in his turned-off oven, keeping warm. This time, even my brother left his own house. And The Lasagna stood alone. As I drove around with my mother, niece, and girlfriend, my mother's refrain throughout the hours was, "What a shame, barely through the antipast and we're at one another's throats. The Lasagna. The Lasagna. The Lasagna, Johnny made The Lasagna," knowing the sacrilege of it all that my brother had been involved in for days in preparation. The Lasagna alone in the oven had a magnetic force. The act of making The Lasagna was a ritual transmogrification, a calling together of the ancestors, of everything we were, and making it all work. The Lasagna stayed home alone, symbol of our disintegration and terminal glue. The Lasagna held us together.

I sat down to open the box of Grandma's writings, handwritten like cuts into stone, blue ink cut into church envelopes, good thick paper, her *q*'s and 2's studiously cursive, each letter full of care and slowly fashioned, all the *t*'s crossed and all the *i*'s dotted by a hand that held a pen tentatively. "There was no such thing as scratch paper, so she wrote with care, she took her time," my mother observed. Grandma Rose never purchased writing paper in her life. Never read a whole book in her life. She wrote on confiscated, found, reused paper: recipe after recipe on numbered church envelopes embossed with "This is my weekly sacrifice"; on cut paper bags, the whole rim intact so you could wear them like armbands; on the back of electric bills; on an envelope with a postmarked Christmas stamp.

I looked at my grandmother's recipes and began to decipher them, knowing they would serve me no good. I don't have my grandmother's hands, but I had watched them. The recipes could offer me only clues. She grew up holding crops. I grew up holding crap, things that never lasted. This is the difference between us. My grandmother held everything as if there were life inside it. Plastic she held like an egg. Plastic she held as if it had grown right out of the ground I'm standing on. Her hands broke eggs like no one I'd ever seen. Her right hand cracked an egg into another egg held by her left hand, and the left egg was the only one that broke every time. Once I brought her two dozen eggs, played a sound track of church bells, and asked her to crack the eggs while my partner, Audrey, videotaped her hands. Not one yolk was broken. The sound track of bells brought up *campanilismo,* the connection you have to who and what is within earshot of the local church bell. Those are your *paesani*, those are whom you trust, and we created that sense of loyalty on our Bronx blocks where our block was our world. I call this video "Eggs and Bells," and it's a meditation to watch the disappearing hands: *guarda questi mani a scomparsi!*

Grandma's recipes are titled "Regulations." *Regole dei cartellato. Regole die biscotti a l'aniso.* I read them aloud and studied them, sounding out the words and hearing her voice saying them in her accent and intonation until I broke the code. I carried them around in plastic sheets and asked for help from old Italian women who took an interest. Grandma wrote in a combination of phonetic English as she heard it, Acquavivese, and Italian. She never measured anything. She cooked *al'occhio* (by the eye). Yet the regulations had some measurements. Biscotti calls for "3 *tispunno begn polvere*." "Three tisPUNNO," I could hear her say. Okay, Grandma, I'm with you, three teaspoons. But what is *begn polvere*? What language are we talking here? I consulted Mrs. Mancini, my friend's mother. "*Polvere* is powder," Mrs. Mancini explained, but we were stuck on *begn*. I listened for Grandma's voice and recited it over and over out loud, "BEHnyay, BEGin, BEGehn, BEGehneh," imitating Grandma's voice, BEGehNAH. C'mon, Grandma, talk to me. "*Begn polvere*," Mrs. Mancini said, "is baking powder." Wow. Rosetta Stone material. "They didn't use baking powder then in Italy, you understand, so it was new to her in America. She had no word for it." She spelled it as she heard it. The regulations for *cartellato* calls for "1 *bottiglia di pruno guise,* and 1 *bottiglia di greppe giuse*." I laughed as I heard Grandma speaking: 1 bottle of prune juice, and 1 bottle of grape juice. "Sure, cooked wine will put you right to sleep when you have a cold," Mrs. Mancini told me. In life, I never saw Grandma follow a recipe, so these papers she left behind in an old Christmas gift box were an enigma. On the bottom of many, she had written, *Non li fate bruciare* (Don't make them burn). Who was she talking to? Did she think that one day we'd read these, we, the inept AmeriCAHN hands that she never wanted touching her bisCUT dough, calzone crusts, *cavateel*? *Non li fate bruciare.* She wasn't taking this note for herself. Grandma didn't give the time or the temperature, just the warning: *Non li fate bruciare.* Although I'll try to resurrect a couple of these recipes, I will spend more hours writing about them then actually cooking with them, since that's what my hands do. Her measurements for flour translate as *ponte* (mounts) or, in other recipes, "Put enough flour how much it will take." My mother remembers: "She never measured! She made a well of flour and pulled it as needed." My mother also relates the story of a friend who, after futile implorations to her mother to measure out the ingredients, quickly put a measuring cup under her mother's hands as she tossed flour in, just "to get a rough idea of how much flour to put." Grandma's directions for spices have no specificity. "*e conderle,*" she instructed, "and spice them up." Did she think we could do that much? These so-called recipes are as open to interpretation as the Constitution. And rightly so. Each eye and hand that comes to them must approach with an inherent knowing.

My mom and I, mourning the loss of Grandma's plain circle cookies, of which we could never get enough, set out to follow the unnavigable regulations. We chose a bisCUT recipe and the one for riGUTH cake. The work! We kids had taken for granted that we could eat all we wanted. On Holy Days, there were endless hills of

Grandma Rose's recipe from her friend Caterina. The recipe dates from 1975; the church envelope paper, from 1974. (Photograph courtesy of Annie Lanzillotto)

Grandma's signature unglazed bisCUT. How much work it was! Shopping, carrying, washing bits of flour and water off the rolling board, standing for hours *sopre il forno caldo*. Mom and I had a shot of anisette with the neighbors and pulled out Grandma's old wooden rolling board, kept deep within her closet. We washed our hands with the half bar of brown soap she kept by the kitchen sink at the ready to disinfect anything and anyone. I wiped my hands on the dish towel that would accompany me the whole evening, slung over my left shoulder. I took care to work the dough around the board so not to waste any bit of flour, as Grandma would have done. I channeled her as I did this. I rolled up my sleeves and donned an apron after beginning to work with the flour. Grandma was ambidextrous. She used every thing and every part of herself. In the middle of the work, it struck me . . . Who am I doing this for? Who will eat these? Who is all this work for? My brothers on Christmas? I'm doing it for my own communion with my mother and grandmother and great-grandmother. My hands remembered her hands. You move your hands how you think. In the act of working the dough, my hands became inhabited.

My mother peeked under each bisCUT with a spatula, and offered me a hot one. "No, you," I said. "You get the first taste." She almost broke down in tears. "I never thought I'd taste these again in my life," she said, then commenting on my baking effort. "The first thing that struck me is, I'm used to somebody so small—I see the hands flying—but there's someone so tall! That's my daughter! The dough, the rolling board, is so familiar, and there are the flying hands, but I can't see the face at the same time cause you have to look up to see the face!"

A month later, my mother took out a tin of the biscuits. I looked at her, squinting, "You still have some of these? How could you? Didn't you bring them to Charlie's for Christmas?"

"No," she said. "I guess it was subconscious. With their no-carbohydrate diets, I don't trust them. I should take a chance they're gonna throw out Grandma's cookies? Never!"

"You mean nobody tasted them for Christmas?"

"I guess not."

I was reading *Cristo si è fermato a Eboli* (*Christ Stopped at Eboli*), in which Carlo Levi describes the relatively upper-class peasants' salutation to one another in the streets and piazza: *Cosa mangi oggi?* When I read this, I put the book down, stunned. I took a walk around Brooklyn with Scaramooch and Cherub, contemplating this as they lunged at the nightly garbage bag full of bagels on the curb outside the bagel shop. Grandma Rose was not upper-class Acquavivese. She was more like the peasants in Ignazio Silone's *Fontemara*. As a girl, she worked in fields owned by others. She didn't trust administrators who wore shoes and "pushed paper and made life difficult and ate well." She was from *gli oumini che fanno fruttificare la terra e soffrono la fame, i fellahin i coolies i peonies i mugic i cafone* (the peoples that make the land bear fruit and who suffer hunger, the fellahin [Arab landless peasants], the coolies [Chinese and Indian unskilled laborers], the peonies [impoverished Jews in China], the *mugic* [Russian peasants before 1917], the *cafone* [Italian landless peasants, such as my grandparents]). In the Bronx, Grandma reinvented her life in a land and a time and circumstance where she could try on the relatively upper-class greeting *Cosa mangi oggi.* Muslims greet one another with a wishing of peace; Greeks, with the time of day; and *campesino*s who for the first time could eat, with—What did you eat today? No longer was Grandma Rose where peasants, if they happened to be greeted this way, would pinch and twist the air in response, as Carlo Levi describes to indicate "little or nothing." No longer was she where she had to make jokes, as when I asked her what she ate as a kid and her eyes sparkled as she gave me a *sfragganize,* a peasant wisdom phrase, updated into standard Italian so I could get it: *Oggi, patate, riso, e fagioli. Ieri, riso, patate, e fagioli. E domani, fagioli, patate, e riso* (Today, potatoes, rice, and beans. Yesterday, rice, potatoes, and beans. And tomorrow, beans, potatoes, and rice). In America, there were a multitude of food responses. There was an element of surprise. Life was unpredictable, but eating was not. And so to Grandma, *Cosa mangia oggi* was a greeting of abundance, of arrival. I never knew that. All along I had taken it like a daily test, hard if not impossible to live up to. When Grandma was over one hundred, she began to tell us of her childhood, pointing to each one of us: "You got a goat; she got a goat; he got a goat; I got a goat. In the mornin', we each bring the milk from the goat and put it in the pail and put the stick in. Whoever is highest on the stick takes the milk and makes the *formaggio,* and takes the biggest piece." Then we'd ask a clarifying question, like what kind of stick, and she'd start over, not changing a word, "You got a goat; she got a goat . . ." Hunger had driven Grandma Rose across the ocean—literal hunger, starvation, coupled with the hunger of the heart for a life she couldn't predict. I didn't know either hunger at all.

Cooking, basting, shaping dough connects me to my ancestors. It is the language my dead speak. But I can stretch an essay better than a dough. I contemplate the hours I saw my grandmother and mother peeling stalks of broccoli rabe and cutting crosses in the stems with the shoemaker's knife to open the stems to the heat. I thought of the son-in-law at La Foccaceria, and I knew that he was right. When it comes to preparation and cooking, broccoli rabe is labor intensive. There's nothing worse than broccoli rabe gone wrong; the bitterness won't leave you. But when it's done with perfection, it's as juicy and satiating as a well-cooked steak, except you feel cleaned inside. Cleaned inside. By eating the rabe, you realize that you've cultivated the desire to live rather than to die. In my Brooklyn kitchen hangs a portrait of Grandma Rose wearing a crown of garlic, from when we performed together at the Guggenheim, with three words rubber-stamped above her, which for me have become as eternal as the Delphic inscription, the salutation with which the god addresses visitors who enter the temple: Know thyself. *Cosa mangia oggi.*

From the Big Bagel to the Big Roti?

The Evolution of New York City's Jewish Food Icons

JENNIFER BERG

THROUGHOUT A one-year period, I questioned native New Yorkers, newly transplanted New Yorkers, non–New Yorkers, New Yorkers living elsewhere, and tourists in New York about which foods they associated with New York City and which made them think of New York. Surprisingly, the results were quite similar. Few individuals described extravagant meals, but many respondents suggested a singular, iconic food such as pizza, egg creams, bagels, deli, Junior's cheesecake, knishes, and Nathan's hot dogs—all foods that today serve as icons and cultural markers for New York. This suggests an enigma to me, for New York City boasts a plethora of varied dining experiences.

New York—with more than 8 million residents,[1] more than 20,000 restaurants,[2] and more than 170 immigrant groups[3]—creates a city, cuisine, and palate virtually impossible to generalize. On the one side of dining culture, Per Se, Masa, and Le Bernardin, catering to the gustatory desires of the wealthy and elite, exemplify the contemporary economic power of the members of some social and business circles who can comfortably pay $400 for a restaurant meal. Countering this phenomenon are the $2 Yemeni hummus sandwiches offered on Atlantic Avenue in Brooklyn, the $4 Punjabi *alu roti* (potato-filled bread) served on "Curry Row" in Manhattan, the Sicilian cannoli sold on Arthur Avenue in the Bronx, and the bowls of steaming *tom kha gai* (Thai chicken coconut soup) available along Roosevelt Avenue in Jackson Heights, Queens. However, most unusual is that even though New York, America's largest and most cosmopolitan city, epitomizes both haute cuisine and ethnic variety, neither of these extremes serves as a vehicle to symbolize or demarcate New York to the outside world.[4]

The two paradigms of food choices do coexist in New York City, but egg creams, bagels, deli, cheesecake, knishes, and hot dogs do not fall into either category. In this chapter, through an exploration of the history of these simple, inexpensive foods, I show that while they originated from one immigrant group and became popular during the same era, they also slowly evolved into icons that represent New York City.

Icons

The term "icon," first used during the Middle Ages as a religious word, suggests images, figures, signs, or objects representing sacred elements. They are fabricated items meant to re-create or suggest something or someone consecrated or divine. Icons themselves are pictures, signs, or resemblances of ostensibly more significant things or people. They are slightly different from symbols or indexes in that they have meanings of their own; however, they develop elaborate meanings when used in reference to something more significant. We display icons, tangible signs of something larger, as pictures, objects, and even food, whereas indexes and symbols have meaning only in relation to another object. It is through the icon that people gain access to and learn about the object.[5]

Recently, the word "icon" has lost most of its religious and spiritual attachment. Today we see icons in secular settings, including examples found throughout popular culture in movies, books, stories, clothing, music, celebrities, and food. Yet similar to religious objects, icons still may have great symbolic power and meaning that create an atmosphere. When consumed or even just imagined, a specific iconic food immediately suggests links to specific places, culturally bound groups, or communities. In cultural contexts, icons help us explore how specific foods mirror express groups of people, as opposed to their original religious meanings and connotations. Iconic foods and their images obviously have different meanings for different groups of people, whether grouped by nationality, ethnicity, religious affiliation, or ideological beliefs. In this chapter, I discuss specific foods that when consumed, or even just imagined, conjure up associations with New York City.[6]

New York City's Food Icons

The bridge between food and icon is prevalent in food scholarship across the social sciences, but even so, social scientists have written little on iconic food for New York itself, perhaps because many people take these everyday food icons for granted. Nonetheless, egg creams, bagels, deli, cheesecake, knishes, and hot dogs were not always obvious symbols of New York. A list admittedly steeped in nostalgia represents to some a New York City romantically captured in time. For example, not many people regularly drink egg creams anymore, and recent immigrants may not have even heard of them. A mile-high deli sandwich and Junior's cheesecake, both contemporary culprits in the obesity and hypertension war, are no longer frequently consumed by New Yorkers. We see the knishes that once sold throughout New York streets by the dozens now relegated to certain neighborhoods. But all these foods, along with the ubiquitous pizza slice and the de-ethnicized bagel, are inextricably linked to New York. They possess iconic status in the early twenty-first century in part because they represent New York City's mythical success story. Once scorned food from early-twentieth-century immigrant groups, they now symbolize the city's embracing of immigrants and the social mobility of the underclasses. New Yorkers need not consume these foods regularly to appreciate and accept their value as a symbolic representation of their identity.

I use egg creams, bagels, deli, cheesecake, knishes, and hot dogs as "lenses" through which to examine the acculturation and assimilation of European immigrants and their fare over the past century. I argue that New Yorkers subconsciously adopted simple and inexpensive immigrant foods as their own, transforming them along the way from fast, reasonably priced food to New York City icons.

New York's iconic foods that possess little ethnic character have a history linked to varying national and ethnic influences. Most of these simple, everyday foods originated in eastern and central Europe.[7] But once they had been brought to New York by German, Czech, Russian, and Polish immigrants during the mass migration between 1880 and 1920, Jewish immigrants adopted and popularized them. As the production and consumption of egg creams, bagels, deli, cheesecake, knishes, and hot dogs increased across ethnic groups during the twentieth century, they became accepted as nonspecific New York fare. Finally, in the late twentieth century, essentially void of their European history or Jewish influence, these seemingly innocuous everyday foods achieved iconic status. In *The Practice of Everyday Life,* Michel de Certeau reinforces how everyday elemental artifacts, such as ordinary daily fare, take on greater significance.[8]

Today these foods retain little Jewish association, although they achieved iconic status through New York's Jewish immigrant community. Tracing their histories from European food to Jewish immigrant fare to New York City icon shows the impact that one large demographic group can have on an entire city's cultural fabric.

Daily, noncelebratory foods of Jewish origin dictated cultural boundaries for these immigrants, allowing them to acquire cultural, yet selective elements of "Jewishness" through their consumption, sometimes referred to as "gastronomic Judaism."[9] Selective choices of Jewishness might include bagels on Sunday mornings or a four-inch-thick pastrami sandwich. In both cases, consuming these nonhistoric, yet appropriated Jewish foods strengthened the immigrants' ethnic identity.

Ironically, as large numbers of eastern European Jewish immigrants rapidly climbed the socioeconomic ladder during the twentieth century, the foods they used to define themselves were not the western European, "Continental" cuisine popularized during the mid-twentieth century, but the more ordinary foods of Jewish origin. In the early twentieth century, beginning with the mass migration, these immigrants consumed these foods as part of their daily fare. Even after the next generation moved to more upscale neighborhoods, they retained their parents' mores, including living in close proximity to other New York Jewish families. Some of these initial moves, spanning the 1950s to the 1970s, from the Lower East Side or Brownsville, were to more affluent communities in Brooklyn (Sheepshead Bay, Canarsie), Queens (Forest Hills, Rego Park), and Long Island (Plainview, Hicksville, Great Neck). During the mass suburban exodus, many people abandoned their lowly ethnic foods, favoring more mainstream fare. Finally, in a nostalgia craze that began in the 1960s and culminated in the 1990s, with their return to New York City, the grandchildren of the immigrants embraced these foods. In doing so, however, they lost aspects of their own specific group identity while strengthening the identity of New York. Accordingly, I divide the New York City Jewish experience into three chronological periods: phase 1, genesis on the Lower East Side; phase 2, exodus to the suburbs; and phase 3: *Aliyah*, or return to the Upper West Side.[10]

The Lower East Side era, phase 1, begins with the culmination of mass migration in 1920, when New York City Jews overfilled the Lower East Side's tenements. I define this post–European emigration period as a "symbolic passive acceptance" of fate,[11] often characterized by pushcart peddlers, cramped quarters, and simple, Jewish fare. At that time, egg creams, bagels, knishes, and hot dogs did not possess the same degree of symbolic meanings that they developed later in the twentieth century. Perhaps, as an overstated generalization, Jews neither defined themselves through food nor identified themselves through symbolically charged foods.[12] For most, the Lower East Side was a temporary step, a place where they lived until they "came to recognize" other options.[13] When this occurred, Jews left behind the Lower East Side and their symbolic passive acceptance.

The second period is phase 2, when those Jews who had earned and saved enough money to leave tenement life moved out of New York City in droves. I consider this their "symbolic active and physical" period. No longer living their meager Lower East Side existence, socioeconomically climbing Jews sought refuge in places characterized by sprawling suburban malls, tract housing, highways, and convenience foods. During this phase, the seemingly benign foods eaten during the tenement days, once possessing little symbolic value, suddenly took on great meaning. For these suburban pioneers, once-basic and everyday foods now represented a life enthusiastically discarded, so accordingly, along with rejecting their tenement lifestyle, they chose to reject these foods as well.[14]

In the final stage, phase 3, Jews who once eagerly embraced suburban life and climbed rung after rung on the socioeconomic ladder of success no longer had to disdain the ethnic markers from earlier days. A smaller, yet socially and culturally influential group of affluent Jews moved back to New York City, during the "*Aliyah* movement." *Aliyah*, the Hebrew word for "returning," refers to the Zionist movement of Diaspora Jews moving to Israel. The expression "making *Aliyah*" suggests more than just moving to Israel; rather, it indicates a return to Jewish life and a bold acceptance and embrace of Jewish culture. I use this term, *Aliyah,* as an updated and modern return to Jewish culture and heritage in New York.

It is the Jews who "made *Aliyah*" and physically moved back to New York during phase 3 who influenced the widespread cultural embrace of all things Jewish, such as the increased number of Jewish social centers, the revival of the Yiddish theater, and the proliferation of babies named Sadie and Samuel. Their return to Jewish life in New York and their commitment to cultural and, sometimes, "gastronomic

Jewishness" had a great effect on other Jews, such as those remaining in Long Island suburbia. I consider these *Aliyah* Jews as cultural leaders, setting the pace for large numbers of followers.

Along with their physical move back to New York, these *Aliyah* Jews also reincorporated foods that just a generation earlier their parents had abandoned. Although the foods (pickled and smoked fish, egg creams, deli, cheesecake, knishes, and hot dogs) resembled those of previous times, Jews updated them. A generation earlier, they had opened delicatessens and appetizing stores in strip malls throughout suburban Long Island. But these mid-twentieth-century examples of Jewish adopted foods had little to do with Jewish identity. Rather, they mirrored generic suburban American food culture. Just as New York Jews have always manipulated their own acculturation process, they also manipulate the foods that they use to represent themselves. A critical change, however, is how Jews feel about them, the symbolic associations attributed to them, and, ultimately, what we have learned about their acculturation story *because* of using these foods. Perhaps on a more significant level, these foods also demonstrate how food-centered scholarship can be used as a vehicle to explore the subtle and shifting meanings of everyday things that are so often ignored.

Phase 2 Jews manipulated egg creams, bagels, deli, cheesecake, and hot dogs (physically and symbolically) both to distance themselves ethnically and, eventually, to define themselves ethnically. Therefore, in effect, these foods had a dual effect as both the manipulated and the manipulator. In phase 1, these foods had minimal symbolic meaning; they functioned as organic aspects of existence—nearly devoid of symbolic representation beyond daily survival. In phase 2, Jewish foods of New York daily life acquired a negative symbolic ethnicity, representing foods, lifestyles, and customs that Jews wished to shed. Finally, in phase 3, the foods came to symbolize rebirth, reattachment, cultural longing, and nostalgia.

The transformation from immigrant food associated with one specific ethnic group to a widely accepted symbol of New York City as a whole illustrates a special twentieth-century New York immigration story. What began as everyday, inexpensive items sold from pushcarts slowly evolved into the inventories of small storefront operations and finally into the emblematic New York foods that thriving businesses merchandise worldwide.

Natural questions emerge: How do we determine which foods are iconic? How did they become iconic? To whom are they iconic? What gives these foods elevated symbolic status? Foods become iconic only after they are firmly immersed in everyday life. For New Yorkers, iconic foods are not necessarily those that they eat daily but those that define their own "New Yorkness."[15]

New York's iconic foods, along with other popular culture fixtures, help paint a vivid and colorful picture of the city's romantic heyday, an early-twentieth-century New York, gritty with gangs, the Brooklyn Dodgers, squalid tenement brownstones, pungent aromas from pushcarts, and laundry hanging on clotheslines. *New York Times* reporter R. W. Apple recalled his first visit to New York City at the age of seventeen: "I pestered the school friend I was visiting, until he took me to Lindy's for corned beef and cheesecake. I figured that that was the closest an Ohio kid was likely to get to the fragrant, seductively shady world of Damon Runyon and Walter Winchell."[16] Although comic Jerry Seinfeld has spent much of his adult life in Los Angeles, he clearly is a New York City contemporary cultural legend. When he and his band of social misfits in the television comedy series wanted a "real meal" instead of their daily diner fare, they headed for Manhattan's kosher deli, Mendy's. Joseph Papp, New York's arbiter of public theater and creator of the annual Shakespeare in the Park festival, reminisced about earlier days: "Life and culture was not discovered in a library, but at home, in the streets, at school . . . all places rich in culture. There was music, both classical and jazz . . . and taste—The ability to distinguish a good ballplayer, dancer, actor, songwriter, marble player, hot dog or knish from a mediocre one—was ever present."[17]

Whether current or former residents of the city, New Yorkers often describe and glorify their city experiences by citing their favorite foods and the sports and hobbies associated with them. At a meeting in 1996, members of the Los Angeles Alumni Association reminisced about life in New York by playing handball, stickball, slapball, and other street games while noshing on egg creams, hot dogs, and knishes. This loosely based ad hoc organization consists of a group of New York City expatriates (predominantly from Brooklyn). Membership is self-selected; anyone living in Los Angeles with an affinity to New York meets the membership "criteria." They try to gather at least once a year, and the organization produces an annual thirty-two-page newsletter reminiscing about the members' lives on New York City's streets.

Through the plethora of films, books, memoirs, and "alumni" associations, Brooklyn arguably remains the New York City borough most steeped in nostalgia and tradition, claiming several iconic symbols. For the masses who grew up in mid-twentieth-century Brooklyn, the nation's "second largest city" was defined by the Brooklyn Dodgers, Nathan's, Junior's cheesecake, and the only true egg cream, the Brooklyn version.[18]

Just as popular culture and the arts influence those foods that become iconic, so does politics. We see this quite clearly in New York, a city with a rich and colorful political history. In 1999, Mayor Rudy Giuliani of New York and Mayor Skip Rimsza of Phoenix placed a friendly bet on their respective teams' success in the National League Division Series (New York Mets versus Arizona Diamondbacks). As collateral, Giuliani "put a dozen cannoli, a case of Brooklyn Lager beer, a portion of Nathan's hot dogs, and cheesecake on the line for the Mets."[19]

More recently, in July 2004 while New York City was preparing for the Republican National Convention, the host committee's advertising campaigns included a poster announcing "A Knish on Every Corner." This one, along with ten other banners, was intended to give outsiders a quick review lesson in New York City culture.

A sense of community helps define and identify different ethnic groups. Social historian Jenna Joselit reviewed press clippings from Yiddish publications, invitations, advertisements, clothing, toys, furniture, household objects, and food to explore the impact of food and Judaism in creating and defining contemporary American Jewish identity.[20] She argues that popular culture artifacts—including food labels, certain appliances, home furnishings, and clothing—along with consumption and new spending habits, helped shape a new culture for American Jews more similar to that of other ethnic groups.

The choices and decisions that immigrants face when they move to America contribute to the acculturation process. Newly minted New Yorkers have to determine a comfortable balance between their familiar customs, such as their choice of food, clothing, music, and leisure, and the new and unfamiliar ones. They have to determine which traditions they will keep intact and unchanged, which they will abandon, and which they will allow to evolve. The acculturation process facing all immigrants in New York, albeit different for each group, is universally laced with rich food memories, even if food or foodways is not the primary focus.[21] Joseph Heller's memories of growing up in predominantly Jewish Coney Island, Brooklyn, during the 1920s and 1930s are vivid, aromatic remembrances of knishes, hot dogs, and ice cream during sweltering summer days.[22]

Egg creams, bagels, deli, cheesecake, knishes, and hot dogs, although from different European cultures and nations, have a common New York history. Brought to the United States by non-Jewish European immigrants, these foods quickly were adopted by New York Jews, who first made and sold them within their communities and then mass-produced and marketed them throughout the whole city. Gaining in popularity across ethnic, racial, and community boundaries, they slowly emerged as traditional New York foods. Finally, in the late twentieth century, they earned status as iconic representations of New York City culture.

Egg Creams

We know very little about the factual history of New York's egg creams. One common urban legend speculates that "egg cream" is a poor English translation of the French *chocolat et crème* by early-twentieth-century Yiddish actor Boris Thomashevsky, because the correct pronunciation of the drink eventually became "egg cream." However, the most widely accepted explanation is that Louis Auster, a Lower East Side candy shop owner, invented the egg cream in the early twentieth century and named it after the white foam layer on top, which somewhat resembles beaten egg whites.[23] In 1964, this generally accepted belief was contradicted, following an article on egg creams, "The Egg Cream Mystique," by Wallace Markfield, in *New York* in response to an article in the *New York Sunday Herald Tribune*. The magazine printed five letters to the editor concerning the article, one of which is the following:

To the Editor:

Allow me to enlighten you on a few facts.

We are in business since 1892. We started in at Stanton-Lewis Streets on the lower East Side. About 1900, my father originated egg cream chocolate. We made all our syrups, fresh strawberry, then cherry, pineapple and our finest (and the _world's_ finest) _orange_ syrup. Sodas in those days were 2 cents a 15 oz. glass. For 1 cent you got seltzer with a little syrup on top. Chocolate was 2 cents, and egg cream (pure, cream and eggs, proportioned in a batch of syrup, not an egg to each glass) was 3 cents. There were no pumps to keep syrup in. We used gallon bottles.

Sincerely,

Emanuel Auster, Proprietor, Auster's Manhattan (American Dialect Society)

Similarly, one historical text, the 1906 edition of *The Standard Manual of Soda and Other Beverages,* includes a recipe for egg creams prepared with egg yolks, cream, syrup, seltzer, and vanilla.[24] However, most egg cream enthusiasts agree that an egg cream contains neither egg nor cream, and, in fact, traditional egg creams served throughout New York City during the twentieth century contained neither egg nor cream. They were made from only three ingredients—seltzer, chocolate syrup, and milk—and were a traditional beverage and treat consumed by Jews on the Lower East Side, in the Bronx, and in Brooklyn in the early twentieth century.[25] Over the next hundred years, the egg cream evolved into a non-Jewish, nonethnic food and eventually into a New York City icon.

Originally, the egg cream was the phase 1 Brooklyn and Bronx Jewish immigrants' icon, or a representation of the richer and more expensive malted. During the latter part of phase 1 and the beginning of phase 2, as Jewish immigrants moved away from Jewish neighborhoods and immersed themselves in the whole of New York, the egg cream became an icon, or representation, for eastern European Jewish immigrants no longer living side by side. Finally, during the suburban exodus of phase 2, as these Jews and their families moved throughout the United States, the egg cream lost its "Jewishness" and became an icon for all of New York City, but primarily for former New Yorkers of Jewish descent.

The egg cream was consumed primarily outside the home, forcing even new immigrants to begin the acculturation and socialization process. This scanty Jewish substitute for the more lush ice cream soda allowed poor immigrant Jews to get a taste of American culture by frequenting soda fountains, drug stores, and candy shops, clearly made easier because fellow New York Jews owned and operated most of these businesses. In phase 2, as Jews moved away from immigrant neighborhoods and to suburbia, the consumption of egg creams declined. Finally, in phase 3, as New York Jews reembraced Jewish culture and identity, egg creams regained their popularity and became a New York City food icon.

Regardless of their lineage, many New Yorkers know about egg creams and associate them with New York, even if they are unaware of their origin or ingredients. Indeed, understanding and identifying an egg cream with New York need not require ever tasting one.[26]

Although there is no clear date when egg creams were invented, using census material on the number of soda fountains, drug stores, and candy shops operating in New York, along with interviews and memoirs, it can be said that egg creams apparently reached their pinnacle of popularity in New York City from the 1930s through the 1960s. During the 1960s and 1970s, candy shops, drug stores, and soda fountains closed, and egg creams became scarce. Phase 2 and the increased number of cars resulted in throngs of New Yorkers leaving Manhattan and the outer boroughs, abandoning their tightly knit ethnic communities and forging out into the suburbs. Trading in small-apartment life, where much of the socializing took place in drug stores and candy shops, parents with kids in tow packed up their belongings in station wagons and made the pilgrimage to the suburbs. Left behind were egg creams, a symbol of poor, ethnic urban life.

During phase 3 in the mid-1990s, with an upturning economy and real-estate market, it once again became fashionable to live in New York. Upscale ice cream parlors, diners, and luncheonettes offered egg creams. In the mid- to late 1990s, with the growing prosperity, egg creams became "grunge or ghetto chic." Along with ripped jeans, baggy pants, and ghetto-inspired attire, young New Yorkers embraced egg creams, not for nostalgic reasons, but for their reverse economic appeal.[27]

In the 1990s, the consumption of egg creams rose along with New Yorkers' renewed interest in having seltzer delivered to their homes.[28] Although seltzer companies never went out of business, owing to their commercial customers, it was only recently that the residential market has revived. One wholesale soda company now delivers seltzer in glass bottles with hand-operated siphons to four hundred customers.[29]

I argue that the migration of Jews from poor, ghettolike areas to the rest of New York City and then, in phase 2, to affluent suburbs dictated the foods that would remain inside cultural markers and those that would be abandoned. Jews successfully merged into the mainstream American culture and chose to shun some of their cultural markers, including foods that did not designate prosperity, acceptance, and the mainstream American culture. They chose to leave behind the lower-class egg cream and then accepted it again when it was not threatening to their status, sense of self, and others' perceptions of them.

Bagels

Perhaps the most popular New York City food icon is the bagel. Ed Levine, a New York City food connoisseur and chronicler of New York food markets and ethnic delicacies, has written, "No city is so closely identified with a breadstuff as New York is with the bagel. . . . The bagel is to a Sunday in Manhattan as the mint julep is to Louisville, Ky., on the first Saturday in May."[30]

According to widely accepted folklore, bagels originated in Vienna, Austria, in 1683, a product developed by a Jewish baker in gratitude to the reigning Polish king. The round shape was meant to resemble a riding stirrup, *bugel* in German, as riding was the king's hobby. Other sources credit Krakow, Poland, as the bagel's point of origin. In *The Joys of Yiddish*, Leo Rosten cites 1610 as the earliest mention of bagels in print, in a reference to bagels used as gifts for pregnant women.[31] In the United States, according to American food historian John Mariani, the first mention of bagels was in 1932.[32] The most common belief is that Jews from Russia, Poland, and the Balkans brought bagels to America. They were not, however, popular or a common food until they arrived in the United States and, more specifically, until after the Holocaust.

According to Barbara Kirshenblatt-Gimblett, a repository of all things related to bagels, the semiotics of bagels changes the farther they are removed from the original source. Kirshenblatt-Gimblett explains that in New York City, bagels are a "Jewish food"; elsewhere in the United States, bagels are a "New York food"; and finally, outside the United States, bagels symbolize America.[33] Although bagels originally were produced in New York City by independent bagel bakeries, corporate bagel chains later introduced a quintessentially New York food to the rest of the nation. As bagel chains proliferated throughout the United States, bagels lost their Jewish identity, becoming instead a New York food.[34] Unlike the other New York City iconic foods, the bagel is actually of Jewish origin, as opposed to foods originally associated with other ethnic groups that were appropriated by New York's Jewish community.

Deli

Whereas bagels are associated with cream cheese and smoked fish, seeded rye and pumpernickel bread remain the mainstay in New York delicatessens. The term "deli" refers to both particular delicatessen meats and the landmark institutions associated with them. Katz's Deli on Houston Street, founded in 1888, has barely changed over the past century. It is most famous for its meal-ticket system, in which customers are given small red chits upon entering that must be surrendered upon exiting; the weathered signs on the wall, "Send a Salami to Your Boy in the Army";[35] and the store-length counter. For many, Katz's is synonymous with New York because nonkosher New Yorkers and tourists can enjoy an egg cream with a pastrami sandwich.

Along with Katz's, on the scale of delis with epic histories and folklore, is the Second Avenue Deli. Abe Lebewohl opened the deli in 1954 on the northern border of the Lower East Side. This strip, also known as the Yiddish Broadway, honored the many Yiddish theaters on adjacent blocks. At the time, New Yorkers referred to Second Avenue around Tenth Street as Knish Alley.[36]

The popularity of the Second Avenue Deli continued to grow from its opening until Abe Lebewohl's murder in 1996 and its eventual closing in 2006. (It reopened in late 2007, but not in its original location.) Immediately after Lebewohl's death, New Yorkers, in an act of solidarity, paused for silence. His funeral was crowded with hoards of people pouring into the street. The chaotic scene ended when the aged rabbi who had conducted the service collapsed on the street.

While Katz's and the Second Avenue Deli are arguably the two delicatessens most steeped in New York immigrant history and folklore, other delis in tourist locations have attracted greater attention from visitors to New York. The Stage Deli is known for its huge portions (as if the Second Avenue Deli and Katz's skimped on portion size), and the Carnegie Deli was made famous by the crazy names of its sandwiches, including "The Mouth That Roared" for roast beef with onions.

All New York delis and even "New York–style" ones throughout the United States offer similar fare. The two most popular meats found in delis are corned beef and pastrami. Pastrami, a derivation of the Romanian word *pastra*, meaning "to preserve," varies greatly from its original European form. What we know today, coated in pepper and spices, is quintessential New York City. Leo Steiner, owner of the Carnegie Deli, observed, "In Europe they didn't spice meat. Here we use only *flanken,* then we dry it, spice it, smoke it, and steam it."[37] Jewish corned beef, a close relation of Irish corned beef, is still distinguishable. R. W. Apple, the poetic food journalist, wrote, "All the other varieties, to tell the truth, pale in comparison with the moist, garlicky stuff Jewish immigrants brought with them to New York from central and eastern Europe. . . . [A] corned beef sandwich defined eating in Manhattan the way onion soup defined eating in Paris."[38]

Like all foods, deli meats continue to evolve. Arthur Hertzberg, a kosher food aficionado, remembers, "When we were all on the Lower East Side, every mom-and-pop store cured its own . . . that was one thing. Now you get two-week-old corned beef, supermarket corned beef and corned beef and cheese—utter desecrations of Jewish soul food."[39]

Cheesecake

The dairy equivalent of the overstuffed, mile-high deli sandwich is the iconic four-inch wedge of creamy New York cheesecake. Consumed in delis, diners, coffee shops, and restaurants, New York cheesecake, another remnant of early-twentieth-century Jewish immigrant foodways, also serves as a contemporary marker of New York identity. Most notable are the cheesecakes served at the world-renowned Junior's in downtown Brooklyn.

Harry Rosen, originally a Lower East Side egg-cream soda jerk, opened Junior's on the corner of Dekalb Avenue and the Flatbush Avenue Extension in 1950. He named the restaurant, with its memorable orange and white–striped color scheme, after his two sons, Marvin and Walter. Today Walter's sons, Alan and Kevin, run Junior's and have expanded the business to include mail-order cheesecakes and egg cream kits.[40]

In 1973, *New York,* chronicler of city trends, ran a competition for the best cheesecake in New York. Junior's won, and it immediately became synonymous with both cheesecake and New York.[41] Following the competition, the Rosen family wrote *Welcome to Junior's,* further enforcing their restaurant and their cheesecake as a New York City food icon.

Although scholars do not know the exact date of cheesecake's origin, many accept that the recipe for a similar cake dates to fifteenth-century Europe. The first recorded American version was in 1736. But it was not until New York restaurateurs started using cream cheese, an American invention modeled on the French Neufchâtel, that cheesecake as we know it took off.[42] In 1872, a dairyman from Chester, New York, developed cream cheese, made from whole milk and cream. In 1880, A. L. Reynolds, a New York dairy distributor, packaged the cheese in foil wrapping and named it Philadelphia, suggesting quality. In 1920, Isaac and Joseph Breakstone produced cream cheese under the Breakstone label, introducing it to the large Jewish population in New York. Almost immediately, it became a spread for bagels and then the major ingredient New York cheesecake.[43]

Knishes are the most "ethnic" of the iconic foods of New York. They continue to remain less assimilated than bagels, clearly a Jewish-derived food, but now wholly mainstream.

Once sold from pushcarts and various storefronts, knishes are sweet or savory dumplings wrapped in a pastry crust and either baked or fried.[44] One of the best known purveyors of knishes is Yonah Schimmel Knish Bakery on Houston Street. Yonah Schimmel began selling knishes from a pushcart more than one hundred years ago on the Lower East Side. For the past hundred years, five generations of the Schimmel family have been selling knishes from the same storefront. But while Yonah Schimmel's remains an icon from the glory days of the Jewish Lower East Side, there were several knish bakers in the neighborhood. In 1916, the *New York Times* credited Austrian immigrant Max Green with creating and introducing the knish to New Yorkers and even cited a competition "war" between knish rivals.[45]

Originally bakers made knishes with potatoes and chicken fat, but with the advent of Crisco in the 1930s, knishes were "lightened." Crisco allowed for a kosher pareve—nondairy, nonmeat—alternative. As Jane and Michael Stern, deacons of coronary heart disease foods, proclaim, "You can make fine knishes with Crisco, but the secret of grandmotherly knishes is chicken fat . . . when you cut open [the knishes] the warm, comforting aroma of seasoned spuds emerges, it is a smell so conclusively homespun, that anyone who ever had a Jewish grandmother . . . might find themselves plunging into sentimental childhood reveries."[46]

Knishes have been known for at least five hundred years, with some accounts dating back to fifteenth-century Ukraine. At first, they were any leftover food wrapped in dough, and eastern European immigrants brought them to the United States. These pastries were known by the Yiddish term *knish,* derived from *knys,* Russian for "pastry," and *knyz,* a Polish snack.[47] After a short time in America, knishes became synonymous with the Lower East Side and then with the whole of New York City. According to food journalist Suzanne Hamlin, "Where else but on the Lower East Side could such a thing be invented?"[48] A Chicago journalist described a visit to New York with his wife: "Within an hour of arriving, my wife and I celebrated our being in Manhattan by sharing a potato knish bought from a cart on 46th Street and Broadway."[49] Food historian and journalist Cara De Silva has written about the proliferation of breads in New York City: "Whatever you call it, New York these days is a place where loaves round, long, plain and doughnut-shaped, marbled, herbed, topped and stuffed, traditional and also innovative have become as characteristic of Gotham as knishes."[50]

Similar to egg creams, knishes are experiencing newfound popularity among both residents of and visitors to New York. No longer considered an inexpensive immigrant food, knishes, now with lighter and more healthful fillings, appeal to more mainstream customers. In response, Yonah Schimmel's introduced a new advertising line on its Web site—"It takes a Downtown knish to satisfy an Uptown craving"—an example of repackaging and remarketing pedestrian Jewish fare to appeal to upscale, affluent consumers.[51]

FROM THE BIG BAGEL TO THE BIG ROTI?

The final New York City iconic food with European roots that I will explore is the Nathan's hot dog. Even though Americans associate hot dogs in general with the United States, Nathan's Famous—with its roots in early-twentieth-century, predominantly Jewish Coney Island—remains a New York icon. As with the foods previously discussed, Jews did not introduce hot dogs to New York. Instead, German immigrants brought the panoply of bratwursts and sausages to the United States, and it was the adoption of the frankfurter by Charles Feltman that led to the explosion of its popularity.

Eastern European Jews consumed Nathan's hot dogs during phase 1 because—like egg creams, bagels, deli, cheesecake, and knishes—it was an inexpensive food created by a Jew and consumed primarily by Jews. During phase 2, as Jews moved en masse from Brooklyn and New York City, they held onto Nathan's while they disdained other Jewish foods. They did so because Nathan's no longer represented poor immigrant Jewish culture but, like hot dogs all around, had come to symbolize America. Therefore, Jews transplanted from the city to the suburbs could eat Nathan's hot dogs, knowing that they were consuming a food embraced by mainstream American culture. Moreover, they ate Nathan's hot dogs at small kiosks that opened throughout suburban New York, further separating the hot dog from Jewish Coney Island, its symbolic place of origin.

Like the egg cream, the hot dog is associated with many folkloric anecdotes detailing its colorful history. A commonly accepted (yet not completely validated) history begins in 1874, when Charles Feltman, a German Jewish immigrant living in Brooklyn, brought a sausage to New York from his native Frankfurt, Germany. He renamed it the frankfurter, honoring his hometown. Folklorists point out that the unadorned frankfurter did not take off until Feltman introduced an elongated bun to hold it.[52] The hot dog's popularity then surged following the 1904 World's Fair in St. Louis, where the American public first tried frankfurters along with other gastronomic delicacies: hamburgers on rolls, ice cream in waffle cones, popcorn, peanut butter, French's mustard, canned pork and beans, tea bags, and Dr. Pepper.[53]

The colorful legend of hot dogs continues with famed sports cartoonist Thomas "Tad" Aloysius Dorgan, who, some believe, coined the expression "hot dog" in 1905. The story is that he selected this term both because he thought the sausage resembled the low, slinky body of a dachshund and because many people still speculated that frankfurters contained dog meat.[54] Sometime around 1905, concessionaire Harry Stevens, at New York's famed Polo Grounds, had his workers cry out, "Get your dachshund sausages hot." Urban legend asserts that Dorgan, unable to spell "dachshund" accurately, thus called them hot dogs.[55] While this hot dog lore is widely accepted as "truth," more recently, hot dog enthusiasts have presented compelling and contradictory explanations. Gerald Cohen, Barry Popik, and David Shulman have questioned these widely recognized hot dog myths and offered new evidence suggesting that the term "hot dog" was heard at Yale and other college campuses as early as 1895.[56] No matter what their true origin is, it was not until Nathan Handwerker opened his stand near the beach at Coney Island that hot dogs took center stage.

Nathan Handwerker, a Polish Jewish shoemaker who came to the United States in 1912, worked as a delivery boy, dishwasher, and counter man at Ma's Busy Bee, a restaurant on the Lower East Side.[57] On weekends in 1915, Handwerker also worked as a roll slicer at Feltman's German Beer Garden in Coney Island, earning $5 a week.[58] Feltman's restaurant sold hot dogs by the thousands. By 1900, it employed twelve hundred workers and had the capacity to serve eight thousand customers daily.[59] According to more urban folklore, two struggling performers (the singing waiters Eddie Cantor and Jimmy Durante) convinced Nathan Handwerker to open up a competing hot dog stand and charge 5 cents for a hot dog, compared with Feltman's 10 cents.

During Coney Island's Jewish heyday, corresponding to phase 1 and early phase 2, Nathan Handwerker built the business. In 1916, he and his wife, Ida, spent $300 in savings and opened a small stand on the corner of Stillwell and Surf avenues, a block from the beach.[60] Shortly thereafter, Sophie Tucker sang a favorite song from the period, "Nathan, Nathan, Why You Waitin'?" Legend says that as the song became famous and as Handwerker's stand attracted greater crowds, one customer suggested that he call the business Nathan's Famous.[61] At first, it did not work well for the young couple. People were skeptical: What did Handwerker put into his hot dog that he could charge only 5 cents? Handwerker used an early marketing strategy: hiring people to dress up as doctors and nurses, wearing white coats. Positioned in front of Nathan's, these "medical professionals" joyfully ate hot dogs. Hoards of people followed, secure in their belief that if Nathan's fare was safe for medical professionals, then it was safe for the public as well.[62] (The notion that Nathan's promoted its hot dogs with the help of the alleged "medical" community is ironic, considering current health concerns.)

In the late nineteenth and into the twentieth century, Coney Island fell from being an exclusive beach resort for the wealthy, to being an affordable beach attraction for the rising middle class, to being a playground for the masses. Finally, in the 1960s, after the outbreak of several fires, the increase in crime, and the rise of abject poverty, Coney Island was no longer an immigrant Jewish neighborhood. During these demographic changes, Nathan's Famous grew, losing its association as a seller of New York Jewish food and becoming, instead, a purveyor of food for the 500,000 to 1 million people who visit Coney Island in the high summer season. Eventually, Nathan's hot dogs became available at suburban outposts and in supermarkets, evolving from a Jewish immigrant food to a New York icon. Today, Coney Island enjoys urban gentrification, and tourists flock to the original Nathan's, whose hot dogs solidly stand as an iconic food.

In the 1990s, a New York journalist made the following analogies: "What Junior's is to cheesecake, Tiffany's is to diamonds, and Nathan's is to hot dogs."[63] Although from a taste standpoint, Nathan's may not be everyone's favorite hot dog, few people can question its iconic prestige. According to a *Newsday* reporter, "There are some things that the rest of the country considers typically New York—hot dogs as a Coney Island—a bow to Nathan's."[64]

Likewise, a reporter for the *New York Times* stated that "for New Yorkers, Nathan's Famous hot dogs are as celebrated as the Empire State Building and as boisterous as King Kong."[65] In 2000, the Museum of the City of New York created the

New York City 100, a list of the most influential New Yorkers of the entire twentieth century. Luminaries such as Andrew Carnegie, Brooke Astor, Joe DiMaggio, Robert Moses, Irving Berlin, Joe Namath, Alvin Ailey, Fiorello LaGuardia, and Langston Hughes made this list, as did humble Nathan Handwerker, a Polish immigrant credited with creating the famous hot dog.[66]

Even New York City's cultural elite have occasionally embraced Nathan's hot dogs. On the opening night of the New York City Opera in 1969, the company's celebratory festivities took place at a Nathan's outpost on Forty-second Street and Broadway. In lieu of the customary champagne, caviar, and a lavish party, tuxedo-clothed patrons and opera enthusiasts munched on hot dogs and fries.[67]

Politicians have constantly reinforced Nathan's as a New York City icon. Countless photos of local politicians and other national figures, including President John F. Kennedy, snapped at Nathan's Famous, have graced magazines and newspapers worldwide.[68] Notably, New York State's Republican governor, Nelson Rockefeller, and Republican attorney general, Louis J. Lefkowitz, campaigned aggressively in overwhelmingly Democratic Coney Island in 1966. They ate countless hot dogs and shook hands for hours, in what was their most successful day on the campaign trail.[69] "No one can hope to be elected in this state without being photographed eating a hot dog at Nathan's Famous," predicted Rockefeller, amid cameras clicking during a campaign stop.[70] These examples, while not precisely proving that everyone across New York consumes Nathan's hot dogs, are important because they demonstrate that Nathan's is a New York cultural symbol.

Conclusion

Bagels, deli, cheesecake, knishes, and hot dogs, brought over from Europe by non-Jewish immigrants, "became" Jewish once in the United States because they were marketed, sold, and consumed by Jews. What originally made these foods Jewish is that New York Jews appropriated them, adapted them, and, in some way, gave them the Jewish "seal of approval."

In time, many of these foods became entrenched as New York foods. Just as Jews moved from being newly immigrant outsiders to being established New York residents, these foods became New York icons. Within just a few decades, it became impossible to visualize New York City without imagining an egg cream, a bagel, an overstuffed deli sandwich, a four-inch wedge of cheesecake, a knish, or a Nathan's hot dog.

In many ways, the three-phase model of New York Jewry closely resembles the pattern of many immigrant groups: the first generation retaining close ethnic ties, the second generation creating distance, and the third generation embracing heritage. Here, however, I suggest that the different pathway taken by New York Jews during phases 1, 2, and 3 allowed their food to become New York icons. For example, Poles, Italians, Arabs, and Germans who moved away from their original ethnic enclaves during the mid-twentieth century returned to them for weekly or monthly food procurement and adventures. During phase 2, most Jewish New Yorkers stayed away from their traditional neighborhoods. Grateful that they had escaped the poverty and crime in Brownsville and the Lower East Side, they embraced and even created new food choices in suburbia. Unlike other immigrant groups, they generally did not take ethnic pride in or find a positive identity by returning to their former neighborhoods. In addition, because the Jews left in such large numbers, these communities drastically changed, retaining few reminders of their history as Jewish enclaves. Some phase 2 Jews returned to the Lower East Side to forage for clothing bargains, but with the exception of patronizing some pickle stands, delicatessens, and smoked fish stores, few Jews regularly returned to shop for food.

I do recognize that this three-phase model may not be the end of the story. During the preceding decades, the population of New York City has changed dramatically, with more than 70 percent of foreign-born New Yorkers arriving here since 1980.[71] In *From Ellis Island to JFK*, Nancy Foner compares the immigrants who arrived between 1910 and 1920 with the recent wave from 1970 to 1990. Her analysis shows that race played a major role in both periods, influencing economic successes and highlighting gender inequalities. In regard to demographics, West Indians, Asians, and Central Americans are now New York's most numerous immigrant groups, replacing the early-twentieth-century immigrants: Jews, Italians, and Irish.[72]

Earlier I cited an incident in 1999, when Rudy Giuliani, for collateral, "put a dozen cannoli, a case of Brooklyn Lager beer, a portion of Nathan's hot dogs, and cheesecake on the line for the Mets" versus the Arizona Diamondbacks in the National League Division Series.[73] The tradition of betting New York iconic foods in exchange for rival cities' fare is now popular with many politicians. In 2003, Gifford Miller, the speaker of the New York City Council, had to ante up a "large New York cheesecake and an assortment of authentic New York bagels" when the Yankees lost the World Series to the Florida Marlins. Mayor Giuliani found himself betting on amateur sports as well, with a "case of Nathan's Famous hot dogs (240 franks) with buns and mustard and twelve dozen assorted H&H bagels" on the outcome of the Little League World Series.[74] Michael Bloomberg, new to the mayoralty in 2002, also joined this tradition for the American League Division Series (Yankees versus Anaheim Angels), wagering Nathan's hot dogs and H&H bagels for Anaheim oranges and Anaheim chilies.[75]

Giuliani's, Miller's, and Bloomberg's choices suggest the golden age of New York immigration, when Jews, Italians, and Irish reigned as the city's principal immigrant groups. While many of these foods remain strong icons in both New York and beyond, a more inclusive ethnic menu slowly is emerging. For the World Series showdown in 2003, both Mayor Bloomberg and Governor George Pataki made bets. Pataki remained loyal to traditional New York icons, wagering Coney Island hot dogs and a bushel of Empire State apples. Bloomberg, however, added to his wager of cheesecake and pastrami sandwiches, "Peking Duck, lobster, and roast pork from a restaurant in the Bronx, just down the street from Yankee Stadium." As he stated, "Since Miami is really New York's farthest suburb, I thought all those transplanted New Yorkers might be tempted by a taste of home."[76] The expanding iconic wager basket may mark a new era for New York's immigrant population and food icons, reflecting demographic changes as well as immigrant recognition.

FROM THE BIG BAGEL TO THE BIG ROTI?

Egg creams, bagels, deli, cheesecake, knishes, and hot dogs were basic foods of sustenance eaten by immigrants. They were simple—with few ingredients and limited spices as well as easy to prepare—and thereby nonthreatening for other New Yorkers to try for the first time.

Today we are experiencing a new mass migration that in numbers alone will overshadow the ethnic changes that New York experienced one hundred years ago, when most of the immigrants were Italian, Irish, or Jewish. The new immigrants represent hundreds of nationalities and ethnicities; the tastes and flavors of these newest New Yorkers seem boundless.

When we consider the eclectic variety of foods they offer and then add to them the more adventurous and sophisticated palates of contemporary New Yorkers, it becomes more difficult to isolate any one food as a candidate to become a new icon for New York City.

Even if the recognized iconic foods of today start to lose their symbolic significance, will the empanada, roti, or bubble tea ever be able to replace the knish, bagel, and egg cream as icons of New York City? Only time will tell.

NOTES

Sections of this chapter come from "From Pushcart Peddlers to Gourmet Take-Out: New York City's Icon Foods of Jewish Origin: 1920–2005" (Ph.D. diss., New York University, 2006).

1. For the past decade, New York City has maintained a population hovering close to 8 million people. My population data come from the census, both the ten-year surveys and the yearly estimated supplements. The most recent population estimate (2003) is 8,085,742. See U.S. Census Bureau, "State and County Quick Facts," http://quickfacts.census.gov/qfd/states/36/3651000.html.

2. The New York City Department of Health and Mental Hygiene, which oversees inspections and licenses, estimates the number of restaurants in New York's five boroughs. See New York City Department of Health and Mental Hygiene, "Restaurant Inspection Information," http://www.nyc.gov/html/doh/html/rii/index.shtml. As with the population, the numbers of restaurants fluctuate widely.

3. Nearly 43 percent of foreign-born New Yorkers immigrated to the United States during the 1990s, and more than 70 percent of foreign-born city residents immigrated during the 1980s and 1990s combined. See New York City Department of City Planning, Population Division, "The Newest New Yorkers 2000: Immigrant New York in the New Millennium," Newest New Yorkers' Briefing Booklet, DCP 04–09, http://www.nyc.gov/html/dcp/pdf/census/nny_briefing_booklet.pdf. This considerable increase in immigration numbers, which drastically changes the makeup of New York's human landscape, rivals that of 1910, the height of the mass immigration from Europe. The Taub Urban Research Center at New York University equates the immigration activity in the late 1990s with the 40 percent of foreign-born New Yorkers in the city during the heyday of mass immigration (Mitchell L. Moss, Anthony Townsend, and Emanuel Tobier, "Immigration Is Transforming New York City," December 1997, http://urban.nyu.edu/research/immigrants/immigration.pdf). At no other time since 1910 has New York had this many immigrants.

4. Mitchell Davis explores the New York restaurant scene, arguing that only high-end ethnic restaurants receive recognition, in "Eating Out, Eating American" (chapter 16, this volume).

5. Richard J. Parmentier, *Signs in Society: Studies in Semiotic Anthropology* (Bloomington: Indiana University Press, 1994); *Collected Papers of Charles Sanders Peirce*, ed. Charles Hartshorne and Paul Weiss, 6 vols. (Cambridge, Mass.: Harvard University Press, 1931).

6. Jennifer Berg, "Icon Foods," in *Encyclopedia of Food and Culture*, ed. Solomon Katz (New York: Scribner, 2003), 2:243–44.

7. I chose not to include the pizza slice—a quintessential, although primarily late-twentieth-century food icon of New York—because pizza has no association with New York's immigrant Jewish community. Cara De Silva, a food historian, addresses pizza "Fusion" (introduction, this volume).

8. Michel de Certeau, *The Practice of Everyday Life*, trans. Steven Rendell (Berkeley: University of California Press, 1984).

9. I define "Jewishness" as a contemporary view and adaptation of general American Jewish culture, relying on Jewish customs, celebrations, traditions, and, most significantly, twentieth-century foodways. It is not a religious categorization and does not conflict with religious participation. Rather, the distinction comes from the strength and importance with which Jews define themselves, by either their level of adherence to religious practice or their predilection for cultural markers that are ostensibly Jewish. I build my definition of Jewishness on that of Jenna W. Joselit, who defines Jewishness as a new "identity emerged . . . with feeling 'Jewish at heart' [more] than with formal ritual" (*The Wonders of America: Reinventing Jewish Culture, 1880–1950* [New York: Hill and Wang, 1994], 294).

I use the terms "gastronomic Jews" and "cultural Jews" in much the same way as I discuss Jewishness. This group defines their Jewishness not because of religious devotion but because of what they eat. A similar term is "cardiac Jews," referring to the link between the typically salty and fatty foods of eastern European Jewish origin and hypertension.

10. A more conventional breakdown of chronological periods is found in Eli Faber, *A Time for Planting: The First Migration, 1654–1820*, vol. 1 of *The Jewish People in America* (Baltimore: John Hopkins University Press, 1992); Hasia R. Diner, *A Time for Gathering: The Second Migration, 1820–1880*, vol. 2 of *The Jewish People in America* (Baltimore: Johns Hopkins University Press, 1992); Gerald Sorin, *A Time for Building: The Third Migration, 1880–1920*, vol. 3 of *The Jewish People in America* (Baltimore: John Hopkins University Press, 1992); Henry L. Feingold, *A Time for Searching: Entering the Mainstream*, vol. 4 of *The Jewish People in America* (Baltimore: John Hopkins University Press, 1992); and Edward S. Shapiro, *A Time for Healing: American Jewry Since World War II*, vol. 5 of *The Jewish People in America* (Baltimore: Johns Hopkins University Press, 1992).

11. Clearly, emigrating from Europe and settling in the United States was not a passive move. Instead, the passive acceptance arose once the immigrants had arrived and settled into the Lower East Side and similar neighborhoods.

12. Again, it is important to add that not all eastern European immigrant Jews followed this pattern. I use this model to explore many, but not all, Jews during this period of immigration and acculturation. For example, I do not address those Jews who moved to America before the mass migration of 1880 to 1920 or the more recent émigrés from Russia and Israel. In addition, I recognize that not all immigrant Jews followed this path and that many who moved to the suburbs stayed there.

13. I use the Lower East Side as a somewhat mythical marker, representing first- and second-generation immigrants. Some Jews moved to Brooklyn and the Bronx but, during this period, maintained their "symbolic passive acceptance" of fate, and their decision to use food symbolically to alter their identity was not always a conscious one.

14. Although phase 1 begins at a set time (after the mass migration), the two other phases do not. Contrary to the historical emphasis on stringently defined beginning and ending years, phases 2 and 3 differ for individual Jews and families. Phase 2, the exodus to the suburbs, occurred during the 1950s to 1970s, and phase 3 began in the 1980s and continues. Although in most cases, we use distinct historical events to define eras, in my cultural analysis, individually evolving decisions based on personal ethnic identity (resistance and acceptance) were the impetus for change.

15. I define "New Yorkness" as a cultural marker used to identify New Yorkers, by both themselves and outsiders. Loyalty and affinity to New York City, not birth place, determine "New Yorkness."

16. R. W. Apple, "Bagging the Endangered Sandwich," *New York Times,* September 15, 1999, F1.

17. Joseph Papp, "The Shakespeare Marathon: The Coach's View," *New York Times,* February 19, 1989, sec. 2, p. 9.

18. L. Goodman, "Egg Cream Dream? U-Bet," *Daily News,* February 15, 1998, 1; Marvin Rosen, Walter Rosen, and Judith Blahnik, *Welcome to Junior's! Remembering Brooklyn with Recipes and Memories from Its Favorite Restaurant* (New York: Morrow, 1999).

19. "Tribune Wires," *Tampa Tribune,* October 8, 1999, Sports section, 6.

20. Jenna W. Joselit, *Getting Comfortable in New York: The American Jewish Home, 1880–1950* (New York: Jewish Museum, 1990), and *Wonders of America.*

21. Historian Hasia R. Diner argues that the Irish immigrant community in the nineteenth century did not follow this similar immigrant story line, overflowing with vivid food memories, in *Hungering for America: Italian, Irish, and Jewish Foodways in the Age of Migration* (Cambridge, Mass.: Harvard University Press, 2001).

22. Joseph Heller, *Now and Then: From Coney Island to Here* (New York: Knopf, 1998).

23. S. Han, "Egg Creams to Go: Junior's Makes the Foam Favorite Available by Mail Order," *Daily News,* June 14, 1998, 52; Goodman, "Egg Cream Dream? U-Bet"; J. Hanania, "Mouthing Off: An Egg Cream Drinking Contest Helps Ex-New Yorkers Settle an Old Score and Celebrate Old Times," *Los Angeles Times,* December 11, 1994, E3; Molly O'Neill, "Where Seltzer Once Thrived, a Few Fizzes Remain," *New York Times,* July 10, 1991, C1.

24. A. Emil Hiss, *The Standard Manual of Soda and Other Beverages: A Treatise Especially Adapted to the Requirements of Druggists and Confectioners* (Chicago: Engelhard, 1897).

25. Some purists say that the only acceptable chocolate syrup is Fox's U-bet, produced by a family-owned company based in Brooklyn. Even today, at Junior's in Brooklyn, the staff always make egg creams with Fox's U-bet, and they highlight the bottles and logo on the menu.

26. The significant and recent change in the composition of immigrants in New York City—including but not limited to Mexican, African, Korean, and Caribbean residents—suggests that egg creams, like the other foods of Jewish origin I discuss here, may not hold the same iconic status for today's New Yorkers that they once did, during the golden age of postwar New York City. Egg creams do, however, still serve as a cultural emblem of New York to outsiders.

27. My own ethnographic research (observing people at East Village candy shops and informal interviews) shows that egg creams are popular with a new group of New Yorkers. Some consumers are descendants of Jewish egg cream enthusiasts, and others are upscale, educated, young, and hip New Yorkers.

28. While seltzer delivery is on the rise, only one company in New York produces seltzer, and there are few deliverymen. Walter Backerman, affectionately known as "Seltzer Man,"

now is himself a New York City icon, featured in several newspaper articles, television appearances, National Public Radio (NPR) broadcasts, and online magazines. See Gabriella Gershenson, "Gomberg Seltzer Works," *New York Press,* http://nypress.com/print.cfm?content_id = 10119. One New York seltzer deliveryman inspired a children's picture book that chronicles the nearly lost home delivery service: Ken Rush, *The Seltzer Man* (New York: Simon and Schuster, 1993).

29. O'Neill, "Where Seltzer Once Thrived."

30. Ed Levine, "Was Life Better When Bagels Were Smaller?" *New York Times,* December 31, 2003, F1, F6.

31. Leo Rosten, *The Joys of Yiddish* (New York: McGraw-Hill, 1968); John Hinterberger, "Voyage of the Bagel—An Old World Staple Adapts, Survives and Thrives," *Seattle Times,* January 5, 1997, Pacific section, 14.

32. John F. Mariani, *The Dictionary of American Food and Drink* (New York: Hearst Books, 1994).

33. Barbara Kirshenblatt-Gimblett, "Food and Performance" (lecture presented at New York University, 1998).

34. Dana Canedy, "The Shmeerin of America: Ethnic Lines Are Crossed as Bagels Become a Breakfast Mainstay," *New York Times,* December 26, 1996, D1.

35. Although Katz's capitalizes on this famous sign, the line itself was adapted from Louie the Waiter, a deli employee. See "Loose-Leaf Notebook," *Washington Post,* November 12, 1943, 13.

36. Richard Shepard, "Nathan's Famous Planning a Broadway Premier," *New York Times,* August 10, 1968, C1; Sharon Lebewohl and Rena Bulkin, *The Second Avenue Deli Cookbook: Recipes and Memories from Abe Lebewohl's Legendary Kitchen* (New York: Villard, 1999).

37. Quoted in Suzanne Hamlin, "The Myth of the English Muffin and Other Foreign Foods," *San Diego Union-Tribune,* July 17, 1986, C6.

38. Apple, "Bagging the Endangered Sandwich."

39. Quoted in ibid.

40. Rosen, Rosen, and Blahnik, *Welcome to Junior's;* Bob Liff, "Junior's Achievement: Corner Named for Eatery of Cheesecake," *Daily News,* March 11, 1999, Suburban section, 2.

41. Liff, "Junior's Achievement."

42. Molly O'Neill, *New York Cookbook* (New York: Workman, 1992), 209.

43. Mariani, *Dictionary of American Food and Drink,* 106.

44. Sharon Tyler Herbst, *The New Food Lover's Companion: Comprehensive Definitions of over 400 Food, Wine and Culinary Terms* (Hauppauge, N.Y.: Barrons, 1995).

45. "Rivington St. Sees War: Rival Restaurant Men Cut Prices on the Succulent Knish," *New York Times,* January 27, 1916, 7.

46. Michael Stern and Jane Stern, "Food: A Taste of America," *Chicago Sun Times,* January 30, 1992, Food section, 6.

47. Hamlin, "Myth of the English Muffin"; J. Kissel, "Local Knish Makers Have Gone into High Gear for Hanukkah," *Pittsburgh Post-Gazette,* December 22, 1997, C6.

48. Hamlin, "Myth of the English Muffin."

49. N. Steinberg, "New York Tradition We're Healthier Without," *Chicago Sun Times,* October 13, 1996, Sunday news section, 20.

50. Cara De Silva, "With Customers in Love with Bread, Many Restaurants Are Opening Bakeries," *Newsday,* June 7, 1995, Dining and Food section, 23.

FROM THE BIG BAGEL TO THE BIG ROTI?

51. Yonah Schimmel Knish Bakery, http://www.knishery.com/main.html.

52. Shawna Brynildssen, "Nathan's Famous, Inc.," in *International Directory of Company Histories,* ed. Tina Grant (Detroit: St. James Press, 1988), 29:342–44; James Trager, *The Food Chronology: A Food Lover's Compendium of Events and Anecdotes from Pre-History to the Present* (New York: Holt, 1997); Alan Davidson, "Frankfurter," in *The Oxford Companion to Food* (Oxford: Oxford University Press, 1999), 316–17; Donald Dale Jackson, "Hot Dogs Are Us," *Smithsonian,* June 1999, 104–12.

53. "A Century of Food," *Arizona Republic,* December 22, 1999, FD4.

54. Trager, *Food Chronology,* 388; "Plaque to Hail Creator of the Term Hot Dog," *New York Times,* April 25, 1971, BQ88.

55. Jackson, "Hot Dogs Are Us."

56. Barry Popik, "Hot Dog" (Polo Grounds Myth and Original Monograph), July 15, 1994, http://www.barrypopik.com/index.php/new_york_city/entry/hot_dog_polo_grounds_myth_original_monograph/ (accessed June 15, 2007).

57. M. Hamstra, "Nathan Handwerker," *Nation's Restaurant News,* February 1996, 76; Anthony Connors, "Why Nathan's Famous," *Daily News,* May 12, 1998, 32.

58. William Freeman, "Nathan's Famous Goes to Yonkers," *New York Times,* July 14, 1964, 52; Murray Handwerker, *Nathan's Famous Hot Dog Cookbook: 150 Recipes from the World-Famous Hot Dog Emporium* (New York: Gramercy, 1983); K. Hoffman, "Nathan's Hot Dogs: It's Love at First Bite," *Houston Chronicle,* July 2, 1999, Dining Guide section, 9.

59. Jackson, "Hot Dogs Are Us."

60. Handwerker, *Nathan's Famous Hot Dog Cookbook;* Hamstra, "Nathan Handwerker"; William Grimes, "A Man, a Plan, a Hot Dog: Birth of a Nathan's," *New York Times,* January 25, 1998, Food section, 4; Jackson, "Hot Dogs Are Us."

61. Jackson, "Hot Dogs Are Us."

62. R. Metz, "Market Place: Hot-Dog Stock and the Relish," *New York Times,* February 14, 1968, 62.

63. Liff, "Junior's Achievement."

64. Peter M. Gianotti, "New York: Where Eats Meets Best," *Newsday,* August 14, 1991, Food section, 65.

65. Anthony Ramirez, "The New Campaign for Nathan's Famous Hot Dog Is a Paean to New York and Its Hectic Ways," *New York Times,* June 30, 1995, D4.

66. Famous' Nathan Handwerker Named Among Top 100 New Yorkers of the Century, Nathan's Famous, press release, http://64.45.18 (accessed July 17, 2000).

67. "Opera Fans Get Down to Nathan's," *New York Times,* February 21, 1969, 36.

68. Shepard, "Nathan's Famous Planning a Broadway Premier" C1; Richard Shepard, "Ida Handwerker Dies; Started Nathan's Famous with Her Late Husband," *New York Times,* December 26, 1976, 51.

69. Jonathan Randal, "Democratic Brooklyn Beaches Visited by Republican Governor," *New York Times,* August 14, 1966, 40.

70. "Famous Nathan," *New York Times,* August 3, 1966, 25.

71. New York City Department of City Planning, Population Division, "Newest New Yorkers 2000."

72. As of 2002, 10 percent of the population of New York City was Asian. From 1990 to 2000, 38 percent of all new immigrants to New York came from Central or South America, Mexico, or the Caribbean, and 22 percent came from Asia. See Rae Rosen, Susan Wieler, and Joseph Pereira, "New York City Immigrants: The 1990s Wave," http://www.newyorkfed.org/research/current-issues/cill-c/cill-6/.html.

73. "Tribune Wires."

74. "Hot Dog! Rudy Bets on Boys," *Daily News,* August 25, 2001, Sports section, 3.

75. Public Information Office, ed., "Anaheim Mayor to Daly and New York Mayor Michael R. Bloomberg Announce Friendly Layoff Wager" (2000), *About Anaheim,* 2002.

76. "Food Is the Series Wager of Choice for Miami, New York Mayor," Associated Press, October 17, 2003, 1.

Cooking Up Heritage in Harlem

DAMIAN M. MOSLEY

THROUGHOUT MOST of the twentieth century, Harlem was the most renowned of all African American communities. The rise of black Harlem was largely a consequence of the massive, northward migration by southern blacks at the turn of the twentieth century. They settled in Harlem for a number of reasons, chiefly for the housing vacated by second-generation European immigrants and because of the strong discriminatory practices existing elsewhere in the city. Less known is the diversity of those black migrants and the presence of many nonblacks who simultaneously contributed to Harlem's transformation. Almost completely unheralded is the extent to which all these parties participated in creating Harlem's food world. Contrary to the dominant perception, Harlem is not now, nor was it then, solely a realm of soul food.

Harlem's current urban-renewal strategies might lead us to believe otherwise. Intent on luring tourist dollars to spur the revitalization of Upper Manhattan, these campaigns have coalesced with the tourism industry to form what is called "Heritage Tourism." As this term implies, developers attract visitors and consumers using a combination of Harlem's inherent assets: history and culture. Yet as these assets are commodified, both history and culture are boiled down into an uncomplicated, simple syrup for the would-be consumer. History thus comes to mean the Harlem Renaissance, and culture is reduced to gospel music, African American art and literature, and, of course, soul food. For example, between 1997 and 2001, the Upper Manhattan Empowerment Zone Development Corporation funded eleven restaurants in and around Harlem. Most of these establishments—Miss Mamie's Spoonbread Too, Wimp's Southern Style Bakery, and Sugar Hill Bistro, to name a few—are complicit with this soul food, neo-Renaissance image. Most of the tourist companies also have capitalized on this image, some even specializing in tours that feature visits to Harlem's black churches followed by outings to its soul food restaurants. The more the food businesses are factored into this urban renewal, the more soul food will become the ultimate face of Heritage Tourism. For some people, this reduction is not palatable.

This chapter is intended to be neither a history of soul food—although the term begs for some definition—nor a treatise on gentrification. Instead, it is an attempt to question a general narrative about food and heritage in Harlem by examining more closely the roles, responses, proprietors, and patterns of its food businesses. Looking at food businesses in this light, first at the height of the Harlem Renaissance—particularly the pre-Depression decade on which most of the current heritage making is modeled—and then at the turn of the twenty-first century, accomplishes several things. It helps lend greater specificity to a food environment then and now that is generally thought to be more homogeneous than it truly is. In reality, the dubious status of early black Harlemites, their low rates of business ownership, and the numerous ethnoracial presences all indicate that soul food not only was one of many components of Harlem's food world, but came to prominence through some unconventional means. Thus I also address the historical accuracy and present-day implications of the Heritage Tourism strategies glorifying Harlem's southern African American food roots above all other components of and contributors to its food world. Last, as several camps posit the community's future, perhaps this work—which scrutinizes some of the ways in which the past is interpreted in order to engineer heritage—provides an (implicit) indication of how Harlem's current food businesses may respond. My chapter, then, primarily challenges popular perceptions, but it also looks at where this road may lead. This matters because as long as Harlem is in the midst of economic changes, food businesses are increasingly at the fore as recipients of funding, harbingers of community change, or simply focal points of controversy. The reason is that restaurants in Harlem are the principal sites where culture is articulated, sites that always exist at the interface of cultural production and consumption.

Historicizing Harlem: Who Were These Migrants, Their Predecessors, and Their Contemporaries?

Urban renewal creates and promotes tourist destinations by marketing unique cultural institutions and capitalizing on history, so an evaluation of how soul food fits into Heritage Tourism must begin with a historical account. Harlem is a community that has experienced extreme change. Over time, it has seen a number of populations move in, settle, evolve, and depart. Yet, even though it was considered for much of the twentieth century to be the most significant and symbolic enclave for black Americans, its original and ensuing composition is often obscured. Southern black migrants moved into a Harlem that had existed for decades, and they did not take it over in its entirety, as is sometimes assumed. Although Harlem is known today for abundant soul food eateries where collards and cornbread are consumed mere moments after Sunday church services, its food world had—and still has—many other components.

At the turn of the twentieth century, Harlem already was filled with Irish squatters on the riverbanks, various central and eastern European Jews—first German and later Russian and Polish—above Central Park, and an accumulation of Italians on the East Side. As is often the case among immigrant groups, they tended to cluster together, in part comforted by familiarity and in part excluded by social networks beyond their communities' borders. Often the most vivid impressions that one ethnic group made on another revolved around food: ingredients, cooking methods, eating etiquette, and aesthetics like smells and fragrances. With food playing important roles in these ethnic enclaves, residents supported culture and tradition by establishing a number of food businesses, from butcher shops and bakeries to taverns and teahouses. As Hasia Diner has noted in regard to migrants and the foods from their origins, "They find ways to prepare them, cooperating with each other to make them available on a community basis. Their stores, bakeries, boarding houses, cafes, and restaurants all bear witness to the desire of the newcomers to relive the foodways of places left behind."[1]

Another presence in Harlem at the turn of the century was its scattered "Negro population," consisting of migrants from other parts of the city and descendants of slaves who had tended to Upper Manhattan's farmland and built the wagon road linking it to New York City during the previous century. These early black Harlemites were not concentrated in particular areas, as most of the European immigrant communities were, and certainly did not yet resemble the vast contingent they would become during the ensuing decades. They occupied some whole blocks but rarely huge patches of Harlem's landscape. Thus, despite some black housing tenements and a few churches, they did not open a great number of formal food businesses early on. Rather, the roles of northern blacks in the food-service industry were mostly as wage earners, not proprietors. Of the 3,802 black males in New York City's workforce in 1905—the beginning but hardly the apex of substantial migration—365 (11.2%) of them were listed as waiters, and another 144 were employed as bartenders, cooks, and "dining car" cooks. The bulk of these positions, either evolving out of domestic-service opportunities or existing within the matrix of white-owned businesses, were not usually connected to any specifically African American notions of cuisine.[2]

In the second and third decades of the century, Harlem's population underwent more significant changes. Blacks from lower Manhattan had initially trickled uptown only when a few astute investors and realtors persuaded absentee owners—that is, owners who were less committed to segregation because they themselves did not inhabit the buildings—to accept black tenants. These absentee owners also were initially persuaded to overlook discrimination by charging blacks higher rents. Soon blacks moved en masse to Harlem, where apartments were bigger and, more important, open to them in large numbers for the first time. Harlem's former European immigrant population, now largely in its second generation, was moving to more spacious, previously unaffordable neighborhoods in other boroughs. Coinciding with both these shifts, southern migrants moved to New York City in droves. In his study of Harlem, Gilbert Osofsky wrote that between "1910 and 1920 the Negro population of the city increased 66 per cent (91,709 to 152,467); from 1920 to 1930, it expanded 115 per cent (152,467 to 327,706). In the latter year, less than 25 per cent of New York City's Negro population (79,264) was born in New York State." Arriving in Harlem at startling rates, these southern migrants upset the balance and thus were not always welcomed to their new surroundings.[3]

There were other tensions besides those between black and white Harlemites. As in other northern cities where southern migrants encountered native black populations, some of the new arrivals' most caustic relations were within the race. Northern blacks had created a social hierarchy and a rapport with whites, both of which were upset by the influx of Southerners not yet acquainted with New York's social customs. Longtime black Harlemites who had achieved harmony—or at least tolerance—with white Harlemites found discrimination returning with new vigor as increasing numbers of blacks moved into their communities. Because these new and revisited exclusionary practices lumped new and native blacks together, the natives looked for ways to separate themselves from the migrants. In this tense environment, the food habits that the migrants brought with them from the South were sometimes the most visible points of contention between the natives and the migrants. Whether this contention was in the guise of a bourgeoisie and a proletariat, natives and newcomers, or the intellectual and the unlearned, there was always a group that disdained those "who didn't dress properly, whose finger nails were dirty, and who didn't eat properly, and whose English was not good." Ironically, this was not altogether different from how new European immigrants disgusted their more established, second-generation brethren with the odors emanating from their "stinking fried fish joints" and "vile tenements."[4]

The native blacks already had their established channels of social and economic access, and the migrants certainly brought their own understanding and aspirations northward with them. One indication of the migrants' speed in affecting Harlem's food world was the rate at which they entered the grocery, restaurant, and food retail businesses. Two studies of merchants and consumers—one by the National Negro Business League in 1928 and the other by economist Paul Kenneth Edwards in 1932—emphasized the frequency with which blacks went into these food businesses in southern cities. Edwards reported that "more Negroes are engaged in the retailing of groceries in the urban South than in the retailing of any other type of consumer merchandise. The belief that a retail grocery establishment can be set up with less capital . . . and that its operation requires no specialized training and little or no previous experience has entered into the calculations of many of these merchants." In Virginia, which supplied New York City with more migrants than did any other southern state, black-owned food businesses were common. Huge numbers of "fish dealers" and "produce dealers," along with peddlers of dry goods, lined the streets of Richmond, most of them mobile merchants.[5]

Native black New Yorkers did not always exhibit the same willingness or desire to go into retail food businesses as proprietors, so some migrants took advantage of this entrepreneurial dearth. Perhaps the most famous example is Lillian Harris, more commonly known as "Pig Foot Mary," who migrated first from the Mississippi

Delta to Manhattan's West Side and later to Harlem. She peddled southern food, probably to other migrants, and amassed enough of a fortune to invest in property and become one of the wealthier black landlords in Harlem. Here is an interesting historical moment and, perhaps, a moment of coalescence for soul food. For if Lillian Harris migrated from Mississippi—a state that supplied New York City with a negligible number of black migrants, as few as one for every forty from Virginia or South Carolina—there must have been something transcendent about her food and its appeal to Harlem eaters for her to have amassed a fortune. Defining this transcendence, however, is more difficult. Was it that her food—the ingredients, the preparation, the prices—was familiar to Virginia-born, and perhaps even Jamaican-born, blacks? Is it possible that she prepared a less regionally specific version or that the regional differences were not as great as they may seem in hindsight, given the prevalence of hogs and hominy across much of the South? Or was it simply that she did not have many competitors in Manhattan? It may not be possible to know exactly who dined daily on Harris's pigs' feet and boiled corn, but it raises interesting questions about the compatibility of regionally diverse food cultures in a climate rife with xenophobia—a climate in which the consumers were familiar with one or another regional cuisine and surely grappled with notions of authenticity.[6]

Although Harris's financial success may have been unusual, her entrepreneurial effort was not. Many migrants, their backgrounds providing the impetus, similarly pursued the ownership of food businesses. In New York City in 1909, "of 330 proprietors [of black-owned businesses] whose birth-places were ascertained, 220, or 66.66 per cent, were born in Southern states and the District of Columbia." Yet even as many followed "Pig Foot Mary" with varying degrees of success, relatively few southern migrants translated their aspirations and acumen into formally recognized food businesses. In fact, by 1930, blacks still owned less than one-fifth of all Harlem businesses. Thus my question: When and how did southern African American cuisine—widely, even if unofficially, called soul food today—establish its dominance in Harlem, especially among competing influences and low rates of business ownership? The uncritical answer may be that as these southern migrants moved in and other groups moved out, the new inhabitants took over residences and transformed businesses. While there is little doubt that the Southerners' migration and successful food businesses were related, a closer look reveals something more subtle: a food world in Harlem built by a number of parties, including some of those who most staunchly resisted the cuisine that would come to be known as soul food, a food world, in other words, in which an odd mix of contributors had their hands in the cultural production process.[7]

There are a number of reasons why migrants were not immediately able to parlay their numbers into a formidable legion of food businesses. One reason is that they had significantly less purchasing power in Harlem than they had had in southern cities. Astronomically high rents, higher on average than those in the rest of Manhattan, plagued black Harlemites in the early decades of the twentieth century. High rents were one of the main causes of the overcrowded tenements: the more wage earners who shared a living space, the easier the costs of living were to bear. The struggle to pay high rents also meant that blacks often had far less expendable income to spend on food. In 1929 in the cities of Atlanta, Birmingham, Richmond, Nashville, Montgomery, Mobile, Chattanooga, Durham, and Columbia, South Carolina, the combined average "Negro" expenditure for food was 27.2 percent of their total purchasing power. But in New York City, where "rents, traditionally high in Harlem, reached astounding proportions in the 1920's," the migrants likely had neither the capital to open businesses nor the steady buying power in their communities to sustain them. This change in buying power may have been the most disconcerting to migrants accustomed to getting food on credit in the South, as either sharecroppers purchasing from landowners or shoppers buying from local stores.[8]

Another reason that the migrants' cuisine did not always translate into formal food businesses is that their communities in New York were less homogeneous than they had been in the South. This again belies the dominant narrative, because although black Harlemites often encountered discrimination as if they were one undifferentiated mass, they in fact constituted a world divided along socioeconomic, ideological, regional, and even national (and linguistic) lines. Moreover, these divisions were emblematic of their nuanced population. By 1930, New York City's "Negro" population was exponentially larger than it had been at the turn of the century, but foreign-born blacks constituted a full quarter of that population. They hailed mostly from the Caribbean, although also from West Africa (often by way of Europe), and there was no shortage of differences—or, at least, *perceived* differences, which surfaced in the form of palpable xenophobia—between these black immigrants and their African American contemporaries.[9]

Two of the main perceived differences between native and immigrant blacks were culture—of which cuisine is surely a part—and entrepreneurial drive. Some of the dissimilarity in neighboring peoples' cuisines is arguably an expected, perhaps even universal, experience. No doubt, the immigrants' food stood out. "Certain dishes," writes Ras Makonnen, "such as pig-snout, salted fish and pigs' tails were available wherever there was a West Indian community established, just as the West Africans who have gone to Britain to settle have maintained their various dishes of yam and rice."[10] But it was not only on the basis of consumption that West Indians were distinctive. From the turn of the century through 1930, they consistently secured jobs and opened businesses at rates that exceeded their percentage of the population. Thus it was not uncommon to hear food-centered epithets or remarks about what some native blacks considered job and economic infringement: "When a West Indian 'got ten cents above a beggar,' a common local saying ran, 'he opened a business.'"[11]

The importance of this rift is manifold and emphasizes tension and heterogeneity in Harlem. Quite simply, if there were many distinct peoples, there also were many distinct cuisines. Yet since they lived with one another—and even within the two major groups of blacks, there were many subcategories (for example, Southerners could be divided further into Virginians, Floridians, and beyond, while immigrants were Jamaican, Haitian, and Barbadian)—Harlem's neighborhoods may not have provided the same cultural solidarity as had the southern communities. To migrants, this could have seemed an unfavorable environment for opening a food business, particularly where animosities were known to exist. Southern migrants, in particular, may have been discouraged from trying to sell their goods on a block featuring stores with "bins on bins of plantains, cow-peas, dasheen, cassava root, all sorts of peppers for chile, and stalks of sugar cane for chewing on as candy."[12] The presence of industrious immigrants like the Jamaican-born W. A. Domingo (pepper sauces, chutneys, and condiments) and the Ugandan-born U. Kaba Rega (cocoa and kola nuts), both of whom imported various foodstuffs to satisfy their tastes and appeal to their communities, signified a variegated food world. Furthermore, the foreign-born blacks not only were culturally distinct, but opened their own businesses more quickly than did the southern migrants. They therefore may have been influencing Harlem's food world in another way, by pushing native African Americans as a group to celebrate, emphasize, and take pride in their own food culture as a foil against the outsiders' economic success and cultural inroads.[13]

Beyond the differences and contentions that characterized black Harlemites, an emerging Puerto Rican presence was flanking and even circumscribing the Italian section of East Harlem. About the community's growth, Winston James writes that "from a mere 1,513 in 1910, the Puerto Rican population in the United States increased more than thirty-four fold, to almost 53,000, within two decades. The overwhelming majority settled in New York City, but no one knows what proportion of this population was black."[14] This population was compared with the Italian sector for both its proximity and its cohesiveness. With the language difference creating an additional barrier, Spanish Harlem not only was culturally distinct from black Harlem, but, as a community, remained largely separate and self-sufficient. As Jamaican-born author Claude McKay wrote, "The Spanish quarter in Harlem is as definitely Spanish as the Italian quarter is Italian. . . . The Spanish group contains a bulging belly of middlemen-traders. There are 300 grocery stores, 200 restaurants, 50 dry goods stores. . . . The casual observer may imagine that there are far too many."[15] Even though this description may not be based on a systematic tallying of food businesses, it does capture both the wonderment and the scorn of one group of Harlemites when looking, from outside, at another group. Furthermore, these figures are evidence of a substantial and unique food presence—which is particularly germane because Spanish Harlem still exists, somewhat separately, today—that coexisted with black Harlem.

A third important reason for the southern migrants' slow transition into Harlem's food world as proprietors was the lingering presence of second-generation European immigrant business owners. Even though most German Jews and Irish and some Italians left Harlem (or moved to its periphery, in effect expanding its boundaries) as blacks and Puerto Ricans moved in, many held on to their businesses as absentee owners. Some European immigrants retained residences on the fringes of Harlem: to the extreme west, to the south adjacent to Central Park, or clinging to the East River. Others commuted from new homes in other boroughs to operate their businesses. But when their original customers moved out of Harlem, these proprietors generally had to make concessions in order to survive amid the rapidly evolving milieu. Perhaps Jane Jacobs, speaking generally about this phenomenon, captured it best: "For small manufacturers . . . they must serve a narrow market at the point where this market exists, and they must be sensitive to quick changes within this market. Without cities,

they would not exist."[16] Sensing that their own existence was in jeopardy, these European immigrant business owners—the ones who remained in Harlem—did make
such adjustments.

One of the places where these changes in immigrants' businesses are most visible
is in their advertising during the period. Surveying the *New York Amsterdam News*
and the *New York Age,* two of Harlem's main newspapers in the 1920s, it becomes
evident that many food businesses began to target a new market—migrants from the
South. Many of these businesses were the very same groceries and restaurants that
once served the scores of European immigrants. For the grocers, it was sometimes as
simple as offering a different range of products, goods more familiar to the new population, and remaining competitive with the market price. This does not mean that
each grocer had to stop selling long-standing goods to accommodate new customers.
If the original European immigrant customers still patronized the grocery, the new
ethnic products could be placed alongside the old ones.

Two such products, appearing multiple times in print advertisements between
1925 and 1930, are Alaga Syrup and Murdock's Pepper Sauce. Alaga, a cane syrup,
was specifically and aggressively marketed to southern migrants. Its ads, which appeared in many different forms, and even in many cities where southern migrants
lived, use unambiguous language that leaves no question of their target: "Every drop
of ALAGA carries a rich store of delicious Georgia Cane flavor—a flavor not equaled
by any other syrup, and which has made ALAGA the South's favorite syrup for over
22 years"—and this from a company operating out of Alabama.[17] And while this
language reveals some things about the syrup's consumers, other information in the
ads identifies its vendors. Regularly urging readers to buy the syrup from their local
grocers, one ad lists all the purveyors within reach of the newspaper's readership.
Not coincidentally, there were as many groceries carrying the cane syrup in Harlem
as there were in the rest of Manhattan, Brooklyn, Flushing, Jamaica, Freeport, and
Mount Vernon combined.[18] In the late 1920s, because only one-fifth of the businesses
in Harlem were owned by blacks, let alone southern migrants, many European
immigrant-owned stores carried Alaga Syrup and other such products indispensable
to African American consumers.

Murdock's Pepper Sauce also appears to have been marketed to non-European
consumers, albeit using more subtle language than Alaga Syrup did. Even though
the Murdock's advertisements read rather blandly, "Appetizing and Pure for Fish
and Meats," they apparently were directed to black immigrant readers and certainly
signal that Murdock's was available in Harlem.[19] One indication that Murdock's was
linked to the West Indian presence in Harlem is the aforementioned food importer
W. A. Domingo, who processed, marketed, and sold his own pepper condiments
during this period. About Domingo's lucrative business, Makonnen has noted that
it "consisted of importing from the West Indies the ingredients for pepper sauce,
and in his own little factory in Harlem he would chop them and produce the various
chutneys and sauces. You can see something of his ability by the fact that Wool-
worth's took his products."[20] This by no means precluded European grocers from
continuing to sell their own ethnic products and produce, but it meant that they could

easily—and, in fact, had to—incorporate new products into their inventories in order to survive.

The situation was more complicated for restaurants and establishments serving prepared food. For example, rather than simply stocking cane syrup next to maple syrup or pepper sauce next to pickles, restaurateurs often had to serve entirely new foods, a change that may even have necessitated the hiring of cooks and servers more knowledgeable about them. At the same time, menu changes were not always permanent. Even if too few of the original customers of restaurants owned by European immigrants still lived near enough to patronize the businesses regularly, these customers might still return on trips into the city on weekends or holidays. Here, the language of advertisements is again informative. It is interesting that during the 1920s, restaurant advertisements evolved from vague, nonspecific language to a stronger, aggressive sort. Thus we find a noticeable transition from generic wording like "tasty meals" and "homelike surroundings," which commonly appears in the early and mid-1920s, to more specific advertisements like "Chicken and Waffles."[21] Surely, restaurant ownership is not always immediately discernable in advertisements. But sometimes, when restaurants advertised repeatedly over time, it becomes evident that the same establishments that served European immigrants—or at least European fare—were increasingly turning to what would later be called soul food. Accordingly, the Marguerite Tea Room, which sometimes offered chicken and waffles also advertised "Consomme d' Marguerite" and "Potage a la Rine" for Thanksgiving.[22]

In those places where southern migrants were discouraged from opening businesses—because of low investment capital and lower purchasing power among their ranks, heterogeneous communities featuring widespread competition, or limited openings left by still thriving European immigrant businesses—they brought their versions of African American cuisine to the forefront of Harlem through different means, sometimes even with the aid of others. These migrants catered and peddled foods in their community; they featured southern dishes at rent parties and social gatherings; some entered the workforce as cooks and servers; and together they pressured the market, forcing existing stores to carry their favorite food products. In these ways, this cuisine was a major influence on Harlem's food world. Although it never reigned without peer during the Renaissance years, it eventually became ubiquitous in Harlem with the eventual exodus of many of the remaining European immigrants and the most upwardly mobile of the black West Indian immigrants. What is now called soul food continues to bear the imprint of other influences:

In Harlem . . . [the immigrant] has introduced to the food culture of the Negro community native vegetables and fruits, yams, West Indian pumpkins, Guatemalan black beans, pigeon peas, mangos, pawpaws, ginger root from which ginger beer is made, choyos which look like large green peppers, plaintains, papaya, guava, eddo, alligator pears, breadfruit, cassava, black pudding, red fish and tannias.[23]

No matter how much they are downplayed, these diverse influences remain a part of Harlem's food legacy. Again, as we turn to twenty-first-century Harlem when Heritage Tourism initiatives direct a new legion of businesses, soul food's rise to the fore- 283ground is not solely the work of the cuisine's progenitors and couriers themselves.

Understanding and Evaluating Heritage Tourism

An eastward stroll along 116th Street in today's Harlem reveals a smattering of soul food joints evolving into a wave of West African restaurants and markets before ultimately giving way to bodegas, *dulcerias,* and Latino bakeries. Each cluster is a reflection of its community, its customers. Each carries more than a modicum of cultural information, history, and significance, although each plays a distinct role in Harlem. One, with its hand squarely in the pot of development funding, is the endearing face of the community; another fights for an equal part in this era of urban renewal and commodified culture; and still another finds itself all but ignored, sometimes not even considered a bona fide facet of Harlem's food world. These are by no means the only groups or types of food businesses to be found in contemporary Harlem, nor is any one of them so hermetically sealed from the others. But their experiences typify an environment whose heterogeneity is increasingly obscured.

Certainly, since its earlier days, Harlem has undergone a substantial transformation. With only scant new construction after the European immigrants' departure, disinvestment started to take a serious toll on housing and businesses, beginning in the Depression. Until recent decades, decaying buildings and abandoned properties lingered, and many still linger, often regarded as blemishes on the community's former beauty. The community's reputation has shifted from that of a renowned black enclave to "Harlem the ghetto, one of the largest concentrations of black working-class and poor inhabitants in the U.S."[24] At different times in the ensuing years, efforts at revitalization have proved fleeting, whether those of philanthropic foundations or community-development corporations. Only recently has economic policy begun seriously addressing Harlem's plight, and today many observers are astounded by the changes.

During the 1990s, a series of federal tax policies were designed to revitalize economically depressed communities across the country. The area including Washington Heights and West, Central, and East Harlem was designated as the Upper Manhattan Empowerment Zone (UMEZ) during this initial round of policy making. The plan was to provide tax incentives to new and existing businesses, encouraging them either to move into depressed zones like Upper Manhattan or, for businesses already in such zones, to broaden their scope and economic viability. These new, relocated, and refurbished businesses, it was reasoned, would create jobs and stimulate the markets of these "distressed areas." Although federally legislated, the tax policies were to be implemented mainly at the state and local levels. In other words, tax incentives and grant programs would be administered differently in each empowerment zone, the logic being that specific economic needs varied regionally. In the Upper Manhattan Empowerment Zone this would mean, first, that the task of allocating funds would rest largely on the shoulders of the Upper Manhattan Empowerment Zone Development Corporation—a mix of commercially motivated and nonprofit community

COOKING UP HERITAGE IN HARLEM

representatives and outside investors—and, second, that market stimulation might be best achieved with a strategy that displayed the area's heritage. This strategy became evident early on with the UMEZ's creation of the Cultural Industry Investment Fund (CIIF). If the mission of the development corporation was the "economic revitalization" of Upper Manhattan, then establishing the CIIF would be central to its objectives.[25]

Remarking on the duplicity of the term "heritage," Barbara Kirshenblatt-Gimblett explains heritage making as being much more deeply committed to present-day economic aspirations than to an especially accurate portrayal of the past:

> While it looks old, heritage is actually something new. Heritage is a mode of cultural production in the present that has recourse to the past. Heritage thus defined depends on display to give dying economies and dead sites a second life as exhibitions of themselves. A place such as Salem, Massachusetts, may be even more profitable as an exhibition of a mercantile center than it was as a mercantile center.[26]

Although this description initially may seem to erode, by way of caricature, any benevolence inherent in the Heritage Tourism initiatives, a glance at the UMEZ's own language—both generally and specifically in regard to what it calls "cultural funding"—shows that its intention coincides directly with Kirshenblatt-Gimblett's account: "Through the CIIF, UMEZ celebrates Upper Manhattan's rich past while creating new legacies. The work of the CIIF is two-fold: community building through a cultural and economic lens; and, a marketing of place that repositions Upper Manhattan as one of New York City's primary cultural districts." Expanding its objectives, the UMEZ listed four areas of cultural funding: "Reinventing/re-envisioning cultural historic sites; Strengthening and advancing primary institutions; Developing and building the next generation of mid-size organizations; Nurturing and growing cultural resources through service organizations."[27]

Enter Harlem, widely considered to have the richest heritage and greatest potential for attracting tourists of all the communities in Upper Manhattan. It is equipped with a unique historical backdrop—the Harlem Renaissance, with its storied mélange of arts, literature, and nightlife—and a viable network of cultural institutions. Many have always looked back longingly to the Renaissance as the experimental, flourishing stage of a nascent black Harlem. Juxtaposed to the poor, troubled Harlem of the 1970s and 1980s, the Renaissance looked even more glorious to 1990s policy makers and financiers. To draw tourists, they had to change the perception of Harlem as a downtrodden ghetto—what better way, some thought, than to foster a neo-Renaissance based on the days of old. Of this heritage making, Arlene Dávila writes that intent on "transforming Upper Manhattan communities into tourist destinations with cultural, entertainment, dining, and recreational attractions, this initiative has been an impetus for current discussions about how and in what ways the area should be marketed and redefined for these ends."[28] Participating in these discussions are a number of stakeholders—from Congressman Charles Rangel, who was an original supporter and writer of the tax policies and remains a member of the empowerment zone board of directors; through the variously allied UMEZ staff and the many tourist companies that shuttle consumers to and from the area; to, not to be forgotten, Harlem's residents, entrepreneurs, and cultural institutions—all with different links to, and interests in, Upper Manhattan.

If, as Dávila says, the "marketing of culture through cultural industries, be they museums, restaurants, or even parades, is increasingly central to the operations of tourism," then the debate over which cultural institutions are the most likely to attract tourists—and, thus, the most worthy of funding—is a spirited one.[29] Among Harlem's cultural institutions are some famed establishments that have survived as relics of an earlier era. The Apollo Theater and the Schomburg Center for Research in Black Culture are examples, two pillars of Central Harlem's cultural realm. But soul food businesses also are hugely important to this economic initiative. It is evident in the expanding media coverage of a new, sometimes upscale, food scene in Harlem.[30] It is discernable in the marketing literature from both development corporations and tourist companies. And it is part of studies that seemingly scrutinize every component of the New York tourism industry. For example, a study of tourism in Manhattan conducted in 2003 reveals a great deal about the role of food businesses as cultural institutions and, thus, the viability of food venues in the implementation of Heritage Tourism strategies. The study was based on "a one-page questionnaire . . . administered to individuals at several visitor-oriented locations in Lower and Upper Manhattan."[31] In Upper Manhattan, where Heritage Tourism is being actively carried out, the market researchers intercepted nearly one-quarter of their respondents at restaurants where patrons were seeking an authentic Harlem dining experience. Conversely, in Lower Manhattan, no questionnaires were distributed at restaurants: food was an accessory to other attractions, not the main draw.

The Upper Manhattan restaurants that served as points of distribution and collection for the survey—Sylvia's, the Lenox Lounge, and Jimmy's Uptown (now closed)—are a legendary soul food eatery, a Renaissance nightlife throwback, and a neo-Renaissance upstart, respectively. That they together attracted nearly 25 percent of Upper Manhattan's first-time or repeat tourists is a testament to the integral role of food in the Harlem tourism experience. Yet these establishments hardly stand alone in the new vanguard of soul food producers. To encourage the spread of the kind of success enjoyed by Sylvia's, a restaurant that existed long before the economic initiatives, the UMEZ lent money and business expertise to an entire wave of enterprises under the auspices of Heritage Tourism. The UMEZ aided the development of many of those in need of funding, such as Wimp's Southern Style Bakery, Sugar Hill Bistro, Manna's Soul Food Restaurant, and Miss Mamie's Spoonbread Too.[32] Besides having to demonstrate their economic viability and capacity to create jobs for residents—both strict prerequisites for funding that favor large, established businesses—a more implicit requirement for these establishments to receive funding appears to have been their overt espousal of Harlem's heritage and, also important, agreement with the UMEZ's definition of that heritage.

There is, nonetheless, some incongruence between the image of Harlem that the UMEZ conveys—an image that is predominantly, if not completely, African American, a legacy belonging solely and uncomplicatedly to southern migrants—and the reality, a Harlem that exists as the confluence of cuisines and cultures. First, soul food is not the only occupant of Harlem's gustatory space. The most obvious evidence of this is the sizable Latino community—not burgeoning but indeed well established, with its share of venerable food locations—that composes as much as 50 percent of the population of Upper Manhattan and nearly all of it in East Harlem. Yet as Dávila argues, these are not the Harlemites who emblematize Harlem's heritage or benefit from Heritage Tourism: "It is East Harlem's bordering neighborhoods of West and Central Harlem that carry a national and international reputation among prospective tourists." Taking this a step further, I would emphasize that it is an older, largely mythologized version of West and Central Harlem that carries this reputation. And of the $25 million that the UMEZ Development Corporation funneled into Harlem through its Cultural Industry Investment Fund, it is estimated that only $1.5 million was for East Harlem's development. In addition to being completely inequitable, this sends the divisive message that the cultural institutions of East Harlem are not as valuable as those of Central and West Harlem. Furthermore, it is not just tourists but also residents and business owners who are receiving this message.[33]

Second, even where the number and placement of restaurants give soul food the appearance of being culturally hegemonic, it continues to bear the mark of myriad

Worded in this way, signs like the one over this 125th Street eatery connote a distinction between dishes. But if "Jerk Chicken" is the signature item, "American Dishes" may be peripheral to West Indian ones. (Photograph courtesy of Damian Mosley)

With this signage, the difference between "Jamaican" and "Southern Style" foods is clear, even though it is not clear why both cuisines are offered in one restaurant. (Photograph courtesy of Damian Mosley)

influences. Some of those influences belie a narrative that makes African Americans the sole progenitors of soul food and the protectors of its legacy. One example is the abundance of restaurants with curiously hybrid offerings: "Jamaican and Southern Cuisine," "Caribbean, Soul, Barbecue," "West Indian and American Food." These textual oppositions always feature soul food as the second or last element; they always feature it in opposition, or at least as a complement, to the lead cuisine. And undoubtedly, the first item is constituted, defined, and distinguished in part by the second term. In Spanish Harlem, too, signs display such compromises as "Spanish and American Food." In this case, "American" is not necessarily the equivalent of "soul," but it still reveals this interdependence of cultural production and its reliance on opposition. There is more than a hint of inclusiveness here, something more methodically and organically spawned than a cursory fusion concept. Not surprisingly, these are not the restaurants that Heritage Tourism touts as the backbone, face, or even extremities of Harlem's soul food culture.

There are many ways to read the menus that list southern or soul food dishes separately from West Indian dishes. One interpretation is that although southern black migrants and Caribbean black immigrants never quite reconciled their cultural differences, realizing the unlikelihood of either group's economic survival if they failed to patronize each other's businesses, they agreed to offer different foods under one roof. This might imply that Jamaicans and their descendants stick to their own foods—oxtail, jerk chicken, plantains, rice and peas, pepper sauce—and that Afri-

In yet another iteration of the Caribbean versus American concept, "Tree," whose *T* is depicted by a palm, and "Patties" evoke this restaurant's West Indian aesthetic better than does its nondescript American one. (Photograph courtesy of Damian Mosley)

can Americans remain with their own foods. Another reading is that the two groups, southern migrants and black immigrants, despite initially grappling for a place in a new, sometimes hostile, environment—a contest that would have included disputes over the right to many things like labor, worship, and cultural expression—found themselves adjusting to a world in which they were dislodged. In this case, they may have had to adjust to new ingredients and new prices, sometimes importing foodstuffs and entering into business themselves, ultimately creating their own brand of soul food. This Harlem soul food may not, then, be synonymous with southern cuisine or African American cuisine, or with versions of soul food in other metropolises not subject to the same influences.

Yet another reading, particularly when taking into account that a soul food restaurant might have menu items that extend beyond the scope of any of its most heralded influences, is that soul food in Harlem might be just as cosmopolitan as it is traditional. There is sure irony when one enters, for example, Manna's Soul Food Restaurant—funded in part by the UMEZ Development Corporation[34]—and finds not only chitterlings and peach cobbler alongside jerk and curried chicken, but also sushi and vegetable fried rice. The irony is perhaps twofold. On the one hand, as much as Heritage Tourism tries to circumscribe it, soul food continues to resist definitions that are either rigid or ahistorical. On the other hand, because Heritage Tourism markets in line with a narrative that does not completely coincide with the actual dining land-scape, tourists arrive in Harlem with a thirst for the authentic—a thirst not likely to be satisfied as well at Manna's as at a restaurant whose menu is more in line with consecrated images.

Conclusion

Soul food resists definition not only by developers and cultural industry investors, but also in conversation, popular and scholarly, and it has resisted definition here as well. I have dodged definition because it was never my intention to examine and characterize soul food broadly across time and terrain, but certainly also because it is not easily definable. Many people have their notions of soul food, positive or nega-tive, concrete and dubious. As I have used the term loosely in this chapter, soul food refers to a cuisine that has roots in slave culture, even though it may not have been referred to by the term "soul food" until some hundred years after Emancipation,[35] and that, in its present form in northern cities, is widely and perhaps uncritically con-sidered a vestige solely of southern migrants. If at one time it was regional—or, more accurately, if it arose out of a number of regionally specific cuisines centered on corn or rice, sugarcane or sorghum, pork or shellfish—soul food as we now know it has little attachment to place. Its current regional affiliation is often simply "the South," even though this oversimplified geography surely belies strong and lasting influences from elsewhere. Yet soul food derives its distinction from other foods and cuisines of the American South in the way that it—particularly the word "soul"—connotes race. Perhaps, then, it is an ethnic or, maybe more precisely, an ethnoracial cuisine. At the same time, though, we could argue that soul food is at least partly a national cuisine, often specific to an African American rather than a diasporic blackness.

Ironically, then, soul food as the designated iconic cuisine obscures the number and range of cultural producers in the Harlem of today, just as it did in the Harlem of yesteryear. In both instances, the primacy of soul food culture was achieved by businesses with varied backgrounds, proprietors, and intentions. Whereas one pe-riod featured competitive cultures, the next is characterized by competitive grants and economic initiatives. To be fair, the economic changes spurred by the empower-ment zone legislation are plentiful and varied. Many other food businesses—full-service wine stores, coffee shops, large-scale groceries, caviar bars, and organic mar-kets—might not exist in today's Harlem without the direct and indirect impact of the empowerment zone. But Heritage Tourism, with its focus on a narrowly conceived African American food culture, seems to propagate a reductive image of Harlem to the greater world.

The mere idea that initiatives drive the commodification of culture means that de-velopment corporations must attribute value to the cultural institutions they feel are most marketable. Some questions that I did not begin this chapter asking—and, thus, in some cases only flirt with the answers—go beyond a determination of whether heritage in Harlem is derived correctly from history: How has knowledge of the Harlem Renaissance been produced and reproduced, thus making Heritage Tourism susceptible to faulty readings that overprivilege the role of soul food? How exactly has soul food been subjected to redefinition—from regional, to ethnic, to national, and now, to cosmopolitan cuisine? If heritage making requires an almost singular focus on the past, are not some of Harlem's cultural producers situated anachronistically, rendered out of place in this cosmopolitan space? At the same time that they are out of place, might they also be kept *in* their places, performing their roles?

NOTES

1. For a further description of the European immigrant communities already inhabiting Harlem, see Gilbert Osofsky, *Harlem, the Making of a Ghetto: Negro New York, 1890–1930* (New York: Harper & Row, 1968), 81–84; for a general discussion of migrants creating businesses to supply their communities with familiar foods, see Hasia R. Diner, *Hungering for America: Italian, Irish, and Jewish Foodways in the Age of Migration* (Cambridge, Mass: Harvard University Press, 2001), 9.

2. On the wagon road and native black Manhattanites, see Osofsky, *Harlem*, 83; regarding northern blacks in food professions, see George Edmund Haynes, *The Negro at Work in New York City* (New York: Columbia University Press, 1912), 74–76. Black women, who vastly outnumbered men as cooks, are not included, possibly indicating that these professions were sometimes extensions of domestic service.

3. For a discussion of the increased movement uptown, see David Levering Lewis, *When Harlem Was in Vogue* (New York: Penguin, 1997), 26–28; for specific numbers for the changes in Negro population by decade, see Osofsky, *Harlem*, 128.

4. For a discussion of the tension between native and migrant blacks in another major city, see Tracy N. Poe, "The Origins of Soul Food in Black Urban Identity: Chicago, 1915–1947," *American Studies International* 37 (1999): 4–33. She says that "natives [of Chicago] . . . felt besieged. In the twenty-five years prior to the Great Migration, the native black community had developed its own churches, institutions, political base, and class structure. . . . In fact, one of the things on which natives prided themselves was the high level of integration in Chicago restaurants, which they attributed to their unassailable manners and refined tastes. Natives resented it bitterly when migrants' unseemly behavior caused the city's finer establishments to restrict all Negroes" (8). Osofsky discusses the same phenomenon in Manhattan: "With the increased migration of Negroes from the South, the brighter side of race relations in the city— the softening of institutionalized prejudices—came to an end" (*Harlem*, 40). Lewis quotes Arthur Huff Fauset about one group of blacks looking down on another in *When Harlem Was in Vogue*, 193. The "stinking fried fish joints" are mentioned in Claude McKay, *Harlem: Negro Metropolis* (New York: Dutton, 1940), 29; the "vile tenements," in Osofsky, *Harlem*, 82.

5. Paul Kenneth Edwards, *The Southern Urban Negro as a Consumer* (New York: Negro Universities Press, 1969), 124–25, 122.

6. For information on "Pig Foot Mary," see Roi Ottley and William J. Weatherby, *The Negro in New York: An Informal Social History, 1626–1940* (New York: Praeger, 1969); Osofsky, *Harlem*, 33; and Lewis, *When Harlem Was in Vogue*, 109–10. All depend heavily for their information on the WPA biographical sketch of Harris written by Odette Harper.

7. For information about black proprietors of food businesses, see Haynes, *Negro at Work,* 100.

8. On purchasing power, see the table "Rough Approximation of Negro Purchasing Power in 1929 in Nine Important Southern Cities, and Its Distribution for Principal Groups of Items of Cost of Living," in Edwards, *Southern Urban Negro,* 123; for a discussion of the differences between rents for black and white New Yorkers, including the "traditionally high" ones uptown, see Osofsky, *Harlem,* 136.

9. Osofsky, *Harlem,* 134.

10. Ras Makonnen, *Pan-Africanism from Within* (Nairobi: Oxford University Press, 1973), 89–90.

11. Osofsky continues, "As a group, West Indians became noted for their ambition, thrift and business acumen. . . . Contemporary surveys of Negro business in Harlem and Columbus Hill demonstrate that a disproportionate number of small stores—the traditional 'Race Enterprise'—were owned by Negro immigrants" (*Harlem,* 133). Other discussions of West Indians being employed and opening businesses at higher rates than American-born blacks can be found in Haynes, *Negro at Work,* 100; Winston James, *Holding Aloft the Banner of Ethiopia: Caribbean Radicalism in Early Twentieth-Century America* (New York: Verso, 1968), 82; Lewis, *When Harlem Was in Vogue,* 41; and Ira Reid, *The Negro Immigrant: His Background, Characteristics, and Social Adjustment, 1899–1937* (New York: AMS Press, 1970), 118–19. Although all these authors account in some way for this difference between natives and immigrants, their explanations of West Indians' entrepreneurial aggressiveness range from those emphasizing the importance of education to West Indians before immigrating to those centered on the generally radical Caribbean social milieu, which produced not just business owners but also polemicists and soapbox orators.

12. Kate Simon, *New York Places and Pleasures: An Uncommon Guidebook* (New York: Meridian Books, 1959), 106.

13. For brief discussions of these black immigrant food importers, see James, *Holding Aloft the Banner of Ethiopia,* 89; and Makonnen, *Pan-Africanism,* 86–94.

14. James, *Holding Aloft the Banner of Ethiopia,* 197.

15. McKay, *Harlem,* 137.

16. Jane Jacobs, *The Death and Life of Great American Cities* (New York: Random House, 1961), 145. According to Lewis, absentee business owners did not completely adjust to the new residents of Harlem: "Harlem remained a colony where absentee landlords and commercial barons hid behind Afro-American managers, where the largest department store, Blumstein's, even refused to hire black elevator operators until forced to, and where H. C. F. Koch's, another large department store, eventually chose liquidation over integration" (*When Harlem Was in Vogue,* 109).

17. *Amsterdam News,* February 5, 1929, 2; for Alaga ads in Chicago newspapers, see Poe, "Origins of Soul Food," 22.

18. *Amsterdam News,* October 27, 1926, 7.

19. *Amsterdam News,* July 25, 1928, 5.

20. Makonnen, *Pan-Africanism,* 89. Also speaking of the prevalence of pepper sauce concoctions among black immigrants, Reid states, more generally, that "to the Harlem cuisine the immigrant has added the use of condiments" (*Negro Immigrant,* 129).

21. *Amsterdam News,* November 2, 1927, 13.

22. Ibid.

23. Reid, *Negro Immigrant,* 129.

24. Richard Schaffer and Neil Smith, "The Gentrification of Harlem?" *Annals of the Association of American Geographers* 76 (1986): 351.

25. Department of Agriculture, *Notice Inviting Applications for Designation of Rural Empowerment Zones and Enterprise Communities* (Washington, D.C.: Office of the Secretary, Department of Agriculture, 1994), 1. See also Department of the Treasury, Office of Public Affairs, Testimony of Treasury Deputy Assistant Secretary for Tax Analysis John Karl Scholz Before House Ways and Means Committee Oversight Subcommittee, press release, 1997, 1.

26. Barbara Kirshenblatt-Gimblett, *Destination Culture: Tourism, Museums, and Heritage* (Berkeley: University of California Press, 1998), 7.

27. Upper Manhattan Empowerment Zone Development Corporation, "Expression of Interest and Qualifications," October 3, 2005, 1.

28. Arlene Dávila, *Barrio Dreams: Puerto Ricans, Latinos, and the Neoliberal City* (Berkeley: University of California Press, 2004), 11–12.

29. Arlene Dávila, "Empowered Culture? New York City's Empowerment Zone and the Selling of El Barrio," *Annals of the American Academy of Political and Social Science* 594 (2004): 49.

30. Eric Asimov, "Foie Gras and Short Ribs: Harlem's Rich New Menu," *New York Times,* December 13, 2000, F1.

31. Audience Research and Analysis, "Visitors to Lower Manhattan & Upper Manhattan," research study prepared for NYC & Company, February, 2003.

32. Empowerment Zone Heritage Tourism Initiative; Asimov, "Foie Gras and Short Ribs"; Kirk Johnson, "Uneasy Renaissance on Harlem's Street of Dreams," *New York Times,* March 1, 1998, sec. 1, p. 1. The UMEZ has funded more than eleven restaurants throughout its stint as financier in Harlem, and, to be fair, not all of them are soul food establishments. On this point, see Upper Manhattan Empowerment Zone Development Corporation, "Empowerment Zone Lends $350,000 for Harlem's First Modern and Healthful Asian Restaurant," October 3, 2005, 1.

33. Dávila gives estimates of the disparities in funding in "Empowered Culture?" 51. Nonetheless, I do not mean to speak of Upper Manhattan's Latino population as *one* people—when, in fact, they are Puerto Ricans, Dominicans, Mexicans, and so on—except to distinguish them culturally from black Harlemites, who, as has been established, are not one people either.

34. Johnson, "Uneasy Renaissance."

35. Doris Witt, *Black Hunger: Soul Food and America* (Minneapolis: University of Minnesota Press, 2004), 82.

Eating Out, Eating American

New York Restaurant Dining and Identity

MITCHELL DAVIS

IS IT ANY wonder in a city where apartments are built without kitchens and restaurant reservationists receive extravagant gifts from strangers that dining out in New York is inextricably linked to identity? In the realm of culturally marked behaviors, eating in New York is a triple whammy: you are *what* you eat, you are *where* you eat, and you are *because* you eat out.

As culinary-minded cultural theorists have shown, eating out is an exercise in the performance of identity.[1] Beyond the consumption of nutrients for sustenance, dining in a restaurant is a sociocultural activity. When we choose to consume food outside the home in a public place, we are saying something about who we are, whether that place is a fancy French restaurant on a tony Manhattan block or a hole-in-the-wall eatery in a far-out borough.

In New York, where most cultural activities are supercharged with self-conscious identity-making potential and there are an estimated thirty thousand restaurants,[2] eating out means that much more. Restaurants are a part of the city's cultural literacy, discussed at dinner parties, debated on the radio, and explored in depth by food-scholar types like those who have contributed to this book. In the same way that they talk about theater and opera and art, New Yorkers talk about restaurants, whether or not they have eaten in them. To be taken seriously as a New Yorker, you have to know where to eat.

How did New York come to be *the* town in America where you are only as good as the last restaurant you ate in? Where you *are* the last restaurant you ate in? The answer lies beyond the traditional historical analysis of immigration patterns and waves of economic prosperity that have been used in the past to explain trends in the restaurant industry. True, these ebbs and flows have had, and continue to have, an effect on restaurants and dining behavior,[3] but they do not completely answer the question of why eating out in New York is such a popular and compelling act of identity formation.

Unwilling or unable to eat and/or entertain at home, many New Yorkers play out a large part of their daily lives in restaurants. In theory, all they need is some cash—and a reservation also helps, if they can get one—to be able to eat in any restaurant in town. This semipublic nature of restaurants makes them sociocultural stews in which people from diverse backgrounds simmer in close proximity while performing one of life's most intimate and important acts: ingesting food. The relative accessibility of restaurants, our need to eat, the disincentives to eating at home, and our human tendency to align ourselves with or separate ourselves from others make New York restaurants a natural venue for constructing identity. Markers of status, class, ethnicity, power, sophistication, and taste become wrapped up in just about every aspect of the dining experience: where you go, what you order, how much you drink, how you behave, and how you tip.

Further adding to the impact of restaurant dining on the identity of New Yorkers is that New York is the quintessential American city. Although New Yorkers try to deny any relationship to the rest of the country, life in New York has come to represent the American urban experience, at least as it is depicted on television, in movies, and in other forms of popular culture—which, in a particularly New York display of cultural cannibalism, are devoured by the people who live here. Although this will not win me any fans in California or Kansas, it follows that New York food is American food, and not only because the concentration of media in the city makes it seem so. Like America, New York and its cuisine are modern and multicultural. The way in which restaurants, but not necessarily the food they serve, have become a natural part of life in New York represents an American culinary ideal. And even though in certain parts of the country the only dining options are fast-food and chain restaurants, the increasing number of meals eaten outside the home is evidence that Americans everywhere are emulating this important aspect of New York life. Ironically, given all the ways New Yorkers consider themselves and their city exceptional, to eat out in New York is to participate in a type of dining discourse that I believe helps us understand what constitutes American cuisine.

Eating Modernity

In his afterword to *Golden Arches East,* a collection of anthropological essays about McDonald's in Asia, Sidney Mintz grapples with the success and ready assimilation of McDonald's and other American fast-food restaurants in culinary-minded Asian cultures, which already had long traditions of food prepared quickly for eating on the go. He concludes that the fast-food restaurants are appealing in part because they are "recognizably 'Western' in every way; they are also modern, in terms of furnishings, the processing and serving of their products, their distinctive attention to their customers." Mintz concludes, "In these ways, 'Western' and 'modern' are linked experientially. Such institutions appeal to at least some of their patrons as representations of modernity, modernity being one of the commodities they purvey, even though they do not sell it as such."[4]

Although eating a Big Mac at a McDonald's in Seoul and dining in an expensive Asian-fusion restaurant in Manhattan seem very different on the surface, underlying both experiences is a similar desire for modernity. New York's obsession with the newest, the latest, and the trendiest restaurant, food, and other cultural products is about staying ahead of everyone else, about believing that as a New Yorker you know what is to come. In short, it is about consuming modernity. Nowhere else do local magazines vie so desperately to secure exclusive advance information about restaurant openings. Nowhere else are restaurants packed on opening night, by which time the people who attended preview dinners have already weighed in with their opinions. Everybody I know has had the experience of showing up at a restaurant that they have seen pictures of or read about, only to learn that the dining room is still a hard hat–required site.

But being ahead of the curve is only one aspect of modernity. Modernity implies a set of ideals, in contradistinction to tradition. Despite the current traditional backlash in politics, America is itself a modern concept. It is a place where the forces of capitalism and democracy converge to produce the ambition that fuels the audacity and entitlement that is New York. These days, although cities like Tokyo and Shanghai may seem more modern on the surface because of their sleek new buildings and technologically advanced infrastructures, not to mention their spectacular restaurants, New York is widely regarded as the place where anything goes—theoretically, at least. This openness is reflected in New York restaurants, where the range of cuisines, the adoption of trends, and, even more important, the pride that New Yorkers have for being open to anything, whether or not they really are, are supremely important.

For almost fifty years, perhaps the most modern, most New York, restaurant of them all has been the Four Seasons, located, significantly, at the base of Ludwig Mies van der Rohe's masterpiece of modernism: the Seagram Building.[5] Designed by Mies and Philip Johnson, the Four Seasons remains the center of an elite New York world of the rich and powerful. Like the Concorde—many of whose passengers no doubt stopped by for lunch on their way to and from Kennedy Airport—the Four Seasons set the bar of modernity in terms of technology and design so high that no other restaurant could ever come close to it. It was (and remains) the most expensive restaurant ever built—costing $4.5 million at the time, or approximately $30 million in 2005 dollars.[6] The bank-like space at the foot of a skyscraper is a celebration of capitalism that still oozes ambition and power. Only the patina of age has dulled its audacity, but the foliage, the uniforms, the linens, and the menu still change with the seasons.

The Four Seasons was the first modern American restaurant. Although the organization of the kitchen and the style of service still were based on the French model, they borrowed everything that being a New Yorker meant and put it into a dining experience. Not only was every aspect of the quality of the food, service, and design taken into consideration, but so were the aspirations of its clientele, many of whom still eat there several times a week. The lead to former *New York Times* restaurant critic Craig Claiborne's first review of the restaurants is as true today as it was in 1959:

Since it opened in 1959, the Four Seasons's combination of modernist architecture and grand ambition has captured a spirit of New York that defined New York dining in the twentieth century. (Photograph courtesy of the Four Seasons Restaurant)

"There has never been a restaurant better keyed to the tempo of Manhattan than the Four Seasons."

The members of the team behind the Four Seasons were asked the same question posed by this chapter: What is the relationship between who New Yorkers are and how they eat in restaurants? What was so unusual, so modern, about their answer was that they commodified the intangibles of a New York restaurant experience. It was not the high quality of the food or the design as such that brought people into the Four Seasons, but the idea that it was the *best* food and the *best* design that mattered. That is what New York deserved. Even though James Beard consulted on the original menu, and the restaurant has always prided itself on using local American ingredients, it has never been a gourmet destination—unless a gourmet happened to be closing a large book deal. Instead, it has always been a New York destination.

Before the Four Seasons, there were other beloved New York restaurants, of course, perhaps none more so than Le Pavillon. Opened in 1941 by Frenchman Henri Soulé, Le Pavillon grew out of the critically acclaimed restaurant in the French Pavilion of the 1939 New York World's Fair. In fact, to staff his restaurant at 5 East Fifty-fifth Street in Manhattan, Soulé hired several compatriots with whom he had worked at the fair. Le Pavillon was an instant sensation, for both its food and its

LUNCHEON AT THE FOUR SEASONS

The Appetizers

COLD

Oysters on Horseradish Ginger 1.85　Small Clams with Green Onions and Truffles 1.65　Winter Farmhouse TERRINE 2.25
Large CHINCOTEAGUES, A Platter 1.95　BLUE POINT Oysters 1.50　Little Neck Clams 1.50　Cherrystone Clams 1.50
Lobster Chunks on Dill 2.95　Iced Brochette of Shrimp 1.95　Virginia BLUE CRAB Lump 2.85
BURGUNDIAN GRAPEFRUIT, Honey Dressing .95　Winter HORS DOEUVRE, A Sampling 2.50　ICELAND HERRING, Pommes Vapeur 2.25
Mousse of Chicken Livers 1.85　A Tureen of MARCH FRUIT .95　Parfait of STRASBOURG PÂTÉ, Garnitures 3.50
A SERVICE OF Scottish Smoked Salmon 2.75　Prosciutto with Bosc Pear or PINEAPPLE 2.50

HOT

COCOTTE of Goose Liver and Grapes 2.25　Snails in Pots—DIJONNAISE 1.85　Cabbage Roulade of Calf's Brains 1.85
BALPICON of Sweetbreads in Pastry 1.75　Deviled Oysters on the Half Shell 1.95　Our Coquille St. Jacques 2.25　Cromesquis of Game 1.65
CRISPED SHRIMP Filled with Mustard Fruits 1.85　Beef Marrow in Bouillon or Cream 1.65　THE FOUR SEASONS Mousse of Trout 2.25

SOUPS AND BROTHS

Lobster Bisque 1.10　Vermont Cheese Soup 1.35　Double Consommé with Madeira 1.25
Consommé, TURKEY ROYALE 1.25　A March Vegetable Potage 1.10　Onion Soup with PORT Gratiné 1.25
CHICKEN and FENNEL Madrilène .95　SWEET POTATO Vichyssoise 1.10　Watercress VICHYSSOISE 1.10　Oyster Gumbo—COLD 1.35

THE MAIN COURSE

EGGS AND SOUFFLES

Omelette with CHICKEN LIVERS 3.65　Omelette Ratatouille 3.25　EGGS BROUILLÉS with Julienne of Truffles 3.75　Eggs Benedict 3.25
NEW ENGLAND LOBSTER TARTS 3.95　Green Crêpes with Prosciutto 3.25　Fondue Soufflé 3.25　Omelette Grand'Mère 3.50　SHIRRED EGGS with Game Beignets 3.75

SEA AND FRESH WATER FISH

FILET OF SEA TROUT, Sauté Grenobloise 3.85　WINTER SOLE, Four Seasons 4.95　CRISPED SHRIMP, Mustard Fruits 4.00　Steamed Clams in Crock Honfleur 3.50
Frog's Legs PROVENÇALE or Sautéed with VERMOUTH and TRUFFLES 5.25　The Classic Truits au Bleu 5.50　Crabmeat Casanova Flambé 5.75
BOUILLABAISSE MARSEILLAISE 4.75　RED SNAPPER STEAK—Grilled 3.65　BARQUETTE OF FLOUNDER with Glazed Fruits 4.95　LOBSTER AROMATIC Prepared Tableside 6.50

A VARIETY OF SEASONALS

BROCHETTE OF SWORDFISH with Green Peppers and Mushrooms 3.75
SAUTÉED VEAL CUTLET with Prosciutto and Gruyère 3.95　POTTED BEEF, Provençale 4.25
ROAST LEG OF LAMB, Purée of Minted Beans 4.00　POACHED YOUNG CHICKEN and Almond Rice, Sauce Supreme 3.85

STEAKS, CHOPS AND BIRDS

Three French Lamb Chops 5.25　JERSEY POULARDE 3.95　CHOPPED SIRLOIN, Vegetable Garland 3.50
AMISH HAM STEAK, Apricot Glaze 3.65　Calf's Liver Steak, Sage Butter 3.65　Two Quail en Brochette, Purée of Marrons 6.50

BEEFSTEAKS OF ALL KINDS

BUTTERFLY STEAK Paillard, Four Seasons 6.25　Sirloin Steak or Filet Mignon 7.00　Beefsteak SCANDINAVIAN 7.25
Skillet Steak with Smothered Onions 7.25　Twin Tournedos with Woodland Mushrooms 6.50　Entrecôte à la MOELLE 7.50
Sirloin Vintners Style 7.25　Filet of Beef Poivre Flambé 8.00　Steak and OYSTERS 7.50

VEGETABLES AND POTATOES

SEASONAL GATHERINGS MAY BE VIEWED IN THEIR BASKETS:　Buckwheat, Forestière .95　Broccoli Flowers, HOLLANDAISE 1.75　Squash with Lemon Butter .95
Beignets Varies 1.25　Onions in Onions .95　Bouquet for One 3.25　Wild Rice 1.50　Beets with Orange .95　Brussels Sprouts and Bacon Cracklings 1.10
POTATOES:　French Fried .85　Baked in Jacket .85　Vapeur .85　Rosti .85　Mashed in Cream .85　Tangerine Sweets .85

WINTER SALADS

Our Chef's Salad 3.50　Winter Hors d'Oeuvre, a Platter 3.65
RACK OF VENISON, Cumberland 4.75　JULEP OF CRABMEAT in Sweet Pepperoni 4.75
BEEF IN BURGUNDY Aspic 4.25　Lobster and Wild Mushrooms 4.95
Julienne of Turkey Breast and Pineapple 4.65　PLANKED STEAK TARTARE 4.75　Bouillabaisse Salad 4.00
✳ ✳ ✳ ✳
WINTER Greens 1.00　Zucchini and HEARTS OF PALM, Lemon Dressing 1.50　Beefsteak Tomato, Carved at Table 1.25
Nasturtium Leaves 1.50　BELGIAN Endive and Grapefruit 1.50　Raw Mushrooms, Malabar Dressing 1.75　Dilled Cabbage and Ham .95
OUR FIELD GREENS ARE SELECTED EACH MORNING AND WILL VARY DAILY　Salad Dressing with Roquefort or Feta Cheese .50 additional

The Desserts

MARCH FRUITS AND CHEESES

Corbeille of Fruit, ON VIEW 1.00　Compote of Fresh Fruits, CART SERVICE 1.25
Melon from Valencia .95　PEAR Bordelaise 1.50
DOUBLE GLOUCESTER—an English Cheese 1.10　Fresh Brie or Vermont Store Cheese .95　A Tray of International Cheeses 1.10　Appenzeller .90

SOUFFLES, CRÊPES AND CRÈMES

SOUFFLES:　MINTED CHOCOLATE, Serves Two 4.00　MINCE MEAT, Serves Two 4.00
Soufflé Praline Glacé 1.65　Candied Harlequin Crêpes 1.95　Frosted Mandarin Soufflé 1.95　Coffee Cup Soufflé 1.75　Sugarloaf BEIGNETS 1.35
Crêpes Aurora 2.25　Zabaglione with Amaretti 2.50　CANDIED CHESTNUT Couronne 1.50　ROSE PETAL PARFAIT 1.25　PAIN PERDUE Caprice 2.25

FROZEN DESSERTS

Quince, Melon, Double Chocolate and USUAL ICE CREAMS .95　FOUR SEASONS Coupe Filigrée 1.65　FROSTED HOLLY in Snow 1.85
CAFE GRANITO .95　Pomegranate Sherbet or Tangerine Ice .95　Parfait Santos 1.25

PASTRIES

FRUIT TART 1.25　Napoleon NONPAREIL 1.50　THE FOUR SEASONS Fancycake 1.35　ENGLISH Pound .95
Petits Fours 1.00　Chocolate Velvet 1.50　GÂTEAU St. Honoré 1.10
Other Sweets from the Wagon
✳ ✳ ✳ ✳ ✳

Café Cognac CHANTILLY 1.75　Iced Coffee, Whipped Cream .75; with Rum 1.50　The Steaming ARCHBISHOP, Serves Two 3.25　Espresso .75
Pot of English, Linden or Chinese Tea .50　Coffee FLAMBOYANT, Serves Two 3.00　Pot of Coffee .50　Irish Coffee 1.50
Cover 1.00

C46 INC. 1960　　201

The menu from the winter of 1960, the first winter for the Four Seasons, used regional product designations and traditional American foods to create an American cuisine in the context of classic French cooking. (Courtesy of the Four Seasons Restaurant)

Beginning in the 1960s, the Four Seasons has provided a stage on which New Yorkers and their admirers could perform rituals of status and class while enjoying fresh, seasonal food. (Photograph courtesy of the Four Seasons Restaurant)

clientele. Through the 1960s, it remained a favorite restaurant of New York's dining elite, including Joseph Kennedy, who tried to hire away one of its chefs—Jacques Pépin—to cook for his son at the White House.

By all accounts, Le Pavillon was a good restaurant. But because it was a French restaurant, it was forever compared with restaurants in France. Thus what made the Four Seasons unique was that it could not be compared with any other restaurant; its ambition was uniquely New York. It was the first restaurant to package New York's self-conscious need to be number one, and it established a model for dining in the city that in the ensuing years percolated down to the tiniest neighborhood eatery. That model allows the food to take a back seat to the social status or other intangible markers that one gains by eating in a particular restaurant. Even when the cooking is superb, as it often is, the people eating in a restaurant in New York usually are there because they know they should be; because they are entitled to be; because, this being New York, the restaurants are good, and they, being New Yorkers, should eat in good restaurants.

The experiential linkage between modern and Western that Mintz attributes to fast food in Asia also holds for restaurant dining in New York. Eating out in New York reinforces a certain Westernness tied to, but also distinct from, the concept of modernity. It is New Yorkers' ability to literally and figuratively digest the food of other cultures and incorporate that food into their own cooking, into their own identities, that has become an emblem of New York's culinary superiority.

In her philosophical ruminations about eating ethnic food, Lisa Heldke concludes that the Euro-American foodie drive to experience, master, and celebrate the cuisines of other cultures is a form of cultural colonialism. She considers two aspects of the food colonizers' attitude to be particularly important and problematic: "their often obsessive interest in and appetite for the new, the obscure, and the exotic; and their treatment of dominated cultures not as genuine cultures, but as resources for raw materials that serve their own interests."[7]

While I find it difficult to accept that every meal that a (presumably white) American or European consumes in an ethnic restaurant is exploitative, I do believe that New Yorkers incorporate these ethnic experiences into their personal and collective identities. Even though not everyone will venture to the outer boroughs to have an Egyptian or a Chinese or a Middle Eastern meal—I know because I have asked many to join me—New Yorkers are proud that such dining experiences are possible. It is as though the presence of a Chinatown populated by "real" Chinese makes the Chinese experience at some lousy restaurant on the Upper West Side that much more authentic. And that self-proclaimed authenticity makes it that much more New York.

New York has a curious relationship with authenticity when it comes to food— not that the notion of authenticity is ever without complication. While New York is the city where anything goes, where various culinary traditions smash into one another and fuse into something called modern American cuisine, New York is also the city where you are supposed to be able to eat utterly authentic re-creations of foods from around the world. Some places, such as the celebrated Swedish restaurant Aquavit in Midtown, conveniently provide both. From a recent lunch menu at Aquavit, I could have ordered traditional gravlax or a selection of herring or Wagyu beef carpaccio served with truffled taro root puree, green papaya salad, and shrimp mushroom broth. A few years ago, while standing in line to check into the MGM Grand Resort and Casino in Las Vegas, I watched a reel of in-house commercials advertising the hotel's offerings. In addition to games of chance, Broadway-quality shows, and the hotel's other amenities, the MGM Grand promised "Italian food so authentic, you'll swear you were in New York!" Although I believe that the Italian restaurants in Italy ought to provide the benchmark of authenticity for Italian restaurants elsewhere, the syllogism behind such a humorous statement underscores that an appreciation of a perception of authenticity in the realm of ethnic food is somehow a part of what it means to eat in New York.

At one time, the authenticity of New York's ethnic restaurants was rooted in the city's immigrant population. Ethnic restaurants served a taste of home to diners from faraway places. In her study of immigrant foodways, Hasia Diner notes that for Italian immigrants to New York, "regional loyalties informed the food culture, and merchants used the imagery of specific Italian places to demonstrate the authenticity of their goods."[8] But at some point, the rest of New York got a whiff of something good to eat in these restaurants, and soon the idea of ethnic eating was co-opted by other citizens as a sign of sophistication. This process was apparently well under way by 1938, when the cover of the April 2 issue of the *New Yorker* depicted diners in eight types of ethnic restaurants and listed forty-nine ethnic dishes that could be enjoyed in the Big Apple—everything from German *apfelstrudel* to Japanese *miso shiru*.

These days, when the foods of the world, or at least the talk about them, have been firmly woven into the fabric of New York life, and a certain sect of New Yorkers constantly travel the globe, ethnic eating (or a familiarity with ethnic food) has become an even more important sign of New York–style cosmopolitanism. That the food is not always accurately re-created is beside the point. The current restaurant critic of the *New York Times,* Frank Bruni, recently pointed out that in the new, trendy places, "what is sold and heralded as ethnic variety is often just ethnic blending, with a frapped result that changes little from one restaurant to the next."[9] Bruni noted a prevalence of tuna tartare, foie gras, and risotto on the menus of restaurants purporting to serve ethnic cuisines that traditionally would not include any of those dishes, preparations, and/or ingredients. Token words and flavors are used to add a smidgen of authenticity, as when an Indian-themed restaurant that served fennel risotto added a garnish of tomato-cardamom reduction to provide at least a hint of subcontinental cooking. Although Heldke considers this culinary misappropriation to be evidence of the dominant culture's arrogance, Bruni's observation highlights that in the realm of identity formation, what people are eating is not the point. Rather, it is what they believe they are eating that helps construct who they are.

White middle-class New Yorkers are not the only ones clamoring for cosmopolitan culinary knowledge by consuming all sorts of food in New York restaurants. Because of the role that eating in restaurants plays in asserting a modern, Western, sophisticated American lifestyle, immigrants to New York use restaurants as a form of assimilation. As one subject in Krishnendu Ray's study of Bengali-American immigrant foodways noted, "I can eat any kind of food when I am outside of my house. But at night for dinner I want my Indian food—rice, dal, vegetables, and chicken or fish curry. One meal I must have my own food."[10] Dividing their meals in this way—between eating out, which implies eating American, both because the food is consumed outside the home and because it is likely not traditional Bengali food, and eating in, which implies eating the food of their home, both because it is consumed inside the home and because it is, in this case, Bengali—helps immigrants negotiate their identity in America. Diner found a similar use of restaurant dining to assert an American identity among late-nineteenth- and early-twentieth-century Jewish immigrants to New York, for whom "just as surely as public education and democracy, these eating places symbolized America's novelty."[11] The constant flow of immigrants to New York and the importance of restaurants to New York life suggest that eating out is and will continue to be an effective tool in the acculturation process.

Although identity is marked by the behaviors and practices of daily life, of which eating is one, the interpretation of those behaviors and practices occurs in the realm of discourse. It is in discourse that the things we do are contemplated and constructed by the people around us and that their meaning and their effect on our identity take shape. It also is usually in the realm of discourse that we reflect on and react to our own identity, and this mulling over in turn has an impact on our practice. This relationship between discourse and practice is one reason that New Yorkers can believe they are eating authentic, ethnic food and use that belief to construct some sort of cosmopolitan identity, even when, as Bruni points out, they are eating the same tuna tartare from one restaurant to the next. In New York, the impressive amount of restaurant discourse serves to reinforce the importance of restaurant dining in the construction of a New York identity.

The sheer number of restaurant reviews in newspapers, magazines, and travel books; on radio programs and Blackberrys; and in other forms of media means that even the least culinarily curious person cannot escape information about where to eat. New Yorkers proudly pull out their tattered copies of the current *Zagat Survey* to find high-scoring restaurants to try. Online food enthusiasts and bloggers not only provide recommendations of restaurants but also discuss other people's recommendations. A whole online community has developed to dissect Bruni's weekly reviews in the *New York Times*, of which the eccentric www.brunidigest.com is perhaps the most obsessive. We know only that this blogger, June, is "fiscally irresponsible, which means I have weak bones and a dorsal fin. And a penchant for dining out, even though I am, in the words of many rich people, a 'poor people.' I make a different face when speaking each of the foreign languages in which I am shittily proficient."[12] We also know that she is obsessed with Bruni and his reviews, commenting on the grammar, syntax, word choice, judgment, and humor as well as other aspects of each weekly review. In fact, June has become an expert not on restaurants but on a restaurant reviewer—her commentary is picked up on other blogs and was even included in an article about Bruni's power that appeared in the *New York Observer*[13]—and thereby shows that the value of New York restaurant information has extended beyond people like me, whose job it is to stay on top of it.

Representations of the restaurant industry in mainstream books such as *Kitchen Confidential* and *Garlic and Sapphires,* on television shows such as *Top Chef,* and in movies such as *No Reservations* bring even more outsiders into the conversation about New York restaurants. They depict a gritty, dramatic, food-centered world in which New York is as much a protagonist in the story as are the temperamental chef and the actors waiting on tables. They reinforce the bond between life in New York and life lived in restaurants. And they provide a reflexive benchmark against which New Yorkers can measure the perceived validity of their own lives.

Much the way Stephen Mennell has shown that the culinary "revolution" that took place in eighteenth-century France had more to do with the advent of a public discourse about chefs and restaurants than with the French Revolution,[14] this constant chatter about New York restaurants keeps such restaurants at the forefront of our day-to-day existence. It means that everyone knows that to be a New Yorker is to have a relationship with restaurants, whether as a diner, an employee, a detractor, or a consumer of vicarious restaurant information. The unsettling probability that most people who read restaurant reviews are not likely to eat in the restaurants—just as those who read book reviews often do not read the books—gives further constitutive power to discourse. Talk about restaurants, in the broadest discursive sense, provides a figurative space in which to create restaurants. It also makes the restaurants better. Mennell theorizes that in France, discourse produced public opinion about matters of culinary taste and restaurants that restaurateurs could manipulate to establish their reputations. In turn, this manipulation created competition that pressured chefs to improve and innovate.[15] In New York, although many restaurateurs claim that everyone would be better off without all this restaurant noise, the truth is that because of processes similar to those in France, they are better for it. The role of quality dining in creating (some would say affecting) a New York identity helps guarantee that the restaurants are good. This is New York; they better be.

One of the most important tools of France's culinary hegemony—besides the fact that French chefs really do know how to cook delicious food—was the printing press. As Mennell's close reading of historic French and English cookbooks through the ages demonstrates, these cookbooks both reflected and refracted trends in food and in the profession of cooking, as well as the role of food in creating a national identity. Cookbooks codified and transmitted the social and cultural markers embedded in their culinary information. Today, in the age of television and the Internet, books play a smaller role in shaping culinary discourse. Cooking shows, food blogs, podcasts, and other media are more pervasive, more participatory, and, as a consequence, more powerful. One wonders whether the shift in culinary hegemony from France to America (more on that later) can be explained in part because of Americans' mastery of these new technologies. Regardless, the result is that culinary discourse has exploded in the United States, as has the number of restaurants.

The relationship between discourse and restaurant practice gives American restaurant critics a unique power to determine taste, especially because as a nation, we do not have a common, unified cuisine . . . yet. Without centuries of a culinary culture to inform the dining public, the American conversation about restaurants often begins with a pronouncement by a critic. Because the most powerful (that is, the most widely read and best funded) critics are located in New York, the city tends to set the taste for the country. (This was true historically of Paris vis-à-vis France before anything that could be called French cuisine had coalesced, and it remains to some extent true there for the same reason that the media are concentrated in the capital city. For more on the media's consecrating influence on matters of aesthetic judgment, see Pierre Bourdieu's discussion of the market of symbolic goods.)[16]

Despite what restaurant publicists have told me anecdotally about the waning power of the *New York Times* review to affect sales negatively or positively, the Gray Lady still carries weight in the realm of restaurant discourse. As I have shown in my survey of the history of restaurant reviewing at the *New York Times*,[17] Craig Claiborne, the paper's first restaurant critic, whose tenure in the Food section began in 1967 and ran for roughly thirty years, established a methodology for evaluating restaurants that became the model in the United States: multiple, anonymous visits and a journalistic tone that reports and comments on the entire progression of the meal. Until Claiborne, the most popular American reviewers emphasized cleanliness above everything else.[18] Although Claiborne trained in Switzerland, his method for reviewing was developed in New York. His model no doubt privileged aspects of dining in New York and might have been different if it had been developed elsewhere, just as restaurant reviewing is different in Europe, where, for instance, anonymity is not as highly valued as in America. Among Claiborne's innovations was the insistence that meals be paid for by the newspaper, and not out of the advertising budget. While other voices have contributed to the discourse on restaurants since Claiborne's reign, including those of the "people" in the form of surveyors for *Zagat* and online chatters, the conversation still is directed largely by the media institutions with the most money (or those willing to fork it over to pay for the repeat visits deemed essential according to Claiborne's model) and the most clout. Thus the conversation is directed by New York. As Anthony Bourdain, the author of *Kitchen Confidential,* told Tom Scocca of the *New York Observer* for an article about the firing of a chef after Frank Bruni had demoted the restaurant from four stars to three, "It's *The New York* fucking *Times,* man! People actually care what they say."[19]

Eating America

Since the French first consecrated cuisine as part of their national patrimony sometime in the eighteenth century, the question of whether other countries could lay claim to a national cuisine has been on the table. Various people have attempted to answer this question for the United States, from cookbook authors and food personalities like James Beard, whose *American Cookery* was an attempt to catalog regional American cooking in the hopes that it might evolve into a cuisine,[20] to academics like Priscilla Parkhurst Ferguson, who concluded that America has "indigenous foodways" and a "culinary culture" but no national cuisine to speak of.[21] I have already stated that the idea of an American cuisine is hard to pinpoint. But part of the reason for the difficulty, I believe, is that people are looking in the wrong place. Instead of home kitchens in the heartland, they should focus on restaurants in New York.

The quest for a national cuisine based on the actual ingredients people use and the dishes they cook is, by definition, a French exercise, the French having literally written the book on gastronomy. A more American pursuit, in keeping with Octavio Paz's characterization of Americans as "the children of a vision of a society rather than heirs to a concrete history" whose cuisine "amounts to a transubstantiation of the democratic virtues of the founding fathers . . . a universalism made up of ethnic, cultural, religious, and sexual exclusions [that] is reflected in its cooking,"[22] would be to find a vision of a cuisine—that is, a culinary ideal or an approach to eating that at once is indicative of an identity we wish to affect and has come to stand for who we are. Paz insisted that Americans inhabit a space somewhere between an ideal and reality, and the same is true of American food.

James Beard must have had an inkling that such a metacuisine existed in the United States when he used the phrase "an American attitude toward food" to describe our country's unique gastronomic contribution.[23] "The truth of the matter is that the way people eat is an unconscious reflection of the way people live," he wrote, advising his readers "to avoid treating the much-touted 'new American cuisine' as if it were some patriotic endeavor one simply must pursue. It's mostly journalistic hype."

Betty Fussell characterizes this American attitude toward food as a preoccupation with speed, hybridization, and portability: "From the start, colonists, pioneers, and then industrial entrepreneurs labored to annihilate seasons, distances, and the particularity of places in order to make food portable over long periods of time. The mammoth enterprise of American cooking was to produce food-in-motion for a people constantly on the move."[24] Even after the start of the culinary revolution that produced what Beard referred to as "new American cuisine," Fussell notes, "the best of the New American cooking is as muddled and as shifty as the old."

Old and new, this dynamic American cuisine, ever changing and in constant motion, touches down and becomes real, however briefly, in restaurants. It is the restaurant, ironically an adopted French form, that gives meaning to American cuisine by locating it in a place. In *The Taste of Place,* anthropologist Amy Trubek argues that the experience of American chefs cooking in restaurants has produced a new model of regional cuisine that is emerging from the intersection of social values and entrepreneurial activities rather than from the relationship of the farmer to the land.[25] As perhaps nowhere else in the world, our national cuisine is constituted at the locus of consumption rather than at the locus of production—in the restaurant, not in the field. French cuisine is what French people cook; American cuisine is where Americans eat. This shift gives restaurants in the United States a unique relationship to cuisine. It also is part of what gives restaurant critics a unique power over taste. And because New York is the restaurant capital of the country, it gives New York a big say in what defines American cooking, despite New York's detachment from most agricultural activities and, at least as most New Yorkers are concerned, from most of America.

It is possible that restaurants became so important in New York life, in New York identity, because of their unique relationship to American cuisine and the unique relationship of New York to America. If, as a country, our attitude toward food emphasizes speed, hybridization, and portability, and restaurants are the site where this attitude becomes food that is eaten, then where else but in a city known for its fast pace, multiculturalism, and constant motion would American restaurant dining take hold?

In his popular history of restaurants in the United States, John Mariani observed, "There's always the gimmick, the draw, the come-on in American eateries. The American restaurant is never merely a place to eat. It is a place to go, to see, to experience, to hang out in, to seduce in, and to be seduced."[26] In a sense, Mariani is saying that like our cuisine, our restaurants are not exactly real. They are fantasies, places of hope and possibility. As such, they provide the perfect stage on which to play out our ever-malleable social identities. Restaurants are not just where we go because of who we are, but where we become who we want to be. Enter the Four Seasons, the ethnic dive, the endless online debate about which pizzeria has the best slice. Joseph Baum, who masterminded the Four Seasons as well as such other venerable New York dining institutions as the Rainbow Room and Windows on the World, was famous for saying that restaurants are theater—a notion corroborated more recently by Arnold Aronson, a professor of theater arts. As a model restaurateur, Baum provided the stage and the show. In so doing, he gave form to a particularly American set of values that, in turn, helped create what has become American food.

If American cuisine is really New York restaurant cuisine, and vice versa, then it would stand to reason that the influence of American gastronomy on gastronomy elsewhere—especially during what we like to think of as the American century—would be to change the way people dine out around the world. The impact of fast food in Europe and Asia is well documented. Although fast-food restaurants are not native to New York, they embody the principles of speed, hybridization, and motion that Fussell attributes to American cuisine and that New York has come to represent both here and abroad. Although many New Yorkers proudly (and wrongly) believe that nobody ever eats in a McDonald's in New York,[27] much of what the company claims to stand for—speed, efficiency, and quality—are principles that New Yorkers hold dear. What else would explain why so many people in the world think that all Americans eat is hamburgers?

Beyond fast food, a more recent export has been a particular New York style of restaurant. For the past decade or so, many of the trendiest restaurants in Paris, Milan, Tokyo, Sydney, Shanghai, and elsewhere have had a decidedly New York feel about them. Whether it is their "loungey" environments, their models-as-servers hiring practices, or their deconstructed fusion menus, the similarity of these far-flung restaurants to New York restaurants is undeniable. You could dismiss the trend as some sort of hip, international style that is part of the "wallpaperization" of the middle-class world. But I think the particular style of hip that these establishments purvey ties into an identity more closely aligned with New York than with anywhere else. The international, cosmopolitan, anywhere-cool style is about as New York as it gets, and as if to underscore my point, these restaurants often use New York in their names.[28]

Not only are we exporting a style of eating and restaurant particular to New York life, but lately we also are exporting our chefs. Chefs who have made their name in the Big Apple have opened restaurants in major culinary cities around the world: Paris, London, Hong Kong, Shanghai, Tokyo, Mexico, Tel Aviv, Dubai, and many points in between. With apologies to Nobu Matsuhisa, one of the most prolific and lauded global chefs, whose creative Japanese cuisine ushered in a Japanese fusion-food trend that has reverberated around the world, the diner eating at Nobu in Tokyo is consuming a set of modern, Western, New York ideals that are very similar to those consumed by the diner eating at a McDonald's nearby.

The great French chef Auguste Escoffier noted in his memoir that "the expansion of French cuisine worldwide is chiefly due to the thousands of French chefs who work in the four corners of the globe." He was proud to have been able to "implant over 2,000 French chefs all over the world. Most of them took root in their new countries, and I can say that each can be likened to grains of wheat sowed in barren ground. France is today reaping the resulting crop."[29] Perhaps the grains of wheat now being sown around the world are New York chefs and their restaurants, although in typical American capitalistic fashion, they are being planted to reap large profits rather than a chauvinistic sense of culinary pride. More significant than short-term financial gains, perhaps the crop we will soon be able to harvest is a bona fide New York–American cuisine about which we ourselves can be proud—fast, fused, and in constant motion.

NOTES

1. Joanne Finkelstein, *Dining Out: A Sociology of Modern Manners* (New York: New York University Press, 1989); Lisa M. Heldke, *Exotic Appetites: Ruminations of a Food Adventurer* (New York: Routledge, 2003); Rebecca L. Spang, *The Invention of the Restaurant: Paris and Modern Gastronomic Culture* (Cambridge, Mass.: Harvard University Press, 2000); Alan Warde and Lydia Martens, *Eating Out: Social Differentiation, Consumption and Pleasure* (Cambridge: Cambridge University Press, 2000).

2. Bureau of the Census, 1997, quoted in http://www.nyseafood.org/doc.asp?document _key=NYSeafoodIndustry.

3. Michael Batterberry and Ariane Batterberry, *On the Town in New York: The Landmark History of Eating, Drinking, and Entertainments from the American Revolution to the Food Revolution* (New York: Routledge, 1999); John F. Mariani, *America Eats Out: An Illustrated History of Restaurants, Taverns, Coffee Shops, Speakeasies, and Other Establishments That Have Fed Us for 350 Years* (New York: Morrow, 1991); Waverley Root and Richard de Rochemont, *Eating in America* (New York: Morrow, 1976).

4. Sydney Mintz, afterword to *Golden Arches East: McDonald's in East Asia,* by James L. Watson (Stanford, Calif.: Stanford University Press, 1997), 198.

5. For a comprehensive history of the restaurant, see John G. Mariani, *The Four Seasons: A History of America's Premier Restaurant* (New York: Crown, 1994).

6. Ibid., 36. The real 2005 value of the 1959 expenditure was calculated using the Consumer Price Index. Using other standard indexes, the real 2005 value ranges from $24 million to $110 million.

7. Heldke, *Exotic Appetites,* 7.

8. Hasia R. Diner, *Hungering for America: Italian, Irish, and Jewish Foodways in the Age of Immigration* (Cambridge, Mass.: Harvard University Press, 2001), 66.

9. Frank Bruni, "Looks Like Diversity, but It Tastes Like Tuna," *New York Times,* October 20, 2004, F1.

10. Kirshendu Ray, *The Migrant's Table: Meals and Memories in Bengali-American Households* (Philadelphia: Temple University Press, 2004), 87.

11. Diner, *Hungering for America,* 201.

12. June, at http://brunidigest.blogspot.com/.

13. Tom Scocca, "Off the Record," *New York Observer,* May 16, 2005, 6.

14. Stephen Mennell, *All Manners of Food: Eating and Taste in England and France from the Middle Ages to the Present* (Urbana: University of Illinois Press, 1996), 134–65.

15. Ibid., 143.

16. Pierre Bourdieu, "The Market of Symbolic Goods," in *The Field of Cultural Production: Essays on Art and Literature* (New York: Columbia University Press, 1993), 112–41.

17. Mitchell Davis, "Power Meal: Craig Claiborne's Last Supper for the *New York Times*," *Gastronomica* 4, no. 3 (2004): 60–72.

18. Duncan Hines, *Duncan Hines' Food Odyssey* (New York: Crowell, 1955), 28.

19. Scocca, "Off the Record," 6.

20. James Beard, *American Cookery* (Boston: Little, Brown, 1972).

21. Priscilla Parkhurst Ferguson, "A Cultural Field in the Making: Gastronomy in 19th-Century France," *American Journal of Sociology* 104 (1998): 634.

22. Octavio Paz, "Eroticism and Gastrosophy," *Daedalus* 101 (1972): 71, 74.

23. James Beard, "'American' Cooking," in *The Armchair James Beard,* ed. John Ferrone (1982; repr., New York: Lyons Press, 1999), 311–12.

24. Betty Fussell, *I Hear America Cooking: A Journey of Discovery from Alaska to Florida—The Cooks, the Recipes, and the Unique Flavors of Our National Cuisine* (New York: Viking, 1986), xxxi.

25. Amy B. Trubek, *The Taste of Place: A Cultural Journey into Terroir* (Berkeley: University of California Press, 2008).

26. Mariani, *America Eats Out,* 13.

27. According to several McDonald's Web sites, the Times Square location, one of forty-six in Manhattan and the largest in the country, is also one of the top grossing. See http://www.mcfun.com/releases_news/news_121701.shtml.

28. Consider the chic New York Grill atop the Park Hyatt Tokyo, featured in Sofia Coppola's film *Lost in Translation.*

29. Auguste Escoffier, *Memories of My Life,* trans. Laurence Escoffier (New York: Van Nostrand Reinhold, 1997), 187.

Hungry City

JANET POPPENDIECK AND JC DWYER

IN HIS LYRICAL novel *Invisible Cities,* Italo Calvino presents a series of dialogues between the young Venetian traveler Marco Polo and the aging Tartar emperor, Kublai Khan, in which Marco Polo recounts his real and imagined travels, giving each city the name of a woman. This is how he describes one of his urban mistresses:

> The ancients built Valdrada on the shores of a lake, with houses all verandas one above the other, and high streets whose railed parapets look out over the water. Thus the traveler, arriving, sees two cities: one erect above the lake, and the other reflected, upside down. Nothing exists or happens in the one Valdrada that the other Valdrada does not repeat, because the city was so constructed that its every point would be reflected in its mirror, and the Valdrada down in the water contains not only all the flutings and juttings of the façades that rise above the lake, but also the rooms' interiors with ceilings and floors, the perspective of the halls, the mirrors of the wardrobes.[1]

New York City is a bit like Valdrada. Beneath the skyscraper city of glass and glamour is another city, submerged in a flood of misery and need: the city of the poor. One in five New Yorkers lives below the federal poverty threshold. Gathered into a city of their own, the 1.6 million officially poor New Yorkers would comprise the fifth largest city in the United States, larger than Detroit, Dallas, and even Philadelphia—larger, in fact, than the population of any city in the nation except New York itself, Los Angeles, Chicago, and Houston.[2]

The poverty threshold that demarcates this other New York is such a notoriously stingy measure of need that not-for-profit organizations routinely use a figure of twice the federal poverty line to designate people likely to suffer economic hardships,[3] and even federal programs like the Food Stamp Program set eligibility ceilings at 130 percent of the poverty line, not at the line itself. For a family of three, official poverty means getting by on a monthly income of less than $1,312 and doing so in a city in which the fair-market rent for a two-bedroom apartment is $1,133 a month. It means getting by on a little more than $300 a week[4] in a city in which child care is expensive, a round trip on the subway costs $4, and it is difficult to find a cup of coffee for less than a buck.

How do they eat? Many a tourist confronted with a double-digit tab for a sandwich and a glass of milk in a hotel dining room has wondered the same about New Yorkers in general. Indeed, food costs in New York are high: 36 percent above the national average in a recent year.[5] The challenge confronting the average New Yorker with a median household income of $41,509, however, pales beside the challenge confronting the residents of low-income New York. What is the taste of New York for the poor and the very poor? How does the food system work in the submerged mirror image of Gastropolis?

Urban planner Kameshwari Pothukuchi conceptualized the urban food system as a convergence of several "streams" of food that come together to supply the city.[6] The largest and most obvious is the "conventional" stream, composed of the grocery stores and restaurants where most residents obtain most of their food. The second is what we might call the "food-assistance" stream, and it has two major currents: a public current and a private current. The public current consists of federal, state, and municipal nutrition-assistance programs that provide food (or food-specific purchasing power) to designated groups within the population. The private current, much smaller in volume than the public current but simultaneously much more visible to many observers, is the "emergency" or charitable food system, the network of soup kitchens and food pantries, food banks and food rescue organizations that offer private food assistance to people in need. Some food pantries and soup kitchens receive some of their food and/or some of their funding from government sources, so there is a significant overlap between the emergency food system and the public food-assistance network. By and large, however, emergency food providers are private, charitable organizations, often faith based. Finally, there is the "alternative," or community, stream, made up of direct agricultural marketing such as farmers' markets, community-supported agriculture (CSA), and food-producing urban gardens.

Let us look at the ways in which these three streams serve or fail to serve the needs of impoverished New Yorkers. Because the spatial dimension of neighborhood is so important to food access in cities, we will "zoom in" on one particular poor neighborhood, East Harlem, to see how these three systems interact there. The physical manifestation of the boundary line that defines poor and near-poor New Yorkers is nowhere more evident than on East Ninety-sixth Street in Manhattan, the traditional division between East Harlem and the tony Upper East Side, to its south. Like Calvino's mirrored water, Ninety-sixth Street offers visitors a chance to gaze simultaneously on one of the richest and one of the poorest neighborhoods in the nation. In East Harlem, 38 percent of the residents live below the poverty line, while just 8 percent of Upper East Siders share this fate. In 2004, a stunning 78 percent of

East Harlem newborns were living in households below the poverty line, while only 5 percent of those below Ninety-sixth Street had this misfortune.[7] The Upper East Side is home to famous actors, politicians, and the city's social elite, and its reputation as an inexhaustible well of political contributions is well documented. But East Harlem, profiled as an archetypal ghetto for decades in works like Piri Thomas's *Down These Mean Streets,* has captured the popular imagination in different terms, as one of New York's most vibrant yet toughest neighborhoods. Its strong cultural heritage as "Spanish Harlem" and its gentrification in recent years obscure the fact that high rates of poor health and material deprivation continue to call East Harlem home. By crossing Ninety-sixth Street, it is possible to see what food means to New Yorkers who cannot afford the gastronomic paradise on the other side of the mirror.

The Mainstream Food System: Price, Quality, and Access

In 1963, David Caplovitz shocked many Americans with his book *The Poor Pay More,* a study of retailing in New York's East Harlem. It is one of those titles, like *Blaming the Victim,* that entered the culture and became a shorthand for an entire analysis. Caplovitz showed convincingly that the image of "cheaper" goods in low-income neighborhoods masked a counterintuitive reality. Poor people, he demonstrated, could not afford to take advantage of many of the real bargains in American society, were victims of usurious time-payment plans, were sold "durable" goods whose materials and construction rendered them useless before they were paid for, and were frequently offered damaged or flawed goods rejected from markets in more affluent neighborhoods.

Caplovitz's work focused on predatory credit practices, not food retailing, but it sparked an ongoing interest in the food prices paid by poor people. Early efforts to find predatory practices comparable to those that Caplovitz had identified in retail furniture marketing gradually gave way, as the research accumulated, to structural explanations. The poor were paying more for food not because unscrupulous grocers took advantage of them but because poor neighborhoods had few supermarkets and many small stores, and the prices in small stores are generally higher than those in supermarkets—an average of about 10 percent higher, a careful review by economists at the Department of Agriculture estimated.[8] These higher prices reflect unit costs; small stores do not have the space to stock the very large sizes of packaged goods that bring down the price per pound, nor can they take advantage of the largest-volume, lowest-cost deals offered by their suppliers. The high prices reflect the costs of doing business—rent, insurance, waste management, and losses to crime—and the fundamental relationship between volume and price. Large suburban supermarkets rely on high-volume sales to thousands of mobile customers; small stores, whether in inner cities or in small towns, get by on much lower volume by charging higher prices.

New York is no exception to the inner-city, small-store price squeeze, and the availability of larger stores with supermarket prices definitely varies with neighborhood affluence. A *New York Times* analysis of data from the New York State Department of Agriculture and Markets in the mid-1990s found that the poorest quarter of the city's community-planning districts had approximately 1.5 chain grocery stores for every 100,000 people, whereas the wealthiest quarter had a bit more than 7 per 100,000 people. The poorer neighborhoods had more small, independent grocery stores, 8.4 per 100,000 compared with 3.4 per 100,000 in the richer neighborhoods.[9] A few years earlier, the city's Department of Consumer Affairs had estimated that having to shop in a poor neighborhood typically raised the food bill for a family of four by 8.8 percent.[10] A more recent analysis by the magazine *City Limits* found that the number of square feet of grocery-store space per resident varied dramatically among the city's neighborhoods. The residents of relatively prosperous SoHo (per capita income, $40,820) had 17.3 square feet of grocery store each, but those in Washington Heights (per capita income, $13,297) had only a little more than 0.5 square foot each.[11] The study counted as a "grocery store" any food market of 4,000 square feet or more; the average for American supermarkets is in excess of 48,000 square feet.[12]

Price differentials and limited access to the cheaper-by-the-dozen jumbo packages are not the only disadvantages that poor New Yorkers face as consumers. Smaller stores not only are pricier but carry far less variety and tend to have an especially limited supply of fresh produce and meat. It makes sense. Produce wilts and rots, but a Twinkie lasts forever—or at least for a very long time. With the mounting concern about high rates of obesity and type 2 diabetes, the limited availability of health-promoting foods in poor neighborhoods has come under scrutiny, both nationally[13] and in New York.[14] Recently, the Brooklyn District Public Health Office undertook a study of food access in two low-income neighborhoods whose rates of diabetes and obesity were exceptionally high. The survey found that supermarkets constituted only 6 percent of available outlets; bodegas accounted for 80 percent; and the rest were gas stations, drug stores, and specialty stores. In a search for healthful choices, the survey found that only 33 percent of bodegas, but 90 percent of supermarkets carried reduced-fat milk; leafy green vegetables were available in only about 6 percent of the bodegas but in 66 percent of the supermarkets.[15] After releasing the report, the Department of Health announced a program to enlist bodegas in several high-risk neighborhoods to carry and promote low-fat milk.[16]

Of course, some enterprising residents travel out of poor neighborhoods to do their shopping, but poor New Yorkers are especially unlikely to own cars—even affluent New Yorkers are far less likely than their suburban counterparts to own cars—so such long-distance shopping costs some combination of money and time to use public transportation. It may be easy to get to a larger market by public transportation, but hauling home a load of groceries by bus and subway is daunting, especially if the shopper is accompanied by small children. Residents of underserved areas have to do the math fairly carefully. How much must they save by shopping at a market out of the neighborhood to warrant the round-trip subway or bus fare of $4, and how much to come out ahead if they take a taxicab home with their packages? And if tired shoppers decide to grab a bite from a restaurant on the way home, the Health Department study suggests that in low-income neighborhoods, they will find mostly fast-food and take-out options. Chinese take-out establishments, Latin American restaurants, pizza parlors, and fried chicken places were among the most common choices.

East Harlem provides a showcase for these trends. A recent study examining all of East Harlem's food outlets, conducted by Carol Horowitz, now a professor of health policy at Mount Sinai Medical Center, revealed not only a discrepancy in the availability of healthful foods across the neighborhood but also a difference in prices when compared with those of neighboring stores on the Upper East Side. Horowitz found that overall, healthful food was nearly absent in most East Harlem establishments and that, when present, it tended to cost more than it did south of Ninety-sixth Street. Her numbers were startling: 87 percent of the food outlets in East Harlem were under 4,000 square feet, essentially corner bodegas. Only three stores contained more than 20,000 square feet of space and so would be defined as "supermarkets" by most Americans.[17]

The major outlier in Horowitz's study, and the exception that "proves the rule" in East Harlem, is the 125th Street Pathmark. After years of concerted effort by advocates whose criticisms predated Horowitz's scientific study, this store was built (over the objections of many small-business owners) in 1998. Its 54,000 square feet

Fast-food restaurants surround each of the three major supermarkets in East Harlem. (Photograph courtesy of JC Dwyer)

of shopping space immediately changed the access equation for all who lived near it. Today this Pathmark is one of northern Manhattan's largest and most fully stocked food outlets, and shopping there has become a weekly rite for many East Harlem residents. The amount of shopping space dwarfs the neighborhood average, with all that this implies: the food is usually more fresh, healthful, and inexpensive than that available at any other nearby store. In the Pathmark's aisles, alongside the packaged and processed foods, it is possible to find decently priced staples and fresh produce— even organics made affordable by the store's own "California-fresh" brand. A mango purchased here for 67 cents would cost $1.79 at a bodega only a few blocks away, startlingly close to the price for a full meal from the McDonald's Dollar Menu.

McDonald's has plenty of competition for that dollar. Most of the 217 restaurants in East Harlem fit the lay definition of "fast food," selling cheap, filling eatables like pizza and fried chicken. The intersection of 125th Street and Lexington Avenue is a perfect model of these choices. On one corner, the Pathmark sells hundreds of varieties of produce. Yet surrounding Pathmark is a veritable gauntlet of high-fat, "quick-service" restaurants. As elsewhere in East Harlem, they tend to be clustered in areas of commerce, capitalizing on their convenience and the "quick fix" of a cheap meal for weary shoppers.

The Poverty Food System: Adequacy Versus Access

Fourteen separate federal food-assistance programs operate in New York. This federal reservoir is the source of the major public current that nourishes poor people in the other New York, but it is not what most people think of at the mention of hunger or food programs in the Big Apple. Tourists who have ridden the New York City subways are likely to think of the spiel they heard from a man describing a persistent but unsuccessful job search while collecting change in a coffee cup, or from a pale, emaciated woman asking for help to feed her children. Or they might remember the man who introduced himself as a representative of the United Homeless Organization, offered sandwiches from a paper bag to anyone who was hungry, and solicited donations to keep the good work going.[18] College students who have come to New York to "feed the hungry" on Alternative Spring Break or other service-learning programs are likely to think of one of the city's several hundred soup kitchens. Maybe they remember a big one like Holy Apostles, which serves more than a thousand meals each day (and was voted "best soup kitchen" in a survey of homeless clients conducted by the Grand Central Neighborhood Social Service Corporation),[19] or perhaps a smaller, restaurant-style program like POTS (Part Of The Solution) in the Bronx, where diners are seated at tables of four and served by volunteers. *Meshulachim* who come to Brooklyn from Israel to raise funds for charities back home may think of the welcome and hot meals provided to them at Masbia, Brooklyn's kosher soup kitchen.[20]

In the affluent suburbs north of the city, residents might think about handing out sandwiches and soup to homeless people on the Midnight Run, a Dobbs Ferry–based charity that sends, in the middle of the night, vans loaded with volunteers, food, clothing, and toiletries to Manhattan to stop at gathering places frequented by homeless people.[21] Closer to home, corporate groups that have participated in team-building excursions might remember a day spent in the repack room of the Food Bank for New York City, identifying "shiners" (cans without labels) or helping to break down bulk donations into quantities useful to food pantries. The thousands of other New Yorkers who volunteer regularly might think of gathering at a food pantry to help unload one of the Food Bank's delivery trucks when it arrived with packaged and canned goods and fresh produce to restock the pantry shelves or of packing pantry bags or serving soup kitchen meals. Less directly involved New Yorkers might think of sending a check, perhaps a donation, to enable City Harvest's big green-and-white trucks to pick up food from restaurants, hospitals, campus cafeterias, corporate dining rooms, hotels, groceries, bakeries, or other food-service establishments and transport it to soup kitchens, shelters, and pantries for immediate distribution. They might think of the letter carriers' annual Help Stamp Out Hunger food drive, the Daily News Readers' Care to Feed the Hungry of New York food drive, or the requests they receive for contributions of canned goods from their churches, synagogues, mosques, or temples.

Unless they have been poor themselves, however, have worked with one of the city's half dozen hunger-related advocacy organizations, or have been employed by the Human Resources Administration (HRA, also known as "the welfare"), they are far less likely to think of the Food Stamp Program or WIC (Special Supplemental Nutrition Program for Women, Infants and Children) or the Child and Adult Care Food Program or senior meals or even school food. Nevertheless, it is these public programs that are the main line of defense against hunger in the Big Apple. There is an enormous amount of activity in the poverty food system. Picture a typical weekday. By the time the sun rises, hundreds of cafeteria workers have begun to prepare breakfast for an average of 190,000 schoolchildren. At 8:00 A.M., dozens of senior centers begin serving five thousand breakfasts. By 9:00, at more than 130 WIC sites around the city, secretaries are scheduling appointments; phlebotomists are drawing blood; nutritionists are offering nutrition education, breast-feeding support, and dietary counseling; and vouchers are being dispensed for the highly nutritious foods needed especially by pregnant women, infants, and growing pre-schoolchildren. By 9:00, the twenty food stamp centers also are open, and workers begin to conduct thousands of recertification interviews with food stamp participants and to receive applications from hundreds of prospective recipients. At midmorning, the children in more than 3,200 day-care centers and 5,500 licensed family child care homes—and some of the adults in adult day programs—are eating a federally subsidized morning snack. While the toddlers are getting back to the business of playing, their grandparents and great-grandparents are stepping out. By late morning, senior citizens are converging on the 325 centers around the city that serve "congregate meals," arriving on foot or in specially adapted vans and minibuses. Using federal Senior Nutrition Program funds, New York's Department for the Aging sponsors thirty thousand center-based lunches each weekday and arranges for the delivery of seventeen thousand more to homebound seniors through Meals on Wheels. Meanwhile, back at the schoolhouse—the city's more than 1,450 school sites—more than 634,000 lunches are being dished up, 560,000 of them free or at steeply reduced prices to children from low-income families. In the afternoon, many schools serve snacks in afterschool programs, as do the day-care centers and family day care homes; and the food stamp offices continue to process people and papers, four of them until 6:00 P.M.[22]

The activity in the "emergency" food system begins earlier, with the first shift arriving at the Food Bank at 5:00 A.M., and runs later: the last City Harvest trucks do not finish their rounds until 2:00 or 3:00 A.M. The total volume of food in this charitable system, however, is dwarfed by that in the public-sector programs. While the Food Bank estimates that the emergency food-assistance network provided 98 million meals or meal equivalents in the fiscal year ending June 30, 2005, the Food Stamp Program alone accounts for more than eight times that number, 842 million meals a year.[23] Add to this equation the school meals served free or at reduced prices, and the federal sector is nearly ten times larger than the private. Factor in 156 million WIC meal equivalents and 70 million meals at day-care centers and family child care homes, and the federal government provides about 1.1 billion more meals than does the private emergency food system, with the latter accounting for 8 percent of the total, or one meal in twelve. This figure is not unlike what Mathematica found nationwide in its massive study of the emergency food system, released in 2002, in which it reported that charitable food assistance provided one, and federal food assistance nine, of every ten meals served.[24] None of these calculations takes into account the fact that through federal donations, state grants, and city funds, the public sector directly contributes to or pays for a great deal of the food distributed through charitable programs. The Food Bank for New York City calculates that in fiscal year 2005, 41 percent of the total distributed through its facility was private donations, and 59 percent was public.[25]

It is relatively easy to explain the disproportionate share of attention accorded to the private current in the food-assistance stream by residents of affluent New York. Private food-assistance organizations raise much of their revenue and collect some of their food by interaction with the public, through food drives, direct-mail solicitations, food-tasting events affiliated with high-profile chefs such as the Taste of New York, the Check Out Hunger coupons at supermarket cash registers, and the ubiquitous barrels and boxes and receptacles for donated food. In a sense, these organizations are the bridges between the New York of the poor and that of their affluent neighbors "upstairs," collecting resources, food, and money from the city of the rich and transferring them to the city of the poor. All these activities make private food assistance "visible" in the above-ground New York in a way that public food assistance is not. In fact, invisibility is an aim of the design of public food-assistance programs. Food stamps were more visible when they were actual paper vouchers that had to be detached from a booklet and handed to a cashier. The advent of EBT (electronic benefits transfer) plastic swipe cards makes the food stamp shopper less distinctive, a major goal of the conversion to electronic technology. School meal programs are required by law to protect the privacy of children who are receiving free and reduced-price meals in order to make these subsidies "invisible." New York City has solved this problem at breakfast and at lunch in some schools by using "Provision

Two"—that is, making the meals free to all children. Even in the remaining schools, since the great majority of students in the system qualify for free or reduced-price meals, it is the paying customers who stand out.

For the residents of the city of the poor, those who depend on the food-assistance stream for much or all of their nourishment, the distinction between private and public sources is more practical. In one sense, it is a trade-off between access and adequacy, best illustrated by comparing food stamps with food pantries. The average monthly food stamp benefit in New York City is $112 a person, or $336 a month for a household of three.[26] A typical food pantry allocation is a three-day supply, and many pantries restrict clients to one visit a month. Clearly, food stamps are likely to put substantially more food in the cupboard, but they are also much harder to obtain. Pantries usually have a registration process. Some require a referral from an agency that is equipped to screen applicants; others make their own assessment of need on the spot. Some accept a client's profession of need; others require some evidence of income or the lack thereof: a pink slip, a notice of termination of benefits. Most ask for documentation of household size.[27] But it is rare to see a food pantry application that exceeds one page. These requirements are usually very simple and pale beside the rigors of applying for food stamps. Responding to the urging of advocates, New York State recently simplified the food stamp application itself, reducing it from fourteen pages to four. But filling out the application is only the first step in an arduous process. Many of the items requested in the application must be documented: income, rent, utility charges, household composition, medical expenses. This frequently takes more than one visit, and waiting times at food stamp offices are notoriously long. A recent study by the Urban Justice Center details the experiences of clients who were prescreened and judged eligible but who, two months later, had no application on file in the system. Multiple visits, rude behavior, loss of documents, and absurd requests (such as applicants proving that they do not have bank accounts) deterred many from completing the process.[28] The requirement for fingerprinting discouraged others and made the process humiliating for many whom it did not; with its overtones of criminality, it is particularly daunting for immigrant applicants. Poverty rates are high among immigrants in New York, but the complexity of the food stamp law as it applies to immigrants and the frequent changes in the law over the past decade mean that the barriers that confront all applicants are higher for immigrants.[29]

Access also may be conceptualized in space and time. There are only twenty locations in New York where food stamp applications may be filed, but there are at least nine hundred food pantries. All but four of the city's food stamp offices are open only during regular business hours, and these four have extended hours—until 6:00 P.M. on weekdays and from 9:00 A.M. to 5:00 P.M. on Saturdays. Only 13.7 percent of the city's food pantries are open after 4:00 P.M., but a full 33 percent are open on Saturdays, and more than 20 percent are open on Sundays.[30] The issue of time of day and day of week is most significant for working people. Despite the stereotypes of hungry New Yorkers as unemployed panhandlers, many are working or are seeking work. Employed people were overrepresented among those who were found eligible for food stamps at prescreening but had no application on file.[31]

Overall, despite a professed desire by city administrators to increase participation in the program, the culture of the food stamp bureaucracy still seems mired in the bad old days of antiwelfare sentiment, when the city's commissioner of human resources declared that food stamps were a form of "dependency" and discouraged people from applying for them. Overall, an estimated 760,000 New Yorkers are eligible for but not enrolled in the Food Stamp Program, a number larger than the total population of San Francisco![32]

Food stamps are an entitlement; that is, if a household is eligible, it has a legal right to the benefits. Congress normally appropriates enough money to provide the benefits for all who apply and are found eligible. Furthermore, the full food stamp benefit is paid by the federal government. States and municipalities contribute only administrative funds, and only a portion of those. Thus it is easy for advocates to argue that the entire city would benefit from a successful effort to enroll eligible individuals and households in the program. It would draw additional federal dollars into the economy, dollars that would begin circulating immediately and generate additional economic activity for each dollar of food stamp benefit. Advocates typically refer to the city government's failure to conduct vigorous outreach and to reduce or remove barriers to participation as "leaving money lying on the table in Washington."

The sums currently lying on the table are substantial: if all 760,000 eligible but unenrolled New Yorkers were to receive the average monthly benefit of $112, there would be more than $850 million to be gained by full participation. Since participation rates are higher among those eligible for larger benefits, it is likely that the remaining households that are eligible but not enrolled would qualify for less than the current average. Nonetheless, reducing the projection by one-third, to an average of $75 a month, still means that New York City is forgoing $650 million annually in food stamps.

The current administration has joined with advocates to obtain a large grant from the federal government to experiment with applications submitted through the Internet, a potential solution if vigorously administered, which would permit people to apply from food pantries, public libraries, hospitals, and other public facilities. Currently, at least one charitable food provider in each borough has joined the city in this experiment, processing clients' applications from the relative comfort of their agencies and working faster than most HRA offices can manage. If this initiative succeeds, New York, which currently has a participation rate for working families substantially below the national average, may become a model for other cities.

Once a food stamp application is submitted, and all the documentation filed, food stamps still take a long time to arrive. The law allows thirty days, or seven for those who qualify for "expedited food stamps" because of urgent need, but in New York, one case in twelve is not served within the legal time limit.[33] By contrast, people seeking help almost always leave a food pantry with a bag or two of groceries, even if they have not yet been determined to be eligible.

The apparent trade-off between adequacy and access, however, overstates the case. On the one hand, food pantry benefits are not as accessible as a figure of nine hundred pantries would suggest. Few offer food 5 days a week; on average, pantries are open 2.5 days a week,[34] and most are open only 1 or 2 days. Furthermore, few are open all day; a three- or four-hour window of opportunity is typical. In order to help people in need negotiate this confusing array of options and find a pantry that is open when they can get there, the Human Resources Administration operates a "hunger hotline."[35]

Ironically, the investment in hotline staff has taken place just as the ability of pantries to respond has been severely impaired by resource constraints. Both the New York City Coalition Against Hunger and the Food Bank for New York City report a growing demand and steady or declining supplies. In response, pantries increasingly find it necessary to turn away clients. A study conducted by the Food Bank of its member pantries found that in 2005, 45 percent had turned away clients who were seeking food, with 84 percent of them citing a lack of food as the primary reason for doing so. More than 50 percent of the pantries reported problems with food supplies sufficient to threaten their daily operations.[36] The Coalition Against Hunger found that 47 percent of the pantries surveyed had had to turn away people or ration services by cutting sizes of portions or reducing hours of operation.[37] Even at the "wholesale" level, the charitable food system is stretched thin. City Harvest, which currently delivers food to more than five hundred agencies, has more than forty would-be recipients on its waiting list. The Food Bank points to the government's falling contributions in the face of mounting need.[38] In short, the failure of resources to keep pace with demand has reduced both the adequacy and the accessibility of the emergency food system.

On the other hand, the food stamp benefit is not as generous as its program design and promotional literature imply. Food stamp benefits are calculated using the same basic assumptions that underlie the calculation of the federal poverty line. They assume that households have to be able to spend only the equivalent of the cost of the Thrifty Food Plan (TFP) to obtain an adequate amount of food and that they allocate to food purchases 30 percent of their disposable income after specified deductions. The benefit for any household is the cost of the TFP for the household size, discounted by 30 percent of food stamp–relevant income. The cost assigned to the TFP is uniform nationwide; it is not adjusted for differentials in cost of living. Notwithstanding, studies have repeatedly shown that most households spending at the level of the TFP are not able to obtain an adequate diet. And efforts to adjust eligibility and benefits to reflect local housing costs are limited by a rule known as the "excess shelter deduction cap"; that is, families can deduct the amount they spend for shelter that is over 50 percent of their income, but only up to a set ceiling, which is not enough to account for real housing costs in New York. Furthermore, the formula for calculating food stamp benefits is obsolete in the same way that the poverty line is obsolete: it reflects life in the United States in the early 1960s, not as it is today. Food stamp recipients tell food pantry staff that their benefits usually last for two weeks or less,[39] after which families turn to emergency providers for help.

For the hungry household, of course, the two currents of food assistance, the public and the charitable, are not mutually exclusive. A study conducted in 2004 found that 30.5 percent of emergency food-assistance clients were receiving food stamps. By 2006, a study of only those in agencies served by the Food Bank found a significantly higher participation rate, 46 percent.[40] Part of the difference may reflect differences in the clientele served by the non–Food Bank pantries included in the earlier study, but at least part of the difference is due to a vigorous outreach campaign aimed at enrolling eligible emergency food clients in the Food Stamp Program. At soup kitchens and food pantries throughout the city, staff members from an array of advocacy groups and volunteers trained by the Coalition Against Hunger, the Food Bank, or FoodChange have prescreened thousands of clients, estimated their probable benefits, and presented them with a computer printout to take with them to a food stamp office.

Together, the hard-pressed emergency food stream and the underutilized federal programs are striving to fill the gap but have not succeeded in closing it. The federal government annually assesses household food insecurity, and New York's numbers, like those of the nation, have been rising. Despite all the activity in the food-assistance system, the latest figures show that 1.2 million New Yorkers live in "food-insecure" households; the Food Bank has estimated that at least 2 million of the city's residents are "at risk" of going hungry.[41]

At the neighborhood level, the relative merits of the private and public currents of food assistance are woven into daily life. In the middle of an East Harlem night, families in the most desperate straits know only one option for emergency food: the Yorkville Common Pantry (YCP), which never closes. From behind a small window in the atrium of a squat, whitewashed building next to Central Park, this program has received significant acclaim as the only continuously accessible charitable distribution point in the city.

But the 24/7 program is only a tiny part of YCP, the largest nonsectarian food pantry in the city, and its efforts represent a fraction of the more than 1.25 million meals that YCP distributes to East Harlem residents and others each year.[42] While YCP is certainly the largest local program, it is by no means the only one. East Harlem is home to fifty other charitable food outlets, which are fairly evenly distributed, so that no East Harlem resident lives far from one. In 2005, however, 67 percent of these other programs reported not having enough resources to meet demand,[43] a rarity at YCP. In other ways, YCP is very typical of its cohorts. Despite the acclaim of the 24/7 program, it is also one of the first providers to admit that "emergency food" is a mischaracterization of its role in the community.

Like many emergency food programs, those run by YCP grew out of the temporary distribution of surplus government commodities (like cheese) in the early 1980s. As such, these programs were not designed to be long-lasting and were not organized with chronic needs in mind. In the intervening years, however, such programs have become a regular source of food for many of their clients. For East Harlem residents, YCP is "as much an anti-eviction program [as anything else]," asserts Jeff Ambers, its former director. Yet even though many East Harlem residents are forced to return to YCP month after month, private funders still conceive of these programs as emergency based, leading to what Ambers calls a fixation on "quantity, not quality" of food and service.

Still, for East Harlem families in need—whether on an emergency or a recurring basis—a little flexibility in a program's hours of operation is a welcome innovation. In the post-1990s economic environment, as New York's wages stagnated and housing prices soared, soup kitchens and food pantries reported that one of their fastest-growing client populations was the working poor. These families have little time to manage their needs, and so the relatively even geographic distribution of charitable food outlets in East Harlem would seem to be a boon for them. Yet this distribution in terms of space masks an insurmountable obstacle in the dimension of time, as few centers are open outside weekday business hours. This problem is typical of New York as a whole. As a result, East Harlem residents who are employed but not earning enough money to get by have extremely inconsistent access to emergency food.

If you happen to be hungry in East Harlem at 1:00 P.M. on a Wednesday, there are ten programs to choose from. But if you are in need after a hard day's work, you will be lucky to find just one. As a result, when East Harlem families try to pull themselves out of poverty by holding one, two, or three jobs, the charitable food system actually works against them. Program directors like Ambers doubt that this situation will change soon.

Thus more working families are finding it worthwhile to skip work in favor of waiting in line for hours at the local food stamp office. Since the average food stamp benefit granted at the HRA office on 126th Street dwarfs what most food pantries

	Sun	Mon	Tues	Wed	Thurs	Fri	Sat
8:00 AM					2		
8:30 AM					2		
9:00 AM		3	2	2	6	2	
9:30 AM		4	3	3	8	4	1
10:00 AM		5	3	4	8	5	1
10:30 AM		6	4	5	8	6	1
11:00 AM		5	3	6	8	5	1
11:30 AM		5	3	6	8	4	1
12:00 PM		5	4	7	8	4	1
12:30 PM		4	4	7		4	
1:00 PM		7	7	10	9	8	1
1:30 PM		8	6	8	8	7	1
2:00 PM		4	4	5	6	5	1
2:30 PM		4	4	5	6	5	1
3:00 PM		2	2	4	3	3	1
3:30 PM		2	2	4	3	3	1
4:00 PM		1	1	1	1	4	
4:30 PM		1	1	1	1	4	
5:00 PM					1	3	
5:30 PM	1				1	3	
6:00 PM	1					1	
6:30 PM						2	
7:00 PM			1		1		
7:30 PM			1		1		
8:00 PM			1		1		
8:30 PM							

Key (number of agencies):

1-2	3-4	5-6	7-8	9-10

Charitable food providers in East Harlem help the hungry—but only during working hours.

can provide, families force themselves to survive the frustrations and humiliations of
the application process. They know that access to food stamps means access to the
East Harlem stores (both bodegas and supermarkets, as well as one farmers' market)
that accept this benefit, allowing them not only flexibility and dignity in their food
purchases but also the temporal convenience that the charitable system lacks.

The Green Food System: Alternative and Critique

It is no secret that many of New York's low-income neighborhoods are epicenters
of the city's diet-related diseases, due largely to the inaccessibility of conventionally
healthful food. In an effort to remedy this, many have begun calling for increased
access in these communities to so-called green food. The green food movement—
broadly defined as a movement to provide closer, more direct relationships between
consumers and producers—has responded by bringing its unique critique of the
conventional food stream, along with many farmers, into New York's least healthy
neighborhoods.

By virtue of an alternative marketing and distribution system typified in farmers'
markets, community gardens, and community-supported agriculture (CSA), green
food is often more fresh and healthful than its conventional equivalent. An outsider
might assume that such superior food would be too expensive or too inconvenient
for low-income diets. Many still equate these resources with the organic movement,
which until recently was characterized as a high-income concern. The fine artisanal
cheeses and organic meats sold in New York's flagship farmers' markets have done
little to dispel this myth. But more than eighty farmers' markets operate in New
York during the summer, many of them in or near low-income neighborhoods.[44] To
be sure, there still are fewer markets than necessary to constitute a real rivalry with
mainstream providers. In addition, most of them set up on only one or two days a
week, generally during business hours, and for only a few months a year. But the
number of farmers' markets has grown dramatically in recent years, contributing to
a national growth of 111 percent between 1994 and 2004.[45]

With the exception of those at fancier locations like Union Square, the prices at
the farmers' markets tend to be competitive with those charged by mainstream providers, as there is no middleman to drive up margins. Efforts by the New York City
Council now under way would expand the pool of money available to farmers who
venture into low-income neighborhoods by outfitting more of these markets with
EBT card access. There is still far to go in this regard, however, for in 2006, only
eight markets in the city had equipped all their vendors to accept food stamps. This
political effort is reminiscent of the WIC Farmers' Market Coupon Program, which
first institutionalized the notion that the government could successfully encourage access to healthful food. With the inclusion of other state-sponsored incentives—such
as Senior Farmers' Market Coupons and Health Bucks, which rewards food stamp
shoppers with extra purchasing power—New York's farmers' markets are actually
beginning to provide some healthy competition for their mainstream rivals. Perhaps
equally important, they are offering a lifeline to local small farmers.

The undeveloped space in low-income neighborhoods, of which many farmers' markets take advantage, also benefits the city's large number of community gardens. Many of them occupy formerly empty lots that were the sites of buildings victimized by landlord-initiated arson in the 1970s. Despite their illicit beginnings, these gardens have been known to unwittingly speed up the gentrification process by transforming vacant, trash-strewn lots into urban oases. Yet while the city's gardens are concentrated in low-income areas,[46] scarce open hours and limited public access mirror the constraints in the charitable food system. And even though the food produced by these gardens is usually free (or sold at a very low cost), occasionally there are health concerns associated with growing vegetables over the mounds of lead paint that used to be buildings.

The poverty (and, as a result, empty space) that allows for the promotion of farmers' markets and community gardens presents a significant barrier to CSAs. Community-supported agriculture operates as a shared-risk buying club, charging customers up front for an entire season's worth of vegetables from a single farmer. This gives the farmer financial stability while practically guaranteeing the delivery of fresh vegetables weekly to the consumer.

By design, these arrangements tend to thrive among populations that can afford the required investment, a rarity in low-income neighborhoods. The city has forty-two CSAs,[47] but few make the recruitment of low-income members much more than an afterthought. Only when local institutions like schools or churches step in is there an opportunity for low-income residents to participate in a CSA, and then rarely as true investors. To counteract this tendency, citywide groups like the New York City Coalition Against Hunger have begun to leverage their resources in neighborhoods like West Harlem to create "revolving loan funds" for the purchase of CSA shares. These funds provide the needed security for the farmer and can be replenished over the growing season by low-income members using food stamps and cash.

Ultimately, the importance of these alternative modes of food production and distribution may be not in the answers they provide low-income consumers but in the questions they raise. Even the most popular of these green alternatives generate only a fraction of conventional grocers' sales. The direct connection they provide between consumers and producers, however, highlights both the systemic nature of food access in cities and the public policies that have allowed this access to fail.

East Harlem is fortunate to have three farmers' markets and a fourth nearby. One of them universally accepts food stamps (a result of the City Council's largesse), and two others have at least one farmer who also accepts the benefit. Greenmarket, the entity that oversees two of East Harlem's markets, does not track its markets' gross sales receipts, but anecdotal evidence suggests that the total sales for these four markets come nowhere near to those of even the neighborhood's smaller supermarkets. Another East Harlem farmers' market, located in the very center of the Wagner Houses housing project, was forced to close after one season because of poor sales. As Greenmarket's supporters like to say, Rome was not built in a day—and neither were the city's most profitable green institutions. But the performance of the farmers' markets in East Harlem brings up important questions about the nature of food environments at the same time that the markets' very existence says something about the dominant food system surrounding the neighborhood.

East Harlem boasts more than twenty community gardens. But like the offices and pantries in the charitable food system, the majority of the gardens are open to the public at odd and inconvenient times. As a result, most provide food only to those who tend plots, an investment of time that not every family can make. Similarly, there is no CSA arrangement in East Harlem. There are two in nearby Central Harlem, both of which are partly supported by local nonprofit organizations. This is typical, for without the space and care (as well as financial support) provided by these institutions, Harlem residents would not have the opportunity to invest in an entire season of produce. These failures—to provide the necessary consumer investment to support a CSA or the critical mass of gardeners to make community gardens a significant food source—demonstrate the inability of East Harlem residents to accumulate the assets of time and money that are often required to make green alternatives viable.

Conclusion

Despite round-the-clock activity and effort, despite thousands of employees and tens of thousands of volunteers, despite billions of meals in the public food-assistance stream and millions of meals in the private stream, despite visionary efforts to make CSA shares and urban gardens available to poor people, food security continues to be out of reach for the residents of the other New York. They are still drowning in misery. By definition, being poor means not having enough money to get by, and poor New Yorkers routinely face choices that would completely paralyze their comfortable neighbors "upstairs": the choice between eating or paying the rent, between food and medicine, between groceries and utilities, between healthful food in insufficient amounts or unhealthful food in quantities large enough to fill a child's belly. The fundamental inequality that makes the lives of some New Yorkers completely unimaginable to the denizens of the other New York pervades the food system. The celebrated luxury of fine dining in Gastropolis masks the dreary reality of scraping by on a combination of food stamps, pantry bags, and soup kitchen meals. For too many New Yorkers, "food security" means the 24/7 food pantry in East Harlem.

There are bridges. The WIC Farmers' Market Coupons are a bridge between the residents of poor neighborhoods and the fresh produce of the greenmarkets. Charitable donations are a bridge between comfortable New Yorkers and their less privileged fellows. Food stamps are a bridge that permits impoverished New Yorkers to shop in mainstream stores. But these bridges do not lead out of poverty. A visit to the abundant choices of the supermarket in an affluent district is followed by a return home to the limited options of the bodega in a poor neighborhood, with the cost of the trip in time and money one more expense to be figured into the calculus of want. The $20 worth of WIC Farmers' Market Coupons are an essential source of revenue for the city's farmers' markets, but they are a token addition to the food-purchasing power of WIC families. Nor do these bridges really unify the city, as rich and poor New

Yorkers seldom share a meal, but spend their days at separate tables. Like Valdrada, Gastropolis is two cities, so close together, but yet so far apart.

NOTES

We wish to thank the many colleagues in New York's antihunger community who provided information for this article. Our thanks especially to Joel Berg of the New York City Coalition Against Hunger, Aine Duggan of the Food Bank for New York City, Charise Lawrence and Joyce Chin of the New York City Department for the Aging, Edie Mesick of the Nutrition Consortium of New York State, Agnes Molnar of the Children's Defense Fund–New York, Nicole Rottino of City Harvest, and Rosario Valenzuela of United Way of New York City.

1. Italo Calvino, *Invisible Cities,* trans. William Weaver (New York: Harcourt Brace Jovanovich, 1974), 43–44.

2. "Top Fifty Cities by Population and Rank," *Information Please,* www.infoplease.com/ipa/A0763098.html (accessed June 11, 2006).

3. Heather Boushey, Chauna Brocht, Bethney Gundersen, and Jared Bernstein, *Hardships in America: The Real Story of Working Families* (Washington, D.C.: Economic Policy Institute, 2001).

4. According to the Bureau of the Census, this is the poverty threshold (2005) for a family of three persons composed of one adult and two related children under eighteen. The poverty income thresholds used for counting the poor differ slightly from the poverty income guidelines published by the Department for Health and Human Services for use in calculating eligibility for benefits and other administrative purposes. The poverty *guideline* for a family of three for 2006 is $16,600 a year, or $1,383.33 a month.

5. Diana Pearce, "The Self-Sufficiency Standard for the City of New York, 2004" (report prepared for Women's Center for Education and Career Advancement, in conjunction with Wider Opportunities for Women's Family Economic Self-Sufficiency Project, November 2004), 6.

6. Kameshwari Pothukuchi, *The Detroit Food System: A Handbook for Community Planners* (Detroit: Department of Geography and Urban Planning, Wayne State University, 2003), 3. See also Kameshwari Pothukuchi and Jerome L. Kaufman, "The Food System: A Stranger to the Planning Field," *Journal of the American Planning Association* 66 (2000): 119.

7. Citizens' Committee for Children of New York, *Keeping Track of New York City's Children 2005* (New York: Citizens' Committee for Children of New York, 2005).

8. Philip R. Kaufman, James M. MacDonald, Steve M. Lutz, and David M. Smallwood, *Do the Poor Pay More for Food? Item Selection and Price Differences Affect Low-Income Household Food Costs,* report AER-759 (Washington, D.C.: Economic Research Service, Department of Agriculture, 1997). See also Michael S. Finke and Wen S. Chern, "Do the Urban Poor Pay More for Food? Issues in Measurement," *Advancing the Consumer Interest* 9 (1997): 13–17; and Chanjin Chung and Samuel L. Myers Jr., "Do the Poor Pay More for Food? An Analysis of Grocery Store Availability and Food Price Disparities," *Journal of Consumer Affairs* 33 (1999): 276–96.

9. Constance Hays, "Congested, Expensive, Out of Date," *New York Times,* May 29, 1994.

10. John T. McQuiston, "Food for Poor Is Said to Cost More," *New York Times,* April 15, 1991.

11. Ironically, in New York, some of the highest-income areas also lack full-service chain supermarkets because rents are so high and traffic congestion makes deliveries very difficult.

12. A Wal-Mart supercenter typically is 175,000 square feet, with 40 percent (70,000 square feet) of it devoted to food. See Food Marketing Institute, "Supermarket Facts, Industry Overview," 2005, www.fmi.org/facts_figs/superfact.htm.

13. See the work of Kimberly Morland and colleagues, especially "Neighborhood Characteristics Associated with the Location of Food Stores and Food Service Places," *American Journal of Preventive Medicine* 22 (2002): 23–29.

14. Carol R. Horowitz, Kathryn A. Colson, Paul L. Hebert, and Kristie Lancaster, "Barriers to Buying Healthy Foods for People with Diabetes: Evidence of Environmental Disparities," *American Journal of Public Health* 94 (2004): 1549–54.

15. Ibid., 1–3.

16. Marc Santora, "New York Pushing Better Diet in Poorer Neighborhoods," *New York Times,* January 20, 2006.

17. Horowitz, Colson, Hebert, and Lancaster, "Barriers to Buying Healthy Foods."

18. They probably would not realize that such solicitors pay the United Homeless Organization a "fee" of $15 for the right to solicit in its name each day; anything else they collect is for themselves.

19. "Best Homeless Services," in "Best of Manhattan," *Manhattan Living,* July 12–18, 2006.

20. Melissa Grace, "Kosher Food for Needy," *New York Daily News,* June 11, 2006.

21. For more information, see www.midnightrun.org.

22. For up-to-date figures on school meals and senior meals, see the Mayor's Management Report, http://www.nyc.gov/html/ops/html/mmr/mmr.shtml. For statistics on WIC and the Child and Adult Care Food Program, contact the New York State Department of Health. For the number of people who receive food stamps, see Human Resources Administration, "HRA Facts," http://www.nyc.gov/html/hra/downloads/pdf/hrafacts_2007_03.pdf.

23. The Food Bank estimate was provided by Aine Duggan, vice president, Division of Government Relations, Policy and Research, Food Bank for New York City. There are 1.09 million New Yorkers enrolled in the Food Stamp Program. Mathematica Policy Research Inc. (MMPRI) has calculated that on average, food stamp benefits provide 65 percent of each month's meals. Assuming 90 meals a month, this means that the Food Stamp Program provides recipients with an average of 58 meals a month, or 766 a year. In New York City, that comes to 842 million meals annually.

24. James Ohls, Fazana Saleem-Ismail, Rhoda Cohen, and Brenda Cox (MMPRI), *The Emergency Food Assistance System—Findings from the Provider Survey,* vol. 2, *Final Report* (Washington, D.C.: Economic Research Service, Department of Agriculture, 2002), 165–67 (available at http://www.ers.usda.gov/publications/fanrr16-2/). Because the MMPRI was using food stamp data from 2000, when only 17 million people participated nationwide, and because food stamp participation has increased by 49 percent, or nearly half, since 2000, the MMPRI's nationwide ratio would now be closer to New York's: one meal in twelve, not one meal in ten.

25. In turn, the Food Bank handles about 55 percent of the food in the system, so simple arithmetic suggests that at least 33 percent of the food in the charitable food stream in New York is composed of federal commodities or other food purchased with public funds.

26. State Senator Liz Krueger, foreword to *A Better Recipe for New York City: Less Red Tape, More Food on the Table,* by Rebecca Widom, Ella Ewart, and Olivia Arvizú Martínez (New York: Urban Justice Center, 2006) (available at www.urbanjustice.org).

27. The food pantries that distribute commodities through the federal Emergency Food Assistance Program are required to make sure that households are eligible under standards set by the states.

28. Widom, Ewart, and Martínez, *Better Recipe for New York City.*

29. Almas Sayeed, "In the Capital of 'Ethnic' Cuisine, Are Immigrants Eating?" *SAMAR: South Asian Magazine for Action and Reflection,* no. 22, March 20, 2006, www.samarmagazine .org.

30. Food Bank for New York City, Division of Government Relations, Policy and Research, "Hunger Safety Net 2004: Measuring Gaps in Food Assistance in New York City," 18, 19, www.foodbanknyc.org.

31. Ibid.

32. Estimates of the number eligible but not enrolled vary. The Children's Defense Fund estimates 528,440. See Children's Defense Fund–New York, "Hunger in the Midst of Plenty . . . The Need for Full Utilization of Federal Food Programs in New York City," June 2006, 5. The estimate of 760,000 used here comes from Krueger, foreword to Widom, Ewart, and Martínez, *Better Recipe for New York City,* v. The Investigation Division of the City Council has set the range of eligible New Yorkers who do not receive food stamp benefits at between 425,000 and 925,000, and the resulting amount of funds forgone by the city at between $577 million and $1.25 billion. See New York City Council, Investigation Division, "Empty Cupboards: New Yorkers at Risk of Hunger Face Continued Barriers to Food Stamp Enrollment," staff report to Honorable Eric Gioia, January 2006, www.nyccouncil.info/pdf_files/reports/ foodstamps4.pdf.

33. Joe Berg, executive director, New York City Coalition on Hunger, testimony before City Council, General Welfare Committee, Hearing on Hunger, November 21, 2005.

34. Food Bank for New York City, "Hunger Safety Net 2004."

35. The hotline system asks whether the caller would like to be connected to each pantry by phone in order to verify hours and availability. During regular business hours, callers can ask to be transferred to a live operator, although the waits are reported to be substantial. See Public Advocate for the City of New York, "New York City Hunger Hotline: Service Leaves Callers Empty Handed," May 2004, www.publicadvocate.nyc.gov/policy/reports.html.

36. Food Bank for New York City and City Harvest, "Hunger in America 2006: The New York State and City Report," http://www.foodbanknyc.org/download.cfm?DownloadFile =294BF288-3048-2A6C-8D968589B9FE1D0B.

37. New York City Coalition Against Hunger, "The Hunger Squeeze: Skyrocketing Costs, Sinking Wages Increase Hunger in New York City," Annual New York City Hunger Survey, November 2005, 12, http://www.nyccah.org/survey2005/final_report.doc.

38. Ibid., 7.

39. Food Bank for New York City and City Harvest, "Hunger in America 2006," 9.

40. Food Bank for New York City, "Hunger Safety Net 2004," 2; Food Bank for New York City and City Harvest, "Hunger in America 2006," 5.

41. Food Bank for New York City, "Hunger Safety Net 2004," 2, 4, 56.

42. For more information about the Yorkville Common Pantry, see www.ycp.org.

43. New York City Coalition Against Hunger, unpublished survey data, 2005.

44. New York State Department of Agriculture and Markets, unpublished data, 2006.

45. United States Department of Agriculture, unpublished data, 2004.

46. Council on the Environment of New York City, unpublished data, 2006.

47. For more information about CSAs in New York, see Just Food, www.justfood.org.

CONTRIBUTORS

BABETTE AUDANT is a lecturer in the Department of Tourism and Hospitality at Kingsborough Community College, City University of New York. After graduating from the Culinary Institute of America, she worked as a chef in New York City for eight years before returning to school to earn a master's degree in public administration. Audant is a doctoral candidate in the human geography program at the Graduate Center of the City University of New York, where her work focuses on the creative urban food economy.

JENNIFER SCHIFF BERG has directed New York University's graduate food studies program since its inception ten years ago. A born and bred New Yorker, Berg's interests include food in cultural contexts, the social history of New York City food, American Jewish immigration, competitive eating contests, and community-focused food education. In 2006, she earned a doctorate in food studies at New York University. Her doctoral dissertation, "From Pushcart Peddlers to Gourmet Take-Out: New York City's Iconic Foods of Jewish Origin, 1920–2005," explores the acculturation of eastern European immigrant Jews.

Having worked at the James Beard Foundation since 1993, and now its vice president, MITCHELL DAVIS has seen many of New York's dining trends come and go. An adjunct professor and doctoral candidate in the Department of Nutrition, Food Studies, and Public Health at New York University, Davis is doing research on restaurant criticism and its role in creating taste. He has written four cookbooks, the latest being *Kitchen Sense: More Than 600 Recipes to Make You a Great Home Cook* (New York: Clarkson Potter, 2006), and is a regular contributor of articles to periodicals, both scholarly and consumer oriented, on a variety of food-related topics.

CARA DE SILVA is an award-winning journalist who writes about a broad range of subjects, especially New York City and its food. Also an independent scholar, she is the editor of *In Memory's Kitchen: A Legacy from the Women of Terezin* (Norvale, N.J.: Jason Aronson, 1996), an unknown genre of Holocaust literature that went on to become one of the *New York Times*'s notable books of 1996. In addition, she is a lecturer and consultant and has often appeared on television and radio.

JONATHAN DEUTSCH is a chef and an assistant professor in the Department of Tourism and Hospitality at Kingsborough Community College, City University of New York. He is the author, with Rachel Saks, of *Jewish American Food Culture* (Westport, Conn.: Greenwood Press, 2008). Deutsch received a doctorate in food studies and food management at New York University and is the secretary of the Association for the Study of Food and Society and the education editor of the journal *Food, Culture and Society.*

JC DWYER has worked with antihunger and food policy organizations as small as Food Not Bombs and as large as the United Nations. His most recent work at the New York City Coalition Against Hunger was creating the nation's first interactive online map of charitable food providers as well as writing two reports on the geographic relationship between urban food access and malnutrition.

MARK RUSS FEDERMAN is not a writer, but is the proud founder—and probably sole member—of FRALS (Fellows of the Royal Academy of Lox Slicers). Federman is a graduate of Alfred University and Georgetown Law School. He was born on the Lower East Side of New York just two blocks from Russ & Daughters, the family's "appetizing store," which he has owned and managed for the past twenty-eight years and which is now run by the fourth generation of the Russ family.

JESSICA B. HARRIS is the author of ten acclaimed cookbooks documenting the culture and foodways of the African diaspora. She has lectured at museums, colleges, and conferences on the topic and contributes often to both scholarly and popular publications. Harris's current research centers on the history of African Americans and food in the continental United States. She is a professor of English at the City University of New York.

ANNIE HAUCK-LAWSON is a native Park Sloper whose life has always revolved around food and New York. She is the vice president of the Association for the Study of Food and Society and an associate professor at Brooklyn College, where her scholarship is grounded in the food voice, a term she originated. As a research tool, the food voice looks at foodways as channels of communication describing individual and group identities. Hauck-Lawson was the curator of the foodways component of the 2001 Smithsonian Folklife Festival, dedicated to New York. She is a Master Composter. These days, with her family, she continues to live, work, study, and grow food in Brooklyn.

ANNIE RACHELE LANZILLOTTO is a writer and food performance artist. Her most recent works are published in *Works of heART: Building Village Through the Arts,* edited by Lynne Elizabeth and Suzanne Young (Oakland, Calif.: New Village Press, 2006); *Hidden New York: A Guide to Places That Matter,* by Marci Reaven and Steve Zeitlin (New Brunswick, N.J.: Rivergate Books, 2006); and *Our Roots Are Deep with Passion: Creative Nonfiction Collects New Essays by Italian-American Writers,* edited by Lee Gutkind and Joanna Clapps Herman

(New York: Other Press, 2006). Lanzillotto's food performances include "Pocketing Garlic," "Opera Vindaloo!" "How to Cook a Heart," and "a'Schapett! Wiping the plate clean with the heel of the bread / savoring what's left when the meal is over." Lanzillotto has received grants and fellowships from the Rockefeller Foundation, the New York Foundation for the Arts, Franklin Furnace, and Dancing in the Streets and was a 2007 Santa Fe Art Institute Writer in Residence.

MARTIN F. MANALANSAN IV is an associate professor of anthropology at the University of Illinois in Urbana-Champaign. He is the author of *Global Divas: Filipino Gay Men in the Diaspora* (Durham, N.C.: Duke University Press, 2003), and his current projects include a book tentatively titled "Altered Tastes: Beyond a Palatable Multiculturalism," an ethnography of Asian American immigrant spaces, fusion and ethnic cuisines, and olfaction in New York City.

ANNE MENDELSON is a culinary historian of wide-ranging interests and the author of *Stand Facing the Stove* (New York: Holt, 1996), a biography of Irma Rombauer and Marion Rombauer Becker, the authors of *The Joy of Cooking*. Her latest book is *Milk: The Surprising Story of Milk Through the Ages* (New York: Knopf, 2008).

DAMIAN M. MOSLEY is a doctoral candidate in food studies at New York University. He lives in Harlem, where food, along with those who distribute, display, and devour it, is a matter of constant contestation. In this one space alone, he finds countless opportunities to assess his many interests, notably ethnicity, disgust, and the symbiosis of proprietary and corporate capitalists.

FABIO PARASECOLI lives in Rome, where he is a journalist for the food and wine magazine *Gambero Rosso*. After working as a correspondent in foreign affairs and political issues, focusing on Islam and the Far East, he concentrated his research on the interactions among food, culture, politics, and history. Besides writing *Food Culture in Italy* (Westport, Conn.: Greenwood Press, 2004), Parasecoli contributed to the Council of Europe's *Culinary Cultures of Europe: Identity, Diversity and Dialogue* (Strasbourg: Council of Europe, 2005). He is on the advisory board of the journal *Food, Culture and Society* and is president of the Association for the Study of Food and Society.

RAMONA LEE PÉREZ is a doctoral candidate in cultural anthropology at New York University whose research focuses on food, family, and flavor in the United States–Mexico border region. She is the coauthor of "Cocinas Públicas: Food and Border Consciousness in Greater Mexico," *Food and Foodways* (July 2007), and contributed to *Encyclopedia of Food and Culture*, edited by Solomon H. Katz and William Woys Weaver (New York: Scribner, 2002). Her interests include kitchen-table ethnography and sensory ethnography, Latino culinary cultures, and domestic nurturing work as feminist praxis.

JANET POPPENDIECK is a professor of sociology at Hunter College, City University of New York. Her primary concerns as both a scholar and an activist are poverty, hunger, and food assistance in the United States. She is the author of *Breadlines Knee Deep in Wheat: Food Assistance in the Great Depression* (New Brunswick, N.J.: Rutgers University Press, 1986); *Sweet Charity? Emergency Food and the End of Entitlement* (New York: Viking, 1998); and articles on hunger, food assistance, and public policy. She is writing a book on school food.

NAN A. ROTHSCHILD is a historical archaeologist and the director of Museum Studies at Columbia University. Her fieldwork was in New York City and New Mexico. Rothschild is the author of *New York City Neighborhoods: The 18th Century* (Clinton Corners, N.Y.: Percheron Press, 2008) and *Colonial Encounters in a Native American Landscape: The Spanish and Dutch in North America* (Washington, D.C.: Smithsonian Books, 2003), as well as several other books and many articles. Her research centers on social archaeology, including the study of food, colonialism, and the role of museums in the contemporary world.

JOY SANTLOFER's contributions appear in *The Oxford Encyclopedia of Food and Drink in America* (New York: Oxford University Press, 2004), *Il gusto degli altri* (September 2006), *Food, Culture and Society* (summer 2007), and *The Business of Food* (Westport, Conn: Greenwood Press, 2007). Santlofer was a consultant for the Museum of Chinese in the Americas for the 2005 exhibition "Have You Eaten Yet? The Chinese Restaurant in America." An adjunct instructor in food studies at New York University, she is currently writing a history of food production in New York.

ANDREW F. SMITH teaches culinary history and professional food writing at the New School in Manhattan and is the general editor of the Food Series at the University of Illinois Press. He has published fourteen books on culinary topics, including the *Encyclopedia of Junk Food and Fast Food* (Westport, Conn.: Greenwood Press, 2006) and *The Turkey: An American Story* (Urbana: University of Illinois Press, 2006). He is the editor of *The Oxford Companion to American Food and Drink* (New York: Oxford University Press, 2007) and is the chairman of the International Association of Culinary Professionals' Culinary Trust.

HARLEY SPILLER's international collections of Chinese restaurant memorabilia, spoons, chocolate bar wrappers, toothpicks, and more have been exhibited at such museums as the Smithsonian Institution and the Museo de Bellas Artes in Caracas, Venezuela. The *New York Times* has written about him many times, most notably when he escorted William Grimes and Italian cooking doyenne Marcella Hazan to under-the-radar dumpling joints. A graduate of Northwestern University, Spiller is the associate editor of *Flavor and Fortune* and has worked in Fun City as an arts administrator and freelance educator since 1981.

SUZANNE WASSERMAN is a historian and filmmaker with a doctorate in American history. She also is the director of the Gotham Center for New York City History at the Graduate Center of the City University of New York. Wasserman's films include *Thunder in Guyana* and the short *Brooklyn: Among the Ruins,* both of which were broadcast on public television. She was a historical consultant for Ron Howard's *Cinderella Man* and the coauthor, with Peter E. Dans, of *Life on the Lower East Side: Photographs by Rebecca Lepkoff, 1937–1950* (New York: Princeton Architectural Press, 2006).

INDEX